The Search for the Man in the Iron Mask

Delaplace del.

Berthet Sculp.

The First Composite of Eustache Dauger

The Search for the Man in the Iron Mask

A Historical Detective Story

Paul Sonnino

ROWMAN & LITTLEFIELD
Lanham • Boulder • New York • London

Published by Rowman & Littlefield
A wholly owned subsidary of The Rowman & Littlefield Publishing Group, Inc.
4501 Forbes Boulevard, Suite 200, Lanham, Maryland 20706
www.rowman.com

Unit A, Whitacre Mews, 26-34 Stannary Street, London SE11 4AB, United Kingdom

British Library Cataloguing in Publication Information Available

Library of Congress Cataloging-in-Publication Data
Names: Sonnino, Paul, author.
Title: The search for the Man in the Iron Mask : a historical detective story / Paul
 Sonnino.
Description: Lanham : Rowman & Littlefield, 2015. | Includes bibliographical
 references and index.
Identifiers: LCCN 2015035816| ISBN 9781442253636 (cloth : alk. paper) | ISBN
 9781442253643 (electronic)
Subjects: LCSH: Man in the Iron Mask. | France—History—Louis XIV, 1643–1715. |
 Political prisoners—France—17th century—History.
Classification: LCC DC130.M25 S66 2015 | DDC 944/.033092—dc23 LC record
 available at http://lccn.loc.gov/2015035816

Printed in the United States of America

Contents

Illustrations

~

Principal Characters

(In Order of Appearance)

Eustache Dauger: Man in the iron mask

Nicolas Fouquet: Brilliant and elegant minister of finance, disgraced by Louis XIV, fellow inmate with the iron mask

Saint-Mars: Governor of Pinerolo, Exilles, Sainte-Marguerite, and the Bastille; guardian of Fouquet and the man in the iron mask

Marquis de Louvois: Son of Michel Le Tellier, who succeeded his father as minister of war under Louis XIV

Anne of Austria: Daughter of Philip III of Spain; married at the age of fourteen to Louis XIII of France; mother, according to the legend, of the man in the iron mask

Louis XIII: King of France, cold and distant husband of Anne of Austria

Duchess de Chevreuse: Beautiful and cunning companion of Anne of Austria who survived disgrace, exile, and revolution to become a key participant in the mystery of the iron mask

Cardinal Richelieu: Prime minister of Louis XIII, the nemesis of Anne of Austria

Cardinal Mazarin: Italian adventurer who gained the confidence of Cardinal Richelieu and Louis XIII and, after their death, managed to gain the confidence of Anne of Austria, helping her and her son Louis XIV to emerge victorious over the revolt of the *Fronde*

Cardinal de Retz: Archbishop of Paris who exploited the revolt of the *Fronde* in order to become a cardinal and paid the piper after its failure

Claude Roux: Indomitable Protestant from Nîmes who became infuriated at Louis XIV and tried to set all Europe against him at the height of his power

Jean-Baptiste Colbert: Ambitious bureaucrat who became Mazarin's private secretary and used the position to poison his mind and that of Louis against Fouquet

Henrietta Maria: Sister of Louis XIII, wife of Charles I of England, who had to return to France and live there in extreme poverty

Oliver Cromwell: English gentleman who became a general in the English Civil War and was primarily responsible for the trial and execution of Charles I

The Count de Charost: Captain of the guard of Louis XIV, Governor of Calais, whose son married the daughter of Nicolas Fouquet

Antoine-Hercule Picon, Clerk of Colbert: Treasurer of Cardinal Mazarin, chief clerk of Colbert under Louis XIV

Eustache de La Salle: Guard of Louis XIV in the company of the Count de Charost, who fired his weapon in the vicinity of the king and was suspected of being an accomplice of Claude Roux

Charles II: Eldest son of Charles I and Henrietta Maria, restored to the throne of England in 1660, whose restoration helps to explain the arrest of Eustache Dauger in 1669 and solve the mystery of the iron mask

~

Chronological Table

1601
Birth of Anne of Austria (September 22)
Birth of Louis (XIII) (September 27)
1602
Birth of Giulio Mazzarino (July 14)
1615
Marriage of Louis XIII and Anne of Austria (November 24)
1617
Arrest and killing of Concini (April 24)
1620
Reconciliation of Louis with his mother
1621
Death of Luynes
1623
Bishop of Luçon becomes Cardinal Richelieu
1624
France moves against Spanish in Switzerland
1625
Buckingham's flirtation with Anne of Austria
1626
Conspiracy in favor of Louis XIII's brother Monsieur
1630
Day of Dupes (November 11)

1631

Louis XIII's mother leaves France

1635

France allies with Dutch and Swedes against Hapsburgs

1638

Birth of Louis (XIV) (September 15)

1641

Mazarin becomes cardinal

1642

Civil war in England; Queen Henrietta Maria, sister of Louis XIII, supports
husband Charles I

Death of Richelieu (December 4) succeeded by Mazarin

1643

Death of Louis XIII (May 14)

Anne and Mazarin continue war

1644

Henrietta Maria takes refuge in France

1646

Mazarin pushes his luck, scares Dutch allies

1648

Beginning of *Fronde* in France

Dutch make peace with Spain

French sign Peace of Westphalia, but not with Spain

1649

Execution of Charles I in England (January 30)

Court of France abandons Paris

Mazarinades in full swing

Return of court to Paris

1650

Anne and Mazarin arrest Prince de Condé and other princes

1651

Frondeurs, friends of Condé, and Monsieur drive Mazarin into exile

Anne sticks with Mazarin

Rebels fall out among themselves

Return of Mazarin

1652

Battle of the Faubourg Saint-Antoine (July 2)

Condé joins Spanish

Failure of *Fronde*

1653
Mazarin, with help from Colbert and Fouquet, recovers losses
Cromwell turns England into Protectorate
1657
French ally with Cromwell against Spain
1658
French and English take Dunkirk
Death of Cromwell
1659
Peace of Pyrenees with Spain (November 7)
1660
Restoration of Charles II as King of England (May 8)
Marriage of Louis XIV and Maria Theresa (June 9)
1661
Death of Mazarin (March 9)
Personal reign of Louis XIV
Arrest of Fouquet (September 5)
Chamber of Justice (November 15)
1662–1664
Trial of Fouquet
Arrest of Barbès
Prosecution of Desfontaines and Hoyau
Banishment of Fouquet
1665
Saint-Mars in Pinerolo receives Fouquet
1666
Death of Anne of Austria (January 20)
1667–1668
War of Devolution
Peace of Aix-la-Chapelle (May 2, 1668)
Morland informs on Claude Roux
1669
Louis XIV plans war against Dutch
Arrest of Eustache de La Salle (June 16)
Execution of Roux (June 22)
Decision to arrest Eustache Dauger (July 19)
Saint-Mars in Pinerolo receives Dauger
1671
Saint-Mars in Pinerolo receives Lauzun

1672
Louis XIV and Charles II begin Dutch War
1674
Charles II abandons Louis XIV
1675
Dauger becomes valet of Fouquet
1678
Louis ends Dutch War
1680
Death of Fouquet (March 23)
1681
Release of Lauzun (April)
Saint-Mars brings Dauger and La Rivière to Exilles
1683
Death of Colbert
1687
Saint-Mars brings Dauger to Sainte-Marguerite
Death of Mattioli in Sainte-Marguerite
1689–1697
Louis XIV holds off Europe in Nine Years War
1698
Saint-Mars brings Dauger with him to Bastille
1701–1713
Louis XIV barely survives War of the Spanish Succession
1703
Death of Eustache Dauger
1715
Death of Louis XIV

Map

The World of Eustache Dauger

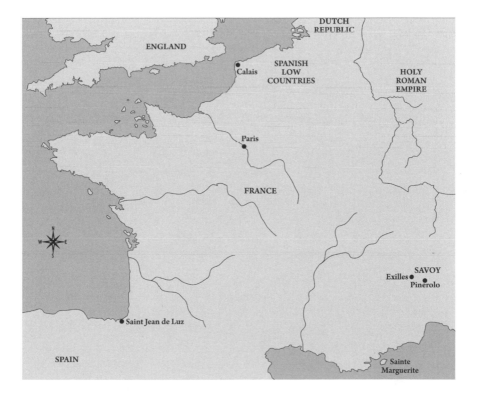

~

Introduction

The State of the Question

On or about August 20, 1669, the major of the garrison of Dunkirk, accompanied by three of his soldiers, delivered a prisoner to the citadel of the fortified town of Pinerolo in northern Italy. Pinerolo was an intimidating place. Long a possession of the dukes of Savoy, only twenty-one and a half miles southwest of their capital in Turin, it had intermittently, and since the year 1631, been an outpost of the kings of France. They, in turn, used it for three practical purposes: to keep the dukes in line, as an entry point into Italy, and as a prison. In that last capacity, the *donjon* (or castle) of the citadel was at that moment occupied by the notorious Nicolas Fouquet, one-time superintendant of finances under Louis XIV, whom this king had put on trial for corruption and treason, and banished to Pinerolo under extraordinarily strict guard. The latest prisoner was by no means so notorious. Nevertheless, he had arrived and was kept in such secrecy that within eleven days of his arrival, the governor of the citadel reported with some amusement that he was rumored to be a marshal of France or a presiding judge. The outside world would hear no more about this prisoner until 1687. By that time Fouquet was dead, and the author of a handwritten news letter began to spread another rumor. According to him, the governor, whom he referred to as Cinq Mars, had picked up a prisoner *wearing an iron mask* in Pinerolo and transported him to the island of Sainte-Marguerite off the Mediterranean coast. The author, moreover, intimated that this prisoner was Fouquet, who was, therefore, still alive. This was the beginning of the legend of the man in the iron mask.[1]

1

The legend had wings. In January of 1688 from Sainte-Marguerite, the governor reported even more whimsically that people suspected his prisoner to be one of two long-deceased celebrities—either the rabble-rousing Duke de Beaufort or a son of Oliver Cromwell. In 1692 an anti–Louis XIV scandal sheet ostensibly published in Cologne asserted that Cardinal Richelieu, desperate at the infertility of King Louis XIII, had provided a lover for his queen, Anne of Austria, which affair had produced the present usurper to the throne of France, promising to continue the story with the misfortunes of the lover. Evidence of some sort of prisoner, moreover, eventually surfaced. When, in September of 1698, the governor, whose name happened to be *Saint*-Mars, assumed a new position as governor of the Bastille in Paris, he brought the prisoner with him, and this event was broadcast all over Europe by the *Gazette d'Amsterdam*. Nothing about a mask, but the original rumor must have had a life of its own, for in October of 1711, the sister-in-law of Louis XIV repeated it, specifying that the man in the mask was an English lord involved in a plot to assassinate King William III.[2]

During the reign of Louis XV that followed, the educated public in France and in Europe believed it had become more enlightened. Whether this was the case or not, it had certainly not become less gullible. The enterprising Voltaire took advantage of this. He may have been a great humanitarian and an even greater wit, but his desire to appear omniscient knew no bounds. His conflicting qualities earned him almost a year in the Bastille and an even longer sabbatical in England, after which he began thinking about writing a history of the age of Louis XIV. In the course of his researches, he talked to whomever he could find—Saint-Mars's successor at the Bastille, a former secretary of state for foreign affairs, the flamboyant Marshal de Richelieu, an old doctor—picking up any secondhand information that they deigned to pass on to him. Aside from such casual conversations, he relied mainly on published sources, always inclined to jump to conclusions about them. He jotted down his findings in a scrapbook, which further reflects his cavalier approach to scholarship. But he had not failed to pick up the legend of the iron mask. At one point he noted,

Man in the Bastille with an iron mask.

At another point he seems to have either read the Cologne scandal sheet, picked up more rumors, or gotten more creative himself:

Prisoner in the Bastille always wearing an iron mask.
Suspected of being the elder brother of Louis XIV.

When he finally got to the first edition of his *Siècle de Louis XIV*, Voltaire did not dare to be so bold. This did not stop him, however, from being inventive. According to him this mysterious prisoner had been taken directly to Sainte-Marguerite shortly after the death of Cardinal Richelieu's successor, Cardinal Mazarin, in 1661. He was tall, handsome, noble, and wore a mask equipped with a flexible iron jaw. Transferred with Saint-Mars to the Bastille in 1690, still masked, but always treated with respect, he lived there in grand style, loved to wear lace, and strummed on the guitar. The old doctor told Voltaire that he had never seen his face, but that he was a fine figure of a man, and never complained about anything. Voltaire completed his account with information garnered from the son-in-law of Michel Chamillart, one-time controller-general of finances and minister of war. When ostensibly begged by his son-in-law to tell him about the man in the iron mask, Chamillart had supposedly replied that it was a secret of state and that he was sworn never to repeat it.[3]

Voltaire was not the only collector of tall stories. Even as he was writing up his own for his *Siècle de Louis XIV*, he was beaten to the punch by a humorously titled *Mémoires secrets pour servir à l'histoire de Perse*, which was a transparent parody on the recent history of France. Its anonymous author implied that the prisoner in the Bastille was a bastard son of Louis XIV, the Count de Vermandois, who had officially died in 1683. According to this account the young man was put in the hands of the commander of the citadel of *Ormus* (Sainte-Marguerite) with orders to keep him out of the way. He was treated with great respect, but no one was allowed see his face. One day, in desperation, he engraved his name on a plate, which fell into the hands of a slave, who delivered it to the commander. After a number of years at *Ormus*, the prisoner was transferred to the fortress of *Ispahan* (the Bastille), where he was visited by *Ali-Hamajou* (the Duke d'Orléans, regent for the young Louis XV), and throughout his captivity the prisoner wore a mask, even though he treated the commander with great familiarity and was always treated by him with great deference.[4]

By the year 1752 Voltaire too claimed to have heard the story of the plate, now more aristocratically made out of silver, from a certain Mr Riouffe, and Voltaire inserted it in the following editions of his history. Subsequently, he received a letter from one of his admirers in Avignon who had the courage to correct Voltaire by informing him that the mysterious prisoner had begun his imprisonment in Pinerolo. But as much as he had done to improve on the chronology, the admirer contributed even more to the legend, for he claimed to confirm the story of the plate, which he now transmuted into pewter. He had heard it from "several old men of the area," who also claimed to have heard it from the deceased Mr Riouffe, who claimed to have heard it from the very fisherman who had found the plate. Voltaire did not take any note of the correction, as much as he may have appreciated the confirmations.[5]

While Voltaire and his competitors were thus accumulating their rumors, the Jesuit Henri Griffet, former chaplain of the Bastille, was discovering some more respectable evidence. He had at his disposal the journal of Etienne de Junca, second-in-command of the Bastille from 1690 to 1706, who, on September 18, 1698, noted the arrival of Saint-Mars accompanied by an old prisoner who was masked and who had been with Saint-Mars since his days in Pinerolo. We read nothing more in this journal about this prisoner until November 19, 1703, when Junca noted that the prisoner, "who was always masked with a black velvet," had died and was quickly buried under the name of "Marchioly." Griffet published these entries in 1769, and they proved two things: such a man was on record, and he had worn a mask. Voltaire seems to have got wind of the book even before it was published and on this occasion he did take note, and in his edition of 1768 he corrected the date of death accordingly. But he persisted in his insinuations. In his *Questions sur l'encyclopédie*, which he wrote between 1770 and 1774, Voltaire suggested that the doctor of the Bastille was not allowed to see the prisoner's face "for fear of recognizing in his looks too striking a resemblance."[6]

In the middle of these debates Baron Heiss, a former officer in the regiment of Alsace, came up with an entirely new suspect, sending an article to a periodical published in Liège, claiming that the man in the iron mask was Ercole Antonio Mattioli (or Matthioli), a minister of the Duke of Mantua. To prove his claim, the baron attached a news letter from Italy disseminated by a French Protestant refugee in Leyden in August of 1687 announcing that Mattioli had been kidnapped on the outskirts of Turin, masked, and imprisoned in Pinerolo for having tried to dissuade his master from selling his "capital city" to Louis XIV. Given the name of Marchioly under which the prisoner had been buried, this account seemed to be much more credible than the all the claptrap about the royal brother.[7]

The candidacy of Mattioli may have had some plausibility, but it could not compete with the more exciting legends. During the early days of the French Revolution, when it was open season on the monarchy, the mystery of the iron mask first hit the stage in Paris in the *Théâtre de l'Ambigu-Comique*. The play was in pantomime, but the audience, with the aid of a printed program, was merely regaled with the old story about the Count de Vermandois. Theoretically better informed was the Abbot Soulavie. He was a former secretary to Voltaire's friend, the Marshal de Richelieu, who had himself spent some time in the Bastille. Pressed by Soulavie, Richelieu had once come up with the cryptic statement that "the prisoner was not as important when he died as he had been at the beginning of the personal reign of Louis XIV, when he was arrested for great reasons of state." Pressed even further the marshal added, "Read what Mister Voltaire has published recently!" The marshal had died in 1788, and after his death Soulavie devoted himself to revising his late employer's memoirs for publication. In his revision, he has the marshal brag about how he got his mistress, who was the daughter of the Duke d'Orléans (the *Ali-Hamajou* of the Persia parody), to get her father, who was incestuously in love with her, to give her a document containing the secret of the iron mask. This putative donation, which Soulavie inserted into his edition, sounds more like someone who was accumulating all the rumors of the century and adding a few more for good measure, notably that the man in the iron mask was a *twin* brother of Louis XIV, abducted at birth to be raised in Burgundy. It all made perfect sense as the monarchy was heading for its downfall, and Soulavie's version was quickly integrated into a second play about the iron mask in another Paris theater.[8]

Another side effect of the French Revolution, however, was that it rendered the archives of the old monarchy more accessible. A former general, Pierre Roux-Fazillac, took advantage of this in order to see what they had to offer. In one archive, he found more details on the arrest of Mattioli. It seems as if he had tried to sell the stronghold of Casale (a kind of seventeenth-century Brooklyn Bridge) to the King of France without authorization from its overlord. In other archives Roux-Fazillac found references to the prisoner of 1669 and how Louvois, the secretary of war, had ordered him to be held so secretly. Roux-Fazillac found this amazing, but not amazing enough to suspect that this prisoner could have been the man in the iron mask. Roux-Fazillac was also able to throw more light on the captivity of another notable prisoner in Pinerolo, the Count de Lauzun, but he could not pin anything on him because he had ultimately been released. Thus, with all his better evidence on the arrest of Mattioli and with the similarity of names between Mattioli and Marchioly, Roux-Fazillac was almost certain that Mattioli was his man.[9]

⌇

In the breathing spell after the French Revolution, when the kings of France temporarily regained their throne, the historian Joseph Delort continued to probe the archives and he found even more papers of Saint-Mars. They provided still more details about life in the citadel of Pinerolo and the prisoners who inhabited it. One of the most interesting regarding the one who had arrived in 1669 was that his name was Eustache d'Auger and that, in spite of the extreme secrecy surrounding his imprisonment, the secretary of state for war Louvois had referred to him as "miserable" and indicated that he was a valet. Why such a fuss over a miserable valet? None of this, however, was sufficient to awaken Delort's suspicions. He too had come across the new documents on the arrest of Mattioli and had fallen under their spell. They confirmed him in the opinion that the man that Saint-Mars brought to the Bastille in 1698 was indeed Ercole Antonio Mattioli. It seemed at that point as if Roux-Fazillac and Delort had solved the mystery.[10]

They had not. The restoration of the monarchy saw a great revival of popular fascination with history, and on August 3, 1831, at the Odéon theater in Paris, for the third time, the mystery of the man in the iron mask hit the stage. The authors of this play were Auguste Arnould and Narcisse Fournier, and for their story they went right back to the explanations of Voltaire and Soulavie, to which they added their own dramatic twists. For example, they invented a Protestant gentleman who had accidentally learned about the twin birth and who rescued the unfortunate brother from where the evil Cardinal Mazarin was keeping him.[11]

Little by little, more bits and pieces kept coming out. In 1837 a self-styled book lover, who went by the pen name of Jacob, tried to revive the rumor that the man in the iron mask was Fouquet. He even published a letter that roughly supported the idea. He was up, however, not only against Arnould and Fournier, but also against a more formidable playwright, Alexandre Dumas, who was about to turn his attention to the writing of history. Arnould and Fournier were his collaborators and, in a series of books that they undertook on famous crimes, it fell upon Arnould to write the essay on the iron mask. In his essay, Arnould recapitulated all the theories of the day, including Jacob's, and he came down squarely on the side of Soulavie. "No system," proclaimed Arnould, "is preferable to his nor based on better assumptions." Certainly it was the one that best suited the philosophy of Dumas and his collaborators, whose priority was to intrigue the public.[12]

As the fame of Dumas spread, he advanced from essays on famous crimes to full-fledged novels, the most successful of which, as we all know, was *The Three Musketeers*. He himself was a liberal monarchist at the time, and he delighted in a story in which three musketeers of Louis XIII, aided by their new friend D'Artagnan, helped to cover up the queen's flirtations with the Duke of Buckingham and save her from the machinations of Cardinal Richelieu. The novel came out in installments and the public kept calling for more. Thus Dumas obliged with a sequel which carried the musketeers into the heyday of Cardinal Mazarin, and then another sequel which carried them past the death of Mazarin into the personal reign of Louis XIV. It was there that Alexandre Dumas came face-to-face with the man in the iron mask.[13]

I can state categorically that if Voltaire begat Soulavie, and Soulavie begat Arnould, it was Arnould who begat Dumas, who then begat every film about the iron mask that has ever been made. Dumas took the Protestant gentleman and transformed him into Aramis, one of the three musketeers, who had come to the conclusion that the current Louis XIV was up to no good. Dumas also resuscitated the reputation of Fouquet, who, after Aramis had ingeniously managed to substitute the lovable twin brother for the current king, faithfully retrieved the original and consigned his double to an iron mask. It was a bit of a stretch, I have always felt, for an even a less than perfect Louis XIV to reward such a loyal minister by banishing him to Pinerolo, but I suspect that under the pressure of deadlines, this was the best that Dumas could do.

During the second half of the nineteenth century, France kept on changing governments while the scholars kept on debating just as inconclusively. On the one hand you had Jules Loiseleur, who was a good archivist, but he could only come up with a perplexing proposal which satisfied nobody. On the other hand there was Marius Topin, who found a fascinating letter that seemed to eliminate Mattioli and seemed to point the finger at two "jailbirds" and "gentlemen of the lower tower," yet kept on insisting that Mattioli was the man. Then there was another general, Théodore Iung, the first historian to gain access to the archives of the ministry of war. He came up with more documents about the prisoner whose name he found spelled as Eustache *Dauger, Danger,* or *D'Angers,* but other than that, he could do no better than a hypothesis that was even more far-fetched than that of Loiseleur. There was never any shortage of candidates. By 1872 there were at least nineteen different theories about the man in the iron mask, each one more preposterous than the other.[14]

In the midst of all this darkness, there were occasional flashes of light. In 1868, among the offerings of a multivolumed collection flamboyantly marketed as the *Archives de la Bastille,* François Ravaisson published a previously undiscovered letter from the Archives of War in which Louvois asked Fouquet in Pinerolo whether Eustache had revealed to another valet "what he has seen," "what he was employed at doing," or anything about "his past life." That should have told somebody something, but no one seemed to notice. Then, thirty-two years later, Jules Lair published an excellent biography of Nicolas Fouquet, which was extremely sympathetic to the disgraced superintendant. Lair too did not pick up on the remarkable letter, but unlike all the pundits who had preceded him, he did pick up on Eustache, whom he dubbed "Dauger." Who was this person, Lair wondered? He was French, Catholic, and a valet. He must have been employed at something sordid. Lair also noted a significant detail, namely, that Eustache had been used as a valet to Fouquet, but carefully kept away from the Count de Lauzun.[15]

These nuggets of truth, however, found few listeners, as the number of implausible suggestions kept proliferating. The highly reputable Franz Funk-Brentano remained loyal to Mattioli. The Englishman Andrew Lang came up with the suggestion that Eustache Dauger was the valet of Roux de Marsilly, a diehard Protestant out to turn Europe against Louis XIV. The fact that Eustache was clearly a Catholic, and that Roux's valet was last heard of refusing to leave England, did not deter Lang or the supporters of his thesis. Then there was Andrew Stapylton Barnes, who published a letter strongly suggesting that Mattioli had died at Sainte-Marguerite in 1694, while claiming that the man in the iron mask was an Italian handicapper of English horse races. Likewise unlikely was the discovery by Maurice Duvivier of a certain Eustache d'Oger de Cavoie, dissolute nobleman, who, however, was ultimately discovered vegetating in a Paris insane asylum. It was not until 1952 that a very sober historian, Georges Mongrédien, not only concluded that the obscure valet was the one and only man in the mask, but also republished the "curious" letter about him. Still he did not comment on it, and it was not until 1970 that another very sober historian Jean-Christian Petitfils, observed that "Danger," as Petitfils insisted on spelling his name, must have committed a crime that Fouquet may have been aware of.[16]

In 1986 as I was getting my manuscript *Louis XIV and the Origins of the Dutch War* into press, my former student Ron Martin drove up to Santa Barbara and asked me, "Since you have just finished covering the years 1667 to 1672, do you have any idea of why, in the middle of his preparations for the war, the king would have wanted to arrest a mysterious nobody and keep him in an iron mask for the rest of his life?" My first thoughts, not surprisingly, were of Roux de Marsilly or Mattioli but, in 1987, while I was visiting relatives in Naples, I stumbled across the evidence that I recount in chapter 2 of this book, which led me into my first brush with death on the Boulevard de Sébastopol. Ron, however, would not let me off that easily, and subsequently, during another visit to Santa Barbara, he pulled the Mongrédien book out of his briefcase and read the eye-opening letter to me. This little encounter, which I shall never forget, also produced his own indispensable insight. Since both Nicolas Fouquet and Eustache Dauger shared the same secret, he deduced, it followed necessarily that the secret of the iron mask referred to something that had happened *prior* to Fouquet's arrest on September 5, 1661. This was still far from a solution, but it opened the possibility that the irrepressible Voltaire had accidentally guessed right, and that the secret of the iron mask went back to the time of Cardinal Mazarin.

∼

It has taken me twenty-six years to follow up on this insight, and one might wonder why I have even bothered. In the long run, what does it matter? In the long run, of course, we will all be dead. Still, I would suggest that we can talk all we want about *longues durées*, discourses, and representations, we can create all sorts of models, paradigms, and structures, but we don't know very much about the age of Louis XIV until we can liberate ourselves from the mystery of the man in the iron mask. I shall try, in the nine chapters that follow, to do so.

Paul Sonnino
Santa Barbara, California

~

CHAPTER ONE

The Sex Life of Anne of Austria

The first thing I would like to do in attempting to solve the mystery of the man in the iron mask is to deal with the persistent rumor that identifies him as an offspring of Anne of Austria, a rumor to which the character of Anne of Austria and her relationship to the men in her life gives a certain respectability.

Anne of Austria was the eldest daughter of King Philip III of Spain, and she had been raised with all the affection and respect that she could possibly desire. But at the age of fourteen, in the interest of a reconciliation between the two leading Catholic monarchies, she had been married to Louis XIII of France, a king who was, to put it mildly, bizarre. Thus it is hardly surprising if she found few emotional incentives either for discarding her partiality to her native land or for loving her incomprehensible husband. She enjoyed admiration; she enjoyed finery. The only quality she shared with her husband, who was five days younger than she, was their age. Everything else about them was different. He had been neglected by his intimidating father, the oversexed Henry IV, who was taken from Louis before he was ten by an assassin's knife, and a self-indulgent mother, the distant Marie de Medici, who preferred consorting with her Italian favorites, Concino Concini and his wife, Leonora, to becoming a bulwark for a bewildered boy. From his childhood Louis found his primary pleasure in falconry and other forms of hunting. He knew he was king, but his primary goal in that capacity seemed to be to defend his status inconsistently and sporadically: he had no loftier goal or vision for his state. He seemed to crave the company of he-men, developing a particular dependence on the Sieur de Luynes, who indulged him in a passion for blood sports, without, however, attempting to mold him in any particular direction.[1]

It's not that Louis XIII was impotent, and it's questionable that he was gay. We have a very reliable record of his sexual activities from his doctor, Jean Héroard, covering—with some unfortunate gaps—the years 1615 to 1628. It results from the doctor's journal that Louis, in spite of some initial jitters, claimed to have consummated his marriage with Anne on their wedding night, November 25, 1615, after which Héroard, on the conventional wisdom that it was unhealthy for fourteen-year-old boys to engage in too much sex, discouraged him from further relations with his wife until he and she became more mature. This was not much of an imposition, since the young king much preferred to stick to his hunting, falconry, and Luynes, who himself must have had very mixed feelings about the potential influence of a strong wife on the malleable personality of his prize. The queen mother had similar reasons for keeping the young queen isolated. She therefore found herself very much a spectator, surrounded by her Spanish ladies-in-waiting, who managed to make themselves unpopular. She watched in silence on April 24, 1617, as the impulsive king, with Luynes assisting, engaged in his first great act of self-assertion by ordering the arrest of Concini, who did not go down without a fight, and whose wife was subsequently beheaded as a witch, while one of Marie de Medici's principal advisers, Armand du Plessis, the Bishop of Luçon, fell into disgrace. The furious queen mother then withdrew to Blois, where she attempted to stir up as much trouble for her son as she could. But if the elimination of an evil mother-in-law had its advantages for Anne, the king's shyness became less of a virtue as time went on, since he displayed no libidinal tendencies of any kind. On the contrary, he exhibited great timidity, covered by a mantle of piety, much to the dismay of his subjects, his court, the court of Spain, and the Holy See, and to the satisfaction of whatever Huguenots or other Protestants who did not want the marriage to produce a new era of collaboration between the two Catholic monarchies.[2]

Freed from Marie de Medici, Anne still had to cope with Luynes, who attempted to control her by means of his own new bride, the teenage Marie de Rohan, who was on the way to becoming one of the most beautiful, brilliant, and conniving women of all time. In 1618 Luynes got Louis to put her in charge of the queen's household. Anne was initially very indignant, but not for long. The two women became fast friends. Marie set an example of infidelity—she quickly took on a lover—which Anne was reluctant to follow, but they shared, I would suspect, a comforting sense of superiority toward their respective husbands. Marie's friendship helped Anne to compensate for another assertive action by Louis XIII, the sending of her Spanish ladies back to their native land. As for Luynes, he had much more reason now to be eager for the king to reproduce, especially since Luynes had no control at all over the king's brother and heir apparent, the Duke d'Orléans, Monsieur, as he was called. Luynes was a timid soul, but on this occasion he acted. On the evening of January 25, 1619, he grabbed Louis XIII by the scruff of the neck and dragged him into the queen's bedroom. The action worked. Louis XIII came out, and his doctor recorded two ejaculations. The news went out like a trumpet blast all over Europe. The king, moreover, seemed to be getting the hang of it. From February 3 to March 18, he and the queen had sex (often twice) on six separate occasions. As the celebration abated, however, there was no sign of a pregnancy and, under this last date, the doctor began to worry: "For all her charms," he jotted down in Latin, "nothing comes of it."[3]

Anne's friendship with Mme de Luynes, however, was all the more useful, since her husband was consolidating his position as the royal favorite. In August of 1619 Louis XIII promoted him to the rank of Duke and Peer, and from this lofty perch, Luynes went on to place one of his creatures, the Marshal d'Ornano, as governor of the king's brother Monsieur, a vital precaution in case of Louis's untimely death. But Luynes, as I have suggested, was rather timid. His wife was unfaithful: he did nothing about it; Louis ridiculed him for it; he took it in silence; and after a little armed skirmish with the queen mother's supporters, in which they were roundly defeated, he preferred to negotiate a peace with the Bishop of Luçon, which paved the way for her return to court and for her favorite bishop to become a cardinal. The reemergence of Marie de Medici was not good news for Anne, and it was made even worse by the fact that, in the course of an unsuccessful siege against some Huguenot rebels, the Duke de Luynes came down with scarlet fever and died suddenly on December 15, 1621. Within six weeks of his death the queen mother reentered the council. The barren queen now had only Luynes's widow, who quickly married one of her lovers, the Duke de Chevreuse, as an ally against a resurgent mother-in-law for the attentions of a conscripted lover.[4]

These continued, such as they were, and early in 1622 there were even signs of a pregnancy, but after a girlish romp around the Louvre with the new Duchess de Chevreuse, in which Anne suffered a fall, she miscarried, the sole evidence for which was some semblance of an embryo identified by the doctors. On this occasion Louis behaved like a compassionate husband and let the blame fall on the much too impetuous duchess, but soon thereafter he went off on another campaign against the Huguenots. Throughout this campaign, Louis's correspondence sounds less accommodating to his wife than to his mother, and as it drew to a close, her agent, the Bishop of Luçon, received his cardinal's hat, assuming the name of Cardinal Richelieu. All this time the prospects for the marriage of Louis and Anne to produce an heir were dimming, and by March of 1623 the queen mother did not fail to take advantage of the king's good graces. She began to press for the quick marriage of her younger son, the Duke d'Orléans, to a rich French heiress, Mademoiselle de Montpensier. That was the last thing Anne wanted, fearing to become even more of an outcast, and that was the last thing Monsieur wanted, preferring a marriage to a foreign princess which would provide him with a connection to an independent dynasty.[5]

As time went on, however, the most dangerous consequence of the reconciliation of the queen mother was the emergence of the man who had arranged it. Working behind the scenes, whether by conviction or by strategy, and probably out of both, he advised the queen mother to support in the council an increasingly hostile policy toward Spain, now ruled by Anne's brother, Philip IV. Richelieu may well have been thinking of Marie de Medici's interest in getting along with her son, but this strategy was also the key to his own success. He had hit upon the very quality in Louis XIII that Luynes had been too timid to channel, namely, the king's impetuous urges to defend his supremacy. Before long, Richelieu, too, entered the council, and the new cardinal convinced the king to send French troops into the Val Telline in order to expel the Spanish troops that had occupied this important passage between Italy and the Holy Roman Empire. Still another uprising of the Huguenots in France forced Richelieu to give up the enterprise, but he had shown his hand. Anne of Austria now found herself contending for her husband's love not merely with a meddling mother-in-law but with an enemy of her house and of her native land.[6]

What was an attractive, lusty, and reasonably intelligent young woman in her midtwenties to do? Well, she could flirt. First, there had been Henry II, Duke de Montmorency, a twenty-three-year-old charmer, then the sixty-year-old Duke de Bellegarde, who made a fool of himself, but the most egregious flirtation came up in 1625 when the court of France succeeded in arranging a marriage between Louis XIII's younger sister, Henrietta Maria, and the Prince of Wales, soon to be Charles I of England. In preparation for the marriage, and in order to bring his new bride back to England, Charles, now king, sent his late father's and his own favorite, the dashing Duke of Buckingham, to the court of France. His specialty was the seduction of beautiful women, the higher on the social scale the better, and he immediately set his sights on Anne of Austria. Louis XIII planned to accompany his sister as far as Amiens, the queen mother and the queen even farther, but on the way to Amiens, he fell ill. The Duchess de Chevreuse advised Anne to remain with her ailing husband. So did Henri de Loménie, the later Count de Brienne, who was fond of the queen and who considered Buckingham a boorish fop. But Anne preferred to listen to another lady in her entourage, a certain Madame de Vervet, and accompanied the procession to Amiens, where the queen mother also fell ill and took to her bed. The scene was set for the memorable incident, which took place in a garden, sometime between June 7 and June 16, 1625. Anne and the Duke of Buckingham were strolling. For a period of time—it is not clear how long—they fell out of sight of their attendants. There were sounds of a scuffle, and a woman's cry was heard. The attendants came running, and Buckingham disappeared. It would seem as if on the following day the queen referred to him as a brute and expressed fears that she was pregnant, which makes some sense given that he himself was later to brag that in the course of his life he had made love to three queens and had browbeaten them all. The attendants did their best to cover up the incident but, like so many cover-ups, it only added fuel to the fire. And Buckingham made matters worse by coming back from Calais, where he, the Chevreuses, Loménie, and others had gone in order to accompany Henrietta Maria back to England, for an impromptu visit at the bedsides of the queen mother and the queen.[7]

The Duchess de Chevreuse and Loménie had spoken wisely. In a hereditary monarchy, there was even more reason than in the Roman republic for Caesar's wife to be above reproach, because any uncertainty about the legitimacy of the succession could be used in order to overthrow the ruler, all the more so if his predecessor's capacity to reproduce was in question. And Louis, who was an insouciant husband but not a permissive one, was enraged. He dismissed Mme de Vervet, but not the Duchess de Chevreuse, who had managed to cover herself, and whose husband was one of Louis's favorites.

⌣

The emergence of Richelieu, moreover, had created a new state of affairs at the court of France. He was very much an authoritarian, and he seemed to dominate Louis XIII more thoroughly than Luynes ever did. The remnants of the Luynes party, the Duchess de Chevreuse and the Marshal d'Ornano, began to conspire. They seemed to want to get Monsieur into the council, which they succeeded in doing, or even, in order to prevent his marriage to the heiress, out of the country. Richelieu got wind of the plot, and Louis ordered Ornano's arrest at Fontainebleau on May 4, 1626. The conspiracy, however, had spread to other great nobles such as Louis's illegitimate half brothers, César, Duke de Vendôme, and Alexander, the Grand Prior, who began to talk of killing Richelieu and maybe even the king. Richelieu, after managing to assure himself of Louis's cousin, the Prince de Condé, who was next in line to the succession after Monsieur, proceeded to arrest the half brothers. Another member of the conspiracy was de Henri de Talleyrand-Périgord, Count de Chalais, a handsome young man in his late twenties and madly in love with the Duchess de Chevreuse. The court having moved to Nantes, he was arrested there on July 8 and, upon being interrogated, he panicked and spilled even more than he was sure of, relating the plans of the conspirators, and especially the Duchess de Chevreuse, to marry the queen to Monsieur, who himself confessed that he had heard the same thing. He got away by agreeing to marry the rich heiress, who provided him with a daughter before making him a widower. Chalais retracted his statements about the "ladies" before his decapitation, but the scene was set for an interrogation of Anne before the council. There she denied all charges, and made a statement that did not reflect too flatteringly on either her husband or his potential successor. "I would have gained *too little*," she said, "in the exchange." That proved to be good enough, for the queen mother and for the husband. Anne cried, and they all embraced. The Duke de Chevreuse softened the blow for his wife, by getting her exiled to Lorraine. She was furious at the inconvenience, and took her revenge by becoming the mistress of its duke, in whose company she fomented an international coalition against France, forcing Louis and Richelieu to think better of her exile and allow her return to her *château* of Dampierre, near Paris. She repaid his concession by holding secret meetings with Anne in the convent of Val-de-Grâce and seducing one of the king's principal advisers, the fifty-year-old Marquis de Châteauneuf. Other conspirators did not get off that easily. Ornano and the Grand Prior died in prison. The Duke de Vendôme, who lacked the courtesy to die and whose royal blood made it embarrassing to decapitate, remained in prison until 1630, from where Louis and Richelieu sent him into exile.[8]

Anne, however, gradually found an unexpected ally in her struggles against the cardinal. Marie de Medici, much to her own surprise, discovered that the loyal servant whom she had inserted into the council was slipping away from her. And to make matters worse, Richelieu was embarking the king on an ever more confrontational policy against Spain for, in 1629, he led his army into Italy in order to assist Charles I, Gonzaga, the new Duke of Mantua, against the Spanish and the Duke of Savoy. Between June and September of 1630 the queen mother, with the support of her daughter-in-law, took the occasion of an illness which brought Louis to the brink of death in order to terrify him into dismissing the cardinal. It seemed as if they would succeed, but the king regained his health and on November

11 he staged the famous "Day of Dupes" from which Richelieu emerged in triumph, while Monsieur escaped to Lorraine, where he secretly married the sister of its troublemaking duke, and Marie de Medici took refuge in the Spanish Low Countries. Monsieur then staged his own little invasion of France, which failed miserably and for which he once more escaped with a slap on the wrists, while his aristocratic supporters, including Anne's early admirer, the Duke de Montmorency, paid with their heads. This left Anne as the sole rallying point of the anti-Richelieu party. Her little court became a crossroad between Richelieu's spies and his diehard enemies. Her mail was intercepted and her husband, who could have had found a thousand willing mistresses anywhere on the continent, compounded her humiliation by developing an open passion for two of her ladies-in-waiting: first for the befuddled fourteen-year-old Mlle de Hautefort, then for the older and more pious Mlle de La Fayette, who could not even escape his attentions by entering into a convent. As to the Duchess de Chevreuse, both the king and Richelieu became exasperated with her continued intrigues and forced her to abandon Dampierre for the more distant Château of Milly near Tours. One of Anne's few aspiring champions at this time was the young Prince de Marcillac, the later Duke de La Rochefoucauld, who hated Richelieu even more than she did and was prepared to do anything for her and her ladies in his chivalrous dreams.[9]

Enter Giulio Mazzarino, Mazarini, or Mazarin, as the name evolved. He came at best from the squirearchy of the Abruzzi, in the service of the very noble house of Colonna, but he quickly became convinced that his own charm, intelligence, and skill could carry him to great heights. He accompanied one of his patrons on a mission to Spain, where he learned the language and almost found himself a wife, but he was suddenly called back to Italy by his father's bankruptcy, and then entered the service of another eminent house, the Barberini, which had ascended to the papacy in the person of Urban VIII. In this capacity Mazarin became a diplomat, attempting to execute the policy of the Holy See, which was to keep the French and Spanish monarchies from staging their wars on Italian soil, and it was therefore as a peacemaker, in January of 1630 in Lyon, that he entered into the life of Anne of Austria. When Cardinal Richelieu introduced him to her, the cardinal maliciously jibed, "You will like him madame, he resembles the Duke of Buckingham!" Richelieu may have been malicious, but he was certainly correct. Here was a man who had come to advance the cause of peace between France and Spain, and a charming, handsome man to boot. They barely saw each other during this stay, but she did not forget him. Moreover, Mazarin gained a certain amount of international fame later the same year, when he managed to arrange a truce between a French and Spanish army which were preparing to give each other battle in front of the fortress of Casale. But, in the course of his diplomatic activity, his allegiance, guided by his ambition, shifted. In spite of the fact that he continued to act as a papal agent, Mazarin directed his efforts at furthering the policy of Cardinal Richelieu, achieving a notable success in this direction when, in 1631, he helped to negotiate the Treaty of Cherasco, which transferred the Savoyard stronghold of Pinerolo, future home of the man in the iron mask, to French control. Needless to say, Cardinal Richelieu loved him and made his best efforts to pressure the pope into appointing Mazarin as papal nuncio to France, where Anne got to see him a bit more often between 1634 and 1636.[10]

As Anne and Louis XIII continued to go their separate ways, she found some comfort, whenever she could get to Paris, in the quiet confines of the convent of Val-de-Grâce, where she could be at her ease and correspond more privately, but such independence became more dangerous in 1635, when the king, with a little urging from Richelieu, decided to enter openly on the side of the Calvinist Dutch and the Lutheran Swedes into their separate wars against the Spanish and Austrian Hapsburgs. Suddenly, her loyalty to her family and to her native land came into open conflict with her obligations to her husband, and whatever correspondence she was maintaining with her family took on the appearance of treason. Early in 1637 Richelieu received further evidence of it and decided to act. He arrested La Porte, Anne's cloak bearer, and questioned him. Richelieu's agents also questioned the abbess of Val-de-Grâce. They found out very little, but Anne and her friend Mlle de Hautefort, in a panic, went so far as to approach their admirer, the Prince de Marcillac, about helping them to flee to the Spanish Low Countries. Interrogated, on August 17, Anne made a full and humiliating confession, while in Tours; her old friend, the Duchess de Chevreuse, also panicked and took refuge in Spain, from where she moved to England, and finally took up residence in the Spanish Low Countries. Louis spent the next four months without even speaking to his wife, much less sleeping with her, but early in December, while she was in Paris and he was hunting his merry way from Versailles to Saint-Maur, he stopped in Paris at the convent of the daughters of Saint Mary to converse, across a grating, with his beloved Mlle de la Fayette. After their conversation, however, a rain and wind storm came up which, along with the darkness, prevented him from continuing on his way. Louis was furious, but the captain of his guards had the gumption to suggest that he invite himself to dine and sleep with the queen. Louis resisted for as long as he could, but he had no choice, and it was that night that he and the queen conceived a child. He was born in

Saint-Germain-en-Laye on September 5, 1638, in the midst of an assembly that could not doubt of the event, named Louis, and nicknamed by an incredulous nation "the gift of God."[11]

The miraculous birth of the dauphin, however, was attended by a second miracle, of no lesser moment. Anne, who had never developed enough affection for her husband to overcome her allegiance to the house of Austria, now discovered in her affection for her son enough of a motive to transfer her allegiance to the house of Bourbon. But if she had undergone such a miraculous transformation, Louis and Richelieu were not prepared to believe it. One more example of the king's spite occurred in 1639 when he exiled two of her favorite ladies-in-waiting, the Marquise de Senecey and Mlle (now Mme) de Hautefort, whom he himself had initially imposed upon the queen. Two years after the first miracle, the birth of a second son did not improve his disposition toward his wife. But Louis XIII, though still in his late thirties, was in declining health. Richelieu, in his midfifties, was doing even worse, and grooming the now Cardinal Giulio Mazarini as his successor. Indeed, when Richelieu died in 1642, Louis immediately made Mazarin his chief minister. As the king saw his own death approaching, it became his primary concern and that of his ministers to avoid another regency similar to that of Marie de Medici, in which the independence of the monarchy to which he had devoted his life would be jeopardized. They could not avoid making Anne regent and placing Monsieur as well as the Prince de Condé in the council. All they could do was for Louis to insert a provision in his testament which would also admit Mazarin and enough of the old ministers to give them a majority vote. This was a dubious undertaking. A healthy and mature king of France could do almost anything. A dead one was subject to the laws of succession, and Louis XIII became a dead king of France on May 14, 1643.[12]

Thus, after twenty-eight years of embarrassment and humiliations, Anne of Austria finally came into her own. How was she going to handle it? Her friends who had supported her through the years of suffering, not to speak of everyone in France who was sick of executions, taxes, and wars, now glimpsed the possibility of a return of what must have seemed like the good old days. Anne, however, moved cautiously and, for the moment, she kept the old ministers, including Mazarin, in place, but she did not hesitate to go behind their backs to unite with Monsieur and the Prince de Condé, neither of whom wished to be constrained by the terms of Louis XIII's will. They therefore took their case before the highest court in the land, the *parlement* of Paris, which jumped at the opportunity to declare the terms of the testament unconstitutional and confirm her, Monsieur, and the prince as the sole decision makers in the council. Anne also recalled her exiled ladies-in-waiting,

Mmes de Senecey and Hautefort, and, notably, the Duchess de Chevreuse. Mazarin was furious at being circumvented and threatened to return to Italy. Anne had to consider. Her closest friends, with the possible exception of the Duchess de Chevreuse's old lover, the Marquis de Châteauneuf, were not very capable of directing a country in the middle of a war. Each of her associates in the regency had his own record of pursuing his own agenda. And there, threatening to leave her at their mercy, was a man who reminded her of the Duke of Buckingham. But whatever libidinal impulse may have driven her in his direction, she also had her reasons. He spoke Spanish. He had the experience of running the government. He was offering, if she would only give him her confidence, to belong entirely to her. Brienne, the old friend who had never abandoned her, read her mind clearly and recommended that she ask him to stay on as her principal minister.[13]

It was very fortunate for Anne that she had become a French woman because Mazarin would not have it any other way. He had no intention of ending up like Concino Concini, a self-serving toady of a pro-Spanish mother and a sacrificial scapegoat to an alienated son. Did Anne, however, have other plans for Mazarin? I believe that she did, because shortly after asking him to stay on she approached him, by his own testimony, with the most suggestive of all questions, namely, whether there was any way to make him happy. To this very explicit invitation, Mazarin might have replied that he loved her, too—which he undoubtedly did in his own way—but that if they surrendered to their passions, this would eventually become apparent and, given the less-than-impressive masculinity of the late Louis XIII, jeopardize the entire succession to the monarchy. The problem, however, was that somewhere in the course of the previous half decade Mazarin, too, had undergone a considerable transformation—he had jettisoned his youthful charm and replaced it with an overwhelming sense of his own worth, and there was no place in the new Mazarin for the amenities of a graceful sensitivity. Thus he feigned not to understand her proposition and turned it into an opportunity to take full possession, not of her body, but of her soul. He told her how sad he was to see how everybody was taking advantage of her kindness and launched into a pompous diatribe against "those who do not do their duty towards her," that is to say, her old favorites. What is remarkable is that she accepted the admonishment with good grace, in the interest of self-preservation, reason of state, and Christian piety. That seems to have been the destiny of Anne of Austria, going from one lover who browbeat her to another, and ending up with a lover who insisted on browbeating her platonically.[14]

Anne's choice of Mazarin to the apparent exclusion of her old favorites was not at all what they expected as a reward for their years of fidelity. The

Duchess de Chevreuse, who would have been happy to corrupt him and could not imagine that any man would resist her, began, by Mazarin's own account, to spread the rumor that he was impotent. Other disappointed aristocrats somewhat inconsistently began to spread the rumor, against all visible evidence, that he was having an affair with the queen. Thus the malcontents, who quickly acquired the nickname of "Importants," found themselves in the ironic position of trying to play on Anne's emotions against Mazarin in the same way that the queen mother and Anne had tried to play on Louis XIII's emotions against Richelieu. The result was the same. On September 2 the Duke de Beaufort was arrested; his father, the Duke de Vendôme (a relic from the Chalais conspiracy), and Vendôme's eldest son, the Duke de Mercoeur, were relegated to their estates. Mesdames de Senecey and Hautefort were quickly sent packing. The Duchess de Chevreuse took it upon herself to withdraw, ending up once more in the Spanish Low Countries, where she resumed her intrigues against the French monarchy.[15]

Anne was not a complete slave to Mazarin. Those friends and supporters who acquiesced to the dominance of Cardinal Mazarin found themselves in secure positions. Indeed she placed her old supporter the Count de Brienne as secretary of state for foreign affairs even though Mazarin could not stand him. But for the most part Mazarin ran the country, skillfully playing Monsieur off against the Prince de Condé and putting his own creatures in key positions. He also managed to find the money to continue the war, and continue it successfully, while sending a delegation to the congress in Westphalia for the purpose of concluding a peace. In fact his conduct of the war was so successful that early in 1646 Mazarin got it into his head that he should add the acquisition of the Spanish Low Countries to his war aims. In pursuit of this prize he decided to besiege a little town on the border of Catalonia in order to intimidate the Spanish and, in November, ordered his plenipotentiaries to postpone signing a peace until the French could take the town. As it turned out, they failed to take it, and his Dutch allies, worried that a resumption of French victories would bring France up to the borders of their own republic, hastened to make a separate peace with Spain. To make matters worse, the Prince de Condé, whom Mazarin had been able to keep under control, died at the end of that same year and was succeeded in his position by his eldest son, a brilliant soldier and a much greater threat than his father had ever been.[16]

〜

The Dutch did not make peace immediately. They simply stalled during the campaign of 1647, which was just what the Spanish needed in order to concentrate on the French. They made the most of it and, exhausted as they were, managed to fight the similarly exhausted French to a standstill. Mazarin had never been very popular, and by this time public opinion in France had reached the conclusion that he was either bloodthirsty or incompetent. And from somewhere or other someone had sent a person claiming to be a gentleman of the chamber of the Duke d'Orléans to the governor of the Spanish Low Countries, challenging the paternity of Louis XIV and claiming the throne on behalf of Monsieur and the new Prince de Condé if they could obtain Spanish help. Mazarin, learning of the plot, treated it as an abominable hoax. Even if it was a hoax, however, this hoax demonstrated that, given the right conditions, the peculiarities of the relationship between Anne of Austria and Louis XIII would come back to haunt the monarchy. In fact, the incident demonstrated that these peculiarities had a life of their own, and for the first time in the history of the reign, the legitimacy of Louis XIV and of his brother had been called into question.[17]

Anne continued to put her faith in Mazarin. He himself would never acknowledge that he had made any mistakes. He ignored his unpopularity to the extent of choosing this time to import some of his own relatives—his sister, his oldest nephew, and three of his nieces—from Italy to France. Whatever criticism he was receiving, he felt, was all the fault of the *parlement* of Paris, which was taking the leadership in criticizing his policies. On August 14, 1648, he wrote to his confidant Servien, who was in Münster putting the finishing touches on the Treaty of Westphalia:

> I kill myself day and night for the greatness of this crown and for the happiness of the French. . . . I have no posts, no governorships, no duchies. . . . They claim that I have amassed treasures . . . and attack me as a foreigner. . . . The state is endangered by the French themselves while God continues to shower us with prosperities.

When, moreover, the government tried to arrest two of its most vociferous judges, Broussel and Blancmesnil, the citizens of Paris put up barricades and obtained their liberation. In spite of the outbreak of this revolt, however, Mazarin managed to salvage a peace with the Austrian Hapsburgs in Westphalia on October 24, 1648, which gave to France its first possession of Alsace, but he still had a war with Spain on his hands and no money with which to fight it. As the disturbances, which quickly acquired the name of the *Fronde*, continued, on January 6, 1649, the court had to abandon Paris, and the embattled cardinal—banished by the *parlement*, his property sequestered, and decried in an explosion of pamphlets—was forced to depend more and more on the support of Monsieur and the Prince de Condé in order to reconcile the *parlement*. They managed to do so by the Treaty of Rueil of March 11, but even after this peace the outpouring of pamphlets, which became known as *Mazarinades*, did not let up. One of these, *La Custode de la reyne qui dit tout*, or "Confessions of the Queen's Bed Curtains," describes an anal encounter between the cardinal and the queen, with the latter sighing in gratitude for his penetrations, and when the government caught and tried to execute the printer, he was liberated by an angry mob. Another pamphlet, *Le Silence au bout du doit*, which I translate as "Mum's the Word," raised Anne's two earliest admirers, the Dukes de Montmorency and Bellegarde, to the status of lovers, and somewhat gratuitously added the name of a traveling Spanish nobleman. Perhaps more authoritative was the composer *of Requeste civile contre la conclusion de la paix*, or "Appeal against the Peace," who claimed to be personally acquainted with a young page whose anus Mazarin had permanently damaged. Under the circumstances, the Duke d'Orléans and, in particular, the Prince de Condé exploited the cardinal's unpopularity for their own advantages, and the once imperious Mazarin found himself obliged to look for his support wherever he could find it. One of the beneficiaries was the Duchess de Chevreuse. She had now become a creditor of the impecunious King of Spain, and was residing in the Barony of Kerpen, which he had mortgaged to her as security for a loan, but she was always interested in returning to France, and the *Fronde* gave her an opportunity to do so. Also, an envoy sent by the *Frondeurs* to the Spanish, the young Marquis de Laigues, had taken the occasion to become her latest lover, and through him she had established a liaison with Paul de Gondi, coadjutor of the diocese of Paris, an ambitious clergyman whose libertine habits did not prevent him from wanting to become a cardinal. By this time Mazarin was so desperate that he made an alliance with this adventurous duo. With their rickety reinforcement, he took the chance of arresting the Prince de Condé and his close relatives, and he himself rushed frantically about the country in a desperate effort to reestablish his own authority. All in vain! Gondi, still angling for his cardinal's hat, and Chevreuse, who was enticed by a promise of a marriage between her daughter and Condé's brother, the Prince de Conti, decided to switch sides. They enrolled the always willing Monsieur in their conspiracy and in January of 1651 turned against Mazarin, obliging him to free Condé and his relatives and go into exile himself along with his own relatives.[18]

For Anne this was one of the worst periods of her life; for Mazarin the very worst. Once again she was completely alone, surrounded by enemies. Even her old friendship with the Duchess de Chevreuse was clouded by the events of the intervening years. For Mazarin, to have risen to such heights and then to find himself once more banished by the *parlement*, his possessions once again seized, and this time having to flee the country, the shift in fortunes must have been devastating. Self-righteous as ever, he became paranoid. He began to fear that Anne had abandoned him, and he began to make plans for a perpetual exile. He need not have done so. He had left Anne with his most trusted advisers: Servien, who had concluded the Peace of Westphalia; Lionne, Servien's nephew, who had served as Mazarin's letter writer throughout that negotiation; Michel Le Tellier, the secretary of state for war; and Zongo Ondedei, a distant relative and close friend. Not that Mazarin was that sure of anybody. Anne and Mazarin, however, had a tremendous advantage over the *Frondeurs*, namely, each other. They shared a common egotism not only for themselves but for the monarchy. The *Frondeurs* did not. Each one of them, with the exception of a few lonely idealists in the *parlement*, was out for him- or herself. On and off, there were calls for a meeting of an Estates-General, which neither the *parlement* nor any leading *Frondeur* supported with much enthusiasm. What each one of them wanted was to control the ministry, to acquire a prestigious office, or, in the case of Gondi, to become a cardinal. Madame de Chevreuse managed to get her old lover, the Marquis de Châteauneuf, reinstated into the council, but no sooner had the Prince de Condé gotten out of prison than he began to act arrogantly toward the very people who had temporarily united in order to procure his liberty.[19]

It was not that difficult, therefore, for Anne and Mazarin to separate them. Acting as if she were completely in the hands of Condé, the queen proceeded to dismiss Châteauneuf, on top of which Condé's sister the Duchess de Longueville or maybe Condé himself combined with Anne to break off the engagement of the Prince de Conti and Mlle de Chevreuse, actions which aroused the suspicion of Monsieur and infuriated the Duchess de Chevreuse, who laid the blame primarily on the Condé clan. She was not, as we have seen, a woman to be trifled with, and having to choose between Condé and Mazarin, she again opted for Mazarin, who was now in Brühl, Germany, and more than willing to forgive and forget. He eagerly accepted her overtures, and with her friendship also came new overtures from Paul de Gondi, the aspiring cardinal. The tensions between the *Frondeurs*, Monsieur, and the Prince de Condé reached a point when the prince, fearing for his personal safety, left Paris and moved into open rebellion, even forming an alliance with the King of Spain. For a brief moment, in September, as the king was about to declare his majority (kings of France became major at the age of thirteen), Mazarin thought he was going to be left behind, but two days after the ceremony in the *parlement* of Paris, the young Louis wrote to Mazarin, inviting him to return. In the midst of this confusion, however, the Spanish had managed to recoup many of their losses, the Duchess de

Chevreuse had relocated herself in France, and Gondi was well on his way to becoming Cardinal de Retz.[20]

It had been Anne and Giulio against the entire nation of France, and it looked as if they had won, but they still had a war against Spain on their hands and a lot of ground to make up. Once more, however, Mazarin showed infinitely more flexibility when he was in a corner than he had ever shown when he had tried to push his luck during the negotiations in Westphalia. He accumulated money and positions, brought in more of his relatives, and sent his trusted Lionne with more moderate demands on a secret mission to Madrid, and this mission only failed when the Spanish insisted on the complete reinstatement of the Prince de Condé. Then Mazarin resorted to the extreme remedy of concluding an alliance with Oliver Cromwell, the man who had been most responsible for cutting off the head of Louis XIII's brother-in-law Charles I and was now the Lord Protector of the Commonwealth of England. In execution of this treaty, the French and the English besieged the Spanish port of Dunkirk, which the French then turned over to the English, giving these heretical republicans a foothold on the continent of Europe. Finally, Mazarin arranged for the marriage of the twenty-year-old Louis XIV to his cousin, Marguerite, sister of the Duke of Savoy, which would have tightened the bonds between France and this important principality in northern Italy. It would appear as if this last move panicked the Spanish, who in order to stop it, played their last card, the hand of Louis's other cousin, Maria Theresa, *Infanta* of Spain, and *potential* (though not too likely at that moment) heiress to the entire Spanish monarchy.[21]

Embattled as she had been between her loyalty to her ancestors and her responsibilities as Queen of France, to see her son marry her niece, and finally bring to fruition the long postponed reconciliation between the two monarchies was more than Anne of Austria could ever have hoped for, and her beloved Mazarin was about to achieve it. There was one problem, however, and that was with the designated bridegroom. Louis XIV had fallen in love with another woman, and that woman just happened to be one of Mazarin's nieces, Maria Mancini. The niece was no less ambitious than her uncle, and considerably less scrupulous. She had no hesitation about succeeding where the *Fronde* had failed, namely, in breaking up the relationship between Anne and Mazarin, not to speak of breaking up the peace. Mazarin would have nothing of it, and on his way to Saint-Jean-de-Luz to meet with the Spanish, he wrote to the king threatening to go back to Rome unless Louis gave up his capricious romance, and in the midst of the conference Mazarin insisted, "If your passion prevents you from coming to your senses, I will have no choice but to carry out my plan." The king relented and Mazarin went on to conclude the Peace of the Pyrenees in 1659. It is difficult not to see the old Mazarin imposing upon Louis XIV the same priorities that, as a young man in Spain, he had once imposed upon himself, and that, upon accepting Anne's invitation to become her minister, he had later imposed upon her.[22]

If the Peace of the Pyrenees and the marriage of Louis XIV was the fulfillment of Anne of Austria's dreams it was only a partial fulfillment for Mazarin. He had not achieved what he had aimed for in 1646, namely, the acquisition of the Spanish Low Countries for France, but it had to do for the moment. And after returning from the wedding ceremonies his health, which had been declining over the previous ten years, began to fail him entirely. He had been assailed intermittently by what contemporaries diagnosed as the gout, the inflammation had now spread into his vital organs, and all of the remedies available to his doctors, which consisted mainly of bleedings and purgatives, only increased his agony. He expired on March 9, 1661, and upon his death, when Louis XIV was asked by the Archbishop of Rouen to name Mazarin's successor, the king replied that he would himself assume full responsibility for governing his own state.

Anne, as we have seen, was no Marie de Medici, nor did she have any desire to imitate her late mother-in-law. As soon as Louis began his personal reign, Anne withdrew to her ceremonial role as queen mother and to her religious observances. She watched in silence as her son rattled his saber at the Spanish, humiliated the pope, and purchased Dunkirk from the English, without presuming to interfere in his affairs. The only sign of her displeasure occurred when Louis, in a reversion to the behavior of his grandfather, took on a mistress and all the embodiments of a sexual athlete. But even in this displeasure, she did not push it to a breaking point. She was ailing, and by May of 1664 she was beginning to show the symptoms of breast cancer, which at least may have spared her from an awareness that her son was about to resuscitate the most ambitious goal of Cardinal Mazarin by setting his sights on the Spanish Low Countries, for she died, on January 20, 1666, before she could see him renew the centuries-old conflict between the French and Spanish monarchies.[23]

The crosscurrents of the libido are difficult to discover and even more difficult to explain, but I have done the best that I can in order to demonstrate that whatever pleasures Anne of Austria may have procured for herself in the course of her difficult life—and there may have been more than meet the eye—if she had given birth to any children other than Louis the Dauphin and his brother Philippe, it would have been impossible for her to have kept them secret in the midst of so few friends and so many enemies. And throughout her entire life, no matter how scurrilous the accusations against her, no one had ever even raised the possibility of such a thing.

CHAPTER TWO

~

The Candidacy of Claude Imbert

Since we have apparently eliminated any offspring of Anne of Austria, we can go back now to searching for a likely valet who was circulating prominently enough in the 1650s to be known by Nicolas Fouquet and Antoine de Lauzun. The place to begin, I would suggest, is with the reports of foreign envoys at the court of France and, quickly enough, we find a suitable candidate. On April 26, 1658, the Abbot Pietro Bonzi, Florentine resident in Paris, reported the following incident to the Balio Gondi:

> Mr Croissy-Fouquet is returning to France at the good pleasure of His Majesty to reside in one of his homes in the province of Anjou. Mr Marigny similarly. It has been rumored that Cardinal de Retz has come close to being assassinated in Cologne by one of his confidential *valets de chambre* named Imbert, induced to this action by Croissy and Marigny.

On May 10, 1658, the Abbot Bentivoglio, the Parmesan resident, filed a similar report to his duke, identifying the corrupter of the valet as Croissy-Marsily (*sic*), placing the incident in Liège, and indicating that the valet had been arrested.[1]

Who was this confidential valet of Cardinal de Retz? His name was Claude Imbert, and it is hard to imagine a more suitable candidate for the wearer of the mysterious mask. He first appears in the contemporary correspondence late in 1651 when Paul de Gondi, then coadjutor of Paris and eager to become a cardinal, is writing, in the hand of his confidential secretary Guy Joly, to their agent in Rome, the Abbot Charrier, who was having some difficulty or other with his fellow agent, the Abbot Barclay. Gondi tells Charrier that he is sending him a copy of his own letter to Barclay as well as "the one that Imbert is writing him." Here, then, is a valet who is literate. Then, early in 1652, when Gondi became impatient with the delays that Charrier was experiencing in obtaining the cardinal's hat and decided to recall him, a mutual friend wrote to the abbot that Gondi's "valet de chambre, whom I met at Notre-Dame, told me that he was writing you today a very important letter on your negotiation instructing you to return." This is a valet who was not only literate; he also knew what he was talking about, for Gondi's intemperate letter, once again in Joly's hand, did go out on that same day, along with a courteous and signed holograph from Imbert. Charrier, however, had the good sense to continue his solicitations, and later in that year Gondi did become a cardinal, while Imbert, well, Imbert became a husband. On October 2 he married Anne-Marie Marès, daughter of a lawyer in the *parlement* of Rouen. The contract, designating Imbert as "first *homme de chambre* of the most eminent Cardinal de Retz" gives us still another specimen of the valet's signature, one of his wife's, and regales us with the new cardinal's, who honored the ceremony with his presence. It was to be the last wedding that Retz would attend for a while. Two and a half months later he was arrested during a visit to the Louvre, initiating the adventure that would keep him imprisoned for over a year and a half, first in the *donjon* of Vincennes, and then in the *château* of Nantes. At Vincennes, he was not allowed his own valet, but we have a description of Imbert following the procession to Nantes. It would appear that there he resided in the town, while attending upon Retz in the *château*. Indeed, in 1654 Imbert was instrumental in the cardinal's escape, one account describing how Imbert offered to share some of Retz's unused wine with the guards and even induced them to drink it behind a tower, as the cardinal slid down a rope to freedom. And, after the escape, Imbert had the coolness to walk out of the *château*, get on his horse, and rejoin Retz in the long odyssey that ultimately brought them both to Rome. In Rome Retz had the opportunity to participate in the conclave of 1655, which he entered, one account tells us, "with the Abbot Charrier, Joly, and Imber [*sic*] his *valet de chambre*." And if we need further proof that this was no ordinary valet, we have only to examine one of the propaganda pieces that the frustrated French court sent down to Rome in order to get the new pope, Alexander VII, to place Retz on trial. In this mock letter to Retz, his putative supporter identifies himself as "the faithful depositary (often to the exclusion of Imbert and Joly) of your most secret thoughts in love and war." Then in 1656, with his welcome in Rome wearing thin, Retz resumed his wanderings, and it is these wanderings that bring us up to the intriguing incident in Cologne, or was it Liège?[2]

As we examine this incident more closely, two remarkable facts emerge. One is that Cardinal de Retz, who was certainly not trying to economize on paper in his *Mémoires*, at no point in their 2,557 surviving pages ever mentions the name of Imbert. On the other hand, the secretary Guy Joly, who had staged his own assassination for Retz's benefit but later became disenchanted with him, composed much shorter *Mémoires*, which dwell extensively on the career of Imbert, and this in order to show the character of Retz in the worst possible light. Imbert, Joly reminisces, had been with Retz for twenty-five years by 1658. In the escape from Nantes, Joly claims, it was Imbert who forced the pusillanimous Retz to go through with it. While in Rome, Joly informs us, Retz sent Imbert on a mission to Genoa, and while the exiles were furtively wandering under assumed names, Joly implies that Imbert was dispatched on a mission to Paris. On the Fouquet-Croissy incident, which is placed in Cologne with no mention of Marigny, Joly categorically affirms Imbert's innocence, recounting how, without the slightest evidence to support his accusation, the jittery Retz had his valet (along with his cook) held in the fortresses of Jülich and Bielefeld for two years, from where the cook eventually escaped and begged relief from Retz's friends in Paris. It was only through their intercession, according to Joly, that Imbert was released. Such a shabby personality was Retz, Joly concludes, that "since his return to France, he has never wanted to hear any of his friends on this subject, nor the prayers of the accused."[3]

If we want to examine this incident still further, the next logical question is, who was the person with the multi-suspicious name of Fouquet-Croissy Marsily? Antoine Fouquet-Croissy was indeed the proprietor of an estate in Anjou named Marcilly (*sic*), as well as one east of Paris named Croissy. He was also a judge in the third *chambre des enquêtes* of the *parlement* of Paris, and had been a member of the French delegation at the peace conference in Münster. This delegation was a house divided, the two French ambassadors, Servien and D'Avaux, constantly at each other's throat; Servien enjoying the confidence of Cardinal Mazarin and D'Avaux drawing his support from the *parlement*. In this squabble, Fouquet-Croissy aligned himself wholeheartedly with D'Avaux, who was instrumental, at one point, in sending the adventurous Fouquet-Croissy on a picaresque mission to Transylvania. Like D'Avaux, Fouquet-Croissy became firmly convinced that Mazarin had, in his own self-interest, avoided making peace with Spain, and after the signing of the Treaty of Westphalia, Fouquet-Croissy returned to France, where he reemerged during the *Fronde* as the author of one of the wittiest of the *Mazarinades*, *Le Courrier du Temps*. As the *Fronde* widened, he became closely associated with the Prince de Condé, being in 1651 one of the signatories in the treaty which he made with the Duke d'Orléans. During Mazarin's exile, Fouquet-Croissy got a chance to prove his thesis that peace was possible by attempting to obtain it himself from the Archduke Leopold, governor of the Spanish Low Countries. The negotiation failed, and with the return of Mazarin, not surprisingly, Fouquet-Croissy found himself excluded from the royal amnesty. In 1653 he came secretly to Paris, and quickly found himself sharing the *donjon* of Vincennes with the Cardinal de Retz. Subjected to torture, he was only released thanks to complaints from his fellow judges and thereupon resumed his exile. He seemed to be perpetually running into Retz, hobnobbing with him in Rome, following him throughout his wanderings, and finally showing up in Cologne. And considering that Fouquet-Croissy had just received permission to return to France, it is not entirely surprising that Retz would have become suspicious. Upon returning to France Fouquet-Croissy immediately proclaimed his innocence in the Imbert affair, but not everyone was convinced of it. Mazarin, moreover, suspected Fouquet-Croissy of continuing to stir up trouble, and once more imprisoned him, this time in Perpignan. An analysis of the *parlement* of Paris, made up around 1660, summed up the popular verdict on this man: "intelligent, defiant, *Frondeur*, had great attachment to the Cardinal de Retz, later suspected of doing him a bad turn." In order to obtain his freedom again, Fouquet-Croissy had to dispose of his judgeship. He seems to have lived out his life in Marcilly and died in 1667.[4]

But there is more to consider about him. In those tumultuous days at Münster, the French plenipotentiary D'Avaux had a chaplain by the intriguing name of François Ogier, an eloquent preacher whose pacifically skewed sermons had annoyed Servien and edified the papal nuncio, the future Alexander VII. Now this François Ogier just happens to have kept a journal of this congress, and this journal leaves us with no doubt about the fact that he and Fouquet-Croissy were also on excellent terms. Then, after the signing of the Treaty of Westphalia, Ogier returned to Paris, where we hear little of him except for his popular sermons and his panegyric of the Count d'Avaux. But in 1662 François Ogier reemerges, if only for a moment, and what does he do? He demonstrates that he was no more fervent an admirer of Fouquet-Croissy and the Count d'Avaux than of Cardinal de Retz, who had just given up his position as Archbishop of Paris for a rich monastery, exulting with him: "Your courage has shown itself invincible to every one but the king. While his authority was in foreign hands, neither promises not threats have been able to shake you."[5]

Now I ask you to let your imagination wander for a minute and consider whether it was possible that in 1656 or 1657, when Imbert may have gone to Paris under an assumed name, he might not have hidden out with François Ogier, and might have conspiratorially begun to call himself *Eustache d'Ogier*? If you do not like that, how about the possibility that around 1660, François Ogier was one of Retz's many friends who came to the support of Imbert, perhaps the one who took him in and who eventually tightened the bonds between him and Fouquet-Croissy, who, whether he had corrupted Imbert or not, should have felt some responsibility for his plight? According to this scenario, therefore, François Ogier was the contact man who provided Imbert with a new identity and, in due time, with a new life as a valet of Fouquet-Croissy. You do not have to believe this, though. It is not essential to my demonstration. All that I need for my demonstration I have already demonstrated, namely, that Fouquet-Croissy had been the Lord of Marcilly.

⁓

For Marcilly or Marsilly was also the title of Claude Roux, Andrew Lang's candidate for the employer of the man in the iron mask. Who then was Claude Roux, or Roux de Marsilly? Claude Roux first came to the attention of the ministers of Louis XIV when, in May of 1668, the French ambassador in England, the prestigious Huguenot Marquis de Ruvigny, warned them about him. Ruvigny had been put on to Roux by Samuel Morland, onetime Cromwellian diplomat and inveterate betrayer of republican causes. Ruvigny had been hidden by Morland in his closet during a visit by Roux to Morland's home in which Morland encouraged the loquacious Roux to talk about himself. Roux had revealed in a thick Languedocian accent that he was a Huguenot born in the vicinity of Nîmes and that he owned a home six leagues from Orléans named Marcilly (*sic*). He further described how Louis XIV owed him some money from an investment he had entered into in the generality of Soissons, how he had numerous conversations both with the King of France and the Prince de Condé, and how he was engaged in a French and Europe-wide Catholic-Huguenot conspiracy—which included a certain Colonel Balthazar in the vicinity of Geveva and the Count von Dohna, former governor of Orange—intended to create a republic in southern France. He expressed the opinion that the area was already on the brink of revolt, that the Swiss were all set to assist; that he had been sent by the conspirators to the Marquis de Castel Rodrigo, governor of the Spanish Low Countries; and that he was now in the midst of negotiations with Charles II, the Duke of York, and the Earl of Arlington. Roux added that he had almost pulled off such a revolt three years before, and that there were "a hundred Ravaillacs in France," referring to the assassin of Henry IV, one of them in the royal guards having two years previously almost assassinated Louis XIV. In the year that followed, no efforts were spared to track Roux down, notably in Switzerland, and to bring him back to France. Finally, on May 12, 1669, a squad sent out by the Marshal de Turenne, working in collusion with the above-named Balthazar, managed to kidnap Roux in the territory belonging to the canton of Berrne and bring him back to the Bastille.[6]

Roux, however, was a remarkable man. Seeing himself transferred to the *Châtelet* and subjected to a quick trial, and foreseeing that he would be tortured into revealing his accomplices, he managed to fashion a sharp instrument with which he intrepidly emasculated himself. The authorities had no choice but to collaborate with his gruesome game. When, on the morning of June 22, they discovered that he was dying, they were forced to conclude that torture would merely precipitate his death, and they rushed in the afternoon to his execution, but he again surprised them by recovering his forces and "railing execrably against the sacred person of His Majesty." As he was being broken on the wheel, he once more succeeded in expressing himself, in spite of his pitiful condition. "I die," he said, "true to my religion and to my aversion to the tyrant of France, exterminator of the Huguenots, consoled, however, that there remain hundreds of others whose spirit will not suffer his undertakings!" The Genoese envoy, who reported these words, compared his courage to that of Mucius Scaevola, and the executioner could only silence him by stuffing a rag into his mouth. It took eighteen blows before he expired, at four or five o'clock in the afternoon.[7]

Here was a man who claimed to represent a local as well as international conspiracy and who had died without revealing it. We can now again let our imagination wander by asking ourselves how the description of this execution must have struck Louis XIV and his ministers. Clearly, they would have had to feel nervous, and there is no question at all that they did. Four days later a certain La Salle, former *exempt* in the king's guards, who had, according to one rumor, passed into Spanish service, was, under suspicion of being one of Roux's accomplices, arrested and put into the Bastille, and there were rumors of more arrests in the offing. Early in July the wife of a grocer turned him in for speaking against Louis XIV, and he too ended up in the royal prison. On the 10th an eccentric-looking priest who tried to approach the king was grabbed by the guards and trundled off to the same place. The captains of the four companies of guards, for that matter, proceeded to weed out every man for whom they could not absolutely vouch.[8]

But as the king and his ministers endeavored nervously to round up the usual suspects, I would suggest that we participate with them in the following game of word association: Roux associates with Marcilly, Marcilly associates with Fouquet-Croissy, Fouquet-Croissy associates with Imbert, and Imbert associates with Retz, the *enfant* the most *terrible* of the entire *Fronde*. I repeat—it does not matter if Imbert had actually been corrupted by Fouquet-Croissy; it does not even matter if Imbert had ever known Roux de Marsilly. All that matters is that, in the course of their roundup, it suddenly occurred to the ministers of Louis XIV to ask themselves, "What ever happened to Claude Imbert?" and a few weeks after the execution, they found Eustache Dauger. But, you may wonder, why not put him on trial, torture him, and get to the bottom of the conspiracy? You forget that seventeenth-century France was a "civilized" country. Frenchmen have rights, and under the provisions of the Edict of Villers-Cotterets, still in full force, torture could only be used in a capital case (no impediment here) and *if* you already had one corroborating witness. And even with torture, if Imbert (who was no sissy) did not confess, he could not be convicted. No, best to call upon that universal panacea of the old regime legal system, the *lettre de cachet*, and get Eustache Dauger out of the way for life.

～

Before I claim my membership in the *Institut de France*, however, there are a number of technical problems to resolve. The first regards the location of Marcilly. It seems a piddling point, but the Marcilly owned by Fouquet-Croissy was in Anjou, the present Marcilly-sur-Maulne, Department of the Indre-et-Loire. Its closest city of reference is thus Angers, not Orléans, which is, moreover, some sixty French leagues away. It must be remembered that Roux claimed that his Marcilly was six leagues from Orléans! Well, the solution to this problem is simple, if we also remember that Ruvigny was hiding in a closet, that Roux spoke in a thick Languedocian accent, that six could well have been *soixante*, that "Orléans" could well have been "Oléron," and that the whole context of the statement could have been different. So far, so good. Second, however, there is a minor matter regarding the dating of Joly's *Mémoires*. At one point in them he refers to "the Sieur de Bouteville (subsequently duke de Luxembourg and marshal of France)," the promotion to marshal an event of 1675. It will be remembered that Joly had said that Retz "since his return to France, has never wanted to hear the prayers of the accused." Does this mean that Joly had personal knowledge of the whereabouts of both Retz and Imbert after 1675? Not necessarily. Joly's had been a bizarre career. After leaving Retz's service he had, of all things, become a royal propagandist and the secretary of Charles Colbert, Marquis de Croissy, following him on missions to Aix-la-Chapelle and to England, where, coincidences never ceasing, he had participated in the hunt after Roux. Thus it is not implausible to assume that Joly was speaking of his last knowledge and that some five years in England had made him lose track of what had ultimately happened to Imbert. And, moreover, on careful scrutiny of the sole surviving eighteenth-century text of Joly's *Mémoires*, it turns out that the disturbing statement about the Sieur de Bouteville *is added in the margin!*[9] What a relief! But third, there is a problem of the remainder of François Ogier's journal. For the Bibliothèque Nationale catalog of the *Nouvelles Acquisitions Françaises* indicates that this journal had a sequel, which, at the time of the printing of the catalog, was in the possession of Viscount Samuel Menjot d'Elbenne. If we could locate this sequel, it might be the place to test our theory of the relationship between François Ogier and Claude Imbert! Well, here is the rub! I located the sequel, the original, covering the years 1648–1656, being in the private collection of Mr Etienne Ogier de Baulmy, and a copy in that of his cousin, Mme de Germiny. Even though the journal tells us much about the connection between the Treaty of Westphalia and the *Fronde*, about Imbert it does not say a word! Well, we recall that, according to our theory, Ogier's contacts with Imbert should only have intensified after 1656. Saved again, but by a hair's breadth!

I must admit, however, that when Mme de Germiny's copy of Ogier's journal was graciously made available to me by her nephew Pierre de Germiny in his express mail facility near Charles de Gaulle airport, I already had an inkling that something was seriously wrong with my theory, because on the previous Friday, April 28, 1989, at the Archives Nationales, after observing a disquieting name in the repertory of Etude LXXIII, I had put in a request for the document in question. It was in *liasse* 538, which contains the minutes of the notary Noël Le Maistre and includes an *Estat De Distribuòn de 200000^# faict entre Messieurs les creanciers de Monsieur le President Gallard*, dated December 28, 1673. The following Tuesday, among the prestigious creditors of this financially troubled judge, I found none other than "Sieur Claude Imbert, bourgeois of Paris & damoiselle Anne Marie Marès his wife," claiming, at a moment when according to my calculations he should have been safely locked up in Pinerolo, repayment of the not too modest sum of 16,199 *livres*, capital and interest owed them since January of 1669. What could I say in the face of this evidence? Was it possible that Louis XIV and his ministers had been so crafty as to have foisted off on the entire city of Paris and on the compliant Anne-Marie Marès another Martin Guerre, not only the spitting image of Imbert, but a perfect imitator of his signature? I am not prepared to pursue this hypothesis.[10]

What, then, is the result of this frustrating initial trek on the trail of the iron mask? I would suggest, first of all, if I may be permitted to let off a little steam, that it arouses in me considerable reflections on the way we practice history. How many theories, much more abstract and intricate than this one, which enjoy wide credence among historians, how many theses about the spirit of capitalism, about rising and falling gentries, about the anthropological significance of cat massacres, how many such theories, I ask, would stand for a moment if they were subject, like this one, to invalidation or verification by a single document? History, unfortunately, is not logic, even less so is it plausibility, least of all is it consensus. We need to start with hypotheses, but these must be hypotheses that we can test before we venture to peddle them . . . all of which brings me back to the search for Eustache Dauger. It seems to me that though I have demonstrated one hypothesis about his identity to be false, the effort has not been entirely fruitless. If Claude Imbert is not the man in the iron mask, and he is not, the man in the iron mask is everything that we ever wanted in Claude Imbert, and more. We are still looking for not just any valet, but a valet who was in the know, the confidential valet of an important personage in the court in the 1650s. And the hypothesis of a relationship, if only in the minds of Louis XIV and his ministers, between the execution of Claude Roux and the arrest of Eustache Dauger is still very much alive. This means that there are two approaches to follow. One is to find another suitable employer for Eustache Dauger. The other is to find out more about Roux de Marsilly. I still believe that where the employer of Eustache and the activities of Roux intersect, there we will come face-to-face with the man in the iron mask.

This chapter was originally presented as a paper at the nineteenth annual meeting of the Western Society for French History, held at Bally's Hotel in Reno, Nevada between November 6 and 9, 1991, and published in the *Proceedings of the Western Society for French History* XIX (1992), 99–108.

CHAPTER THREE

~

The Fouquet Connection

After the candidacy of Claude Imbert blew up in my face, I was in a daze, and as I was making my way through the stalled traffic on the Boulevard de Sébastopol, I was almost killed by an equally dysfunctional motorcyclist, who swished in front of me and missed me by an inch. I do not recall how long it took me to recover from this near-death experience, but when I managed to pull myself together, I concluded that the one thing I was still sure of was that Nicolas Fouquet knew the secret and the identity of Eustache Dauger. That being the case, I had to investigate the life of Nicolas Fouquet in order to determine what he could have known and when he could have known it.

Nicolas Fouquet came from a modest but noble Angevin family with a long tradition of royal service. Two members of the family, Christophe, Nicolas's granduncle, and François, Nicolas's father, had been members of the special tribunal that had tried Chalais—the first as *procureur général* (king's prosecutor); the second as one of the judges. This kind of service had endeared the family to Cardinal Richelieu, and François in particular took full advantage of this favor in numerous capacities, while producing, with his pious wife, an abundant progeny of six sons and six daughters. Nicolas, born in 1615, was preceded only by an older brother, another François, and, by dint of his father's favor, Nicolas at the tender age of eighteen found himself counselor in the *parlement* of Metz, and at twenty *maître des requêtes* at the court of Louis XIII, from where he managed to install a cousin as *procureur général* in his former *parlement*. The masters of requests were a body of bureaucrats who reported to the councils, ran their own tribunal, and went out as intendants on special missions, whether to the provinces or with an army. Since, moreover, Nicolas's elder brother was an otherworldly type, the king named him to be Bishop of Bayonne in 1637, so that when their father died three years later, Nicolas found himself for all practical purposes at the head of his family. Ambitious, capable, and this worldly, he married a wealthy lady by whom he had a daughter before leaving him a widower, and he embraced his family tradition with all of his energy and talent. When the crisis over the will of Louis XIII erupted, Nicolas, who, as a master of requests, had a right to sit in *parlement* on such occasions, had to choose between a dead king and a living queen. He decided for the former and lost, but it was the better decision nevertheless, since it won him the gratitude of Cardinal Mazarin, who promptly promoted Nicolas's brother François to the richer diocese of Agde and then sent out Nicolas as an intendant to the province of Dauphiné.[1]

It was profitable and prestigious to be an intendant, but it was also dangerous, especially in the middle of a long war, when public resentment against royal taxes was running high. Fouquet in his intendancy tried to cut a middle path between enforcing the will of the government and appeasing the complaints of the people, so much so that he satisfied neither and the government recalled him, but he had done well enough to be appointed in the following years as intendant to the army in Catalonia, then as intendant on the northern frontier, and then again, with the danger of insurrection approaching, to a newly created post as intendant to Paris. It was in this capacity that, in the latter half of June 1648, he penned several *mémoires* for Cardinal Mazarin, arguing that it was a time to compromise with the *parlement* since, given the anger of the people, force against them would not work. This was advice that fitted in with Mazarin's intentions at the moment, though he could not resist Condé's subsequent victory over the Spanish at Lens to try the arrest of the two judges, which brought him to the day of the barricades and the outbreak of the *Fronde*.[2]

It would appear as if Fouquet had his reservations about the queen's beloved, but when, in January of 1649, Mazarin and the court abandoned Paris, Fouquet remained loyal to the queen, acting as intendant of the royal army under the Prince de Condé that besieged the city and pressured the *parlement* into concluding the Treaty of Rueil. He was seconded by his younger brother the Abbot Basil, as libertine a type as one can imagine, albeit treasurer of one monastery and beneficiary of another. They both stuck with the cardinal as well when he arrested the princes and tried to remain in power with the support of Gondi and the Duchess de Chevreuse. During this same period, in March, while Mazarin, the queen, and the young Louis XIV were making an armed tour of the provinces in an effort to reassert royal authority, Fouquet appears to have joined the court at Dijon. He seems to have been nurturing plans of his own, intending to purchase the important post of *procureur général* in the *parlement* of Paris, and he was back in August, while the court was at Libourne preparing to besiege Bordeaux, where he took the occasion to obtain the approval of Cardinal Mazarin for his transaction. It was in the course of these movements that Fouquet decided to make overtures to the man who was destined to become his nemesis, Jean-Baptiste Colbert.[3]

At that time, Jean-Baptiste Colbert was merely a rising young bureaucrat. His father was a merchant from Reims who had moved to Paris, and Jean-Baptiste began first as a clerk to a banker in Lyon, then to a notary in Paris, then to a lawyer, and finally to a *trésorier des parties casuelles* (treasurer of the sale of offices) until, in 1640, his father purchased for him the office of commissioner of war. There he began serving under the benevolent eye of a cousin who had married into the family of Michel Le Tellier, whom Mazarin installed in 1643 as secretary of war. Le Tellier may have been one of the cardinal's closest confidants, but he was not necessarily one of his greatest admirers. He was also on poor terms with Mazarin's other confidants, Servien and Lionne, and during the tours of the provinces which the court undertook during the year 1650, Le Tellier had Colbert accompany it as his liaison. Ambitious as he may have been, Colbert thought even less of Mazarin than did Le Tellier and, in a report to him on June 23 from Compiègne, described the cardinal as "a man for whom I have no respect." Curiously, the feeling was not mutual, and Mazarin was content to keep Colbert at his side, alternatively ignoring and mistreating him. Fouquet ran into Colbert during his visit to Libourne, at which time, needing all the help he could get, he asked him to inform Le Tellier that he, Fouquet, wanted to become Le Tellier's friend versus Servien and Lionne. "I thought it best," wrote Colbert to Le Tellier on August 9, "since he is an exceptional man who is likely to go far, to reciprocate on your behalf." By dint of such conniving, Fouquet obtained his coveted post. This was, however, on the eve of Mazarin's exile.[4]

At first, as he was wending his way to the frontier, accompanied by his nieces, nephew, and sporadic escorts of cavalry provided by sympathetic governors, Mazarin kept muttering to all who bothered to listen that he still had the confidence of their majesties, even though, as we have seen, he had his doubts about both the queen and his collaborators whom he had left at her side. But his old collaborators, with the liberated Prince de Condé in the corridors of power, had no alternative but to make up to him, and very quickly Mazarin began to fear that they were looking out for themselves. On March 17, from Bouillon, he was complaining to Lionne about the infidelity of Le Tellier and, even incidentally, of Colbert. Not that Mazarin ever lost faith in the capacity of his enemies to fall out among themselves for, only a few days later, he was predicting to Lionne that the Prince de Condé would scuttle the marriage of his brother with the daughter of the Duchess de Chevreuse, which, of course, turned out to be prophetic. But such confidence was difficult for Mazarin to sustain. By May 12, in Brühl, he was alternating between warning the queen that Servien and Lionne were also betraying him and unveiling a plan on how she could maneuver both Monsieur and Condé into accepting his return. A short time later, he went so far in his despair as to contemplate taking religious orders, which implied that he was reconciled to returning to Rome; then, his emotional pendulum suddenly swinging back, he imagined that he might get the queen to appoint him governor of Breisach, from where it was a shorter cavalcade to Paris. As we have seen, however, he need not have worried. The Prince de Condé not only allowed the Duchess de Chevreuse to slip through his fingers; he also developed enough distrust for Le Tellier, Servien, and Lionne to oblige the queen to dismiss them. It would appear, therefore, that the Prince de Condé knew Mazarin's friends better than Mazarin himself did, and Mazarin may have been forced to come to the same conclusion, since from that time on, he never expressed the slightest doubts about their fidelity.[5]

Mazarin may also have had his doubts about Nicolas Fouquet. Nicolas had just married another wealthy lady in pursuit of his personal fortune, while attempting to steer a dangerous course between Mazarin and the *parlement* in pursuit of his own political survival, but since the *parlement* could never quite figure out how it could be both for an absolute monarchy and against its prime minister, Nicolas was able to navigate between these shoals. When the *parlement* set up its new commission to investigate Mazarin, Fouquet, as *procureur général*, was theoretically in charge, but he directed the investigation through his substitute while doing everything he could to delay the proceedings. And in the very midst of them, he managed to extract an *arrêt* out of the ambivalent *parlement* that lifted its seizure of Mazarin's assets. While Nicolas was playing his double game, however, his younger brother Basil was adding his own dimension to the Fouquet connection. Early in May Mazarin and Basil began to correspond, and early in June he came in great secrecy to Brühl, where Mazarin regaled him with his plan for dividing the opposition and sent him back to execute it. Very quickly Basil became notorious in Paris for his contacts with Mazarin, much to the embarrassment of Nicolas, who was criticized for them on the floor of *parlement*. But Mazarin, who appreciated Basil all the more, was never short of encouragement for people whom he needed. "You will never," he wrote to him on August 13, "have a better friend than I." And Basil reciprocated. At this delicate time, when even the queen showed signs of wanting him to return to Rome, Basil was Mazarin's principal contact with Paul de Gondi and the Duchess de Chevreuse. But what is most enticing in our search for the man in the iron mask is that Basil Fouquet had a valet, who first comes to our attention on December 26, 1651, at Brühl, carrying letters and, we may suspect, verbal messages from his master.[6]

Whatever animus he may ever have conceived against Jean-Baptiste Colbert, Mazarin quickly overcame it. One of his principal concerns before going into exile had been to hold on to his personal wealth and, ever since coming to France, the intendant of his household had been a certain Olivier Euzenat, who had intermittently made use of a small council to assist him, but in those frantic days before he abandoned the court, Mazarin had entrusted Colbert with collecting every last penny that Mazarin could claim from the treasury. Colbert did not waste a minute in proving his worth, and in not too subtly hinting to Mazarin that "it was absolutely necessary to have a person in whom you have full confidence to assume the conduct of *all* [italics mine] your affairs." We can have no doubt whom Colbert had in mind, and neither did Mazarin, who, on March 1, 1651, wrote to Le Tellier from La Fère virtually appropriating Colbert for this purpose. Colbert applied himself with extraordinary tenacity in combining absolute fidelity to Mazarin with horror at how miserably his affairs had been administered up to then. Always careful to limit his barbs to those who were most vulnerable, Colbert in his letters from Paris found a receptive reader in the anxious cardinal in Brühl, who on May 23 informed Le Tellier that he was planning to get rid of Euzenat entirely in favor of Colbert, all the while urging Colbert to demonstrate to the public that "never has any minister thought less of his own interests when it was a question of those of the state." If Colbert had any quarrel with this proposition, he never showed the slightest sign of it. He gradually set up a new council, filling it as much as he could with his creatures, such as his relative the lawyer Gomont, and it is possible to follow Colbert in his correspondence as he appropriated Mazarin's confidence: alarming him, reassuring him, and scolding him, all in the name of Mazarin's love for himself.[7]

This subservient behavior was in sharp contrast to that of Nicolas Fouquet, who on November 9 made the mistake of writing a confidential letter to Jean-Baptiste Colbert, assaulting the character of Mazarin, and accusing him of disgraceful ingratitude to his supporters:

> I am astonished that His Eminence has not changed from his ordinary methods, one of which is of not doing anything for those who are honorably and

faithfully attached to his service, and the other that by keeping them hanging, he thinks he can get them to do even more in order to deserve his good graces.

This was just the opening for which Colbert was waiting. He passed the letter on to Mazarin, regretting that Fouquet was indispensable under the circumstances, and expressing pious shock at his outburst. His own relationship with Mazarin, Colbert puts on an entirely different footing.

> I am preparing a writing on the condition of your affairs when I first took over their direction, so that, since I work for my own satisfaction as much as for yours, I get it by comparing the condition in which I found them with the condition in which I will put them.

No doting mother, no infatuated lover, no Siamese twin could demonstrate more passion for another human being than did Colbert for Cardinal Mazarin.[8]

⌒

Mazarin's return to France was not without its travails. He had to collect a small army with which to defy the decrees of *parlement* that prohibited his return. These could not stand up against his 4,000 to 5,000 mercenaries, but they did keep him from immediately returning to Paris, and the court was obliged to go to Poitiers where, on January 28, 1652, he rejoined it. But he was still intending to return to Paris, and the collaboration with Retz and Chevreuse was in full swing. Mazarin, therefore, was all the more in need of Nicolas and Basil Fouquet for this and for every other intrigue that they could muster in the capital. The hopes for a speedy return were interrupted when the Prince de Condé gained a small victory over the royal army, after which he himself came to Paris in the hope of bringing the *parlement* and the Duke d'Orléans over to his side. Neither was very happy to see him— the *parlement* urged him and Monsieur to compromise with the court over everything except Mazarin's return—and keeping him informed of all these dissentions was Basil's valet, who, on April 11 and 13, carried two important communications between Basil in Paris and the court in Saumur and Gien. So did Basil himself, who, on April 24, was caught outside of Paris by one of Condé's raiding parties, while carrying letters from Nicolas to the king and Mazarin advising them on how best to get into the capital.[9]

I'll have to admit this about Basil: he was a cool customer. He managed to sweet-talk Condé with possibilities of reconciliation with the court, and the prince released him on his honor, free to roam the city. He even refused to let a revolution stand in the way of his love life. Instead, he combined the two. He went to visit the beautiful Duchess de Châtillon in the hope of getting her assistance in his negotiation. She was a daughter of the ill-fated Duke de Montmorency, widow of a Marshal of France, and most important of all, the current mistress of the prince. Basil did not succeed in winning her over but, in the process, he fell madly in love with her.[10]

It was during this intermission that on June 24, 1652, some thirty-five miles outside of Paris in the city of Melun, there occurred another incident that, if we are interested in deep dark secrets, we cannot fail to consider. It is related by our old friend La Porte, the queen's cloak bearer, who had suffered so much on her behalf under Richelieu and was no more enamored of his successor:

> The king having dined at the quarters of his Eminence, and having been with him until seven in the evening, he had me informed that he wanted to take a bath. . . . I understood the reason without his having to tell me. The thing was so terrible that . . . I spent five days trying to decide if I should tell the queen. . . . I finally did . . . and she told me that this was the greatest service I had ever rendered her.

Not even Voltaire, who loved to play the know-it-all, could take this intimation of pedophilia seriously, and neither can I, but this anecdote is extremely instructive for another reason. It is instructive because La Porte, for all his hatred of Mazarin, was not so foolish as to make his suspicion public during his lifetime. No one, of course, could forget how Mazarin and Anne had been depicted in the most explicit of the *Mazarinades*, but even in these, the accusations were only made in general, because the moment that the informant got down to specifics, he or she would have to betray his or her identity, and that would seal his or her fate forever. It would have been foolhardy to speak openly about such things. Indeed, La Porte himself went on to claim that his confidential revelation to the queen had ultimately led to his disgrace. What this incident confirms for us, therefore, is that the secret of the man in the iron mask has nothing to do with lewd or lascivious behavior on the part of anyone. Admittedly, we are left with the possibility that, years after any such transgression, a drunken valet had presented his evidence for it to his audience in a cabaret, but with so much water under the bridge, a sound thrashing would have done the job much more cheaply than a lifetime in solitary confinement.[11]

But to get back to the *Fronde*, at the beginning of July Condé's army of some 5,000 men found itself at Saint-Cloud, some eight miles west of Paris, facing a much larger royal army of 12,000 under the Marshal de Turenne nearby at Saint-Denis some six miles to the north of the capital. The prince, concluding that his position was untenable, attempted on the night of July 1st to march his soldiers directly across Paris in order to reach a more defensible position near Charenton, some four miles to the southeast, but the governor and the mayor, still theoretically loyal to the king, refused to open the gates, forcing the army to march in considerable disorder along the walls. Nicolas Fouquet got wind of this predicament and it was he who informed the court. Turenne was thus able to engage the rebel army at dawn, chasing as far as the Faubourg Saint-Antoine and, in the presence of the young Louis XIV, attacked it in broad daylight. Among the casualties of that day was Paolo Mancini, Mazarin's oldest nephew, mortally wounded, but the royal army was on the verge of a complete victory which would in all probability have ended the *Fronde* then and there. All during this engagement, Monsieur, with his characteristic irresponsibility, was faking an illness, much to the disgust of his twenty-five-year-old daughter, "Mademoiselle," who was observing the battle from the ramparts of the Bastille, while trying to extract a letter from her father, still theoretically lieutenant-general of the kingdom, ordering the governor and the mayor to open the gate. At the last moment she obtained it. The Porte Saint-Antoine opened, the cannons of the Bastille fired on the royal army, and the remnants of Conde's army filed into the city. No one ever forgot what she did on that day.[12]

This decisive action did not, however, save the *Fronde*: it merely postponed its demise. The *parlement* was all the more embarrassed by the presence of the Prince de Condé in the capital and of his army which took possession of the outskirts, while Condé himself, under increasing pressure to make peace with the court, had to rely more and more on violence in order to maintain his pretensions. The situation reached a climax when, on July 4, a mob incited by some of his soldiers stormed the *Hôtel de Ville* (city hall) of Paris, looting and killing in the process. This event was the turning point of the *Fronde*. It coalesced the law-and-order sentiment in the capital. The court exploited it by announcing that Cardinal Mazarin had offered his "withdrawal." Fouquet thereupon suggested that the court should order *parlement* to leave Paris and transfer itself to Pontoise, some eighteen miles to the north. Since, however, neither side was prepared to negotiate in good faith over the details of the withdrawal, the *parlement*, claiming that the king had been made prisoner, redundantly reappointed the Duke d'Orléans lieutenant-general of the kingdom and innovatively named the Prince de Condé to be commander of its army. The Chancellor Séguier lent his name to this hastily assembled regime. Too little, too late. The court executed Fouquet's recommendations and welcomed him and a rump of the *parlement* to Pontoise, Mazarin carried through with an imitation withdrawal within France itself from which he continued to direct the government, while Basil remained in Paris, more in the hope of seducing the Duchess de Châtillon than of bringing the recalcitrant Prince de Condé to the peace table. By popular demand, on October 13, he abandoned Paris, taking his little army with him to the Spanish Low Countries. By equally popular demand, on October 21, the king returned to the capital, prompting the Duke d'Orléans, insouciant as ever of the miseries he had inflicted, to retire to the comfort of his *châteaux* of Limours and Blois. Having gotten rid of the two principal troublemakers, the queen mother now found herself in a position to dispose of the third, Cardinal de Retz, by arresting him. It was only a question of time before Mazarin could return, and if anyone had done more than the bungling disunited *Frondeurs* to produce this happy outcome for him, it was Nicolas and Basil Fouquet.[13]

We do not hear much from Jean-Baptiste Colbert during these death throes of the *Fronde*, but he was there in the background, busily straightening out the private affairs of Cardinal Mazarin. In October of 1652 Colbert was proposing to Mazarin that he invest in a new company for trading in the Levant, through which he could not only make "a considerable profit" but also help to "reestablish commerce in this kingdom." Colbert was also becoming more forward. When Mazarin was considering reentering Paris in the company of the king, Colbert took the liberty of advising him to make his own dignified entrance at a later time, all the while protesting, "Your Eminence knows that I don't interfere with affairs of state." On January 2, 1653, the Duke de La Vieuville, superintendant of finances, died. His death produced numerous candidates to replace him, among them Servien and Fouquet, all claiming this key position as the reward for their services. "No one," wrote Colbert to Mazarin, "should presume to give Your Eminence advice on such a delicate matter," after which he immediately proceeded to do so by advising Mazarin not to bestow the office on anyone who was liable to use his subordinates in order to mislead his superior. We don't need to guess to whom Colbert was referring.[14]

It was only a question of time before Mazarin could make his grand entrance, and it took place on February 3 "with," according to the *Gazette*, "all the glory that his great services deserve." One of his first acts was to settle the competition between the two leading candidates for the superintendancy, and he did so by a Solomonian decision, splitting it up between Servien and Fouquet, who also retained his position as *procureur général*. Servien never got along with his equals, and with Fouquet it was no exception. Mazarin needed money for everything: he wanted to be repaid for his past loans to the government, paid for provisions that he was in the business of furnishing to the armies, and adequately funded in order to ease out local governors of questionable loyalty. For nearly two years the two superintendants managed to satisfy him, in part by a devaluation of the currency, in part by new taxes, but by the end of 1654 the cheaper credit dried up. Mazarin tried to establish some harmony between Servien and Fouquet by separating their functions, the former being responsible for disbursing, the latter for finding the money, but this did not alleviate the worsening financial crisis, and if it demonstrated a greater reliance on Fouquet, it also imposed a much greater burden upon him.[15]

Mazarin was also in need of physical protection, and there was another Fouquet ready to provide it for him. After having honed his skills as a confidence man during the *Fronde*, Basil Fouquet shifted effortlessly into the role of Mazarin's chief of intelligence in its aftermath. It is possible that in July of 1653 Basil organized an assassination plot against the Prince de Condé, and probable that in September he foiled a counter-plot by the prince against the cardinal. Basil's continuing courtship of the Duchess de Châtillon, however, added to the fury of her former lover the Prince de Condé, who gradually turned his assassins directly on Basil. This may have helped to confirm Mazarin's confidence in Basil, in spite of his infatuation with the duchess. In 1654 he obtained for him the right to succeed his relatives as *procureurs généraux* in the *parlements* of Metz and Paris, but toward the end of the following year there occurred an incident that could only have been embarrassing to him. Mazarin, it is not clear how, got hold of a letter from the Duchess de Châtillon to the Prince of Condé, indicating that she was trying to entice her latest admirer, the sexagenarian Marshal d'Hocquincourt, governor of Peronne and Ham, to deliver his strongholds into the hands of Condé. The incriminating letter reached Mazarin and the king in Compiègne, while they were with the army. Mazarin had Basil arrest the duchess but, in an amazing display of indulgence for both of them, kept him on as her jailer. "Everything I have done for her," he wrote to Basil, "has been out of love for you!" Not exactly. Mazarin did not love anyone, except in his own way. He was only using Basil to arouse the jealousy of Hocquincourt, who could not bear to think of his delicate flower in the hands of a reprobate. Hocquincourt's passion, plus a cash reimbursement of 700,000 *livres*, did the trick. Mazarin released the duchess from the clutches of Basil and consoled him for his loss with the governorship of Ham.[16]

If, after this incident, Basil Fouquet was still Mazarin's best friend, Jean-Baptiste Colbert was rapidly catching up with him. Basil had transformed himself from Mazarin's guardian angel in adversity into Mazarin's attack

dog in prosperity. Colbert's domain was less spectacular, but no less important to Mazarin, who was so filled with appreciation as to forget exactly
how old he was:

> I am fifty years old [he was fifty-two] and in desperate need to put my affairs
> in good order. I have never been able to do it myself, so you will have to, for I
> will fail to take care of my personal interests, which I have both by nature and
> by habit sacrificed to the public ones.

That was all the encouragement Colbert needed. About a week later he
began the practice of sending long letters to Mazarin written in a clear
secretarial hand on the left so that Mazarin could casually reply in his own
scribble on the right. Little by little, if one follows this correspondence, one
can see Colbert extending his guardianship from the private affairs of his
patron into the finances, military needs, and security of the state.[17]

∽

The Fouquets had chosen to play a dangerous game, a game of grabbing and
holding on to power in the face of a volatile world, and they chose to play
it without reservations. One of its prerogatives was to live in style. In 1654
Nicolas purchased a lavish residence in Saint-Mandé on the outskirts of Paris,
and in 1656 he began major reconstruction on an old *château* that he owned
in the village of Vaux near the city of Melun. He chose as its architects Louis
Le Vau and Michel Villedo, and over the next few years the magnificent edifice began to take form. He was in the habit of surrounding himself with artists
and men of letters. He frequented beautiful and intelligent women, without,
however, creating scandal. Less sophisticated and more outrageous was his
brother Basil, who chose to obtain his sense of worth exclusively through
the flaunting of high-born mistresses and the intrigues of low-born informers,
but in either case the Fouquets maintained their own identities, as opposed
to Jean-Baptiste Colbert, who dissolved his into that of Cardinal Mazarin.
Unfortunately too for Nicolas and Basil, their family coat of arms featured a
squirrel standing on its hind legs, presiding over the motto "Where shall he
not ascend?" In a hierarchical society, a problem arose for squirrels when they
ascended too rapidly, when they acted too arrogantly toward their former
superiors, when they displayed too much ostentation too quickly. Nicolas and
Basil Fouquet, each in his own way, had chosen to test the system.[18]

Having exhausted the credit of the state, early in 1655 Nicolas had to
resort to a series of new edicts creating offices and inventive new taxes on

every aspect of life. The young king had to go personally to the *parlement* to ensure their registration, and even he was not entirely successful. It was in the course of this confrontation that legend has him bursting into *parlement* brandishing a whip and informing members that "*L'Etat c'est moi!*" which is not entirely accurate. What is accurate is that in spite of the difficulty that Nicolas was experiencing in finding money, Mazarin kept insisting on it, especially when it was a question of being reimbursed for his own advances. The situation reached crisis proportions in the middle of June 1656 when the Marshal de Turenne, with some 20,000 troops, was attempting to besiege the city of Valenciennes in the Spanish Low Countries. The place had a huge perimeter, and he had stretched his forces very thin in order to encircle it when, on the night of July 16, they were surprised by a slightly smaller Spanish army which included the renegade followers of the Prince de Condé. The French were routed; one of their generals was taken prisoner and, according to the Spanish, 11,000 more were killed, wounded, or taken prisoner! It was this event, we may recall, that inspired Cardinal de Retz to leave the security of Rome and send Imbert into Paris, and indeed for Mazarin the defeat meant another round of discontent with his policies and the additional expense of replacing his losses. For Fouquet, it made the difficult financial situation even worse. But, in an emergency, he raked up money, much to the appreciation of Mazarin, who showered his graces upon him. He made Nicolas's elder brother François coadjutor of Narbonne. Another brother Louis replaced him as Bishop of Agde. Basil became keeper of the seals and then chancellor of the Order of the Holy Spirit. It must have seemed to the Fouquets as if they were untouchable. At the beginning of 1657 Nicolas contracted a particularly prestigious marriage alliance—that of his eldest daughter to the son of the Count de Charost, captain of the king's bodyguard and governor of Calais. But Mazarin had not changed. The emergency waned, and his demands for money did not. Mazarin still sympathized with Basil, but Nicolas began hearing rumors that Mazarin was critical about his handling of the finances and about his elegant lifestyle.[19]

Nicolas was too much of a gentleman to grovel. Instead, he resorted to sarcasm. On June 26, 1657, he sent a letter to Cardinal Mazarin ridiculing his complaints about the finances and vindicating his own rights to a little relaxation. Not that the gravity of his predicament had not dawned on him. Contemporaneously with this letter, he composed a confidential *mémoire*, almost to himself, on what he should do. He began it by returning to his one-time estimation of Cardinal Mazarin—naturally suspicious, especially of people of worth; ungrateful to those who had put themselves in the greatest danger on his behalf, namely, Nicolas and Basil Fouquet; and ready to listen to their detractors, by which he undoubtedly meant Colbert. The conscious purpose of the *mémoire*, however, was for Nicolas to instruct his supporters on what to do in the event he was arrested. The first remedy Nicolas had in mind was simple. If he were kept in isolation, listen to Basil. Otherwise Nicolas wanted his family to try to get him a valet, and he named four in order of preference: Vatel, Longchamps, Courtois, and La Vallée. Then he would have wanted books, all the conveniences of life, and a doctor, but as the *mémoire* continues it becomes clear that the purpose of these requests was to gain time during which all of his connections who were governors, such as the Count de Charost, could fortify their strongholds in order to intimidate the government into restoring his liberty. If the government tried to put him on trial, Nicolas wanted these same governors to block all tax receipts and issue a manifesto so as to rouse the people. He was, in short, prepared to start another *Fronde*. Many historians have been struck both by the audacity and the implausibility of this *mémoire*, but none have observed that it is also a key document in the hunt for the iron mask. It is a key document not only because it gives us the names of four of Nicolas Fouquet's valets at that time, none of which was Eustache Dauger, but also because it raises the question of why, if Nicolas was in possession of a secret that could have imperiled the monarchy, he did not make any use of it in this moment of panic. The answer is, of course, that at that moment neither he nor his valets knew any such secret.[20]

While Fouquet was thinking about his survival, Colbert was thinking about Mazarin's legacy. Mazarin, as we have seen, was dead set on vindicating his conduct of the negotiations in Westphalia, and Colbert had been busily collecting the correspondence in order to pass it on to Mazarin's personal historian, the Abbot Siri, who could be guaranteed to interpret it correctly. This was all with Mazarin's approval, and what this tells us is that at this point he was infinitely more conscious of his achievements than of his failings. Colbert also wanted to make sure that no visitor to Paris could ignore the fact that Mazarin had been there. If the *palais Mazarin* was not enough, Colbert now proposed a "grand project" by which he had in mind a school for young nobles, the future College of the Four Nations, to stand on the left bank of the Seine right across from the Louvre. But as agreeable as Mazarin was for his conduct of diplomacy to be remembered, he was a little less enthusiastic about funding an education for the young. The reason? It would be too expensive, and moreover, it would probably not get built during his lifetime. This tells us that, however concerned Mazarin may have been about his legacy, he was even more concerned about participating in it.[21]

If there was ever a time for the Fouquets to watch their step, this was it, yet it was in the midst of his brother's crisis that Basil also got himself into trouble with Cardinal Mazarin. We have seen how Basil always had some difficulty in keeping his love life out of his political intrigues. Now that his side had won, he acted as if he had won, and that gave him the right to inject himself into the lives of the most beautiful and highly placed women to be found. Among these were the Countesses de Fiesque and Frontenac, two ladies-in-waiting of Mademoiselle de Montpensier, the Amazon of the Battle of Saint-Antoine. Since that memorable moment she had quarreled and made up with her father, and, hoping for reinstatement at the court, she was on her way back to Paris, when she heard that the above two ladies had told Basil Fouquet that she had made a will in favor of the Prince de Condé. Mademoiselle was furious. This did not stop her from returning to Paris, where she proceeded to hold court in the family palace of Luxembourg, but she disgraced her two former friends, and Basil, with his king-of-the-walk attitude, came to their defense. Mademoiselle became even more outraged and Mazarin took her side. In his moral universe, some people could allow a defeated army into Paris and be forgiven; others could put their lives on the line for him and fall into disgrace when they got in his way. From La Fère, on July 21, he wrote Basil a scathing letter, warning him, "Your best friend can give you no better advice than to lead a life in keeping with your profession." Here again, out of the blue, a hint on where not to hunt for the man in the iron mask. If Mazarin could reproach Basil for not living up to the standards of his profession, it is hard to imagine that he knew that Mazarin was not living up to his own. In any case, in order to patch up the quarrel, he obliged Basil to make a humiliating apology to the great Mademoiselle.[22]

Toward the end of the year 1657, not content with having been reprimanded by Mazarin, Basil proceeded to pick a quarrel with his brother. It was apparently over money, and in order to obtain it Basil began to conspire with a clerk upon whom Nicolas depended in order to find lenders to the treasury. Mazarin feigned to ignore the family squabble, but he could not dissimulate the damage it could do to the finances. He wrote to Nicolas, "When I have as much confidence in a person as I have in you, I do not question his conduct toward his subordinates," giving him, somewhat superfluously, the freedom to dismiss his clerk. But the very redundancy of this vote of confidence cast doubt upon its sincerity, particularly since the year 1658 was, by Nicolas's own recollection, the most difficult for the finances since the *Fronde*. It is true that in September of that year the king permitted Nicolas to purchase the island of Belle-Isle on the Breton coast and even gave him the right to appoint its governor, but shortly thereafter Nicolas pulled out the *mémoire* that he had written the year before and added his brother to the list of his enemies. This makes the *mémoire* doubly revealing, for not only does it demonstrate that Nicolas was continuing to fear for his own security but, more importantly for our investigation, it demonstrates that he was still not in possession of any secrets that could topple the monarchy. Nor was the future looking any rosier for Basil. As the peace was approaching, so also was the likelihood that his arch-enemy the Prince de Condé would be returning to grace. On February 17, 1659, Abel Servien died, but if this passing relieved Nicolas of a truculent colleague, it also placed the entire responsibility for the condition of the finances on his shoulders. Mazarin kept thanking Nicolas for his efforts, but the Fouquets were no longer to Mazarin what Colbert had become. While he was at Saint-Jean-de-Luz and in the process of negotiating the peace, Mazarin wrote to Jean-Baptiste Colbert and asked him for his advice on what to do about the finances.[23]

Colbert could hardly restrain himself. He had already developed his beloved trinity of finger pointing, quick fixes, and utopian visions. Now he expanded upon it in a confidential *mémoire* that he must have written for the ages. The finger he pointed directly at the superintendant, who, according to Colbert, had not been keeping any books. This device had presumably permitted Fouquet and his clerks to cheat applicants for government contracts out of their advances, buy worthless orders for payment from private parties at a discount only to cash them at the treasury at face value, and engage in other dishonest practices by which he had lined his own pockets and built up his influence throughout the kingdom. For the time being, Colbert had no better advice for Mazarin than the stop-gap expedient of trying to restructure the debt. In the course of the *mémoire* Colbert even admitted that the corruption dated from as far back as the late sixteenth century, but he was totally oblivious to the fact that for the previous eight years he had been doing on behalf of Mazarin exactly what the cohorts of the superintendant had purportedly been doing for him. It seems as if Colbert never stopped to consider whether the problem lay in Fouquet or in the pressing demands of financing a war. For Colbert immediately went on to recommend the obvious utopian reforms that any superintendant, if he did not have to finance a war, would have been more than willing to undertake: redeeming bonds, repurchasing offices, and last but not least, setting up a Chamber of Justice, a special tribunal which would despoil the profiteers of their ill-gotten gains.[24]

Long before this *mémoire* ever reached Mazarin, Nicolas Fouquet had obtained a copy of it. He was himself going to Saint-Jean-de-Luz to discuss the finances, and he took the occasion to complain to Mazarin that Hervart and others, in collusion with Colbert, had been spreading rumors that he was about to be dismissed. He was particularly angry at Colbert, who, after treating him as a friend, had turned against him. The upshot of all this was that he offered to resign both his posts as *procureur général* and superintendant of finances. Given the need for money, it was more of a threat than an offer, and Mazarin, who had just received Colbert's *mémoire*, lied through his teeth that Colbert had never spoken or written in such a manner. Rather than dismissing Fouquet, Mazarin went on to agree upon some additional stop-gap measures to keep the government afloat. But he immediately informed Colbert of Fouquet's complaints, which prompted another confidential *mémoire* from the indignant Colbert. After voicing the usual complaints against Fouquet, Colbert now concluded that "nothing can change him." After denying his own collusion with Hervart, Colbert spoke badly of him too. And, after eliminating all the opposition, Colbert concluded that he "did not want anyone's place." If Nicolas Fouquet was worried about his future, he had every right to be.[25]

It is, of course, extremely difficult to prove a negative, but from what we have seen thus far it is hard to imagine how Nicolas Fouquet could have become privy to any secret that would have imperiled the monarchy in 1669. He never developed the closeness of relationship with the queen, with Mazarin, or with the young king that might have given him knowledge of much more than his own manipulations as superintendant of finances. We have, moreover, been able to identify and exclude his valets. In fact, the one Nicolas prized the most, Vatel, went on to become the *maître d'hôtel* of the Prince de Condé and committed suicide in a spectacular manner in 1671, when the fish failed to arrive for a feast in honor of Louis XIV. As to Basil, he was certainly in a good position to collect delicate information, but if he was not worth imprisoning along with his brother, it is even harder to imagine what earthshaking information any valet of his could have garnered in the course of his errands. The only conclusion I can draw, therefore, is that whoever's valet Eustache Dauger may have been, he was neither the valet of Nicolas nor of Basil Fouquet. And yet, we are still left with the fact that Nicolas knew his secret.

CHAPTER FOUR

∿

Calais

One of the first things that comes to mind, when one learns that Eustache Dauger was arrested by an officer of the garrison at Dunkirk, is that the arrest may have happened while Eustache was arriving from or leaving for Dover, some seventy-five miles across the channel in England. This is certainly a thought that crossed my own mind, so that during the summer of 1990 I made a quick stop in Lille while on the way to the Low Countries on the hunt for Claude Roux in Belgium and the Netherlands. It was a frustrating experience. First, the archives of the Department of the Nord happened to be closed, and when I finally made contact with them, I learned that in 1931 all of the notarial acts for Dunkirk in the seventeenth century had been burned in a fire. It was neither the first nor the last time my researches would be frustrated by the destruction of documents. However, in the winter of that year, Ron Martin drove up to Santa Barbara for one of our *tête-à-têtes* on the man in the iron mask, and it was on that occasion that Ron caught me up on a recent discovery by a Mr Stanislas Brugnon that in 1669 Jean-Baptiste Colbert had reimbursed Captain Vauroy for having picked someone up in *Calais* and delivered him under guard to Pinerolo. So much the better! The city of Calais had all the attractions of Dunkirk as a port of embarkation, it was even closer to England, and we can almost eliminate it as a port of arrival, for if Vauroy had been ordered to go to Calais, he must have known when he could expect to find Eustache there, which would have been impossible for incoming ships. And if this clarifying insight were not enough, there was another striking thing about Calais that quickly attracted my attention. That was the name of the governor, Louis de Béthune, Count de Charost—the man on whom Fouquet depended to hold the city.[1]

Let us begin, however, with the proximity to England by recalling that the first time we ran across the city of Calais in our investigation, it was the departure point of Henrietta Maria on her way to meet her royal husband. The marriage had become a happy one, especially after 1628 when the Duke of Buckingham disappeared from the scene, but the reign of her husband had not. He had encountered a rising tide of parliamentary and Puritan opposition, against which she kept advising him to hold firm. Open hostilities broke out in 1642, and even though at first the royalist side seemed to have the advantage, it was perpetually short of resources. Under the circumstances, the activist queen took matters into her own hands. The previous year in London had seen the marriage by proxy of her nine-year-old daughter Mary to William, the fourteen-year-old son of Frederick Henry, Prince of Orange, Stadholder and Captain-General in the Dutch Republic, a fine Protestant connection to which no Puritan could object. Now, under the pretext of accompanying her daughter to meet her new husband, Henrietta packed whatever jewels she could lay her hands on and sailed from Dover to the province of Holland, where she could pawn or sell them for some ready cash. It was not easy to do, but with the assistance of the prince, she was able to pledge her jewels for the sum of 1,265,300 florins, which enabled her to purchase supplies and raise troops. She also sent her confidant, Henry Jermyn, to France. He managed to extract some 96,000 *livres* out of Cardinal Mazarin, and in February of 1643 they returned to England with their own army of 1,300 men.[2]

Unfortunately for her, they did not do much good, and with her own health deteriorating along with the military situation for her husband, in 1644 she was forced to abandon him in England and return to France, accompanied by the faithful Jermyn. At the beginning of a regency, in the middle of a war, the France to which she returned could offer her little more than sympathy. Anne of Austria sent her 10,000 *pistoles* and assigned to her a pension of 30,000 *livres* a month. When she got to Paris, the government furnished her with an apartment at the Louvre, and Mazarin provided her with 312,000 *livres*. In the spring of 1646 she was joined by her son Charles, Prince of Wales, and a bit later by her little daughter Henrietta, and in November, while she was at Saint-Germain-en-Laye, the Duke d'Epernon lent her 230,000 *livres*, for which she pledged more of her jewels. The following year, on December 4, 1647, she pledged to him the two most precious jewels of her collection, the *grand Sancy* and the *miroir de Portugal*. In 1648 Mazarin managed to furnish her with another 150,000 *livres*. By January of 1649 she and her daughter were freezing in the Louvre while the army of Anne of Austria and the Prince de Condé was besieging Paris, and Henrietta had to have recourse to the *parlement* of Paris in order to obtain 20,000 *livres* for her sustenance. But on the 30th of the same month, across the channel, a rump of the English parliament, dominated by Oliver Cromwell, executed her husband and turned England into a republic. The year before, her younger son, the Duke of York, had barely managed to escape, and on February 13 he joined her at the Louvre. We know by Henrietta's own testimony and that of her son Charles that by 1649 she had run up her debt to Mazarin to the hefty sum of 593,416 *livres*. Apparently she had used whatever assets she could muster to pay the interest on her pledged diamonds and to assist her eldest son, now Charles II, in his futile efforts to reconquer the throne.[3]

Another problem faced by Henrietta was the timidity of the French regency during the *Fronde*. After the execution of Charles I, French and English privateers had begun an undeclared war on each other's shipping, which Mazarin was more than willing to terminate. As he wrote to himself in the middle of 1650, "It is important to come to terms with the English, and if that does not succeed, to ally with Holland." If Mazarin thought something, Servien was never far behind, and some six months later, on January 20, 1651, Mazarin's right-hand man in the area of foreign policy made the complete case for him. As terrible as it was to deal with regicides, if it could be assured that the English would join France in its war against Spain, France should not hesitate to recognize the new republic, the "Commonwealth." This, however, was only ten days before Mazarin went into exile, and even though the French did send an envoy—through Calais—with limited instructions, the English republicans preferred to flirt with the Spanish until early in 1652. At that time, just as Mazarin was rejoining the court at Poitiers, Oliver Cromwell sent an emissary to Dunkirk, offering a bribe to its governor, the Count d'Estrades, or, failing that, to make an alliance with France, in return for turning over the seaport to the English. Estrades, who would not be corrupted, referred the overture to the court, but in what must have been a stormy council session in which the newly arrived Mazarin supported the idea and Châteauneuf, in one of his last hurrahs, opposed it, Anne of Austria sided with Châteauneuf. Three months later Mazarin managed to get her to see the light, but it was too late. With an English fleet anchored in the Downs to intimidate any French effort to relieve the city by sea, on September 16, 1652, the Spanish recovered Dunkirk. Soon thereafter their armies recovered both Barcelona and Casale as well. One stronghold after another, the *Fronde* was rapidly swallowing up everything the French had so painfully acquired since the days of Richelieu.[4]

Under the circumstances, Mazarin was prepared to do almost anything in order to obtain allies against Spain. In December of 1652 he sent a young envoy, Antoine de Bordeaux—again though Calais—to England, ostensibly to settle the undeclared naval war. The Commonwealth, however, was not very responsive. It had a commercial war against the Dutch, which it was winning; it was being courted by the Spanish; and in July of 1653 the desperate Mazarin raised the stakes by ordering Bordeaux to propose an "alliance" with these regicides. Between 1649 and 1651 they had only maintained an obscure resident in Paris—a French Huguenot with the tempting name of Augier—and after his departure, his function was being performed even more obscurely by his nephew, a certain René Petit, so that everything depended on Bordeaux in London. In December of 1653 Cromwell turned the Commonwealth into the Protectorate, with himself as Protector, and soon thereafter Mazarin promoted Bordeaux to the rank of ambassador, as well as sending him a colleague. By now Mazarin was talking about a "close alliance," vaunting the fidelity of France to its Protestant allies, and promising not to help anyone against the new regime. A victorious peace with the Dutch Republic gave Cromwell even more bargaining room, and he concluded, apparently, that it was more in his interest to plunder the Spanish in the West Indies than to torment the French in the Channel, but Bordeaux's negotiation got stalled by the clumsiness of his new colleague—whom Cromwell expelled—and by the persecutions by the Duke of Savoy of some of his Protestant subjects in the valleys of the Vaud, whose protection Cromwell embraced. It was on this occasion that he sent Samuel Morland, through Calais, with letters both to Louis XIV and to the Duke of Savoy in support of the persecuted Vaudois, and it was on this mission that Morland was to make his first contacts with Claude Roux, the man whom Morland would later betray, and who will keep reappearing in our search for the iron mask. Mazarin, who had no scruples about allying himself with regicides, had even fewer scruples about the toleration of heretics . . . if it would produce his victory over Spain. Under pressure from both France and England, the Duke of Savoy suspended his persecution. For Cromwell this was all the more evidence that he had the most to gain if he could get a foothold in Dunkirk with French help. On November 3, 1655, he concluded a treaty with Bordeaux that ended the commercial war against France. On December 30 England declared war against Spain, and on the same day Cromwell designated his own nephew, Sir William Lockhart, as ambassador to Paris.[5]

The abandonment of ethical standards and religious principles was a common practice in the seventeenth century, and those who embraced it justified it under the name of "reason of state," just as our modern practitio-

ners justify similar transgressions under the name of "national security." But
there was no way, even by the morals of the seventeenth century, to justify
the spectacle that accompanied the establishment of the English Commonwealth, namely, the mad scramble of the greedy to acquire the spoils of
the decapitated King of England. In this scramble, from the very beginning,
Mazarin showed himself an eager participant. In May of 1650 the secretary of
the French embassy in London sent Mazarin a list of what was on sale, from
which it appears that the cardinal quickly snapped up six pieces of tapestry
of the *Acts of the Apostles*, after Raphael. A merchant named Jaback acted
as one of Mazarin's principal suppliers. The Commander de Souvré, one of
Mazarin's old cronies, apparently sold him five pieces of Charles I's *History of
David*, after Albrecht Dürer, and no sooner had Bordeaux gotten to England
than he began purchasing horses for Mazarin, quickly moving on to more
tapestries, engravings, paintings, and busts. His and Mazarin's biggest concern seemed to be the exchange rate for letters of credit, as they competed for
the masterpieces of Dürer, Peter Paul Rubens, Hans Holbein, Raphael, Correggio, Titian, Giulio Romano, Anthony Van Dyck, and others. Even the
death of Mazarin's father on November 14, 1654, did not dampen Mazarin's
appetite for this infamous commerce, which frequently passed, whether for
the transfer of money or the transport of goods, through the port of Calais,
and where, from time to time, we find the Count de Charost collaborating.
Early in 1655 Mazarin went so far as to send his personal jeweler, François
Lescot, to England, thus attracting our attention to the Lescots and to their
relation to Cardinal Mazarin.[6]

The Lescots were members of the merchant bourgeoisie. François's father,
Mathieu, is designated in notarial acts as *bourgeois de Paris*, and François's
mother, Estienette, was of similar origins. Mathieu and Estienette had at
least five children, four boys and one girl, who, to confuse the researcher,
married another François Lescot. Furthermore, the civil records of Paris for
this period having been destroyed during the Commune of 1871, it is extremely difficult to determine the children's age or seniority. It would appear,
however, as if a certain Remond Lescot was the elder of the brothers and, at
first sight, the most intriguing, for we encounter him in 1636 and 1638 as a
valet de chambre and jeweler of Anne of Austria and, therefore, if we are still
attracted to that theory, in the best possible position to have made off with
the twin brother of Louis XIV. Also, Remond was known to Mazarin, who
noted in his Carnet sometime in 1645: "Have the queen's Lescot come in to
see me." Whether this means that Mazarin was referring to an obscure valet
or was already distinguishing between the two brothers is an open question,
but we do know that by 1647 Mazarin had enough confidence in our François

to send him off to Portugal on the hunt for diamonds, and that from that time on his connection to Mazarin was a matter of public knowledge. We know that during the *Fronde* Lescot held some of Mazarin's furniture and precious stones in his home and, once the *Fronde* was over, felt familiar enough to joke about who might have absconded with Mazarin's dressing gown.[7]

We are not quite sure whether Lescot passed through Calais, but he had recently arrived in England by May of 1655, by the testimony of both Bordeaux and Colbert. Lescot quickly got to work purchasing furniture, it is not clear whose, and sending it back through the ambassador. Apparently, it was a buyer's market. Mazarin and Colbert expected Lescot to return quickly but he kept delaying his departure. By July 12 they had received twelve packages from him, and they were clearly anxious for more. It is also evident from the correspondence that some of these packages contained diamonds, again of uncertain proprietorship. It also turns out that the energetic Lescot got himself into trouble. He found himself pursued for some of these diamonds by none other than Oliver Cromwell, who wanted them for his own son and, amazingly, on discovering this, Cardinal Mazarin placed the interest of his collection ahead of the interest of his diplomacy. "Mr Lescot," he wrote to Bordeaux, "would need your assistance in order to recover something over there," adding in a postscript in his own hand, "not only is he one of the greatest servants of the king, but one of my best friends." In this manner Mazarin seems to have gotten his jewels, and Lescot seems to have finally returned to France, but by starting with Calais and appearing to get lost in the process, we seem to have stumbled onto an insight into one of Cardinal Mazarin's dirtier passions.[8]

Mazarin's courtship of the Commonwealth, not to speak of his pillaging of her husband's possessions, could hardly have endeared him to the anguished Queen of England, but there was very little that she could do about it. In 1653 the last of her sons, Henry, the Duke of Gloucester, briefly joined her in France, but the lack of support from Mazarin's government as well as her own uncompromising Catholicism alienated even the duke, so that Charles II, with all his brothers, transferred his own little court to Cologne, from where he hoped more effectively to subvert the English regicides. This, however, did not prevent Henrietta and Charles from working together. On March 23, 1654, we find her and her son borrowing 65,640 more *livres* from the Duke d'Epernon, thus running up their debt to him to 433,000 *livres*. It must, moreover, have been a humiliating experience for the English royal family. Henrietta had to suffer the presence of Cromwell's nephew in Paris, treated like an honored guest. His presence at first embarrassed Mazarin as well, but, as unpalatable as it was to besiege Dunkirk only to turn it over to the English, his situation was getting desperate. The frustration of Lionne's mission to Spain, scuttled as it was by the humiliating defeat of Turenne before Valenciennes; the growing financial crisis; and the rumblings of revolt throughout the country—all these things called for desperate remedies and, excruciatingly, after numerous ups and downs, Mazarin and Lockhart came to terms, according to which, in the spring of 1657, the combined forces of France and England would by land and by sea besiege the strongholds of Gravelines, Mardyck, and Dunkirk. England would provide the navy and 6,000 troops, a portion of which troops would be paid by the King of France. Dunkirk and Mardyck would go to England; Gravelines to France.[9]

～

Let us not forget the Count de Charost. He came from a distinguished family. His uncle, Maximilien de Béthune, first Duke de Sully, was a Huguenot follower of the future Henry IV, father of Louis XIII. When Henry, in order to hold on to his throne, decided to become a Catholic, Sully took advantage of the Edict of Nantes to remain a loyal Protestant, while at the same time establishing his own reputation as superintendant of finances. After the assassination of Henry IV, Sully went into retirement, devoting the remainder of his life to composing his reminiscences. However, his younger brother Philippe, the first Count de Charost and father of Louis, had always been a Catholic, which stood him and his son in particularly good stead with a dynasty that had enthusiastically embraced its new religion. Louis, born in 1605, also went by the name of Count de Charost. He chose a military career, gaining distinction under Louis XIII and Richelieu. Such was his reputation that in 1634, the king appointed him to be captain of the second French company of the *gardes du corps*, the royal bodyguard. The bodyguard was made up of 400 men, divided into four companies, each under its captain serving for three months out of the year. The second company served from April to June, giving its officers and its men ample time for other services. Not surprisingly Charost kept rising. In 1636 the king appointed him the governor of Calais, not only a key seaport but at that time very close to the frontier with the Spanish Low Countries. His loyalty and services became even more valuable during the regency of Anne of Austria and the ministry of Cardinal Mazarin.[10]

Charost was no sycophant, however. On August 15, 1648, eleven days before the famous Day of the Barricades, there occurred a scuffle over precedence between the bowmen of the *Hôtel de Ville* and the king's guards in which the Marquis de Gevres, Charost's senior colleague, came to the defense of their subordinates. This was no time for Cardinal Mazarin to pick a fight with the city hall of Paris, and he immediately dismissed the marquis, asking two of his junior colleagues, Charost and Chardenier, to replace him. Both, along with their remaining colleague, refused, which produced a wholesale dismissal of the captains. This was no time for the government to be severe with anybody. Charost retained his governorship of Calais, his colleagues also retained their other positions, and on November 9, 1649, he also regained his captaincy of the guards. So for that matter did his colleague . . . for a while. And, after additional displays of his military prowess, in September of 1650 Charost was promoted to the rank of lieutenant-general, and three days after Mazarin went into exile, on February 3, 1651, he received a *brevet* to the title of Duke and Peer of France. This looks very much like the career of an assertive but loyal nobleman.[11]

Did the Comte de Charost have a valet? Of course he did. Anyone like him had a dozen of them, and in the case of Charost we can quickly identify one of them around this time. His name was François Lamoureux. He was a *valet de chambre*, and on July 4, 1651, he was in Paris in the office of the notary François Le Fouyn to enter into a "convention" under which he would furnish a certain François Angouin of Auvers and his wife with up to 3,000 *livres* for the purchase of wheat over the next five years, each party splitting the profits from its resale. There are a number of intriguing things about this act: (1) It is surrounded in Le Fouyn's minutes by several acts of Charost himself. (2) It informs us that Lamoureux had a sideline. (3) Le Fouyn was also the notary of Cardinal Mazarin. But our excitement quickly ceases. Lamoureux disappears. For all we know, he went full time into the grain trade. And why would anyone want to arrest him under the name of Eustache Dauger? The discovery of Lamoureux, therefore, merely decreases the likelihood that the Count de Charost had anything to do with the secret of the man in the iron mask.[12]

It is always possible, of course, that a captain of the guards could have been privy to some secret and highly volatile information that might have toppled the monarchy, but if Charost was in on it, I cannot imagine what it would be. His very punishment for insubordination would testify against it. Had he been in possession of some major secret, he would have been treated much more leniently or much more harshly. When Mazarin returned from exile, Charost continued in his multiple duties, and from his outpost in Calais, these included maintaining contact with French envoys in England, the defense of the frontier along the northern seacoast against Spain, and, as we have seen, facilitating Mazarin's purchases. In July of 1654, learning that the Spanish had denuded their garrison at Fort Philippes on the outskirts of Gravelines to a mere 120 soldiers, he took it upon himself to attack the stronghold with as many men as he could muster and on the night from the 16th to the 17th stormed the place, taking fifty-eight prisoners, including the governor; grabbing all its cannons and munitions; and demolishing as much as he could of the fortifications before returning in triumph. In a lean year for victories, this feat gained him a headline and six-page accolade in the *Gazette*.[13]

Still, this kind of clue called for an expedition to the archives of the Pas-de-Calais in Arras, which I undertook in the summer of 1991, hoping that neither the Royal Air Force nor the *Wehrmacht* had gotten there before me. They had not, and I found there a good collection of official records, including notarial acts from the city of Calais for the middle years of the seventeenth century. Aside from Charost, I found a number of his subordinates: there was Charles de Calonne, Baron (later Marquis) de Courtebonne; the *lieutenant du roi*, Dominique Benoist; Sieur de Volespine, the major; as well as a Hippolyte de Launoy, who was in command of the powerful citadel. Calais was a garrison town, and the mainstay of its garrison was the regiment of Charost's own son, the Marquis de Charost. One of its officers, Dominique de Cancer, Seigneur de Pignan, behaved so heroically in the raid on Fort Philippes that it won him special mention in the *Gazette*, and he appears frequently in the notarial acts while serving as an officer in other units. I was also able to identify a number of royal officials: Pierre Costé, prosecutor; François Thosse, judge and administrator of the royal domain; and Dominique Fly, commissioner of the navy. Finally, there was a series of notables who dominated the municipal government throughout the years—the Rault, the Hache, and the Caussien. Many of the military were local nobility, and not surprisingly there was a lot of social mixing and doubling of functions between the military, the royal officials, and the municipal notables. Cancer, the heroic officer, was the husband of Isabelle Fly, sister of the commissioner of the navy. Susanne Costé, sister of the prosecutor, was the wife of Fly. The commissioner Jacques Hache, the on and off mayor, was also an adjudicator of the *gabelle* (salt tax) and the husband of Marie Rault, daughter of Antoine the former mayor. All this was very typical. Still there was no great link of clientage or intimacy with the court in Paris that could enliven our search for the man in the iron mask . . . at least at first glance.[14]

Our attention, therefore, must remain with Charost and, given his domination over the stronghold, the marriage, early in 1657, of his son to the daughter of Nicolas Fouquet now assumes more imposing proportions. Admittedly, that the nephew of a legendary superintendant of finances should undertake to form an alliance with a current holder of that prestigious position would hardly be surprising. Having a fortress to defend and the regiment of his son as the mainstay of the garrison, what better arrangement than for the town to be provisioned through the special care of a superintendant who was the father-in-law of an important colonel? On the other hand, the fact that Nicolas Fouquet presumed, as he did in the summer of 1657, that if he were arrested he could count on the garrison of Calais to hold out for him, begins to look much less chimerical if one presupposes a secret understanding between him and the Count de Charost. This hypothesis could also explain how it was that Nicolas Fouquet came to be acquainted with Eustache Dauger.[15]

Moreover, in the course of scouring the notarial acts of the city of Calais, I also came upon another valet of the Count de Charost. This is thanks to a confrontation that took place in the winter of 1664–1665 in the market square between the Sieur de Brannasize, an officer in the garrison, and two brothers, Bathélémy amd Jean Regner, the first of whom was the valet of a local nobleman, the Sieur de Marigny. In the course of the encounter, Brannasize sustained injuries amounting to 800 *livres* in medical and 417 *livres* in additional expenses, and he pursued his attackers in the royal court, which condemned them to costs plus three and seven years in the galleys, respectively. Not surprisingly, the brothers appealed and, just in case, attempted to settle. It is at this point that they chose as their intermediary a valet of the prestigious Count de Charost, a certain Antoine Houdan, who served them well. He got them off with a payment of 1,100 *livres* which, it would seem, also deterred the criminal prosecution. Was Eustache Dauger an alias for Antoine Houdan? The following summer, back in Paris to track him down in the records of Nonnet, the notary who had issued the procuration, I found it and spent the rest of that miserable summer looking for more traces of Houdan and searching for anything suspicious in the rich records of Charost's notary, Thomas. Alas, I found Houdan in the same way I had found Imbert, alive and kicking in 1675, 1679, and 1681, and the many notarial acts signed by Charost that I scoured did not reveal anything out of the ordinary. I did find one interesting tidbit, the name of the Countess de Charost's coachman, François Augier. Could it be that the Count de Charost had another valet named Eustache Dauger, a relative of François, give or take a little particle, whom we have failed to uncover?[16]

This tidbit is too intriguing for me not to share, but not intriguing enough to prevent me from returning to the situation in Calais where, at the end of May 1657, the first contingent of English troops began to arrive in Boulogne, some twenty miles down the coast. At that time Mazarin, fearing the outbreak of another *Fronde*, wanted nothing more than to proceed with the execution of the treaty with England, but he was in the hands of the Marshal de Turenne, who insisted on making a number of feints—his own brief siege of Cambrai, which misfired, and a long siege of Montmédi by his colleague La Ferté, which succeeded—neither of which satisfied Oliver Cromwell, who suspected that Mazarin was in bad faith. In the meanwhile, Charost in Calais found himself under attack by the Spanish and gained even more distinction by stoutly repulsing them with the aid of the bourgeois militia. It was not until September 30 that Turenne got around to the siege of Mardyck, which succeeded with the aid of an English squadron offshore. The French turned this conquest over to an English garrison, thus mollifying Cromwell somewhat, but it closed the campaign and forced the postponement of the more ambitious sieges until the following year.[17]

Thus in the year 1658 the city of Calais became the staging area for one more desperate effort by Mazarin to bring the Spanish monarchy to its knees. He arrived there on May 21 with the young king. Turenne was at that moment at Bergues with his combined Ango-French army of 15,000 preparing for the siege of Dunkirk, which he invested two days later, his troops piling up their circumvallations until the night of June 4–5, when they began digging the trench. The Spanish, whose army in Flanders included the troops of Condé and the English royalists under the Duke of York, was of almost equal size. They had no intention of letting the siege proceed and attempted a relief. Turenne marched out to meet them and on June 14, in a great battle in the dunes outside of the city, the combined Anglo-French army defeated the Spanish, which defeat was followed by capitulation of the city on June 24. He then went on with his army to lay siege before Bergues.[18]

～

These were two impressive victories, but Mazarin's travails were not over. While visiting the siege of Bergues, the young Louis XIV began to experience pain, wooziness, headache, and loss of appetite. On returning to Calais he felt feverish, and between July 1 and 4 his doctor Antoine Vallot subjected the king to an unspecified number of enemas (*lavements*), five bleedings, and repeated infusions of syrup, in the course of which Louis not surprisingly got worse. Mazarin, fearful for his own future as well as that of the king, wrote to Paris for two more doctors. Vallot, for his part, began to suspect some sort of venom, and on June 5 proceeded to a complete purgation, which only resulted in a night of delirium. On Sunday, July 7th, the king was given communion and asked Mazarin, as his best friend, if he was going to die. The same day the two doctors from Paris arrived only to witness another bad night. But Vallot was adamant in his diagnosis and insisted on applying, along with another bleeding, the more radical remedy of a powdered beetle (Spanish fly), spread on the patient's arms and legs to induce blistering through which the poison could exit. This remedy not having much effect, Vallot not only went on to his seventh bleeding, but he proposed another complete purgation of the body combined with an emetic wine, which contained the mineral antimony, in the hope of inducing vomiting. His colleagues were hesitant, but he appealed to Cardinal Mazarin, who supported the remedy. On June 8 Vallot applied it, and miraculously, after twenty-two bowel movements of a green and yellowish substance, the king began to recover.[19]

This almost cataclysmic disaster in the midst of a Herculean labor obliged Mazarin to order Turenne to suspend his operations for a few days, but no sooner had Louis begun his recovery than Mazarin, himself badly tormented by his body, resumed his drive to break the will of the Spanish. On July 22 Turenne took Bergues. A few days later at Cassel, Mazarin met with him and La Ferté, and they decided on the siege of Gravelines. Everything was going splendidly. La Ferté took it on August 28 and Turenne took Oudenarde on September 9, when opportunity suddenly knocked. On the 13th (3 O.S) Oliver Cromwell died, leaving the Protectorate in the hands of his inexperienced son, Richard. With England in disarray, here was another opportunity for Mazarin to achieve his lifelong ambition of taking over the entire Spanish Low Countries. He was almost there. In the ensuing week, Turenne moved with his army in the vicinity of Brussels, but thought better about attempting a siege and decided to go for the more modest conquest of Ypres. In 1646 Mazarin would have been enraged at such timidity, but in 1658 he was no longer the man who was willing to stake his very being in return for a spectacular triumph. "You have done very well to withdraw toward the Lys," he wrote to Turenne. Mazarin would have been content enough at this juncture to see the Spanish Low Countries as a neutral republic.[20]

There are other indications, too, that Mazarin was mellowing. In his correspondence at this time, he shows an unprecedented degree of empathy for the welfare of the soldiers and especially for the wounded. He also seems to have been surrounding himself with a more professional group of subordinates. One of these was Charles de Grouchy, Seigneur de Robertot. He had emerged, like the Lescots, from the circle of Anne of Austria, and Mazarin had qualified him as far back as 1655 as "a person whom I love and who belongs entirely to me." Mazarin was also working hand in hand with two young intendants, Jean Talon and Olivier Lefèbvre d'Ormesson. These were all men of considerable integrity by the standards of any age, but even they were not above reconciling their services to Mazarin with their services to the monarchy. For example, after the fall of Dunkirk, Mazarin discovered that there had been a frigate under construction in the harbor that he wished to acquire for his own navy. When Dominique Fly, the commissioner of the navy, offered to assist him in purchasing the sails, Robertot stepped in, informing Mazarin that he could get them for him at a lower price.[21]

Fly, however, had been around for a long time. We first meet him as far back as 1629 when a commissioner-general of the navy already finds him as a local commissioner in Calais—at least this is how he is designated three years later when he takes on a lease to collect the admiralty rights for the entire province of Picardy. In December of 1653 Bordeaux in England asks for some money from Colbert to pay for a painting by Correggio, since a "bourgeois of Calais" has not yet sent it to him. We can only guess who this bourgeois was, but we do have evidence from another source that Fly was communicating with Bordeaux. In June of 1657, during the Spanish attempt to surprise Calais, Fly distinguished himself as commander of one of the companies of bourgeois militia which assisted the Count de Charost in defending the city. In the next few months we find him corresponding with England over the procurement of weapons, as well as corresponding regularly with Bordeaux. This is noteworthy enough.[22]

What is even more noteworthy, however, is that in the days following Louis XIV's recovery Mazarin had written from Bergues to Charost asking him to provide him with some accommodations in Calais. Charost, of course, rushed to offer his own residence, which offer Mazarin declined, and the next thing we hear from Colbert in Paris is that "while your eminence will be in Calais, I will not fail to address all my letters to Mr Fly." We have no choice, therefore, but to stop and ask ourselves why an ailing Cardinal Mazarin should prefer the hospitality of a mere commissioner of the navy to that of an affluent royal governor. Moreover, before leaving Calais Mazarin left money with Fly for the fortifications of Gravelines, and after leaving Calais the relationship became even tighter. On hearing of the death of Cromwell, Mazarin sent Fly a mysterious package for delivery to Lockhart in Dunkirk. He also sent him letters to forward to the Marshal de Schomberg in Ypres and to Robertot. On September 24 Mazarin thanked Fly for having visited the works at Gravelines. On October 5 he assured him: "I have entire confidence in your competence and fidelity." On October 9, he entrusted him with additional responsibilities for the fortifications of Gravelines. Faced with condemnations from pundits and pious alike for having turned Dunkirk over to the English, Mazarin had a manifesto produced in his own defense, which he had Colbert send to Fly in order to forward it to Robertot. Mazarin even went so far—we are not quite sure when—as to entrust Fly with at least 10,000 *livres* of his personal funds, and he was holding 12,000 at the time of

Mazarin's death. This last is a clue that Sherlock Holmes would certainly keep in mind, and so should we.[23]

Mazarin, however, had an even more intimate relationship with another person who comes under our special scrutiny at this time, namely, Angelo Sanvitani, one of his own valets, who went by the nickname of Lange. He seems to have been from Rome, but we know little else about his origins. We first find him in October of 1656, when he is escorting some linen for the troops to La Fère. He was married in December of 1657 to a certain Marie du Couldray, and in January of 1658 he was distributing payments to Mazarin's own *Mazarin-italien*, and seeing to the provisioning of Mardyck. Once Mazarin got to Calais he associated Lange with Talon and Robertot in the operation of the hospital. After the fall of Dunkirk, Mazarin put Lange in charge of purchasing the frigate that was under construction in the harbor, and during the remainder of the campaign, Lange acted almost like a commissioner of war, seeing, along with Fly, to the fortifications of Gravelines and taking special care of the military hospital at Bourboing, all of which earned him Mazarin's highest plaudits. After the fall of Ypres, Mazarin put him in charge of collecting the king's revenues in the city—in the course of which he fell out with the major of the garrison—as well as collecting the contributions from the countryside. When, late in October, Lange became ill Mazarin was extremely distressed, referring to him as "a faithful and devoted servant." Last but not least, Mazarin employed Lange for the purchase of tapestries and paintings, one of them by Raphael. An insight into the character of their intimacy emerged when he wrote proudly to Mazarin that he had obtained a painting for him by trickery. It is hard to imagine even Colbert describing his handling of Mazarin's affairs with such brutal candor.[24]

Eventually, however, Mazarin got around to asking Lange for his books, excusing himself, as if he needed to apologize, with the amazing assertion that "it is a detail into which I cannot enter." He was apparently better empowered early in 1660, when he dispatched Robertot to Flanders to check on all the contributions. It was a moment of reckoning for Lange, and it would seem as if he had not covered his tracks very effectively, as Robertot wrote to Mazarin on February 17 that Lange had collected 30,000 *livres* more in contributions than he was supposed to and was charging uniforms at their full value to his expenses while deducting them, at least in part, from the pay of the soldiers. Robertot wrote in the same vein to Colbert, and a few days later the Intendant Talon wrote to Mazarin:

> As to the account books of Mr Lange, Your Eminence can see what to make of them by the letters of Mrs Robertot and Vandermetz, who is the most honest

man in Flanders. In a word, Your Eminence has been very badly served by this individual. . . . I have learned things about him in this country that make my hair stand on end.

On receiving Robertot's letter, Colbert forwarded it with his own to Mazarin, which permits us to gain access to Mazarin's private and remarkable reply to Colbert:

I don't think Lange was the only one to take everything he could in that country. Let Robertot know what you think he should do and let me know what orders he thinks I can send him to back him up . . . *in good time* [italics mine].

Given the fidelity that Mazarin expected from his own servants and given the way that Colbert had been writing to Mazarin about Fouquet, the timidity with which Colbert now communicated the sins of Lange is astonishing. It reveals that in the relationship between Mazarin and Lange, there is an unprecedented degree of indulgence than can only make us wonder at the extent of their collusion, if not of their intimacy, especially when we recall that Eustache Dauger was buried under the name of Marchioly. Is this because whatever mask Eustache occasionally wore could not disguise an Italian accent?[25]

Once again, possibility is not proof, and whatever evidence may point to Angelo Sanvitani can instantly be turned into a pumpkin by a single document. And here it is! In a letter written on April 15, 1670, nearly nine months after the arrest of Eustache Dauger by the Duke of Savoy, to his ambassador in Paris, the duke most obligingly begins with the statement: "You have received one of my letters by the hand of M[r] de Lange." Thus to Imbert, to any valet of Fouquet or of his brother, and to any valets of the Count de Charost, we can now add at least one of Mazarin's valets, and certainly one of his most promising.[26]

We may not have found the right valet in Calais, but we have isolated Dominique Fly, a permanent resident of long-standing loyalty, with connections across the channel, who had performed both public and personal services for Cardinal Mazarin. I would suggest, therefore, that if, in July of 1669, any minister of Louis XIV had wanted get a well-known valet out of Paris so as to arrest him without arousing any suspicion, the best way to do it was to send him, as he may well have been sent on many previous occasions, on an errand to Calais to pick up a shipment at the home of Dominique Fly, where Captain Vauroy could be sure to find him. And if this is correct, our foray to Calais suggests that the arrest of Eustache Dauger is an inheritance from the private operations of Cardinal Mazarin, on which operations we are now in a position to concentrate.[27]

CHAPTER FIVE

~

Follow the Money

Cardinal Mazarin's admirers through the ages have tended to see him as an aesthete whose cultivation of the arts was part and parcel of his magnificence, but my more cynical impression of the cardinal is supported by contemporary historians who have investigated his personal finances. Daniel Dessert has pointed out "the extreme greed tainted by abject baseness that Mazarin puts into his frantic quest for wealth," and Claude Dulong has reminded us that "in the seventeenth century gems and precious stones were not merely adornments, they were secure assets in case of need." My excursion to Arras, therefore, in combination with their impressive researches, gave me more reason than ever to take Mazarin's fortune into account if I hoped to solve the mystery of the iron mask.[1]

We have only hints of his fortune during his youth. He had a *palazzo* in Rome, heavily mortgaged, and he certainly did not bring a fortune to France with him. He had an old friend, the Abbot Mondini, to help him manage his assets, and by 1644 Mazarin also had the lawyer Olivier Euzenat to assist him with his private affairs. Mazarin later claimed that around 1641 he had put in the hands of his banker Cantarini some 493,000 *livres* while retaining some 300,000 in Rome. From that time on, we can begin to assess the state of Mazarin's finances by dividing it into three headings: (1) his official salary and his benefices, (2) his investments and acquisitions, and (3) his contributions to the functioning of the state.[2]

As for his official salary, it consisted of a variety of posts: member of the council, minister, cardinal, superintendant of the queen's household and the king's education. Claude Dulong estimated his income from these at 204,000 *livres* a year, plus a whole collection of other offices including, in 1645, the superintendancy of the *Compagnie du Nord*, which sum, with the help of such offices, looks as if it rose to around eight million by 1648. Each of these positions was rife with opportunities to generate more income. Then there were his benefices, and Joseph Bergin has determined that between 1639 and 1648 he acquired fourteen, including the extremely rich abbeys of Saint-Médard de Soissons, Saint-Michel-en-l'Herm, Moissac, Saint-Florent de Saumur, and Royaumont. Bergin estimates his income from this source alone rose from 16,000 *livres* a year in 1641 to 228,000 in 1648. Even if this was net, it is doubtful whether the cost of maintaining the monks and the monasteries, for which he was responsible, rose proportionately. At the beginning of the regency, he rented the modest *hôtel Tubeuf*, which he expanded into the sumptuous *palais Mazarin* and eventually purchased. The queen who loved him was also free with her bounties. In 1644 she gave him 300,000 *livres* outright, which he later claimed he never received. In 1645 she passed on to him the king's right to one-fourth, which the following year she raised to one-third, of the income from all the prizes taken by French privateers. But this was barely scratching the surface.[3]

His investments, closely connected to his official duties, included a little army and a little navy. He had his own regiment, the *Mazarin italien*, to which he later added three more—the *Mazarin-vaisseaux*, five regiments of cavalry, and one of Polish infantry. His had a navy for the purpose, among other things, of privateering, and in 1647 Queen Christina of Sweden gave him a handsome 32 gun frigate the *Jules*, which became its flagship. He speculated in military supplies such as arms, ammunition, cannons, lead, and wheat. He also speculated in copper, from which he could profit thanks to the government monopoly on the minting of coins. His position gave him or his agents the capacity to obtain paper orders for cash or assessments on future revenues from the treasury which he could subsequently negotiate at a discount, redeem, or furnish to his bankers at face value. He was the owner, under an assumed name, of a number of boutiques throughout the city, which he rented to various shopkeepers. Last but not least were his acquisitions of luxury goods, both for himself and for profitable resale. In March of 1643 Mazarin sent the Abbot Mondini to the Spanish Low Countries to recover the furniture and precious stones of Marie de Medici. In September of 1644 Mazarin asked the French resident in the Dutch Republic to be on the lookout for the best bargains in diamonds. We have a record of Mazarin's personal collection by 1645, and it was already impressive. In 1647, he sent François Lescot on his first mission, this one to Portugal, in search of more diamonds. All these enterprises could easily escape import duties and other tolls. By 1648 he had assembled an entire council, made up of Euzenat, Ange de Massac, and the faithful Mondini, for his personal affairs, along with a host of lesser operators, such as Dominique Jobart, the Girardin brothers, and François Le Bas.[4]

Mazarin was not ungrateful for his prerogatives, and there were times when he displayed his gratitude by using the riches which the monarchy was bestowing upon him in order to support it. For example, sometime in 1643 he claimed to have advanced, through his banker Cantarini, 19,000 *livres* to the treasury, for which he later demanded repayment. In 1644 he provided 100,000 *livres* to the Marshal de Schomberg, Governor of Saint-Esprit in Languedoc, in return for transferring the office to Monsieur, whose good graces were necessary at the beginning of the regency. In the summer of 1645 he seems to have outdone himself in secret and pious generosity by donating 300,000 *livres* from his benefices, again through Cantarini, to the Venetian Republic, whose island of Candia (Crete) had just been invaded by the Turks. But if these examples illustrate a certain chivalrous intermixing of the private and the public, others appear considerably more self-serving.[5]

This was the case in his relationship with Henrietta Maria, the embattled Queen of England. We recall that she had been obliged to abandon her husband in order to collect money for his cause. From the very beginning, Mazarin seemed to be willing to help, and it was certainly in the political interest of France to do so. We can also recall, by Henrietta's own testimony and that of her son Charles, that between 1643 and 1649 Mazarin, through his bankers Cantarini and Serantoni, lent her some 593,416 *livres*. It is interesting to note, however, that in 1651 Mazarin asserted only that he had lent her "more than 300.000 *livres*," which is far short of 593,416. What could account for the huge discrepancy? We have a hint in the account book that Cantarini later presented to the commissioners of the *parlement*, where after noting the transfer he adds, "The cardinal has given me his word in the presence of Lord Jermyn, Mr Lionne, Mr Ondedei, and others *to have it paid to me* [italics mine] or to pay it himself." In other words, it was not even clear to Cantarini where the money would be coming from. We have another hint of what was happening in the archives of the French Ministry of Foreign Affairs. There, in the middle of a volume of diplomatic correspondence with England for the year 1653, we find a "List of Jewels of Her Majesty the Queen of England pawned in Holland." It describes the jewels and their holders, and indicates the dates of the interest payments. The full value of the jewels was some 1,627,600 Dutch florins, which is consistent with the original value of the jewels pawned by Henrietta Maria in 1642. The last payment date being November 28, 1646, and more payments being due in May of 1647, this suggests that the document was drawn up between those dates. But who was making the payments? It could have been Henrietta Maria. We remember that on November 11, 1646, and December 4, 1647, she borrowed heavily from the Duke d'Epernon. But what would have been the point of borrowing from Peter to pay Paul? What is much more likely, therefore, is that by this time, Mazarin was gradually taking control over the diamonds that Henrietta had pledged in Holland.[6]

The same kind of money laundering appears in the case of the marriage of Marie de Gonzague, aunt of the Charles II who had succeeded his grandfather as Duke of Mantua, to Vladislav IV of Poland. On the surface this marriage may have seemed like a diplomatic coup designed to augment French influence. The King of Poland demanded 2,100,000 *livres* in cash as a dowry, and in order to satisfy him the King of France contributed 600,000 *livres* outright and advanced 900,000 to be taken from Marie's own inheritance, which was in the midst of litigation, while, in order to let him keep his own possessions in France, which included duchies of Mayenne, Nevers, and Rethel, the King of France required Charles to be responsible for the rest, which, counting the 900,000, amounted to 1,500,000 *livres*. The duke, who was already heavily in debt, was in no position to borrow more, so that the court of France had to intervene in order to help him find the money. But this transaction, too, smells to high heaven. In the first place, one half of the 600,000 *livres* of the dowry which were ostensibly donated by the King of France consisted of overpriced diamonds sold to the Queen of Poland by Mondini, and another half in money ostensibly advanced to the royal treasury by Mazarin. In the second place, the money theoretically advanced by the King of France and the remainder of the dowry owed by the Duke of Mantua, just like the money lent to the Queen of England, went through the hands of Mazarin's bankers, including some 450,000 *livres* contributed by Mazarin, in what form we can only imagine. In the process, Cantarini and his associates became the holders of Marie's rights, while Mazarin was lining his own pockets with 750,000 *livres* in obligations from various parties. In the third place, and most significantly, Charles, who had enough problems protecting his possessions in Italy, was in no position ever to repay, which exposed him to being expropriated by his creditors in due time.[7]

We can also smile at the more frantic mixture of his personal interest with that of the state that Mazarin began in 1647 when his position and his policies were both in jeopardy. When an entire French army in Germany mutinied, he raised 300,000 *livres* by pawning his tapestry and plate in order to control the damage. The next year, he put his money into a last ditch effort to support a revolution against the Spanish that had broken out in Naples. Also in 1648, we find him making a huge purchase of tapestries in Flanders, bargaining over the best price for amber and musk—which were only good for perfume—in Portugal and, once again in order to maintain the French army in Germany, selling to his banker Cantarini no less than 212,950 *livres* in plate and jewelry. All this lends some credence to Colbert's later claims that in 1648 Mazarin had tried to run the state with his own money. During this difficult period, when he needed all the support he could get, he even offered the eldest of his seven nieces, the twelve-year-old Laura Mancini, in marriage to the thirty-seven-year-old Protestant, the Marshal de Turenne.[8]

Mazarin, of course, was by no means the inventor of such practices. His predecessors in his position, from Sully, to Luynes, to Richelieu, had engaged in them as well. And they all justified it in the same way, namely that, in view of the services they were rendering to the monarchy, they were entirely deserving of their prerogatives, and that, moreover, their financial independence and their networks of patronage were an essential part of the security of the state. But we have to say about Cardinal Mazarin that he was carrying the art of profiteering to unprecedented levels, and this without the remotest idea that he was setting a record. We remember his absolute denial, just as the *Fronde* was breaking out, that he had acquired any posts, governorships, duchies, or treasures. And yet, for all of this self-rightcousness, there was still an element of guilt. He did not want to see his finances revealed. He did not want his more sordid operations to be made the subject of public scrutiny. He lived in a world in which no one questioned the morals of the powerful until such time as they fell. Then each of the Ten Commandments came into play. This is exactly what happened to Cardinal Mazarin.[9]

⌁

The court had barely left Paris on January 6, 1649, before the *parlement* proceeded to banish Cardinal Mazarin and to seize his possessions, and on the 12th its commissioners appeared at the home of his principal banker, Cantarini, demanding to see his books. Loudly protesting that he had no funds belonging to the cardinal and that, on the contrary, the cardinal was in his debt, Cantarini finally led them to the residence of Abbot Mondini, where they discovered four registers which indicated that between 1643 and 1648, Cantarini and his partner had received over 26,000,000 *livres* in deposits from the king and 7,808,648 from Cardinal Mazarin, and that Mazarin also maintained an account in the name of Mondini for 136,470 *livres*. The auditors for the *parlement* also claimed to discover that Cantarini owed

Mazarin an additional 442,802 *livres*, whereas on January 23rd Cantarini produced summaries to indicate that Mazarin owed him and his associate Cenami some 120,000. Whoever was telling the truth, there was still a huge discrepancy between Mazarin's official wages of some 200,000 *livres* a year and the eight million or so that he had accumulated. Apparently aware of Mazarin's importation of precious stones, the commissioners inquired as to their whereabouts, Cantarini replying that he knew nothing about them. The commissioners also wanted to know about the sale of 212,950 *livres* worth of plate and jewelry ostensibly made in 1648 by Mondini on behalf of Mazarin to Cantarini, to which the latter replied with a certain amount of plausibility that this was a business transaction occasioned by the cardinal's financial stringency at the time.[10]

The authors of the anti-Mazarin pamphlets had a field day with these revelations. Following the seizure of Mazarin's palace an *Inventaire des merveilles*, a description of the curiosities found in it, ranging from some immodestly nude statues to a high-tech chair that served as an elevator. These at least could be excused as decadent luxuries, but the *Lettre d'un religieux envoyée à monseigneur le prince de Condé*, supposedly the letter written by a monk to the Prince de Condé, exposed the cardinal for running his own business in tapestries, silver plate, and precious stones. A little later, under the date of August 15, 1649, more information about this flourishing sideline came out in Fouquet-Croissy's *Courrier du Temps*, which announced, on top of everything else, that "young Lescot [François's son, Mathieu] has returned from Lisbon and brought Cardinal Mazarin eight hundred thousand *livres* in precious stones in order to maintain the business that Mondini and his other ecclesiastical and lay agents carry out for him." What everyone may have suspected about Cardinal Mazarin, but had not dared to articulate, now became a matter of public scrutiny.[11]

By this time, however, the *parlement*'s investigation into the cardinal's finances had been interrupted by the compromise Treaty of Rueil, and during this intermission Mazarin sought desperately to solidify his position. Having failed to tempt Marshal de Turenne with the teenage Laura Mancini, he then offered the same nymphet to the Duke de Mercoeur, who loved her dearly. He was the elder son of the Duke de Vendôme, of Chalais conspiracy fame. After the arrest of the princes in January of 1650, when Mazarin took the court on a tour of the provinces in an effort to reassert royal authority and the Estates of Burgundy offered the queen 100,000 *livres*, she quickly reserved it for him. In the course of this excursion, his old friend Mondini died, which forced Mazarin to redistribute whatever papers and precious stones had been in Mondini's hands. Mazarin also kept more of his nieces on the market, offering his second one to the Duke de Candale. He was the son of the Duke d'Epernon, creditor of the Queen of England, who was attempting to hold the rebellious seaport of Bordeaux in check for the king. When, at the end of May, the governorship of La Fère, a key frontier stronghold in Picardy, fell vacant, the queen retained it for herself, no doubt intending to reserve it for Mazarin. That same year he lost the *Jules* to the navy of Oliver Cromwell, but the frigate *Anna*, a gift by Queen Christina of Sweden to Anne of Austria, Mazarin had quickly added to his own navy. He continued in his advances to the state, claiming that in 1650 alone he had advanced more than 700,000 *livres*, but as his position deteriorated, he had to turn his attentions to hiding his assets. Some of his most valuable possessions he placed with Tubeuf, former owner of the *palais Mazarin*; others with the queen; still others Mazarin left with his banker Cantarini or with another one of his bankers, Hervart, some even with the Duchess de Chevreuse. The Governorship of Upper and Lower Auvergne, which the queen had just given him *in petto*, he put into the hands of the potential bridegroom, the Duke de Candale. The stronghold of La Fère Mazarin left to the Sieur de Manicamp, the best person he could find in the emergency. The queen was also quick to resume control of the emoluments that she had ceded to him and place his posts in the hands of the most reliable possible proxies. Still, before he left France in January of 1651, he made every effort to obtain guarantees that he could retain all his property and that he would be reimbursed for all of his advances.[12]

The exile of Cardinal Mazarin gave the *parlement* an opportunity to resume its investigation, and by its *arrêts* of March 2 and 11, 1651, it set up a new commission. One of its duties was to investigate any violations of its *arrêts* that may have been committed as Mazarin was leaving the country; another was to investigate his "piracies, finances, and impediments to the peace." Some of its members followed in his tracks; others met in Paris at the home of his old enemy Broussel, where they hauled in Cantarini and demanded all of his previous registers plus all the ones he had not yet presented. He did his best to hold them off but, in the meanwhile, the commission called in more witnesses. On April 27, it interrogated one of Cantarini's clerks, a certain Jehan Carteron, who testified that he had been employed in redeeming letters of change from the treasury and that he had also been coerced by Cantarini and his associates into participating in a fictitious purchase of boutiques in various parts of the city. On May 6 the commission questioned Cantarini's cashier, Ludovici, who turned out to be a model witness for the prosecution. He expounded freely on Cantarini and Serantoni's shipments of large quantities of precious metals out of the country, on Mazarin's personal profits from the Queen of Poland's wedding, on his appropriation of Marie de Medici's succession, on the gifts given to him by Anne of Austria, and on his bloated reimbursements for the *Mazarin-italien*. On May 25 Charron, an agent of Bellinzani, agent of the Duke of Mantua, went so far as to claim that all of the 900,000 *livres* for the Queen of Poland's dowry had come from the royal treasury and that Mazarin had been the recipient of bribes from the Ottoman Sultan. On June 3 a courier testified that in the middle of the war he had delivered a suspicious letter from Mazarin to the Marquis de Castel Rodrigo, governor of the Spanish Low Countries. When on August 4 Cantarini finally came up with his remaining books, any good that they may have done for him was overshadowed by the particularly damaging accusation of a treasurer of the navy who claimed that Mazarin had appropriated the king's ships for his own piratical ventures in the Mediterranean. Before a Chalais-type tribunal with the accused at the bar, all of this innuendo would have been enough to send Mazarin to the block, but in a court caught in its own plodding procedures, the evidence was fragile, full of hearsay, and Mazarin, of course, had an entirely different interpretation, and so apparently did the Duke de Mercoeur, who came to see him in Brühl and blissfully married Laura Mancini. The investigation in Paris, moreover, concluded with an *arrêt* of the *parlement* which ordered that whatever goods of Mazarin could be identified be placed on sale for the benefit of his creditors, and it was probably in consequence of this decree that Cantarini now submitted his summaries, in which the amount he claimed was owed to him by Mazarin had risen to 354,205 *livres*. But by this time the *parlement* was wavering between its hostility to Mazarin and its hostility to the Prince de Condé. Colbert appealed the *arrêt* and got it modified. "This is the first time," he wrote to Mazarin, "that the *parlement* has done something to your advantage."[13]

Just as the *parlement* had been getting into motion, however, there appeared the handiwork of an extremely knowledgeable polemicist whose poem *La Mazarinade* was destined to provide a generic designation for all of the broadsides that appeared in France between 1648 and 1652. The *Mazarinade* is as scurrilous as it can be, accusing Mazarin of every kind of perversion, even though it spares Anne of Austria. But it does seem to have some inkling of Mazarin's adventures in Spain, where, according to the author, Mazarin's flirtation with a woman earned him a beating by one homosexual patron and forced him to return to Italy where he obtained employment from another. When it gets past the smut, the *Mazarinade* also accuses Mazarin of stealing tapestries and precious stones with the help of Mondini. But perhaps the most remarkable of its revelations, and one that we can be certain is not invented, is what it claims to reveal about Mazarin and the Queen of England:

> from their unhappy queen
> her rings you stole

Who was this polemicist who knew so much? There has been some debate about his identity, but it is almost certainly the comic poet Paul Scarron. In his youth Scarron had been in Rome at the same time as Mazarin, which is where he could have picked up the local gossip. Scarron's patrons in Paris included both Anne and Mazarin, but Scarron was also a favorite of Gondi, the Condés, and a host of *Frondeurs*. The wide berth Scarron gave to Anne in the *Mazarinade* is revealing. Mazarin, however, had stopped his pension. Everything fits to make Scarron the author, and the *Mazarinade* is worthy of our closest attention. Gondi, who claims to have persuaded the *parlement* to subsidize Henrietta Maria during the *Fronde*, must have shared his knowledge of her financial straits with Scarron. Mazarin was fortunate that, in all of the commotion, this was one accusation among many, but what would happen if the crown of England would ever be in a position to demand their restitution?[14]

We can also remember how, in his denial of responsibility on the eve of the *Fronde*, Mazarin had flaunted his restraint at not having acquired any governorships or duchies. Even as he was crawling his way back into France, however, he was beginning to make up for lost time. In April of 1652, Anne gave him his long-coveted governorship of Breisach, but this was on paper, since an independent minded *lieutenant du roi* controlled the stronghold. In October, the governorship of the *château* of Vincennes, just outside of Paris, fell vacant, and Mazarin managed to grab it. But most of all, he resumed his campaign for marriage alliances. One of his nieces, Laura Martinozzi, he offered for the son of the fabulously rich soldier, a cousin of Richelieu, the Marshal de La Meilleraye, with whom Mazarin invested in the commerce raiding business. Her sister Anna Maria, he kept offering to the Duke de Candale. But at this point La Meilleraye was reluctant about the marriage and so, apparently, was Candale's father, the Duke d' Epernon. This did not discourage Mazarin from bringing in more relatives—two sisters, three more nieces, and two nephews. Mazarin also resumed his designs on the house of Mantua. His banker Cantarini was going bankrupt and, possibly to counter the testimony of Ludovici before the commission, Mazarin had Cantarini make a private declaration that it was Mazarin who had furnished the mysterious 450,000 *livres* toward the dowry of the Queen of Poland. His more solvent banker, Barthélémy Hervart, he associated with his new superintendants of the finances in the subordinate post of controller-general. Mazarin also advanced toward a more substantial governorship when the queen made him her lieutenant-general and later governor of Brouage and Aunis—including Brouage, La Rochelle, and the iles of Ré and Oléron—which comprised a sizable segment of the northwestern coast of the kingdom.

It cost the government 530,000 *livres* to get Daugeon, the officer occupying the port of Brouage, to surrender it, but the possibilities of this region for the entire gamut of corruption, patronage, and trafficking were staggering. In September of 1653 Colbert left his cousin, Colbert du Terron, there to take charge of the situation.[15]

In spite of all these occupations, we also find Colbert extremely concerned about recovering the diamonds that the Queen of England had pawned in Holland. This emerges clearly from two *mémoires* that he wrote in May of 1653 regarding the exchange rates in that country. At that time, it will be remembered, a war was going on between the Commonwealth of England and the Dutch Republic, and Colbert was concerned about the cost of transferring funds. The best alternative, he concluded, was to "load up with merchandise and transport it to Holland," adding that "presently money is being borrowed in Holland at an elevated interest only to pay it back in six or more months when the interest is much lower." "On this point," he continues, "it would be good to know what interest is being paid in Holland *for the mortgaged precious stones* [italics mine] so as to compare it with the loss." The French pronoun "on," which I translate into the passive voice, leaves open the question of who was making the payments, but we can answer the question because on the same day Colbert received a letter, through Henry Jermyn, from Mazarin, in which Mazarin orders Colbert to give Jermyn a letter of change for 20,000 florins for Holland at the best rate possible. There is no doubt, therefore, that by 1653 Mazarin was in control of the Queen of England's diamonds.[16]

Admittedly, more urgent matters kept intervening, such as getting the not too reliable Manicamp out of La Fère, which had become an especially important outpost in the continuing war against Spain. Nothing, he kept telling Anne, was so important as to get it back into the king's hands. And this time it would take 50,000 *livres*—certainly cheaper than Brouage—in order to ease out the occupant. Mazarin was even prepared to engage his own diamonds in order to do it. Leaving the queen in Paris and taking the fifteen-year-old Louis XIV with him, Mazarin marched up to the place. The superintendants of finance sent him 22,000 *livres*, and he managed by hook and by crook—without having to pledge his own diamonds—to rake up the rest. By this time his activities were taking on all the proportions of a family affair as, from various outposts on the frontier, he directed the reassertion of royal authority throughout the kingdom, the war against Spain, and, almost minutely, the purchase of military supplies. It was becoming increasingly difficult to distinguish his personal profit from the interests of the state, but that he had recovered most of his seized property and was accumulating more is attested by the 216 folio inventory of his possessions that Colbert began in September of 1653. This inventory, which carries though into 1654, also gives us a good impression of the works of art that Mazarin had acquired from the estate of Charles I by that time. We find in it the tapestries of the *Five Senses*; three individual pieces of Raphael's *Acts of the Apostles*, bearing the King of England's claim of proprietorship; six pieces of the *Twelve Months of the Year*; and among the paintings, Van Dyck's *Three Princes of England*, Raphael's *Head of a Young Man*, Romano's *Saint Jerome*, Correggio's *Beautiful Antiope*, and his *Torment of Marsyas*.[17]

Nor were the diamonds of the Queen of England left behind. On October 14, 1653, Colbert wrote to Mazarin that he was preparing another letter of credit for Jermyn. The only question was whether Jermyn should carry it, or Chanut, who was leaving to become the French ambassador at The Hague, or Lescot, who was to examine the diamonds with a view to their subsequent redemption. The war between the Commonwealth and the Dutch was dragging on, and the exchange rates were still too high. Also, Jermyn was asking for an advance of 10,000 *livres* to Henrietta Maria "on account of the 40 from the sale of her precious stones," which suggests that Mazarin was now in charge of selling a portion of them. Mazarin replied that it might be better to wait a little longer, and he generously approved the advance to the queen. One week later, Colbert was still uncertain as to whether to send off Lescot to examine the diamonds, since this "could be postponed until the redemption," to which Mazarin replied even more positively not to do so. He was then expecting to redeem the diamonds in three months, at which time Chanut could examine them and Mazarin himself would obtain a passport for their safe passage from Archduke Leopold, Governor of the Spanish Low Countries. This plan, like many of Mazarin's visions, did not materialize, even though he and Colbert continued to be anxious.[18]

～

Having already made one of his nieces a quasi-princess of the blood, in February of 1654 Mazarin proceeded to make another a full-fledged one with the marriage of Anna Maria Martinozzi to the Prince de Conti, repentant younger brother of the rebellious Prince de Condé. Moreover, a few months later, in April, the opportunity occurred to make up for his lack of duchies when the impecunious Duke of Mantua sent an agent Francesco Bellinzani to try to sell the Duchy of Mayenne to the highest bidder. He found a buyer, but before he could effectuate the sale he was asked by Mazarin, through Colbert, to give Mazarin the first option at the same price. It is hard to imagine a more blatant exploitation of one's position for personal gain, but who could prevent it, and Mazarin, for a mere 750,000 *livres*, got his first duchy. Not only that, but he wanted to make doubly sure that he would not be affected by Cantarini's bankruptcy. Thus on April 22 Colbert made Cantarini confirm it was Mazarin who had furnished the 450,000 *livres* toward the marriage of the Queen of Poland. Soon thereafter Hervart, as a creditor of Cantarini, passed to Mazarin 372,000 *livres* in claims from Cantarini's rights to the succession of Mantua, along with all of Hervart's own rights. On July 28, date of the final settlement of Cantarini's bankruptcy, Colbert, claiming Mazarin as a creditor, obtained more than a million *livres* in demands on the treasury and assignations, which Mazarin had given to Cantarini for the purchase of Mayenne. The net was thus closing on the remaining duchies of the house of Mantua. And while the marriage festivities for Anna Maria were taking place in Paris, Mazarin was making another recovery for the monarchy and for himself, his long-coveted stronghold of Breisach on the right bank of the Rhine. It took 200,000 *livres* to the garrison and 100,000 for Charlevoix, the acting *lieutenant du roi* in order to entice them to march out, and a huge annual pension for the Count d'Harcourt, governor of the nearby province of Alsace, who still remained theoretically in place, but Mazarin was finally able to occupy his coveted Breisach and to insert his own man, Saint-Geniez, into the stronghold. In regard to La Fère, the queen, claiming that she had been unable to obtain reasonable bids for the domain, now sold it to Cardinal Mazarin for 500,000 *livres*, and then proceeded to give him all sorts of additional privileges, including the governorship of the stronghold, unavailable to the previous bidders. The following year Mazarin married off another one of his nieces, Laura Martinozzi, to Alfonso d'Este, the son of the Duke of Modena, establishing his first connection with a princely house of Italy. And to confirm Mazarin's hold upon Alsace, Colbert installed his brother, the twenty-six-year-old Charles, sieur de Vandières, as intendant of the entire province. The kinds of power bases that Anne of Austria had denied to Condé, for fear that he would be in a position to control the monarchy, she was now freely showering upon Cardinal Mazarin.[19]

One of the most striking features of Mazarin's correspondence in this period is his extraordinary dedication to Mme de Chevreuse. She had been no less of a double dealer than Cardinal de Retz, yet Mazarin cherished her dearly, and not, as we have seen, because of her beauty. He regrets not being able to accommodate her, welcomes her lover the Marquis de Laigues, and thanks her for her friendship. On August 22, 1654, after writing Colbert a short note from Peronne, Mazarin affixes a PS asking him to visit Mme de Chevreuse "who has fallen." On October 9 from La Fère, we again find

Mazarin ordering Colbert to visit her, this time to reassure her of his "very humble service" and to inform her that the Marquis de Laigues "has left to go on the voyage that she knows about," to which Colbert replied that he just happened to find her reading some letters from said marquis which she dutifully turned over for transmission to Mazarin. I can only wonder how Mazarin in La Fère could be so well-informed about Laigues's movements and why Laigues's correspondence with his mistress should be of any interest to Mazarin and Colbert unless there something underfoot between them. And the attentions continued. In July of 1655 Mazarin, out of a clear blue sky, asked Colbert to extend his regards to Mme de Chevreuse, who responded with her appreciation for his cordiality. In August Mazarin was reluctant when she asked him to permit an exiled gentleman to go take the waters, but he would do it if she insisted, and in September he ordered Colbert to extend to her his compliments. In November, after using his influence in order to exempt her from paying a tax, Mazarin responded immediately to her letter of gratitude. Such gallantry was understandable enough when he needed her desperately in order to contrive his return to power, but, given the ups and downs of their relationship, one can only wonder at his diligence.[20]

Almost as perplexing is his pursuit of the marriage alliance with the house of La Meilleraye. True, the marshal was a relative of Cardinal Richelieu, to whom Mazarin owed so much. Also, La Meilleraye was rich, a good soldier, lieutenant-general in Brittany, and governor of Nantes, and he had stood by Mazarin during the *Fronde*. But, as governor of Nantes, he was also the one who had allowed Cardinal de Retz to escape, and Meilleraye's son, the prospective bridegroom, was a proving to be a nonentity. That, however, may have been exactly what Mazarin was looking for, and he even went so far as to cut him in on 30,000 *livres* from the sale of a post in the queen's household.[21]

In the meanwhile, Mazarin set his sights on the domain of Auvergne. In May of 1656 the queen, who had once owned it, was in the process of repurchasing it, and the repurchase had a particularly suspicious ring to it. Colbert referred to it as being "made in the name of the queen," which sounds exactly as if it was being made for Mazarin himself. This bonanza, however, was interrupted on July 16 by the unexpected relief of Valenciennes by Don Juan of Austria and the Prince de Condé. We need to remember that this defeat initiated one of the worst financial crises for the monarchy since the outbreak of the *Fronde*, but even these difficult financial straits did not prevent Colbert from asking Mazarin to send him a record of all the advances that he had made to the monarchy prior to 1652 so as to obtain their reimbursement. Nor did it prevent Cardinal Mazarin from considering the jewels and redeeming the tapestries of the abdicated Queen Christina of Sweden, who had gone off to Italy and left them in the Spanish Low Countries, for in October of 1656 he sent Lescot to the area for this very purpose. On this occasion they were redeemed in the name of Hervart. The crowning achievement of all these efforts was his second alliance with one of the princely houses of Italy. On February 20, 1657, his niece Olympia, a particular favorite of the young Louis XIV, married Eugene-Maurice de Savoie, Count de Soissons.[22]

But perhaps the most intriguing of Mazarin's private dealings for the pur-pose of our investigation is in three communications between Colbert and Mazarin, one of July 6, one of September 10, and the third of September 17, 1656. In the first Colbert informs Mazarin that the full amount paid to the Queen of England plus interest was now some 597,416 *livres*. In the second Colbert informs the cardinal that Mylord Jermyn was refusing to sign an obligation for the money, on the grounds that, by the terms of the loans, this obligation would only be due in the event of the restoration of the English monarchy, a refusal which Mazarin most generously accepted. A week later, however, on September 17, Colbert announced to Mazarin that he had given Jermyn a "certification" for 600,000 *livres* that Mazarin had paid to her on various occasions, and that he, Colbert, was worried that Henrietta's son Charles would use this certification to damage the alliance that France was attempting to conclude with the English Commonwealth. To which concern Mazarin replied that this money, having been furnished many years before, would look just fine, and on the very next day Henrietta confirmed that by 1649 she had run up some 597,423 *livres*. Fascinating bit of evidence! Let us again recall that in 1651 Mazarin had only asserted that he had lent her "more than 300,000 *livres*." We can only conclude, therefore, that by 1656 he and Colbert had found a way, just as they had with the money furnished to the Queen of Poland, to appropriate Henrietta Maria's debts to the regency for himself.[23]

In any event, it is obvious that Mazarin wanted to acquire the diamonds of the Queen of England, or at least what was left of them, almost as badly as he wanted to acquire the duchies of the Duke of Mantua, and by the spring of 1657 the repeatedly postponed voyage of Lescot to the Dutch Republic was about to materialize. He was to accompany a new French ambassador, De Thou, and it appears as if Lescot was not going to go empty-handed. He was to carry with him a number of bales, which required a number of porters to load, and we may suspect that these were not bales of hay. We may also suspect that he was going to examine the diamonds of the Queen of England, and bring them back with him, and we have the extract of a letter which he sent from Amsterdam on May 8, in which we learn he has obtained, among other ornaments, two diamond earrings, but these cannot have been part of the queen's collection. Mazarin and Colbert expected him to stay so that he could, among other things, examine the diamonds, but by May 19 he was back in Calais, much to Mazarin's chagrin, for in the meanwhile Colbert had been negotiating for the redemption of said diamonds, which would have required the presence of Lescot in the Dutch Republic. Colbert tried to repair the damage. As he wrote to Mazarin on May 29:

> I will send Mr Lescot with Mr de Vardes who is leaving next Thursday, I don't know yet if he can bring the diamonds of the Queen of England, since this affair is not yet finished.

While this transaction was underway, however, another one was about to fall into Mazarin's lap, and we may well wonder whether it was purely accidental, for all of a sudden, Henrietta Maria found herself pressed by the Duke d'Epernon to repay him 427,556 *livres* out of the 433,000 that she had owed him since 1654. The desperate queen had no choice but to offer to sell the *grand Sancy* and the *miroir de Portugal* to him for a mere 300,000, which did not even cover her entire debt. We have a minute of her offer drawn up by a clerk of the notary Le Fouyn, who, as we well know, was also the notary of Mazarin. And, in a reenactment of the preemptive purchase of the Duchy of Mayenne, we have the phenomenon of this minute remaining unfinished and replaced by another more impressive one, minuted by Le Fouyn himself, in which Henrietta made the same sale for the sum of 360,000 *livres* to none other than Barthélémy Hervart. But as we might expect, the man who had already lent his name to Mazarin in the loans to the Queen of Poland and in the acquisition of the Queen of Sweden's tapestries, was also a stand-in for Mazarin in the acquisition of Epernon's diamonds. Thus, on May 23, Colbert wrote to Mazarin:

> If Your Eminence wants Mr Lescot up there with him, I beg you to let me know if I should have him take the two diamonds of M^r d'Epernon, which I redeemed this morning.

Which brings us back to the diamonds in the Dutch Republic, where we come face-to-face with an old friend who may have merely seemed up to now like a colorful addendum to our investigation, for on May 27 Colbert wrote to Mazarin:

> The affair of the diamonds has been delayed up to the present for many reasons which it would take too long to explain to Your Eminence, and just as it

was on the point of concluding Madame de Chevreuse has said that she could not complete it unless she was paid 150,000 *livres* in cash which she says Your Eminence promised her.

So there we have it! It was the beautiful Madame de Chevreuse, the mistress of two husbands and even more lovers, the single-handed survivor of Richelieu, Mazarin, and the *Fronde*, who had once more managed to make herself indispensable, and to whose pretensions Mazarin, though he was financially at the end of his tether, ended up by surrendering.[24]

Aside from acquiring the diamonds of the Queen of England, Mazarin finished the decade by making even more acquisitions that he had taken to heart, the first of which was the Duchy of Nevers. It too had been long in the making, and in this instance the bankrupt Cantarini and his associates were the instruments of Mazarin's purposes. On September 7, 1657, they obtained a decree from the *parlement* that permitted them to resume his seizures of Charles II's possessions, notably in that duchy, and he attempted to defend himself by launching an appeal. It was a fool's errand and a trap. Mazarin was all ready to step in as an interested party, along with other putative creditors. The duke's lawyer insisted that the 900,000 *livres* lent to the Queen of Poland had come from the crown, and intimated quite courageously that there were "persons more powerful than Cantarini and Serantoni" behind the seizures. But the lawyer for Cantarini was Mazarin's own Jean de Gomont, who cited document after document, including the belated declaration of April 22, to demonstrate that it was Cantarini and his associates, including Mazarin, who had provided the 900,000 *livres* and that the Duke of Mantua had never paid them back. By a decree of March 29, 1659, the *parlement* threw the appeal out of court. The sale to Mazarin for 1,800,000 *livres*, out of which the duke did not receive one penny, with Mazarin taking it upon himself to pay the remaining debts of the duke, was consummated on July 11, 1659. In describing this momentous event to Mazarin, Colbert was not unmindful of the potential dangers that lay ahead:

> Since our courts are inclined to jump to the conclusion that persons of great authority only conduct their affairs with violence . . . this will certainly produce great legal problems in the future against the successors of Your Eminence.

Mazarin, however, was primarily interested in completing his edifice, and his next acquisitions of this period consisted of large holdings in Alsace and nearby areas. Between January and February 1658 the king granted him the lordships of Thann and Altkirch, followed by the County of Ferrette and the Lordships of Belfort, Delle, and Issenheim. The Duke de Candale died about this time, and Mazarin took over the governorship of Upper and Lower Auvergne. At the same time, he maintained his pursuit of tapestries. Servien had managed to acquire for himself a set of seven tapestries of the *Acts of the Apostles*, after Raphael, bearing the arms of England, but his death on February 17, 1659, permitted Colbert to buy them up for Mazarin, on top of which Colbert was also able to acquire another set of seven, which had been owned by the Earl of Holland.[25]

It is hard to imagine in the midst of all these acquisitions that Mazarin could still have found the time to run a government, but by the summer of 1659 the negotiations with Spain had reached a point where most of the major issues, with the exception of the offices of the Prince de Condé, had been resolved. Mazarin now made ready to descend upon the frontier city of Saint-Jean-de-Luz in order to iron out the final details of the peace. If there was ever a moment in his life that he exhibited all of the excess of the parvenu, this was it. He amassed as much money as he could for the voyage. Before he left, on the way, and even after he arrived on July 29, he kept on ordering every kind of ornament for himself, for his suite, or to distribute among his former enemies. Mazarin just had to demonstrate to his opposite number, Don Luis de Haro, that he was his equal, which Mazarin did by bullying him, patronizing him, and repeatedly threatening to leave, but, in the heat of these negotiations, the thoughts of this man of the hour returned to none other than the lady who had once questioned his manhood, but had more recently satiated his greed. At some point in August, he wrote to the Duchess de Chevreuse that he wanted to serve her, and in the middle of trying to squeeze one more stronghold out the King of Spain in exchange for a little more hope for the Prince de Condé, Mazarin fulfilled his promise to the duchess. He cajoled Don Luis de Haro into granting her some 50,000 *écus* (150,000 *livres*), and on September 8 Mazarin wrote triumphantly to Anne of Austria, "Mme de Chevreuse's affair is settled, having obtained from Don Luis, after some argument, some of the money she had given for Kerpen." A few days later he wrote to the duchess herself apologizing for having gotten her so little. When it was all over, and he signed the Peace of the Pyrenees on November 7, 1659, France acquired Artois and Roussillon, Louis XIV a wife, and Condé the government of Burgundy, and the reimbursement of the Duchess de Chevreuse had risen to 165,000 *livres*. As to Mazarin himself, not satisfied with having granted him extensive territories in Alsace, Louis now gave him the governorship of the province and the post of Grand Baliff of Haguenau.[26]

But what about Mazarin's unholy ally, Oliver Cromwell? Well, we recall that he had died late in 1658, and his position as Lord Protector had passed on to his son Richard, who was having great difficulty in retaining it. Both Mazarin and Don Luis, therefore, could afford to ignore him, particularly since, while the negotiation at Saint-Jean-de-Luz was going on, there was brewing an equally intense but more secret negotiation between General Monck, who commanded the best troops of the Protectorate, and Edward Hyde, who was advising Charles II. In the course of his exile, Charles had privately decided to embrace Catholicism, and Henrietta Maria, who had incited her husband into losing his head, now prompted her son to do the same by trying to take over England with a French army, but the counsels of Edward Hyde prevailed, and Hyde came to an arrangement with Monck by which Charles could assume his throne without seeming to impose himself upon his subjects. Thus, on May 29, 1660 (June 8 in Paris), he made his grand entry into London, to the acclaim of a population weary of puritanical blue laws enforced by major generals. But the restoration of an independent monarch of an ancient enemy was a mixed blessing to Cardinal Mazarin, since it must have occurred to him that he was the possessor of the monarch's father's paintings, the monarch's mother's jewels, and the monarch's father's tapestries. The duchies of the Duke of Mantua and many of his other spoils Mazarin might enjoy with relative impunity, but the restored King of England was no Duke of Mantua, and we must remember that Charles Stuart was perfectly aware of Mazarin's dealings with Henrietta Maria, assuming Charles could ever forgive Mazarin for his alliance with Cromwell. No sooner was Charles restored than he made peace with Spain. Thus, of all of Mazarin's ill-gotten gains, the ones he had gotten from the house of Stuart were the first to come back to haunt him, especially as his health was failing and he was sensing the approach of death.[27]

CHAPTER SIX

~

A Tale of Two Families

During the sixteenth century the population of Europe regained and even surpassed its losses from the great plague, but this growth of population was also accompanied by a rise in prices and an increase in expectations which often expressed itself in the form of the Protestant "Reformation." As the enthusiasm for the Reformation's Lutheran form subsided, its more militant Calvinist version established itself in Geneva, from where it spread into France, the Low Countries, and Scotland. In France these Calvinists called themselves Huguenots, and in 1560 they staged numerous coups throughout the country, taking over churches and monasteries, setting up consistories, and fortifying themselves militarily. In the south, the Huguenots were particularly strong in the provinces of Languedoc and the Vivarais. We cannot count their number, but we know that in that same year they already controlled a majority in the Estates (provincial assembly) of Languedoc, and during the civil wars that followed, the Huguenots extorted from the central government the right to govern and to fortify more and more cities all over France. In 1567, in Nîmes, they occupied the cathedral, expelled the bishop, and massacred over one hundred Catholics. By 1597 they controlled politically, religiously, and militarily about fifty fortified strongholds. Out of a population that was approaching twenty million, the Huguenots never consisted of much more than 10 percent. Yet in 1598 when Henry IV, by his famous edict of Nantes, finally brought an end to the religious wars, the best he could do was to set up mixed administrations of Catholics and Protestants in the localities that the Huguenots controlled.[1]

The sixteenth century was also an age of unprecedented social mobility, and the ambitious took advantage of it. In the city of Nîmes one such family was that of the Roux. As we have seen, I had Roux de Marsilly in my sights from the very beginning and, after spending the summer of 1990 trying to find him in Lille, Maastricht, Antwerp, Liège, and Brugge with only limited results, by 1994 I finally decided to confront him in Nîmes, from where I spent the following four summers shuttling between it and Valence, La Rochelle, Montpellier, and Avignon, all of which permitted me to break through the published evidence. I discovered in the course of these travels, as well as by periodic visits to the Church of Jesus Christ of Latter-day Saints in Santa Barbara, that he had a grandfather named Mathelin (or Mathurin) Roux, an illiterate Protestant merchant who by 1608 was rich enough to have recourse to a notary, and in 1611 his son Claude was in a position to marry Anne Pepine, daughter of Antoine Pepin, minister of the church in nearby Monnoblet. The wife's family were not only pious; they were also soldiers for their faith, Antoine's son Etienne having rapidly acquired the title of captain. Claude Roux, however, was of a different stripe. He was a merchant, and a prolific one at that. He and his wife had seven children: Claude (a girl), Jean, Etienne, Claude the future conspirator, Jeanne, Antoine, and Catherine. In spite of the fact, moreover, that the early seventeenth century was a time of narrowing horizons in France, especially for the Protestants, and that Louis XIII succeeded in depriving them of their fortified strongholds, the Roux family continued to flourish. In 1631 the elder Claude may have become consul (city councilman) in Nîmes. In 1638 his eldest son Jean married the daughter of a lawyer in nearby Sommières, and the elder Claude had such confidence in Jean's business sense that he emancipated him soon thereafter. The following year we find the elder Claude identified in a notarial act as "merchant-druggist" and both his sons Jean and Etienne as "merchants." Even in the best of times, life was not without its personal tragedies. Later that same year, Jean Roux lost his young wife.[2]

It was not only ambitious Huguenots who took advantage of a turbulent world. Wherever they prevailed they also encountered a Catholic opposition, whose most energetic families were quick to respond in kind. In the little village of La Figère in the equally Protestant Vivarais, one such family was the Picons. After investigating many more suspects than I have already described, I finally came across the Picons in 2003 in Paris, when I hit upon the contract for the marriage of an Antoine-Hercule Picon, signed by Jean-Baptiste Colbert and by enough high dignitaries to give me pause. It took a while for the pause to sink in, but I kept finding more and more references to Picon in Paris, notably the claims of his family to nobility and, just like in the case of Claude Roux, the trail carried me down to Nîmes, where I returned in 2012 and had the extraordinary good fortune of meeting Jean-Bernard Elzière, whose assiduous genealogical researches delivered me from four more summers of stifling heat in southern France. With his indispensable help, I went on immediately, in Nîmes and Privas, to find many Picons in the closing years of the sixteenth century exercising the modest profession of *practicien*, paralegals—not quite lawyers—often acting as witnesses for notaries. During the sixteenth century the Picons had apparently preserved their Catholicism intact and, early in the seventeenth, some members of the family had moved to Rivières in nearby Languedoc. I found one Georges Picon in 1608 at the wedding of Jacques Coste and Hélipse Plantier, where he is listed as "captain of Rivières." I also discovered in a testament of 1617 that he was the husband of Jacques's sister Marie. Moreover I found his nephew, another Georges Picon, on April 23, 1623, at his own wedding to Alise de Coste, which suggests a more than passing relationship between the Picon and Coste families. Who, however, were the Costes? Well, the father of the bride was the son of another Jacques who was the husband of Hélipse de Budos, the illegitimate daughter of a distinguished nobleman from the province of Guyenne—Jacques de Budos, Marquis de Portes. Raised at the court of Anne de Montmorency, Budos had temporarily toyed with Protestantism before returning to the religion of his ancestors. His daughter Louise had married Henri I de Montmorency. His son Antoine-Hercule, stepbrother of Hélipse, was even more distinguished and even more Catholic. He was raised at the court of France with Henry II de Bourbon, Prince de Condé, and Louise's daughter had married him. Antoine-Hercule fought gallantly with Henry II de Montmorency and Condé against the rebellious Protestants, and in 1624 he was resting from his labors in the *château* of Theyrargues, overlooking the village of Rivières. It is hardly surprising, therefore, that in that same year, when Georges Picon and Alise de Coste had their first child, they chose the Marquis des Portes as the godfather and named their son Antoine-Hercule. A few years later they had a second son, whom they more imaginatively named Gabriel, and still later a daughter, Marguerite. In 1626 Antoine-Hercule de Budos got married, and he chose a distinguished bride, Louise de Crussol, daughter of the Duke d'Uzès, another stalwart Catholic and royalist, who was the *chevalier d'honneur* of Anne of Austria. In 1629 the marquis died fighting against the Protestants at the siege of Privas and, after his death, I found our Georges acting in various capacities for his widow.[3]

By the early 1640s the Roux family too was spreading out. Jean moved to Paris where he courted another lady and continued his business activities, but young Claude seems to have followed in the tracks of his uncle and opted for a military career. In 1642 we find a Claude Roux in a list of recruits furnished by the nearby city of Beaucaire, most probably for the army of Catalonia. I make no great claim for this piece of evidence—his name is crossed out in another copy of the same list—but this campaign in Catalonia by an adventurous twenty-year-old is perfectly consistent with the stories that Roux later told Samuel Morland about his earlier life. As to his brother Jean, in a notarial act of July 8, 1642, we can definitely place him living on the Rue Quincampoix in Paris and leasing a house on the Rue Baillet for a period of ten years. In September he invested the sum of 35,000 *livres* in harvesting the lumber of a forest in Chilleurs on the outskirts of Orléans. He was not only investing; his courtship was successful. His new wife was Marie Chappuzeau, daughter of Charles, a lawyer in the *conseil privé* of the king, who had written numerous learned works of jurisprudence. Her brother Samuel was himself an aspiring writer. The marriage contract, signed on October 21, 1643, is a gold mine. Signing with the bridegroom was Claude Roux, along with his younger brother Antoine. Also present was a cousin of theirs, Pierre de Rode, who styled himself an *écuyer* (squire), son of a sister of Mathelin Roux. The most striking thing about the contract, however, was the signature of two of the witnesses for the bride. One was the Prince de Condé, prince of the blood of France, and the other his son-in-law, the Duke de Longueville. What, however, had brought princes of such eminent stature to participate in such a plebeian celebration? I think I can explain. Originally a Huguenot, the Prince de Condé had become a convinced Catholic, but he had maintained many of his Protestant connections. One of them was Charles Chappuzeau, Marie's father, who had been serving as the prince's lawyer before the *conseil du roi*. Another was his chamberlain the late Daniel d'Aumale-Haucourt, seigneur of Chilleurs, who had died in 1640. His eldest son, Charles, had inherited the *seigneurie*, and both he and his brother Nicolas were currently serving in the army of the Dutch Republic under the command of Frederick Henry, the Prince of Orange. Moreover, the Prince de Condé had served Louis XIII as Governor of Languedoc and as commander of the army of Catalonia, in which his son the Duke d'Enghien, future Prince de Condé, had personally fought in 1642. All this suggests that both the Chappuzeau and the Roux families had more than a passing relationship with the house of Condé.[4]

The Picon family was doing even better. In 1634 Georges Picon's patroness Louise de Crussol remarried. At this time she was already a *dame d'honneur* of Anne of Austria, and she chose as her second husband a rising nobleman named Charles, Marquis de Saint-Simon, elder brother of a favorite of Louis XIII, named Claude, whom the king liked well enough to elevate to the rank of duke. Charles had a governorship in Languedoc, but he lived mainly in Paris near the court or in his *château* of Laversine not far from Senlis in northern France, where he was both *bailly* and governor. His younger brother, the favorite, was governor of Blaye near Bordeaux. Louise de Crussol's absence from the south seems to have worked to the advantage of Georges Picon. By 1634 he had taken over the office of "regent" in the Marquisate of Portes. In Languedoc the term *regent* was often synonymous with *consul* or *syndic*, officials in some way elected by individual communities to direct their local affairs, and Georges apparently did so with the blessings of his patroness. It is interesting to note that whereas I can easily find Georges Picon in Rivières at this time, and I have even found a baptism on February 7, 1644, in which Antoine-Hercule's younger brother Gabriel acts as a godfather, I see no sign of Antoine-Hercule. Moreover, on February 27 I find Georges Picon to be the regent in nearby Theyrargues, and in May of 1644 Charles de Saint-Simon descended upon Rivières with a power of attorney from his wife and executed some thirty-eight notarial acts, which made Georges Picon administrator of a large number of her domains in that area. This leads me to conclude that a young Antoine-Hercule must have accompanied or joined Louise de Crussol at the court of France in the entourage of Anne of Austria, because we know, beyond a shadow of a doubt, that in 1643 he began working for Jean-Baptiste Colbert, who during that year, as we have seen, was serving as a commissioner of war in the entourage of Cardinal Mazarin.[5]

The Roux were also exploiting their connections. After the marriage of his brother, Claude Roux began identifying himself as a "merchant of Paris." He also joined his brother in their exploitation of the forest in Chilleurs. In the course of the year 1644, Claude periodically visited that village. There, through a precious trickle of notarial acts, which I also found in 1990 when I descended upon Orléans, I learned a number of fascinating details about him. First, he was rich enough to have a servant, not named Eustache Dauger, but Pierre de La Roque. Second, Claude was inclined to violence. Toward the end of that year he assaulted a royal sergeant, and had to pay him and his replacement a total of 115 *livres* in compensation. Third, and perhaps most significantly, this is where he discovered the particle of "de" Marcilly. Marcilly was a farmstead in the domain of Chilleurs, which domain, as we have seen, was at this time in the possession of the d'Aumale-Haucourt family. It looks, therefore, as if the Chappuzeau-Roux connection with the house of Condé also involved a profitable connection with the d'Aumale-Haucourts.[6]

Even in the seventeenth century the movement between the *château* of Laversine, Senlis, and the court in Paris was not difficult for anyone possessed of a stable, and the Saint-Simons were certainly in that category.

During the 1640s we find them in all of these places, exercising their various functions. If, as I am assuming, Antoine-Hercule Picon was in their midst, and if as I am sure, in 1643 he began to work for Jean-Baptiste Colbert, we can now understand how an ambitious young man from Languedoc and a rising young bureaucrat ever got together. This was also a good time for Antoine-Hercule to pick up a valet, and although in my pursuit of the Picon family I have found no trace of individuals with the name of Auger or Dauger who might have provided the Picons with a suitable valet for their son in the region of Portes or Rivières, in the region of Picardy surrounding Senlis, we find a village named Auger (today Auger-Saint-Vincent, nine and one half miles northeast of Senlis) and in the city of Senlis, whose genealogical records I only began to consult in 2012, I found several families bearing that name, the most interesting of which had a son who became a hatmaker.[7]

The prospects were not quite as exhilarating for the Roux as they were for the Picons. Late in 1644 Jean Roux went bankrupt. But somehow or other the Roux managed. In March of 1645 Claude in Chilleurs, in conjunction with his brother still in Paris, concluded a sale of wood for 135 *livres*, after which there is no more trace of Claude in Chilleurs. The elder Claude died early in 1647, and the young Claude apparently rejoined his brothers Etienne and Antoine in Nîmes. In December of that year, we find Etienne, Claude, and Antoine there with their mother for the marriage of Claude's cousin Jeanne, sister of Pierre Rode, to a certain Pierre Crommelin. The Crommelins were a Protestant family of merchants from Saint-Quentin in Picardy, which, by what may or may not have been a recurring coincidence, turns out to be another outpost of the d'Aumale-Haucourts. Things were not going well for Jean in Paris, however. In April he made a brief trip to Chilleurs in order to sell 900 *livres*' worth of lumber, after which he too disappears from the Orléannais. The Roux, however, keep popping up. By February of 1649, Claude had found a wife for himself in Montélimar, a bastion of Protestantism in the province of Dauphiné. Her name was Marie Chalamel, daughter of a lawyer, and Claude's life with her in Montélimar was that of a merchant with numerous children and limited means. The opportunities were also drying up in Paris, where Jean lost his second wife. Still, with Jean in Paris, Etienne in Nîmes, Claude in Montélimar, and Antoine, whom we begin to find in Lyon, the Roux were building up a banking network, and in 1651 Claude Roux and an associate obtained a contract from Philippe de Laurens, treasurer of the mint in the Principality of Orange for the manufacture of *liards* (copper coins). The little Principality of Orange was a Protestant enclave in the middle of France, located right between Geneva and the province of Languedoc. Its absent ruler at that moment was the infant William III of

Orange, who as a sovereign prince, had a perfect right to mint such coins, much to the annoyance of the King of France, who kept issuing declarations prohibiting their use in France itself. One can only wonder how much the Roux's association with the d'Aumale-Haucourts had helped him to obtain his contract, but it is certain that, with the *Fronde* in full swing, Claude and his associate could not have found a better moment to ignore the prohibitions against their coins in France. Unfortunately for Claude, he quickly fell out with his associate, littering the court records of the *parlement* of Orange with their internal squabbles, in which Claude's brothers periodically intervened. To make matters worse, he also got embroiled with his suppliers and with the treasurer de Laurens. The Roux, however, seemed to be accustomed to controversy. In the midst of these tribulations, we find Claude as a signatory to the marriage of another one of his valets, a Catholic named not Eustache Dauger but Jean Espinasse.[8]

If the *Fronde* provided a mode of survival for the Roux, it presented a dilemma for the Saint-Simons. On the one hand they were connected to the Condés by the marriage of Henry I de Montmorency's daughter to the father of the current Prince de Condé. Charles de Saint-Simon was even the captain of the Condé *château* of Chantilly. On the other hand they had their traditional loyalty to the king. As it turned out, no sooner were the princes arrested than the Duke de Saint-Simon hastily left Paris for his government of Blaye, but he quickly assured Mazarin of his loyalty and, in the process, alienated the Condé family, which was hoping for his support, by holding the key stronghold of Blaye as a constant threat to the rebellious seaport of Bordeaux. Likewise, the marquis remained loyal, even though he lost control of Chantilly, which was seized by the regency. If Antoine-Hercule had retained any connection with the Saint-Simons, and it seems that he did, he was able to navigate these shoals, because when Mazarin returned from his exile and resumed his control of the government, he himself began to appreciate Picon's qualities.[9]

~

For most of the people of France, both the majority of Catholics and the minority of Huguenots, the failure of the *Fronde* gave them no alternative but to put up with the prime ministry of Cardinal Mazarin. Not that the Huguenots needed to abandon their pugnacity, for we must remember that in this period Mazarin was particularly reticent about alienating Oliver Cromwell, who presented himself as a protector of oppressed Protestants all over Europe. In June of 1653 in Nîmes, for example, a Huguenot consul named Jean Roux (not to be confused with Claude's elder brother) began complaining about the apportionment of taxes in favor of the Catholics, and over the next few months the dispute made its way through the courts of the province. Meanwhile, the Huguenots of Vals, in the Vivarais, who had set up a house of worship in their city, found themselves at odds with the widow of the Marshal d'Ornano, their Catholic feudal lord. She descended upon them from Paris, followed by her son-in-law with a small army, and established a garrison. The Huguenots did not take this lightly. Coming, arms in hand, from all over the Vivarais, Languedoc, and Dauphiné, they assembled around the town of Vallon in a force of 6,000 to 7,000, facing a smaller force of 4,000 to 5,000 that the lieutenant-general of the province had been able to collect. The scene was set for a return to the religious wars of the sixteenth century at a moment when Cardinal Mazarin could least afford it, and sometime during the month of September he sent the Marquis de Ruvigny, a Huguenot of the conciliatory type, in an attempt to pacify the region. He came with promises to restore the Huguenots to their privileges, obtained an amnesty for all, and succeeded in getting the armies to separate peacefully. As to the Huguenots of Nîmes, by May of 1654 their case reached Paris, where the council of finances produced an equivocal decision that did not satisfy either party. Still, in these two incidents, the Huguenots had demonstrated that they were not entirely incapable of resisting the incursions of the monarchy.[10]

What was Claude Roux doing when these struggles were going on? First and foremost he was contending with his personal affairs. These were not going very well in Orange, and in March of 1653 he made a fictitious cession of his half interest in the mint to a certain Guillaume Donnadière (or Donnadieu). But Claude was not ignoring the struggles of his fellow Huguenots. Up to then, he had not shown any particular commitment to his faith. He must, however, have been enough of a Huguenot at heart, because sometime between June and November he took up arms in the Vivarais to defend his coreligionists. And he must certainly have made a name for himself there while the Marquis de Ruvigny was on the spot, since we recall how frightened Claude later was to be recognized by the marquis in London. While in the Vivarais, however, Claude's legal problems in Orange seem to have worsened. When, in November, Jean came down from Paris to try to straighten them out, de Laurens, the treasurer, had him arrested. And yet the Roux persisted. One month later Jean was out of jail and purchasing a mill for the processing of copper.[11]

Life under Cardinal Mazarin was considerably more promising for the Picons. Georges, it is clear, remained in Rivières, still serving as "regent" for the Marquisate of Portes, but both of his sons, Antoine-Hercule and Gabriel, seem to have been making their mark at the court of France. We have an amazing document which indicates that since 1651 Antoine-Hercule had been collecting all of the income from the cardinal's benefices, and by the year 1653 Gabriel was with him, as is evident from a letter of September 10 from Mazarin's secretary, Toussaint Rose, to Colbert's cousin, Colbert du Terron in La Rochelle. The subject seems to have been the purchase of some military equipment.

> I have informed His Eminence of everything it has pleased you to write to me. He has received the letter of change and tomorrow on his return from Dourlens he plans to send the brother of Mr Picon.

And on March 27, 1654, we have a notarial act in which Mazarin seems to be expanding Antoine-Hercule's functions, for he makes him his procurator for

> the collection of each and every sum coming from the goods, revenues, and domains which belong to him at present and which could subsequently belong to him along with the temporal revenue both in the bishopric of Metz as in other benefices which he holds as well as any others to which he may be nominated . . . as well as his pensions.

The only qualification was for Picon's acts to be controlled by Colbert and for Picon to keep account books. A few weeks later, we have another act in which Mazarin purchased the library of his late librarian from his heirs in which Picon, although he is not mentioned in the act, appears as a signatory. On May 24 we find him paying bills on behalf of Colbert du Terron. This shows us that by this time, Gabriel was assuming the functions of an expediter, and Antoine-Hercule was acting both as a personal agent to the Colbert family and as a treasurer for Cardinal Mazarin.[12]

The Picons were not without competition. Colbert seems to have been favoring a certain Louis Berryer, who first appears at this time. The Girardins were still around and Mazarin seems to have been particularly fond of them. In 1653 I find what would appear to be Claude Girardin as a farmer of the *aides*—the indirect taxes on wine and commodities—and furnishing Mazarin with a critical 20,000 *louis* (or *livres*) toward the recovery of La Fère. The following year, after concluding some partial contracts that did not turn out well, I find Mazarin offering what would seem to be the same Girardin a contract (thereby supplanting Antoine-Hercule) to collect the income from all of his benefices. Another servant from before the *Fronde*, François Le Bas, reemerges in 1653 as the tutor of Mazarin's recently arrived nephew Philippe Mancini. During that same year I also find a new name, Simon Mariage, getting an authorization from the king to administer the vacant monastery of Bonnecombe while at the same time acting as secretary to Mazarin's private council. But whatever their popularity, none of these individuals could perform their functions without working through the agency of Antoine-Hercule Picon.[13]

In his attempts to reestablish the authority of the monarchy, Cardinal Mazarin also did his best to reestablish it over the coinage, and he began, not surprisingly, by a devaluation of the copper coins, from which, in the issuing of contracts, he could also derive some personal profit. Thus in April of 1654 the government reiterated its futile declaration of 1649 which required all possessors of domestic and foreign *liards* to "bring them to the offices which would be established" and exchange them for the new ones. Soon thereafter the government contracted with a certain Isaac Blandin to establish the factories throughout the kingdom. Though Claude Roux was theoretically no longer a contractor for the manufacture of *liards*, these actions further complicated his life, since his undercover contract in Orange was about to expire. The treasurer de Laurens, moreover, was demanding his back payments, especially in view of the most recent prohibitions by the government of France, but Jean Roux, now representing Donnadieu, retorted that they could still market them for an additional year. Jean Roux lost this round in court, but he was right about the declaration. It met with widespread resistance and Cardinal Mazarin was still in no position to enforce it vigorously.[14]

But if the French monarchy felt some need to temporize with its subjects, the neighboring Duke of Savoy did not. Since the thirteenth century, when they had become sovereigns of the Vaud, his predecessors had tolerated a certain degree of religious independence among its inhabitants, the Vaudois, and since the Reformation, when the religious conflict had become sharper, the pressures upon them by the Catholic house of Savoy had intensified. This was particularly true with Christine, a sister of Louis XIII and mother of the present duke, Charles Emmanuel II. In 1655 the situation in the Vaud was similar to what it had been in the Vivarais two years before: a disagreement over the right to construct churches. The only difference was that the Duke of Savoy sent in his troops, the Vaudois resisted, and the Catholics won, their troops proceeding, on April 24, to a massacre of the resisters. This atrocity sent a shock wave through Protestant Europe. John Milton called upon God to avenge his saints, and God turned over the task to Oliver Cromwell. It was on this occasion that he sent Samuel Morland, first to the court of France, then to the court of Savoy, and finally to Geneva. It must have been on this occasion too that Claude Roux went down to fight in defense of the Vaudois. As John Pell, Cromwell's ambassador to the Swiss cantons, reported:

We hear that some of Dauphiné and Languedoc have joined themselves with our brethren in the valleys of Piedmont.

The alliance of God, Oliver Cromwell, and Claude Roux was quickly joined by Cardinal Mazarin, who in his efforts to gain the friendship of Cromwell also put pressure on the court of Savoy to relent. Thus, by a number of fortunate strokes, the violent Claude had courted a confrontation with the French monarchy and even, to some extent, gotten away with it. He had also, in the process, broadened his connections, for he took this occasion, it would appear, to make the acquaintance in Geneva of Samuel Morland, who would subsequently betray him to Ruvigny, and General Balthazar, who would subsequently deliver him to Turenne.[15]

In July of 1655 we again find Jean Roux in Orange in court representing his brother's stand-in, Guillaume Donnadieu, but for the remainder of that year and throughout the next, the French monarchy continued to make life difficult for the Roux. During this period we have some difficulty in keeping track of them, but we do have some hints as to how they were coping. In 1656 and 1657, for example, there is a Jean Roux in Corbeil, outside of Paris, working in one of the mints established by Isaac Blandin. As to Claude, it would appear that he had entirely pulled out of Orange, for I find de Laurens attempting to sue him in Montélimar. It is doubtful, however, that Claude was even there, since his notarial acts in that city disappear. It is even doubtful that he was back in Nîmes, where there was trouble brewing between the Huguenot and Catholic consuls. At least, there is no sign of him or any members of his family taking part in it. However, we have an intriguing hint about his whereabouts when we discover that in 1656, the Prince de Condé, fresh from his relief of Valenciennes, was trying to rake up some money in the border town of Charleville through the manufacture of *liards*. Could it be that Claude Roux was one of the investors? We remember that in 1668 he claimed to Samuel Morland that he was on intimate terms with the prince.[16]

The more challenging life became for Claude Roux, the more privileged it became for Antoine-Hercule Picon. In a quittance for 1,144 *livres* received on October 31, 1654, from Adrien Le Normant for the right to operate a mill belonging to Mazarin's abbey of Saint-Denis, we learn that Picon was then living at the home of Jean-Baptiste Colbert on the rue Plastière. We also have acts in 1655 in which Picon served as a cashier for Mazarin's abbeys of Saint-Denis outside of Paris and Saint-Médard in Soissons. The act for Saint-Denis was signed in the interior of the *palais Mazarin*, and Picon for the first time identifies himself specifically as "*tresorier de Son Em^{ce}*." Picon was also participating in the collection of taxes in Mazarin's government of

La Rochelle, which contained the three rich tax districts of La Rochelle, Xaintes, and Sables d'Olonne. In February of 1656 Picon was sending Terron posters in regard to the sale of salt, in which Mazarin had a particular interest, throughout the government. We can get a sense of Picon's rising status from a letter that Terron sent to Jean-Baptiste on March 8 of that year in regard to his account books, but what is even more amazing in the same letter is the name of the person who would seem to be sitting in La Rochelle at the right hand of Colbert du Terron:

> You will assuredly agree that they match the registers of Mr Picon. It is for him to decide . . . if a sum of 150$^\#$ that Mr Bardon gives for the two first quarters of 1655 has to be attributed to the two last quarters as Mr Rode claims.

There is no mistake! This is the cousin of Claude Roux who is now in La Rochelle helping to collect taxes for Cardinal Mazarin. Not only is the cousin of Roux working under Terron, but the brother of Picon is about to join them. At this time the tax district of Sables d'Olonne was defaulting on its *taille*, and on May 21 Terron is accusing Jean-Baptiste of not keeping his promises:

> Since you are no longer talking about Faille or the brother of Mr Picon. I am going to touch base with Le Combe and make a stop-gap treaty with him for 100,000 *livres*.

To this charge, Jean-Baptiste replied:

> Picon's brother will leave in two days. I think that the treaty that you are proposing for the tax district of Sables for 100,000 *livres* is inadequate.

As it turned out, Picon's brother, now styling himself the Sieur de La Boudre, did not arrive until the month of August, but when he did he quickly showed his mettle. Working with Terron and an intendant with the army, they all agreed that quartering troops in the district of the Sables was the only way to get the tax out of the peasants, and their advice was followed.[17]

Antoine-Hercule was also heavily involved with Mazarin's second outpost, namely, Breisach in Alsace where, as we have seen, Jean-Baptiste's brother Charles was the intendant, and at this point we discover Mazarin's first direct communication with Antoine-Hercule Picon. On this occasion we find Mazarin in Compiègne on September 1, 1656, personally sending a short note to Picon in Paris, ordering him to transmit a package (we can only wonder what it contained) to Charles Colbert in Breisach. And given Mazarin's interest in despoiling the Duke of Mantua, it should hardly be surprising if we see Picon, on December 29, disbursing a loan of 15,000 *livres* to the impecunious duke. It is hard, therefore, to imagine anyone, outside of Jean-Baptiste Colbert, who was in a better position than Antoine-Hercule Picon to be intimately acquainted with the private finances of Cardinal Mazarin.[18]

∽

Our tale of two families becomes even more intriguing because on April 9, 1657, Claude Roux's cousin Pierre Rode and an associate signed a contract with Colbert du Terron to collect the temporal revenues of Mazarin's abbey of Saint-Michel-en-l'Herm. This raises the question, was Pierre Rode doing this for himself or was he one more stand-in for Cardinal Mazarin? What makes this latter possibility worthy of consideration is that one month later Pierre Rode appears in Paris to sign a contract with none other than Antoine-Hercule Picon, now styling himself as Sieur de La Farelle, agreeing to split with him one half of his interest in the contract for temporal revenue of the same monastery, which permits us to wonder why Rode would split up a profitable contract with a perfect stranger if Jean-Baptiste Colbert was not behind both Rode and Picon and directing the bulk of the profits into the coffers of Cardinal Mazarin. There is also evidence, as we shall see, that Picon was in association with Rode, with a certain Hache, and with a certain Duchanin, in the collection of the *taille* from the generality of La Rochelle.[19]

Mazarin's circle, of course, was constantly in the process of regeneration. Louis Berryer was hard at work, and on November 4, 1655, he became the administrator of the Duchy of Mayenne. One of his collaborators was Louis Beschameil (or Béchamel), creator of the famous cream sauce that bears his name. Jobart, of whom Colbert was jealous, died in 1656, but others, like the Girardins, were still in the ascendancy. They were helping to collect taxes in La Rochelle and in the Duchy of Nevers. In 1656 Mazarin finally convinced Pierre Girardin to contract for the collections from all of his benefices for one year, and Girardin must have been very good at it because in 1657 Mazarin extended the contract until 1659. Pierre, however, was unlucky. In May of 1657 he was kidnapped on the outskirts of Paris by one of the Prince de Condé's raiding parties and imprisoned in Antwerp, where he died, obliging Mazarin to execute one of the prince's followers in retaliation. After trying to replace Pierre by the brother of the lawyer Gomont, Mazarin finally turned to Pierre's brother Claude, who signed up for the remainder of the general contract. But, through all of these permutations, we can sense the looming shadow of Antoine-Hercule Picon. On October 1, 1657, we have a letter in which Mazarin does not merely charge him with an errand; he discusses it with him and orders him to get into direct contact with Nicolas Fouquet in order to carry it out. A few days later Fouquet writes directly to Mazarin on the same subject, and Mazarin refers to Picon by name in replying. Toward the end of the year Picon is disbursing money to the recently married Olympia Mancini and her husband the Count de Soissons.[20]

Where were the Roux at this time? We tend to lose track of them, although we do have some precious indications. In 1658 the government closed down the various mints and issued a series of *arrêts* that devalued all *liards*, domestic or foreign, that may have been in circulation. If, therefore, Claude Roux had any in his possession, he found himself deprived of a good source of income, and his brother Jean, if indeed he is the Jean Roux working in Corbeil, must have found himself out of a job. Moreover, this is the only time at which we can insert Claude's claim that he had entered into a treaty in the generality of Soissons, and we should know by now that there is always a kernel of truth in his assertions. Indeed, by connecting all these dots with other fragments, I would venture to guess that he had, in imitation of Pierre Rode, entered into a treaty for the collection of *aides*—the indirect taxes on wine and commodities—which the government farmed out to individual contractors. How do I come to this conclusion? I come to it because of his later connection with some wine merchants in the Spanish Low Countries, whom he later identified as his particular friends. If this is the case, the Roux were still trying to accommodate themselves to the regime, even though they were less successful than their cousin, who on May 7, 1658, begins to qualify himself as *conseiller du roi* and *receveur des tailles*. If the French monarchy wanted to provoke its Huguenot subjects into rebellion, it would have to try a lot harder.[21]

Back, therefore, to Antoine-Hercule Picon. On May 1, 1658, a certain Remy Dauge (alas, no relation to Eustache Dauger) receiver of the domain of La Fère, appeared along with the notaries Duprez and Le Fouyn at the home of Jean-Baptiste Colbert to acknowledge receipt of various funds owed to him by Cardinal Mazarin. On the same day Dauge also sold this same office for the sum of 6,000 *livres* to Antoine-Hercule Picon, again styling himself as Sieur de La Farelle. It might seem from this transaction, just as it might have seemed from the contract that he had signed with Pierre Rode in the previous year, that Picon was merely engaging in a little moonlighting on his own. However, almost two months later, we find him appearing with the notaries Mouffle and Le Fouyn, once again at the residence of Colbert, and declaring that even though he had purchased the office from Remy Dauge, "the truth is that he has and pretends nothing from the said office and that the whole of it belongs to His Eminence." One begins to wonder, therefore, whether the practice of using Antoine-Hercule Picon to cover some of Mazarin's less dignified transactions was not becoming a habit. Meanwhile, the effort to extract the maximum taxes from the generality of La Rochelle was also in full swing, and in the district of the Sables d'Olonne Jean-Baptiste Colbert was relying on the combination of the army and the brother of Antoine-Hercule Picon to accomplish this job. As Jean-Baptiste Colbert wrote to his cousin:

> I would have been happy to learn that Mr Picon is receiving hard money because, aside from the pay for the troops, if our receipts are not good while the troops are in this tax district not much is to be expected once they are out.

Gabriel Picon's responsibilities, however, were not limited to hard money. In September a banker named Hache in Paris, who handled letters of credit from La Rochelle, went bankrupt. As Terron wrote to Colbert a few months later:

> I am doing from this end everything that I can to get out of Mr Hache's bankruptcy. M^r [Gabriel] Picon is doing his best too, so that I hope we will get out of it.

The solicitude, however, was not entirely for the benefit of the monarchy. A few weeks later Jean-Baptiste announced to Terron a forthcoming change in the intendant who was supervising the troops who were enforcing the collection of taxes, Fortia being replaced by Pellot. Such appointments were usually made at the discretion of the secretary of state for war, unless someone in greater authority dictated otherwise, and the secretary of state for war was, of course, Michel Le Tellier, entirely subject to the dictates of Cardinal Mazarin. In announcing the replacement, Jean-Baptiste explained the reason: "You know," he reminded Terron, "that Mr Pellot is our relative and all for us." Clearly, Gabriel Picon de La Boudre was part of an exclusive club.[22]

Up to this point, Antoine-Hercule Picon had kept an extremely low profile in Paris, rarely wandering outside of the *palais Mazarin* and its environs. He was, however, about to become more visible. In July of 1659, for example, while Mazarin was in Libourne outside of Bordeaux, Colbert sent Picon to him with a box of jewels and two gold braided sashes. It was not always that genteel. We recall the banker Hache, who was involved in the transfer of funds from La Rochelle and who had gone bankrupt. Apparently, he could not pay up, and on August 6, 1659 Michel Le Tellier signed a *lettre de cachet* remanding Hache to the Bastille. A certain Jean Bosquet, who ran into Hache at the prison, asked him why he was there, and Hache told him that it was because Picon, the treasurer of Cardinal Mazarin, was demanding some money from him. On another occasion Bosquet witnessed a confrontation at the Bastille where Picon asked, "Will you pay?" and Hache replied, "If I owe you anything, show me!" On this occasion Hache went on to complain that Picon was exceeding his authority, and that if he was in default on his debts, he should be placed with others like him in the *Consièrgerie*. This impertinence earned him confinement in a dungeon for some seven weeks, after which he was presented with a bill for 15,000 *livres* which he still refused to pay, so that he was put back in a cell until December of 1660. One of his servants also complained that she had been kidnapped; questioned by Picon and his cohorts, including the notary Le Fouyn; and threatened with hanging. It would seem, therefore, as if Antoine-Hercule was having no trouble in fitting right into the spirit of the Mazarin operation. When, and it took some doing, Hache finally got out, he sued Picon in the *parlement* of Paris, and it is from the interrogatory of this case that we have most of these details, including the testimony of Duchanin that Picon, Rode, Hache, and himself had been associates in the collection of the *taille* in La Rochelle.[23]

Did Antoine-Hercule Picon have a valet? As we have seen, any man in his official position would have any number, and in the case of Antoine-Hercule Picon, I have suggested when and where he may have come in contact with a valet by the name of Eustache Dauger. If so, in September of 1659 he finally comes out of the shadows. At that time Mazarin was in Saint-Jean-de-Luz preparing to impress Don Luis de Haro, and Colbert and Picon were doing their very best to back him up. For that purpose, they sent one of Picon's valets down into the Basque country armed with samples for the presents that Mazarin wished to distribute—plumes, caps made of castor, and combs, along with samples of cloth for a livery—along with a tailor, requesting that Mazarin choose the ones he wanted, to which Mazarin replied with less than ideal syntax:

> You will have seen by the letter that I write to you by Picon's man that I want some beaver skin hats, and I have given some out to be made the same way as this same man will tell you, but also one without white hairs the same size as the hat that he is bringing. I want to have five without white hairs, but I would need six or twelve gray and black ones for the King of Spain made with the utmost care.

Here is a valet known by Picon, known by Colbert, and known by Mazarin. Both Colbert and Picon do not need to refer to him by name, which suggests that he was Picon's only official valet. The very matter with which he was charged may not appear to be very thought provoking, unless we recall the profession of one of the Augers whom we originally met in Senlis. I would suggest, whether this means anything or not, that we are here finally in the presence of Eustache Dauger. All we have to do now is to wonder what else he knew about his three employers besides their preferences in haberdashery.[24]

We do not have to wonder very long, because it will be remembered that in October of 1659, Jean-Baptise Colbert launched his most concerted and most secret attack upon the reputation of Nicolas Fouquet. It will also be remembered that Fouquet got wind of the *mémoire* and complained to Mazarin, who asked Colbert how this had happened. Fouquet, Colbert replied, must have obtained a copy of the *mémoire* from one of the postmasters, for he, Colbert, had taken the most extraordinary precautions regarding its security,

> having absolute confidence in the copyist, who has served me faithfully for 18 [crossed out] 16 years on an infinity of occasions more important than this one.

Who was this copyist in whom Colbert had such confidence? We can certainly suspect who it was, especially if we recall how, back in the 1640s, we found Antoine-Hercule strangely missing from his hometown in Languedoc, but in a subsequent letter to Mazarin, Colbert identifies this copyist positively as Antoine-Hercule Picon and specifies that he had locked him up in a room for three days in order to transcribe the *mémoire*. We can then ask ourselves, if Colbert had sent Picon on an infinity of delicate missions over a period of sixteen years, on how many such missions had Picon's only identifiable man accompanied him?[25]

It would seem as if the closer Cardinal Mazarin came to the end of his life, the more passionately he insisted on leaving it with his fortune intact, and when it came to paying off the creditors of the Duchy of Nevers, Antoine-Hercule Picon played an even bigger part and with an even greater sense of urgency. Thus on January 12, 1661, he appeared suddenly in the company of the notaries Mouffle and Le Fouyn at the home of the Count di Sanazzaro and demanded, in keeping with the conditions of the purchase, a complete list of the creditors. When the count replied that he would have to communicate the demand to the council of the duke, Picon replied that he took the answer as a refusal and threatened further legal action. With their patron about to vanish, however, Colbert and Picon suddenly became less sure of themselves. Two weeks before Mazarin's death, Sannazzaro reported that a clerk of M[r] Colbert had *come back* to see him to inform him that Mazarin was entirely satisfied with his conduct.[26]

The rise of the sons also carried with it the rise of the father. The year 1659 saw Georges Picon buying or otherwise obtaining a number of offices which may or may not have taken him away from his home in Languedoc. He became a *conseiller* and *maître d'hôtel ordinaire du roy*, *commissaire général des armées*, and *maître de requêtes de la reyne*. And almost immediately after the marriage of Louis XIV, Antoine-Hercule became *secrétaire du conseil* of the new queen. He had attached his destiny to the star of Cardinal Mazarin, and it had paid off handsomely. The question was whether he and Eustache Dauger could survive Mazarin's passing.[27]

~

CHAPTER SEVEN

The Testament of Cardinal Mazarin

What a complicated personality! Mazarin had come up from nowhere to become the principal minister in France. He had conquered a woman without making love to her. He had survived a revolution and gained territories in a war. But for what? Certainly not for sex, certainly not for family, not even for material wealth or power. My guess is that it was for vanity. Everything was subordinate to it, even his greed. He simply had to prove to himself that he was the greatest of statesmen, greater than his namesake Julius Caesar, greater than his predecessor Cardinal Richelieu, greater than his fellow upstart Oliver Cromwell. If he had any love it was for French monarchy, but this was simply an extension of his vanity. As to his greed, we have seen that he had been almost as greedy for the monarchy as he had been for himself.

Mazarin had enjoyed good health through most of his life. He had undergone some short illnesses in 1635 and 1644, but had surmounted them. In the summer of 1650, in Nevers, he had by his own testimony come close to dying of an unspecified illness, and the following year, during his exile in Brühl, he is more specific about his symptoms: severe abdominal pain, jaundice, palpitations of the heart, inability to concentrate, sweating, and itching. His capacity to withstand this sort of suffering and to persevere is a testament to his love for the gratifications of this world, for by the time he returned to France the following year, he was claiming to be in perfect health. Pain and gravel stones, however, were his constant companions as he restored his authority over France, conspired with Oliver Cromwell, and accumulated the spoils of Charles I. Mazarin did not look healthy in 1657 and in 1658, after the king's close brush with death in Calais. Mazarin was in agony during the entire siege of Gravelines with what contemporaries diagnosed as the gout. He was bedridden in Bayonne on the way to Saint-Jean-de-Luz, but found a miraculous remission in his diplomatic jousts with Don Luis de Haro. The agony, however, returned in March of 1660 with violent pain in the intestines and periodic fainting spells. The disease, it would appear, was spreading into the vital organs. Even this suffering, however, did not prevent him from making a second voyage to Saint-Jean-de-Luz for the wedding of the king. By this time his thighs and legs were emaciated, and during the trip back he was so weak that had to be carried in and out of his carriage. But he would not abandon the struggle to survive, and on his return to Paris he wrote to his old friend the Marshal de Grammont, expressing a "great desire to recover." He got his wish for about a month, and it almost seemed as if, aided by frequent displacements between Vincennes, the Louvre, and the *palais Mazarin*, he was regaining his health and vigor, but one candid doctor named Guénault had begun to warn him that he was dying. By early October the disease was visible in both feet, both knees, an elbow, and a wrist. Louis-Henri, the young Count de Brienne, describes him in January of 1661, stretched out in his armchair, his arms and legs flailing, his speech incomprehensible. On February 6, 1661, a fire in the Louvre forced him back into his palace, and no sooner was he there than he allowed a consultation by twelve doctors, including Guénault, who now informed him that he had about two months to live. It was only after this consultation, according to Brienne, that Mazarin finally began to think about death, and since Brienne's testimony is too valuable to discard, it behooves us to evaluate him and it with the greatest attention.[1]

Louis-Henri was a young man with an uncertain future before him. The son of the same Count de Brienne who had befriended Anne of Austria during her most difficult days, Louis-Henri too had no love for Cardinal Mazarin, and he too had managed to survive due only to the favor of the queen. In August of 1651, while Mazarin was still in Brühl, Anne of Austria had even granted to the young Brienne the right to succeed his father as secretary of state for foreign affairs, in preparation for which Louis-Henri had taken a grand tour of northern Europe, accompanied the court to Lyon for Louis XIV's pseudo-engagement, and had assisted Cardinal Mazarin during his conferences with Don Luis de Haro. Most importantly for our investigation, the young Brienne was also in attendance at the Louvre, at the *palais Mazarin*, and at Vincennes during the last days of Cardinal Mazarin. In the course of his experiences, the young Brienne kept some sort of diaries, which later in his life he put together into a rambling set of *Mémoires*. In one of the most poignant passages in these *Mémoires*, he gives us an unforgettable portrait of Mazarin's state of mind as he was facing death.[2]

Brienne tells us that, just a few days after the fire in the Louvre, he was walking though the second floor gallery of the *palais Mazarin* with a cousin when Brienne heard the approach of Cardinal Mazarin, which sounded like the shuffle of a man on his last legs. Brienne immediately hid himself behind a tapestry, from where he heard Mazarin say, "I'll have to leave all this!" Then, hesitating as if he were going from object to object, he continued, "And this too . . . I worked so hard to get all these things! Can I leave them without regret? I'll never see them again where I am going!" As much as he hated Mazarin, Brienne felt a twinge of compassion. But he was also so horrified at such a sentiment from a dying man that he let out a sigh. On hearing it, Mazarin cried out, "Who is there?" Brienne came forward and told him that he had a letter from Bartet in England. Mazarin reacted plaintively, "Give me your hand, I feel weak, I can't take it any more!" Then he continued, "Don't talk to me about affairs of state . . . look at this beautiful painting by Correggio, this Venus of Titian, this incomparable painting of the flood by Antonio Carracci. I'll have to leave all this! Good bye dear paintings, you were so expensive!" He also implied to Brienne, who tried to comfort him, that Louis XIV could hardly wait for him to die.[3]

Brienne may have overdramatized. He had an eccentric streak, he was soon to fall into disgrace, and he wrote up his *Mémoires* in old age, but there is a ring of truth to this account that makes it impossible to dismiss. It shows us nakedly and starkly how passionately Mazarin loved life and how he prized riches. Not even his agonies could make him abandon them: he even preferred them to his alternative passion for affairs of state. And we have already run into other moments of his life when he put jewels and duchies for himself over the interests of France. If these were Mazarin's very words, and Brienne claims that they were, it would appear as if to the dying Mazarin there was no conception of an eternal life that could surpass three Italian masters. Or maybe we can contemplate the possibility that, in the depths of his heart, Cardinal Mazarin could not bring himself to believe either in God or in the devil.

What makes the Brienne scenario particularly compelling is how long it took for Cardinal Mazarin to think of his succession. As we have seen, he loved people insofar as they were useful for his ambitions. Not surprisingly, therefore, his closest emotional bond was with the royal family. As to his blood relatives, there was little love and more simple utility. There was his younger sister, Laura Margherita Martinozzi, who had returned to Rome, and her two daughters, Anna Maria, whom he had married to the Prince de Conti, and Laura, whom he had married to the Duke of Modena. Mazarin's youngest sister,

Geronima Mancini, had died in 1656, preceded by her eldest son, who had died after the Battle of the Faubourg Saint-Antoine and who was followed in death by her youngest son, Alfonso, who had died in 1658 while roughhousing with his schoolmates. She had, however, a huge progeny: three daughters—Laura, whom Mazarin had married to the Duke de Mercoeur and had subsequently died; Olympia, whom Mazarin had married to the Count de Soissons; and Maria, with whom Louis XIV had fallen in love and was now destined for the Constable Colonna—a middle son, Philippe, who had recently disgraced himself by attending a wild party during Holy Week, and two more daughters, Hortense and Marie-Anne. Thus, out of this superabundance of nieces, the closest male descendant was Philippe, the debauchee.[4]

On or about February 8, 1661, Mazarin decided to abandon his palace in Paris. He must have cut a pitiful figure as he boarded his carriage for his final destination, the *pavillon de la Reine* in the *château* of Vincennes, a few miles east of the capital. The king and the queen mother quickly joined him. From time to time they would go into Paris, so that when they came back to Vincennes on February 22 they were particularly shocked. They stayed with him for two hours and came out crying. We cannot be sure, but it was possibly at this time that he discussed the disposition of his estate with Louis XIV, and it would appear as if with the last ounces of his strength Mazarin's single-minded motive was to preserve the glory of his name. Thus, for lack of anyone better in his own family, he had decided to bestow the most visible portions of his estate upon the eager son of the Marshal La Meilleraye, on the condition that he marry Hortense Mancini and assume the name and title of Duke de Mazarin. He would receive the Duchy of Mayenne and a host of other incomes and offices held by the cardinal in Auvergne, Brittany, Brouage, and La Fère amounting to some 400,000 *livres* per year. On the other hand, Mazarin merely commended his youngest niece Maria Anna Mancini to the care of Anne of Austria, with the promise of a dowry for her eventual marriage. The greatest loser relatively speaking, because he was the most direct male descendant, would be Philippe Mancini, since he was destined at that moment for the Duchy of Nevers, the county of Férel, the governorship of Alsace, and an eventual marriage with the daughter of the Princess Palatine. Not far from Mazarin's mind, with each agonizing distribution, were his most valuable jewels and notably those of the Queen of England, which he intended to pass on to the crown. How do we know all this? We know it because, apparently, Mazarin's close confidant, Zongo Ondedei, divulged it to the Venetian ambassador. It was the Venetian who informs us of it, as well as the motive of the cardinal in preferring the house of Meilleraye over the house of Mancini. It was in this period, too, that Fouquet visited Mazarin, who commended the interests of the son of La Meilleraye to his care. That these decisions were taken in a panic is illustrated by the marriage contract, containing slightly different conditions, of the future Duke de Mazarin to Hortense, signed in Vincennes on February 28. The marriage was celebrated in Paris on March 1 with Ondedei officiating.[5]

During these last two days Mazarin experienced some relief, which gave him and his close confidants time to consider that, since he had accumulated so many riches and in such questionable ways, it would be extremely embarrassing for him to submit his possessions to the customary procedures for the inheritance of property. Such an operation, at least, required a good lawyer, and the young Brienne, in a document that he composed very late in his life, claims that it was Gomont (whom we have already met on numerous occasions) who came up with a solution. The idea was that Mazarin should draw up the simplest of wills, leaving everything he possessed to the king, who would then be free to dispose as much of it as he wished without anyone having the effrontery to question him.[6]

Whatever relief Mazarin may have been experiencing, however, it did not last long. The passage from March 2 to 3 was so agonizing that on the morning of the 3rd the canon of the church of the *château* had to be called in to administer extreme unction. It is difficult to reconstruct the exact sequence, but apparently Claude Joly, the curate of Saint-Nicolas-des-Champs in Paris, who had met with Mazarin on two previous occasions, was also called in and remained with him for about three quarters of an hour. By nine o'clock, however, Le Vasseur and Le Fouyn arrived to record the testament. It would be wonderful to have the original draft, possibly in the hand of Gomont, or at least the minute in the hand of Le Fouyn, but we do have four complete copies which come extremely close to the original, along with similar copies of a number of other wills and codicils that the notaries produced during the next few days. From the four copies of the simple will, all of which I have designated as Text A, it results that Mazarin humbly begged the king to "dispose of the said goods in keeping with the thoughts and plans of His Eminence, *which His Majesty has heard verbally*" (italics mine), adding that the king was also free to dispose of the goods as he himself wished.[7]

⁓

Had Mazarin died at that point, this would have settled the matter. Instead he lingered, watching his friends playing cards, fondling his beloved diamonds, and trying as much as possible to keep up appearances. Brienne did observe that Mazarin showed less interest than usual in who was winning.

"We've got to bury the synagogue," he kept repeating, "with honor!" The synagogue, of course, was himself. But appearances were deceiving, for it was at this very time that it must have occurred to him and to his confidants, perhaps even to Louis, that Gomont's solution, for all of its elegance, placed too much suspicion upon the king as both the beneficiary and dispenser of a gargantuan estate. Mazarin and his confidants, therefore, now desperately devised an alternate plan—which was not that much of an improvement— namely, for Gomont to draw up a more detailed will. It must have been this will that Mazarin's confessor, Angelo Bissaro, describes in his account of Mazarin's death, specifying that Mazarin worked on it and corrected it on March 4 into the night. It was not until the morning of Sunday, March 6, before the notaries arrived to transcribe the more detailed will.[8]

In this testament, still part of Text A, after thanking God, Louis XIII, Anne of Austria, and Louis XIV for making him the instrument by which Christendom had returned to a perfect peace, and regretting that his illness had interrupted his efforts to undertake a thoroughgoing domestic reform, Mazarin went on to a number of charitable contributions and bequests, such as the donation to the Theatines for a church and the establishment of a college for young nobles before, rather suddenly and unexpectedly, introducing the jewels of the Queen of England, which, along with others in his possessions, he bequeathed to the crown. He did not mention any of the jewels by name, much less where he got them, but obviously he did not feel he could ignore them either, lest the crown in future ages would find it difficult to explain how it had obtained such property. Thus the jewels of Henrietta found themselves mingled with the others under the rubric of "eighteen of the most beautiful diamonds to be found," and these would henceforth contribute to something else which concerned him greatly, namely, that his name would be forgotten by history. It is hard to believe that he did not think that the Treaty of Westphalia, his triumph over the *Fronde*, and the Peace of the Pyrenees would not be sufficient to make us remember him. He needed eighteen diamonds to be named "Mazarins" as well. Less conspicuous, but no less intriguing were all the paintings in his library, which he did not identify, and two tapestries, which he could name without embarrassment, and which he could turn over to the crown with greater modesty.

Mazarin then addressed himself to the members of his own family. The daughters of his surviving sister, Martinozzi, whom he had nicely married, also got something, as did the sister herself, but the desire to preserve the name and, even more, the desire to control things beyond the grave emerges in his treatment of Philippe. He did not get the governorship of Alsace and Ferel. He still inherited the Duchy of Nevers, the governorships of Brouage and La Rochelle, and whatever Mazarin owned in Rome, but all of this under the tutelage of Colbert and under the precise condition that Philippe marry someone approved by the king, and that he and his heirs adopt the name of Mancini-Mazarini. In an intriguing paragraph for our investigation, the dying cardinal took the time to bequeath to his nephew a tapestry of the *Acts of the Apostles,* "made in Paris," and required that it be sent to Rome.

The dying cardinal continued by making provisions for the daughter of his late niece who had married the Duke de Mercoeur (she ended up with the income from Auvergne), for the niece who had married the Count de Soissons, and for the mischievous Marie Mancini, who was at that moment in Paris waiting for her marriage by proxy to the Constable Colonna. This brought him to the heart of every testament, the designation of his universal heirs. They were, as Ondedei had divulged, the son of Marshal de La Meilleraye and Hortense Mancini, who, having been married on March 1, were now the Duke and Duchess de Mazarin. Mazarin, however, could still not make up his mind how to part with his palace, diamonds, paintings, and remaining governorships, "reserving their disposition by codicil or otherwise *however he pleased*" (italics mine).

But perhaps the most striking feature of this entire testament is the confidence that Mazarin places in the person of Jean-Baptiste Colbert. Mazarin puts all his papers, whether public or private, into the hands of Colbert and prohibits that any inventory of them be made, but this confidence goes much, much further:

> My said Lord Cardinal not being able to say enough about the fidelity of Mister Colbert, which he has experienced over more than twelve years, approves everything he has done up to the present. Simply wants him to be taken at his word. My said Lord Cardinal wants and intends that the account books of his household that will be presented be examined by him alone who will sign and approve them.[9]

Not only no inventory of Mazarin's papers, not only that Colbert be taken simply at his word, but as to Mazarin's "goods, furniture, and effects," that no inventory be made of them either, and if his beneficiaries asked for one they would be disinherited! An inventory was common legal practice in the seventeenth century, and required by the customary law of Paris for the benefit both of the heirs and of the creditors of the deceased, so Mazarin in this instance was writing a will in direct contravention of public law and which exempted his estate from any public scrutiny. It is hard to imagine a more brazen indication of guilt combined with a more categorical demand for impunity. It was even too much for Jean-Baptiste Colbert. The challengers to the will would wait for the first opportunity—an untimely death, a weak government, a rebellion—to get their revenge, and for his own security he needed the backing of some executors prestigious enough to form a protective shield. Not surprisingly, they appeared. Mazarin designated Guillaume de Lamoignon, the presiding judge of the *parlement* of Paris; Nicolas Fouquet; Zongo Ondedei; Michel Le Tellier; and Colbert himself. If one did not know the reasoning, the first two choices, especially the second, might appear surprising. But the reasoning was clear enough. Lamoignon and Fouquet were the two men who could exert enough control over the *parlement* to block any challenges to the will and, in order to defend their handling of the assets, it would be in their interest to block any such challenges. At the same time, Ondedei, Le Tellier, and Colbert would be sufficient, in a pinch, to outvote Lamoignon and Fouquet. It was on this coalition of mutual interests that Mazarin relied in order to defend him beyond the grave.[10]

It was still Sunday, March 6th, and while the notaries were transcribing this testament, Mazarin's condition became so grave that Claude Joly in Paris had to be interrupted in the midst of his morning sermon in order to provide Mazarin with some additional spiritual comfort. By noon, however, Mazarin was well enough to add a codicil, still part of Text A, which the notaries had to return in order to record. In it Mazarin finally decided on how to dispose of his palace. It would be divided between the Duke and Duchess de Mazarin and Philippe Mancini. Mazarin also dictated some final letters. The king was there, and he approved both the testament and the codicil. Mazarin even felt well enough to have himself shaved, colored with rouge, and carried in a sedan chair around the gardens of Vincennes, much to the amusement of the malicious onlookers. This act of bravado cost him dearly. Brienne recalled that it left him more dead than alive. He still had enough life in him on the morning of the 7th to add still another codicil to his will, which included an intriguing tapestry for Philippe Mancini. It seemed like the end, and the notaries now read the testament in the presence of the king, the principal beneficiaries, and the executors; Louis XIV, shedding copious tears, expressed his approval of both to the testament and codicils without even bothering to read them. But finally, later on that day, Mazarin's energy ran out. He handed over some presents to the royal family, including the eighteen precious diamonds, which he turned over to the king; said good-bye to the royal family; and asked them not to visit him again. He handed Colbert the keys to a strong box in his apartment at the Louvre, and informed him of more hard cash in his palace in Paris, at La Fère, in the hands of Marshal Fabert in Sedan, and owed to him by President Tubeuf and others. He received a visit from the nuncio bringing a plenary indulgence from the pope and was given extreme unction. From that time on, only his confessor, his personal servants, Colbert, and Joly had access to him, Colbert playing the angel with a fiery sword and barring the passage to his chambers.[11]

Brienne tells us that right after witnessing the administration of extreme unction, he himself mounted his carriage to return to Paris. He must have had his fill of death, and as his carriage was approaching the Faubourg Saint-Antoine, he ordered it to stop so that he could watch the king's musketeers, who were drilling in a nearby field. While he was thus catching his breath, he was surprised to see someone approaching his carriage on foot. It was the cardinal's first *valet de chambre*, Bernouin, who informed Brienne that he was on pressing business for the cardinal and asked him for a ride into the city. Brienne then took him into the neighborhood of the Louvre, where he got off and begged Brienne not to tell anyone about the incident. Brienne claims he thought nothing of it at the time, but learning later that there were five million *livres* in the Louvre, he came to suspect that Bernouin had grabbed the money for himself so as to keep it from the heirs of the cardinal. Brienne, of course, had no knowledge of what had just gone on between Mazarin and Colbert, and this is certainly a wonderful example of how legends begin to spread. Yet Brienne, in his ignorance, provides us with the most precious piece of information that we have yet discovered in our search for the secret of the iron mask, for it shows us the first step in the securing of Mazarin's property and transferring it to the king, and not only that: it shows us the kind of persons who were employed in the process, namely, confidential valets. If I may venture to say so, I suggest that we are closing in on Eustache Dauger.[12]

On March 9, at two or three in the early morning, Mazarin breathed his last. His nieces Hortense and Marie and their brother Philippe were also at Vincennes at this time, and Hortense tells us that whatever regret they may all have experienced, Marie and Philippe said to each other, "Thank God, he's finally croaked!" "To be perfectly honest," Hortense added, "I was not any sadder. . . . I never saw anyone who was so sweet in public and so rude and arrogant with his family." The young Brienne was no more sympathetic. He was back from Paris, and in attendance in Mazarin's antechamber along with other courtiers, as Louis XIV rushed in—it must have been in the middle of the night—shedding copious tears. Spotting the Duke de Grammont, the king grabbed him by the arm, uttering, "We have just lost a good friend, you and I!" Torn between his amusement and his piety, Brienne confessed that he could hardly refrain from laughing.[13]

Brienne, however, continues to provide us with more than food for *Schadenfreude*. He tells us that he was immediately ordered by Louis XIV to transfer a number of key governorships, including that of Brittany, which was possessed by the queen mother, to the Duke de Mazarin. This illustrates the depth of Louis's attachment and that he was prepared to execute the desires of the late cardinal even to the detriment of Anne of Austria who, as it turned out, refused to give up the post. Brienne also gives us insights into the behavior of the new Duke de Mazarin, who initially appeared reconciled to accommodating the queen mother and very quickly changed his tune. He was thus the first of the troublesome heirs who would have to be kept under restraint. Finally, Brienne describes how he was ordered by Louis to inform Fouquet, who was then in Saint-Mandé, to be present the next morning at seven o'clock for a council, along with Chancellor Séguier and the four secretaries of state, who were in Paris. Once again Brienne's testimony is priceless. He tells us that when he visited Fouquet to inform him of the order, the superintendant seemed quite disoriented and begged Brienne for the latest news. If, as we have seen, Fouquet was not in possession of any incriminating secrets as late as 1658, and we have seen how quickly his position had deteriorated over the previous three years, we now enter into a period when, thanks to his being one of the executors, he was finally in a position to learn something. Thus to the entrance of numerous valets into a deep dark secret, we can now observe the emergence of a situation in which Fouquet was finally in a position to have known something about what one of these valets had seen and how he had been employed.[14]

⌣

Apparently, however, Colbert did not feel that Mazarin had authorized him sufficiently, or at least felt that Mazarin's order that he, Colbert, be taken at his word also permitted him to take liberties with what I have identified as Text A of Mazarin's testament. Thus, between March 8 and 12, while the entire continent was waiting to discover the details of the testament, Colbert, with the possible assistance of Gomont and connivance of Le Fouyn, proceeded to enlarge it. The first enlargement was modest enough, and it produced what I have identified as Text B. It elaborated on the confidence that Mazarin had expressed in Colbert and devolved some of it upon Picon. Here is the passage with the additions in bold:

> My said Lord Cardinal not being able to say enough about the fidelity of Mister Colbert which he has experienced over more than twelve years, approves everything he has done up to the present. Simply wants him to be taken at his word. Wants and intends my said Lord **"Cardinal, considering the great affairs which**

since a number of years have prevented him, as he was accustomed, from examining the account books of Mr Picon, that the account books" [continuing more or less as in Text A] **"of his household which will be presented, be examined by the said Mr Colbert, and signed and approved by him alone."**[15]

What is remarkable is that Colbert did not limit himself to inserting this short elaboration, because in the course of these same four days, he added much more extensively to the will, creating what I have designated as Text C. He seems to have had Picon in his heart, for in a section on provisions, he stops to include the detail that they were in the hands of Picon. And the section on Philippe Mancini went from approximately 1,426 words in Text A to 4,362 words in Text C. And, as if he had not sufficiently praised himself, or covered the interests of Antoine-Hercule Picon, Colbert elaborated on his first elaboration even further:

> Further my said lord cardinal testator has declared that after having experienced over nearly twelve years the affection that the said zeal of the said Mr Colbert for his service. . . . His Eminence entirely approves everything that has been done by the said Mr Colbert both by virtue of his general powers of attorney and in keeping with the orders that he has received verbally. And even everything that has been done by everyone who has handled the money of His Eminence and by Mr Picon his treasurer, it having often been necessary to make the expenses without writing. Wants the said Mr Colbert simply to be taken at his word about everything that has been received, spent, done, and directed by his orders in affairs of every nature whatsoever. Further declares my said Lord Testator that it is still his intention that the said Mr Colbert examine and approve all the account books of the said Mr Picon his treasurer from the year 1650 until the year 1657 inclusively in keeping with the power of his general powers of attorney, but that since the said year 1657 affairs of state, the age, and the poor health of His Eminence have prevented him from attending this work, he has wanted and expressly orders Mr Colbert to see, examine, and sign them.

For purposes of our investigation it is important to note that from no mention at all in Text A to one mention in Text B, the name of Picon rises to three mentions in Text C. Thus, next to covering his own interests, Colbert shows no greater concern in his additions to the testament of Cardinal Mazarin than to protect the interests of Antoine-Hercule Picon and the heirs of Philippe Mancini.[16]

Another thing that is evident about this conspiracy is the ambivalence in the minds of the conspirators about what they had done. On the one hand, they were aware that the disclosures in the testament were outrageous; on the other hand, they blithely permitted the notaries to read it before the heirs and executors. The result, not surprisingly, was that someone took notes and began to distribute them. The conspirators knew enough not to give anyone a copy, but were not worried enough to keep the originals under lock and key. Thus the ink was hardly dry on the minute before someone leaked out a complete copy, the ink was hardly dry on the first addition before someone leaked out another complete copy, and this is why we still have four copies of Text A and thirteen of Text B. Finally, the conspirators had never been comfortable with the clauses prohibiting the inventory. The moment Mazarin had passed from the scene, Louis XIV himself began to have second thoughts, and it is hard to imagine that any of the executors wanted to incur the legal responsibility for disposing of so much property without accounting for it. This last dilemma, however, had its advantages. While everyone was reconsidering, there was no move from any source to place any seals upon Mazarin's possessions, as was required by law, which gave ample time for Colbert to finish producing his Text C and for his collaborators to rummage through Mazarin's residences. On March 18 the notaries again read a will before the king, the principal beneficiaries, and executors. Still, no one received a copy. Everyone must have known that they were participating in a charade, but in the glow of the dawning of the personal reign everyone denied it to himself.[17]

On that very day the executors began to assemble, apparently at the Louvre, and they showed every sign of taking their duties seriously. They decided to have regular meetings, and over the next ten days appointed two lawyers, Jacques de Fita and Jean de Gomont, a clerk François Le Bas, and a recorder, the notary Le Fouyn—all, of course, accomplices of Colbert—to keep a register of their proceedings. On March 29 Louis XIV sent the executors an express order to proceed with the inventory, decreeing, as only an absolute monarch could, that this could be accomplished "without causing any prejudice in any way to the dispositions of the testament." On March 31, it was a Thursday, the notaries Beauvais and Le Fouyn appeared at the chambers of the late cardinal in the Louvre. There they were met by four of the five executors, Fouquet, Le Tellier, Ondedei, and Colbert (Lamoignon being absent), and Colbert informed them—as if they didn't already know—of the king's insistence on proceeding with an inventory. The Duke and Duchess de Mazarin were also in attendance and ready to comply with the king's wishes but, for some reason, possibly because they wanted to protect themselves, everyone took the precaution of "protesting," and they never lost an opportunity of reiterating that they were not in any way violating the testament. The executors also excused themselves, because of their other official duties, from showing up every day for the inventory and delegated this task to Le Bas, who immediately called in an entire crew to assist him, among them Joseph Sellory, the keeper of Mazarin's palace, and two appraisers, one of them being François Lescot. It had been twenty-two days since the decease of Cardinal Mazarin, twenty-two days during which it had been open season on his account books and on his treasures, and still no seals on the doors of any of his possessions. All of these individuals were simply sworn in by the notaries and taken at their word that they were faithfully producing and appraising the possessions of the late cardinal.[18]

We do not have the minutes of the meetings of the executors and we cannot be sure where, exactly, the rest of the meetings took place, but we can tell from the report which Le Bas drew up for the Duke and Duchess de Mazarin and which was also preserved by Colbert that between March 18 and August 25 the executors met on at least nineteen different days, sometimes more than once on the same day. They clearly had the will at their disposal, as we shall see by the recollection of Fouquet, although this does not mean that they had a copy of it in their possession. On April 11 and May 7, 15, and 25 they happily agreed to divide Mazarin's papers into three groups, one to inventory and give to the Duke and Duchess de Mazarin, one to inventory and return to Colbert, *and a third not to inventory at all!* On May 7 and 15, and again on June 6, the executors were equally accommodating in regard to Picon's account books, whose signing, in keeping with Mazarin's intentions, they entrusted to Colbert, who happened to be absent at Fontainebleau. The only delicate moment that I can detect occurred on May 25th when some malicious executor asked Colbert to produce evidence of Mazarin's tonsure and his naturalization, which Colbert faithfully promised to locate and never did. On July 6 Picon again appeared before the executors with his account books, hypocritically offering to have them verified by any person of their choosing, which he knew perfectly well they would categorically reject, citing the specific instructions of the cardinal.[19]

Since, moreover, Le Fouyn was both recorder for the executors and notary for the inventory and Le Bas acted as clerk for both, I can only conclude that the executors, and particularly Le Bas and Le Fouyn, must have done a lot of scurrying from one meeting to another. We do not have the original minutes of the inventory, which, as was the custom, were retained in the office of the principal notary Le Fouyn, but we can tell from the two copies which have come down to us that they spent from March 29 to April 2 on the contents of two cabinets in Mazarin's apartment, filled largely with rings, jewels, stones, medals, and other valuables—248 items in all—at which point Colbert appeared and announced that he had been given the keys of these cabinets by Cardinal Mazarin two days before his death, along with the key of a chest containing 70,000 *pistoles* (840,000 *livres*) in cash located in the alcove. Colbert also revealed that the cardinal had kept 60,000 *pistoles* (720,000 *livres*) in his *château* at La Fère, 297,000 *livres* in his palace in Paris, and 100,000 *pistoles* (1,200,000 *livres*) with Marshal Fabert in Sedan, and was owed 100,000 *livres* by President Tubeuf. Among the smaller sums owed to Mazarin, according to Colbert, were 12,000 *livres* by a "M^r flix," our old friend from Calais. All of these assets were presumably to go to the Duke and Duchess de Mazarin, but if we recall Bernouin's little jaunt to the Louvre on the same day that Mazarin gave Colbert the keys to his coffers, and if we recall the twenty-two days between Mazarin's death and the inception of the inventory, and if we recall that there had never been any seals on Mazarin's possessions, we can only wonder just how much confidence we can have that this constituted the sum total of the Cardinal's liquid assets. We do know, however, that the inventorying in the Louvre quickly came to a conclusion, Sellory suggesting that Mazarin's remaining possessions in the Louvre could more easily be inventoried with the bulk of his property in the *palais Mazarin*, a suggestion which occasioned a four-day delay until the move could be effected.[20]

On April 6, therefore, Le Bas and his collaborators moved to the storeroom of the *palais Mazarin*, where they remained until June 3, and where they were presented with the bulk of the items that they inventoried. Unfortunately, for the objects that interest us the most, we do not have a complete catalog of Charles I's collection prior to his execution, the parliament having already disposed of a portion of it before putting the remainder on sale in 1650 at Somerset House. The best that we can do, therefore, is to compare the catalog of this sale with references made by Bordeaux of what he was attempting to purchase for Mazarin with the inventory that Colbert began drawing up for Mazarin in September of 1653, with the inventory after decease of 1661, and with the present holdings of the Louvre or the *Mobilier national*. From such a comparison it would appear as if, in keeping with the mixture of guilt and innocence, there was no concerted effort to keep the possessions of Charles I out of the inventory after decease. For example, sixteen pieces of the *History of David* and five pieces of the *Life and Passion of Jesus Christ* after Dürer, six pieces of the *Twelve Months of the Year* adorned with signatures of the King of England, four pieces from the *Acts of the Apostles* after Raphael and adorned with the royal arms and signatures, ten pieces on *Horsemanship* after Rubens, and the *Five Senses*, all tapestries, made it without a hint of scruple into the inventory, along with Van Dyck's *Three Children of Charles I* and Raphael's *Saint Michael Slaying the Demon* and *Saint George Slaying the Dragon*, all paintings. We should note, however, that since the tapestries were made in numerous copies, it would have been extremely difficult for original owners to lay claim to them, unless they bore clear marks of proprietorship. On the other hand, there are some items clearly from the estate of Charles I which do not appear in the inventory at all. These include some of the most precious: eight pieces of a *Paysage* after Holbein and six more pieces of the *Acts of the Apostles* after Raphael, adorned with the arms of England, all tapestries, along with Raphael's *Young Man*, Titian's *Venus del Pardo* and *Madonna of the Rabbit*, Van Dyck's *Saint-Sebastian*, and Giulio Romano's *Triumph of Titus and Vespasian*, all paintings. The Count de Cosnac, who observed these lacunae, tried to explain them by arguing that these objects must either have been among those in the library bequeathed *en bloc* to the crown or have been somewhere other than the Louvre, the *palais Mazarin*, or Vincennes, but this argument does not hold water since we know from the testimony of Brienne that the *Venus* of Titian was not in the library, but *in the second floor gallery* of the *palais* and that the inventory makes it a point to identify items that Mazarin had already given away or were at that moment in other locations. The items inventoried at the *palais Mazarin* went from a mere 250 entries to the impressive number of 2,224, but this does not take away from the fact that the omissions raise a critical question: Since the omitted items were heavy, who did the lifting? Certainly not Colbert, but if not he, who was available to transport them? Who else in seventeenth-century France was available for such a task if not one or any number of confidential valets?[21]

After one day of inventorying at Vincennes on June 15, Le Bas and his collaborators appear to have moved back to the *palais Mazarin* on the 17th where they addressed themselves to Mazarin's papers. Here Colbert, who personally brought them in, had a completely free hand, and this is evident from the selective character of the entries. The first documents involved the purchase of the *palais Mazarin*, a useful title to pass on to the heirs, but while the inventory contains numerous acts concerning the administration of the domain of La Fère, there is no evidence of how exactly Mazarin obtained it. There are a good number of current leases on the income from Mazarin's benefices, but no documents establishing Mazarin's titles to them. Again, there are numerous acts concerning the administration of the Duchy of Mayenne, but no act of purchase. Of all of Mazarin's governorships and domains, the only ones represented in the inventory are the immense territories in Alsace, which the king began granting to Mazarin in 1658. As to the financial relationships of Mazarin with the court of England, there were two acts, the one of December 1, 1656, and another one of March 20, 1660, in which the exiled Charles II and his mother both acknowledged owing Cardinal Mazarin the sums of 597,416 and 64,150 *livres* but, needless to say, there was no hint of the fictitious transfer of the *grand Sancy* and the *miroir de Portugal*, nor of the acquisition of the *Acts of the Apostles*, with its telltale markings of the King of England, from the estate of Servien. There were four acts concerning the transfer, through Mondini, of the 300,000 *livres* to the Queen of Poland; none, however, from Cantarini asserting that Mazarin had furnished the money. In short, although there must have been at least as many notarial acts and appointments to offices among Mazarin's papers as there were paintings and tapestries in his residences, Colbert had managed to reduce the former in Mazarin's inventory to a mere 134 entries. The work on the inventory concluded on June 22 with the marriage contracts of Mazarin's nieces (except for Marie Mancini's) and the insertion of a short inventory, compiled on the 28th by the local authorities in La Fère.[22]

Considering the convoluted principles of Cardinal Mazarin, the work on the inventory had gone very smoothly. "Never," wrote Le Bas in his report to the Duke and Duchess de Mazarin, "have so many things been executed in such a short time, so fairly, and in such good faith." Never, he might have added, had so many things been executed with such hypocrisy. Everyone who had participated in the process knew about the equivocations in the will, the contraventions of procedure, the delay in beginning the inventory, and the rush in completing it, and even beyond the executors of his will, there was a wide circle of participants, each of whom knew his or her own end of it. Indeed an escalating impression of Mazarin's wealth was public knowledge and public scandal. But what else could his executors do, except to rely on the combination of their own obfuscations and the intimidating presence of the emergent king?[23]

We have thus come across all the actors at the one moment when they came together to participate in a conspiracy that is worthy of the name: Michel Le Tellier, who later countersigned the arrest order for Eustache Dauger; Jean-Baptiste Colbert, who later furnished the funds for Eustache's transfer to Pinerolo; and Nicolas Fouquet, who did not have to be told who Eustache was. How else could these three men, along with Le Tellier's son, the Marquis de Louvois, have shared a sufficiently vivid memory of a valet named Eustache if that memory did not connect them all to a common experience that they could never forget? What else could Louvois have been referring to when he asked Fouquet whether Eustache had revealed anything to his companion about "what he has seen," about "what he was employed at doing," and about "his past life"? And what else could Eustache have seen or been employed at doing except at transporting the possessions of the late Cardinal Mazarin? It seems to me that only two questions still remain: How did Antoine-Hercule Picon survive the passing of Cardinal Mazarin? And why did it take Eustache Dauger eight years to get himself into trouble?

CHAPTER EIGHT

~

The Cover-Up

In inaugurating his personal reign, Louis XIV believed that he had broken definitively with a great abuse which had crept into the French monarchy. To him his quintessential reform was that he had chosen no prime minister, no Cardinal Richelieu, no replacement for Cardinal Mazarin. But even in this new order of things and all the flattery that it elicited, the traces of the old order remained. The most visible vestiges of the cardinal's administration were the principal ministers whom the king chose to assist him—Lionne for foreign affairs, Le Tellier for war, and Fouquet for the finances. There was even the question, should Louis lose his enthusiasm, of which one of them would take over the reins of government.[1]

Then, too, there was the immense network of offices, territories, and marriage alliances through which Mazarin had seen to his own security. The king had, through the reapportionment of Mazarin's estate, regained possession of a part of it, but there were still huge portions in the hands of his heirs. Conveniently, they were young, inexperienced, and grateful enough for their good fortune, but just to make sure that they would not abuse it, there was always Colbert. What he had done for Cardinal Mazarin, Colbert now took over for the cardinal's heirs, and with considerably greater authority. It was the same for Antoine-Hercule Picon, who continued as Colbert's right-hand man and in the council of the new queen. The Duke de Mazarin being the principal beneficiary, he was under the closest supervision. If Jean-Baptiste was not enough, his brother Charles, now Marquis de Croissy, acted as intendant in Alsace, and for the private property inherited by the duke and his wife, Antoine-Hercule's brother, Gabriel, became their treasurer. Philippe, now Duke de Nevers, was put under the watchful tutorship of François Le Bas. The intendant of the household of the Count and Countess de Soissons was a brother of the lawyer Gomont. Under such guidance, any misbehaviors of this privileged lot amounted to, at the most, court gossip.[2]

More serious were the invisible vestiges of the cardinal's regime. The personal reign of Louis XIV was barely five months old before the Count d'Estrades, now French ambassador in England, found it necessary to announce that Charles II was demanding that the Dutch Republic restore all the property of his crown that had fallen into the hands of its inhabitants. Even more alarming was the report that he was preparing to make a similar demand of the French. A different king of France might have rushed to return to Henrietta Maria and to her son all the paintings, diamonds, and tapestries, chivalrously presenting them as family heirlooms that Cardinal Mazarin had heroically rescued from the clutches of Oliver Cromwell. That, however, was not the character of Louis XIV. In a letter penned by Lionne, the king wrote:

> You must skillfully prevent anyone from ever making such a demand of you since, for numerous reasons that would take too long explain, I would not even consider being reimbursed. You must never speak about what I am telling you.

What this reply clearly demonstrates is that Louis was not merely holding on to Cardinal Mazarin's advisers and honoring his memory, he was also consciously identifying himself with the cardinal's moral world with its contradictory combination of shame and self-righteousness. This was the moral world in which the young king had grown up, and he was not enough of an independent thinker to create an alternative one of his own. One wonders how he would have reacted if Charles had pressed his demand. But, fortunately for Louis, the newly restored King of England was not about to pick a quarrel with his French cousin over such a trifle at this time, and the rattling of this particular skeleton was reserved to another day.[3]

Both the visible and the invisible vestiges of Mazarin, however, combined in the person of Nicolas Fouquet. Colbert had effectively poisoned the cardinal's mind against him, but Mazarin had not dared to create an additional crisis for himself by attempting to dismiss him. The personal reign, however, created a fresh opportunity. Colbert could not only redouble his accusations; he could present Fouquet as the one man in the kingdom with enough influence to force himself upon the king as prime minister. As far as Louis was concerned, whatever Mazarin had done to gather power around himself, it had been for the benefit of the monarchy. The young king reserved no such indulgence for Fouquet. Indeed, nothing was so easy for Louis than to excuse Mazarin while transferring all of his transgressions upon Fouquet. The only problem was how to get rid of him. Not only was Fouquet aware of Mazarin's cozy relations with the treasury, but Fouquet also knew about the irregularities of Mazarin's testament and, as one of the executors, had certainly witnessed the many more irregularities that the inventory had so elegantly covered. Moreover, his post as *procureur général* of the *parlement* gave him immunity from prosecution by any kind of extraordinary tribunal, and it was therefore all the more difficult to deny him a fair trial. It was, of course, not excludable for the king simply to thank Fouquet profusely for his services and then consign him to a life of honorable retirement but, once again, this was not in the character of Louis. With Cardinal de Retz still on the loose, with the Prince de Condé returning to his governorships, and with an affluent Fouquet hypothetically stirring the pot of discontent, getting him safely out of the way became the first priority for the king and for Colbert.[4]

If Fouquet had been able to guess what Louis had in mind, his only option would have been to resign the superintendancy of finances and modestly to retain his post as *procureur général*. Fouquet had plenty of warnings from various and sundry informants that his enemies were plotting against him, but he had painted himself into a corner, so that his only remaining option was to try to appease the king by apologizing profusely for his transgressions and then convince him of his indispensability. Louis played along with this game. He accepted Fouquet's apologies, flattered him with additional responsibilities, and waved the wand of royal favor before him. Late in June the king announced a voyage of the court to Brittany in order to hold the estates of the province. His intention, of course, was to get Fouquet out of Paris in order to arrest him more easily, but Fouquet kept right on whistling in the dark. Against the most elementary principles of prudence, he decided to give up his position as *procureur général*. Debilitated by intermittent fevers, he then sealed his fate by hosting an extravagant festival at Vaux which seemed to confirm Louis's worst suspicions about him.[5]

On August 27 the king left his *château* at Fontainebleau for his voyage to Brittany, followed by his entire court. He no sooner arrived in the old ducal palace at Nantes than he began to work with Colbert and Le Tellier on the details of the arrest. They lulled Fouquet into attending an early morning council meeting on September 5, after which, as he was being carried in his sedan chair under the spires of the cathedral, he was arrested by D'Artagnan, lieutenant of the musketeers, and hustled off to Angers. Fouquet's retinue in Nantes was also detained, his wife was relegated to Limoges, and orders were issued to seize his papers in Paris, Vaux, and Saint-Mandé. The best efforts to block the roads, however, did not prevent another one of his valets, La Forêt, from getting back to Paris with news of his arrest. Whether any of Fouquet's family in the area were able to salvage any of his papers is difficult to determine. In any case, his entire family, with the exception of his mother, ended up in exile. Nicolas himself was kept under close guard, but given a doctor and a valet. It was, however, easier to arrest Fouquet than to prosecute him. The commissioners charged with inventorying his papers did not find that much. Aside from an act by some tax farmers promising to pay a pension of 120,000 *livres* a year from the *gabelles* to an unnamed person, their biggest find, hidden behind a mirror, was the notorious project on what to do in case he was arrested. As for Nicolas, he busied himself with his defense, writing to Le Tellier and begging him to read the letter to the king: "I may have made mistakes . . . I did what had to be done. . . . One could not follow any rules with the cardinal, when it came to money. The king has most graciously told me that he pardoned everything. Now I find myself a prisoner." As if that argument would get him anywhere with Louis XIV! Le Tellier answered that the king was too busy, and prohibited Fouquet from writing any more letters.[6]

On November 15, 1661, Louis XIV issued his edict setting up the Chamber of Justice. In a separate document, he also commissioned its members, starting with the Chancellor Séguier and the chief justice of the *parlement* of Paris, Lamoignon. The list went on to include other presiding judges from various courts, councilors of state, masters of requests, and other individual judges. One of the masters of requests was Olivier Lefèvre d'Ormesson, Mazarin's faithful intendant of Picardy. A supplementary commission included the judge Nicolas Pussort, uncle of Colbert. The choice of *procureur général*, or chief prosecutor, was striking. It was Denis Talon, son of a troublemaker and a troublemaker himself during the *Fronde*, who had recently atoned sufficiently for the sins of his father and for his own by declaring himself an enemy of Fouquet. For clerk of the court, the king chose Joseph Foucault, another enemy of Fouquet. One wonders whether Fouquet, as he was transferred from Angers to Amboise, then to Vincennes, where he was held in the tower of the medieval castle, ever contemplated the irony that he now found himself in the hands of the same kind of tribunal over which his uncle and his father had once presided. His request for a volume of ordinances—there was one which prohibited superintendants of finances from being tried by Chambers of Justice—was refused. Even with a hand-picked tribunal, however, it took some time to make heads or tails out of his papers. Talon had to seek the help of Gomont, and it was not until March 4 that the chamber sent two commissioners, under the watchful eye of Foucault, to question Fouquet at Vincennes. It was clearly a fishing expedition, and he fought back stubbornly. At first, he refused to recognize the jurisdiction of the tribunal, then he relented somewhat. Asked about his personal wealth, he estimated that he was currently in debt for considerably more than he was worth. Asked about the mysterious pension, he intimated that it was for the benefit of Mazarin and his valet Bernouin. Presented with the project found behind the mirror, the flustered Fouquet could merely stammer that he was driven to it by the hostility of Cardinal Mazarin, and that it was a "simple project and draft of useless thoughts."[7]

In these early days of his personal reign, however, the King of France was in his glory. The financiers were so intimidated by him that Colbert, for whom Louis now created the new office of controller-general, could proceed to his long-meditated reformation of the state. In October of 1661, in London, the Spanish ambassador had challenged the precedence of the Count d'Estrades. The King of France forced his own father-in-law, the King of Spain, to send an envoy to Paris to make a public apology. In August of the following year, in Rome, the retinue of Louis's ambassador got into a brawl with the pope's Corsican guards. The King of France threatened to invade the Papal States unless the pope gave him satisfaction. By October of that same year, Colbert had managed to collect two million *livres* in cash with which to repurchase Dunkirk from the impecunious Charles II of England, thus giving Mazarin's desperate move in turning over the port to Oliver Cromwell the happiest possible ending. These were the days when Louis took the title of "Sun King." What kind of a chance did the impudent squirrel have against him?[8]

Fouquet's family and his friends never stopped trying. Toward the end of March of 1662 a series of anonymous pamphlets had begun to appear, the first of which was titled *Discours au Roy par un de ses fidèles sujets sur le procès de M. Foucquet*, or "Speech to the king by one of his faithful subjects on the trial of Mr Fouquet." Its courageous author was Paul Pellisson, one of Fouquet's confidential clerks, and Pellisson's points closely mirrored the defense that Fouquet himself had vainly attempted to put before the eyes of the king. Fouquet, Pellisson wrote, had been a faithful subject during the *Fronde*; what Fouquet had done had been under the orders of Cardinal Mazarin, and moreover, as a former superintendant of finances, Fouquet could not be tried by a special tribunal. This argument made no difference as the judges went on to interrogate a series of witnesses in the hope of building a case against him. His mother and wife had made tearful pleas to Louis which may even have had some effect because the king did not object when the Chamber of Justice, which, since Séguier did not appear, was presided over by Lamoignon, granted Fouquet pen and paper, an inventory of his papers that had been seized, as well as the right to be assisted by two lawyers. Moreover, in keeping with his willingness to give Fouquet the appearances of a fair trial, Louis also designated two members of the chamber whom he thought would be appropriately severe, Ormesson and Sainte-Hélène, to act as reporters on the case and eased out Lamoignon, obliging Séguier to preside in person. It was not that easy. Now that Fouquet had a pen and paper, he did not fail to use them. He composed a vigorous *Jugement sur les deux défenses imprimées en faveur de M. Fouquet,* or "Judgment on the two defenses that have been published in favor of Mr Fouquet," claiming that Colbert and his minions had distorted and falsified the inventory of his papers and going on to accuse Mazarin of having enriched himself to the tune of some fifty million *livres.* As final proof he referred to the irregularities of Mazarin's testament:

> The extreme wealth of Cardinal Mazarin appears by the reading of that mysterious testament, which has been kept hidden up to now, none of the heirs, legatees, or executors having been able to obtain a copy, except for Mr Colbert, who manufactured it and, by his omnipotence over his master, had such extraordinary clauses inserted in it, that it is not so much a testament as it is a panegyric of the said Mr Colbert.

By this time the Fouquet family had set up a secret press which published this writing. He requested that the court return his papers to him and began to identify Colbert's henchmen: Ondedei, Rose, Roussereau, Villacerf, Le Bas, Berryer, and Picon. This request, too, was published. He also attempted to disqualify Talon, Foucault, Pussort, and another judge, without success, but the chamber did not abandon its dilatory procedures and ultimately did provide him with some copies of his papers. Finally, by the beginning of April, Talon was ready with his charges, and on the 10th Ormesson the reporter began reading them, aided by a number of his fellow judges, the introduction alone running to sixty-one folios. Its claims were that Fouquet had embezzled the pension of 120,000 *livres* from the *gabelles* along with the pensions on other tax farms, that his clerks had committed similar thefts, that he had lent money to the state at outrageous rates, that he had diverted millions to sustain his lavish lifestyle and, last but not least, that he had contemplated rebellion. One indication that the trial was taking longer than expected: Louis moved the Chamber from its ceremonial quarters in the Palace of Justice to the more military Arsenal, and Fouquet from the chivalric castle of Vincennes to the more ominous Bastille.[9]

~

The reading of the charges was still continuing when the friends of Fouquet produced their most striking evidence up to date, namely, a copy of the mysterious testament of Cardinal Mazarin. How they obtained their particular version can only be a matter for speculation. It was not the earliest text that we have designated as Text A, nor the final text that we have designated as Text C, but a very reliable (save for a few printer's errors) copy of the intermediate Text B. The publication came out in two imprints, both obviously fictitious, one in Cologne and the other in Paris, along with a number of handwritten copies, and for the first time the public became aware of two incriminating facts about Cardinal Mazarin: that he had retained a large number of secret financial documents and, most notably, that he had desperately resisted the compilation of an inventory after decease. There was no question about the impact of these revelations. The Cologne edition was quickly translated into English and Dutch; the English version by James Howell, a publicist for the Earl of Clarendon, chief minister of Charles II, was accompanied by a not too positive evaluation of Cardinal Mazarin's honesty. With the tide of public opinion turning against him, Talon made a bid to reverse it by reducing the charges to the eight principal ones, which it still took from June 25 to July 7 to read and which he published, but Fouquet immediately began to submit his replies, which kept insisting that the prosecution had suppressed all of the evidence in his favor and misinterpreted all of the evidence that it claimed to have against him. To cite just one example, he now employed textual criticisms that would have done honor to a Benedictine monk to demonstrate that the pension on the *gabelles* had gone to Mazarin or to Girardin. To further illustrate Mazarin's cupidity Fouquet claimed that Mazarin

> had used my credit to obtain from Jabec paintings for some three hundred thousand *livres* in 1660 without having paid for them, bequeathing them to the king by his testament, which states that I could work something out with the dealers. Mr Colbert may have decided to alter this portion of the testament . . . but the king and the executors have seen it several times.

For our investigation, this passage is one of the most revealing in all of Fouquet's defenses, for it finally gives us an indication that Fouquet was not only conscious of Mazarin's acquisitions of works of art, including those which he had acquired from Jabec, but also, in spite of his denials, familiar with the details of Mazarin's testament. With regard to the testament, moreover, either Fouquet was referring to the equivocal provision, namely, the paintings in the library of the *palais Mazarin*, or he is referring to a provision which does not appear in any of our texts, providing one more proof for my own claim that Colbert had altered the testament. Toward the end of his response Fouquet once more pointed the finger at Le Bas and Picon, insisting that he could furnish further proof of Mazarin's malfeasance if he were given access to all their letters, with which Colbert had absconded. To this mounting body of evidence, which Fouquet's supporters continued to publish, Talon attempted his counter replies, but he was being drawn more and more into a duel for public opinion. There was an odor of the *Mazarinades* in all of this, and a much more pungent one at that. Louis XIV may have been the most absolute monarch in all of Europe, but he could not find a way to preserve his glittering image in the face of the growing impression that the wrong man was being put on trial. Louis and Colbert needed somebody to blame, and this time it was Talon, whom they ultimately replaced with two other prosecutors, Guy Chamillart and Vincent Hotman. Interesting to note, Chamillart was the father of the future controller-general and minister of war, whose son-in-law would inform Voltaire that the man in the iron mask knew the secret of Nicolas Fouquet.[10]

Nicolas Fouquet, however, was not the only person who was fishing in troubled waters. Early in 1662 a certain Michel Barbès launched a suit for some 7,000 *livres* against Louis Béchamel, Marquis de Nointel. Barbès was a *conseiller* and *maître d'hôtel du Roi*, and *payeur* (paymaster) of the Swiss guards. It would appear as if he had also, at some point, given the Duke de Mazarin a *mémoire* claiming that Cardinal Mazarin and Servien had been skimming from the tax farmers, especially from a Girardin—not clear which one—money which, presumably, should have gone to his heirs. Béchamel was also a *conseiller du Roi*, secretary in the prestigious *conseil de finances*, and, it will be remembered, a famous gastronome, but more importantly for our investigation, he had married into the Colbert family. The suit also involved the Duke de Mazarin, and at that moment Béchamel also found himself employed by the Chamber of Justice as one of its commissioners. It may be no coincidence, therefore, to discover that on July 30, 1663, Le Tellier signed a *lettre de cachet* remanding Michel Barbès to the Bastille. His wife wrote frantically to Colbert, pleading for his release, but to no avail. This little incident makes me presume to designate Barbès as "the first man in the iron mask."[11]

It should be clear by now that there had been in the comportment of Louis XIV and of Colbert a rather bizarre combination of anxiety and nonchalance when it came to covering the tracks of Cardinal Mazarin. On the one hand, we have seen that they had made every effort to keep his testament and his

Louis XIII and Anne of Austria

The Duchess de Chevreuse

A

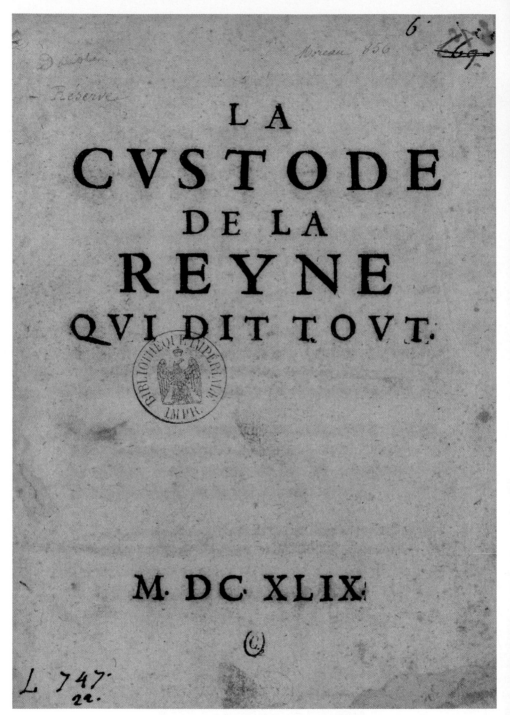

Confessions of the Queen's Bed Curtains (1649)

IEAN-FRANCOIS-PAVL DE GONDY, Archeuefque de Corinthe Coadiuteur de Paris. Abbé de Buze et de Kemperlay, 3. Fils de Philippes Emanuel de Gondy Comte de Loigny, Marquis des Isles dor, Seig. de Dampierre, General des Galeres de France; et de Francoise Marguerite de Silly, et le 4 du nom de Gondy qui possede cette Metropole de Paris, dont il fut consacré Archeuefque Coadiuteur l'an 1644. estant recōmandable pour sa Doctrine et sa capacité dans les affaires d'Estat. Ce que le Roy ayant recogneu, et ne uoulant pas dauantage differer la rescompence deuë à tant de belles qualitez le nōma Cardinal en 1651. et fut promeu a cette dignité le 19 Feburier 1652. par le Pape Innocent X. le premier des XI que créa ce souuerain Pontife. Il a pris le nom de Cardinal de Retz. Fut arresté à Vincennes le 11 Decemb. suiuant.

A prit ce vendent chez L. Boisseuin à la rue S. Iaques proche S. Seuarin. APans chez Daret 1652 auec priuil. du Roy

Cardinal de Retz

C

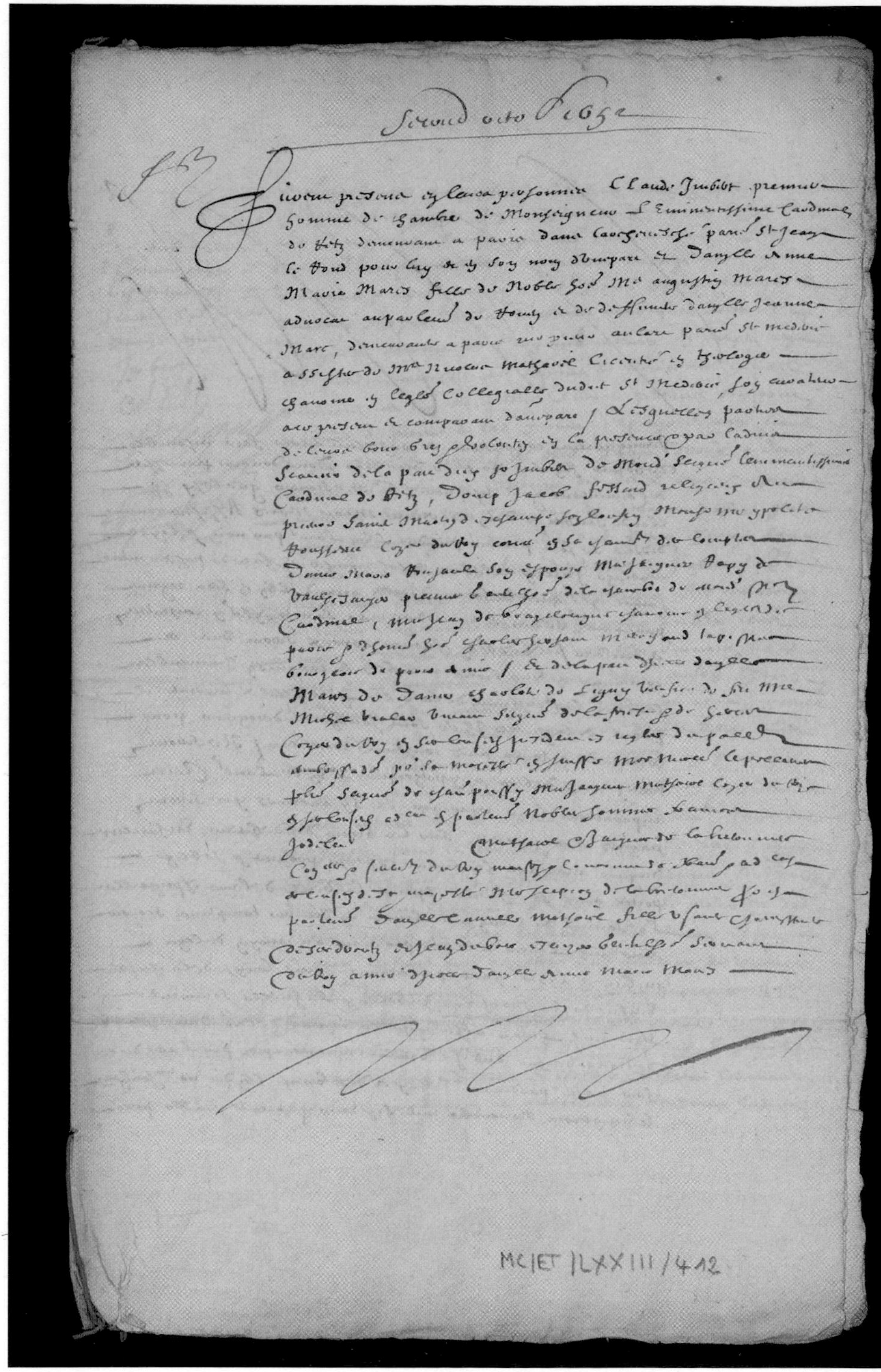

The Marriage of Claude Imbert

Nicolas Fouquet

Basil Fouquet

Jean-Baptiste Colbert

Veüe et perspective du Chasteau de Vaux le vicomte du costé de l'entrée. Fait par Aveline avec privilege du Roy.

Vaux-le-Vicomte

Charles I and Henrietta Maria

Oliver Cromwell

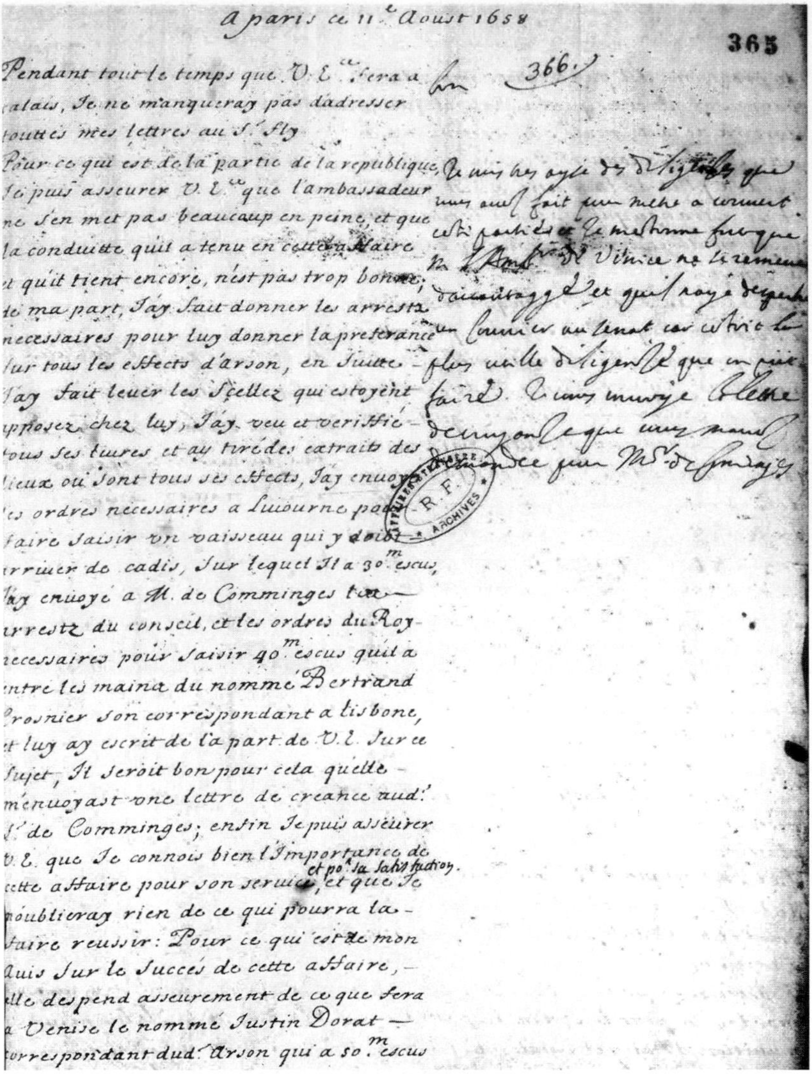

a paris ce 11.ᵉ Aoust 1658

366.

[handwritten letter in French — Colbert to Mazarin]

"While your eminence will be in Calais, I will not fail to address all my letters to Mʳ Fly" New Mailing Address. Colbert to Mazarin, August 11, 1658

De Courtray d'où par trahifon as,
Tu fis fortir la garnifon.
De Lerida deux fois manquees
Quoy que deux fois bien attaquees
Du fruict du grand combat de Lens,
Perdu par tes confeils trop lens.
De la Cataloigne reduite
Au defefpoir, par ta conduite,
Du Duc de Guize mal logé,
Dans Naples qu'on a negligé.
De la dizette des Prouinces,
Du peril que courent nos Princeff.
Qui font à la guerre, tandis
Qu'en ton Palais tu t'ébaudis.
Du Duc de Beaufort mis en cage,
Digne effect de ton grand courage.
D'vn Marefchal de France, pris,
Pour la recompenfe, & le Prix,
D'auoir bien fait à Barcelonne
Du vol du Duché de Cardonne.
D'auoir fait prendre vn faux boüillon,
Au feu Prefident Barrillon.
De la Reyne, perfuadée
De ta fincerité fardée.
Des Anglois, qui n'ont point de pain
Que tu laiffes mourir de faim;
Et de leur Reine defolée
De fes bagues par toy vollée,
Du Venerable Parlement
Traitté par toy peu dignement.
Et de la pauure France, Etiqué,
Par ton auarice Hydropique
De l'argent qu'on a deftourné
Au nom de Portolongoné.
D'auoir, Courretier de Priape,
Supprimé le Neueu du Pape,

C

"From their unhappy queen / her rings you stole." *La Mazarinade* (1651)

I

Cardinal Mazarin in His Gallery

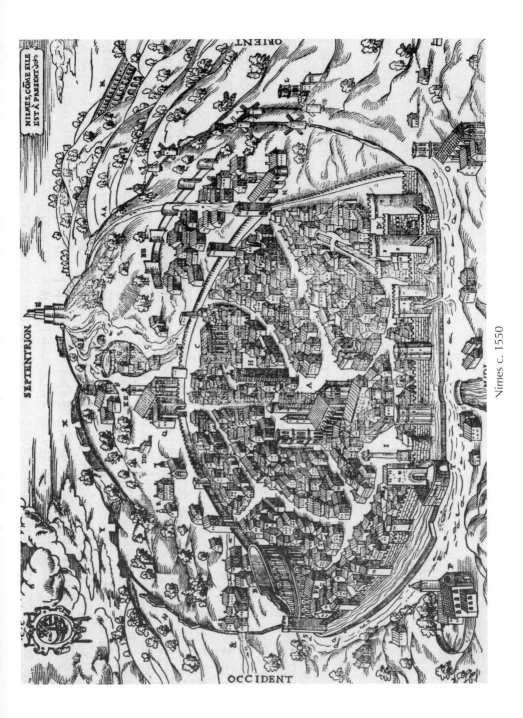

Nimes c. 1550

Picon's Man. Colbert to Mazarin, September 3, 1659, with Mazarin's own hand reply

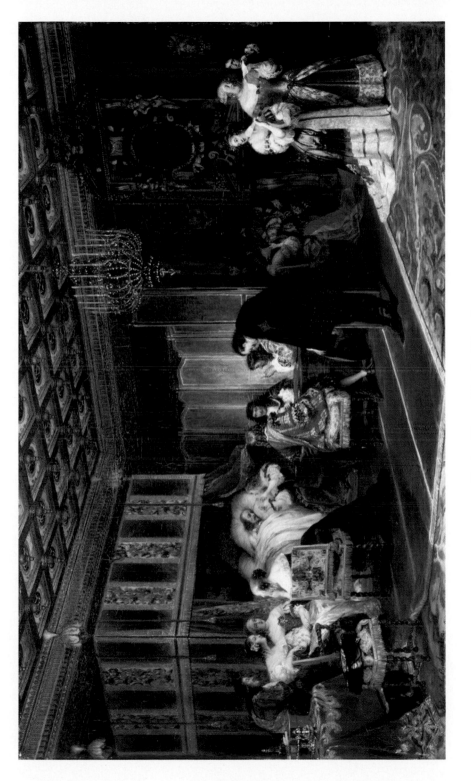

The Last Illness of Cardinal Mazarin

M

de Lyonne pour les affaires d'Estat afin de
les communiquer au Roy, ou à qui Il plaira
a Sa Majesté d'ordonner dans les occurrences.

Mondit Seig.r ne pouuant donner assez
de tesmoignage de la fidelité de Monsieur
Colbert qu'il a esprouué depuis plus de
xii. ans approuue tout ce qui 'a esté par
luy fait Jusqu'a present, et veut qu'il
en soit creu a sa simple parolle.

Veut et entend Mondit Seigneur attendu
les grandes affaires qui l'ont empesché
d'examiner les Comptes du Sieur Picon ⟵
depuis quelques années comme Il auoit
accoustumé de faire, que lesdits Comptes
qui seront rendus de Sa maison soient
examinez par le Sieur Colbert et par
luy seul signées et arresteés.

Mondit Seigneur le Card.al deffend trés
expressement qu'il soit fait aucun Inuen.re
ny description de ses biens, meubles, ou effects
mobiliaires, ny d'aucuns tiltres ny papiers

Picon in Text B

N

Opening Session of the Chamber of Justice

The Marriage of Antoine-Hercule Picon witnessed by the Marquis de Saint-Simon

Pinerolo

Exilles

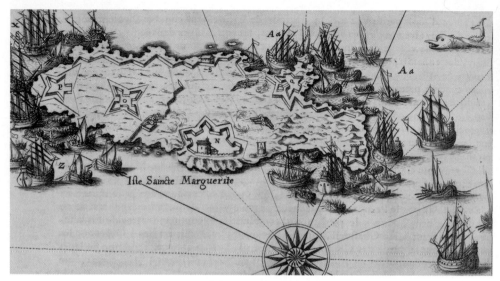

Sainte-Marguerite

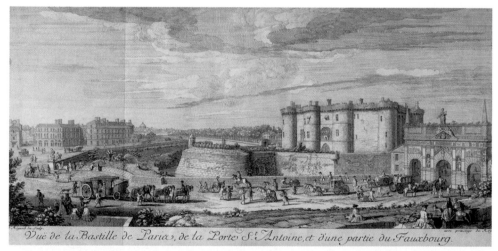

Vuë de la Bastille de Paris, de la Porte S.t Antoine, et d'une partie du Fauxbourg.

The Bastille, the Porte Saint-Antoine, and Part of the Fauburg

inventory under wraps. On the other hand, we have also seen that they had provided the Duke de Mazarin with copies of the inventory and, in June of 1662, to ensure that Philippe Mancini would not be troubled in his inheritance, they had gone to the trouble of exhibiting the relevant portions of the cardinal's testament publicly in the office of a notary in Rome. Later, when Mazarin's jeweler François Lescot died in March of 1663, their anxiety reared its ugly head since it took almost exactly one year for the seals to be placed on his possessions, which suggests that some extraordinary care had to be taken in order to ensure that anything that would concern Cardinal Mazarin was left out of Lescot's inventory. They may have put Barbès in jail for suggesting to the Duke de Mazarin that he should recoup the funds, apparently the pension skimmed from Girardin; on the other hand, in June of 1663 Louis allowed Gomont to go to England in an attempt to recoup the money—apparently the acts of December 1, 1656, and another of March 20, 1660—in which acts the exiled Charles II and his mother both acknowledged owing Cardinal Mazarin the sums of 597,416 and 64,150 *livres*, supported by the "certification" for 600,000 *livres* that that Jermyn had signed in 1656, which the duke now claimed was owed to him as the cardinal's heir. When Gomont got there Charles II, who harbored plans to humiliate the Dutch at sea as a prelude to declaring his Catholicity to his people, admitted that he owed the money, but informed Gomont that he owed it to the French crown, not to Cardinal Mazarin, and also hinted that once he was in a position to repay it, he would also reclaim the heirlooms of his family. We can only imagine how that response struck Louis XIV and Colbert when Gomont repeated it to them, which he undoubtedly did. Nevertheless, in 1664, when the pope's nephew Cardinal Chigi came to France to apologize to Louis XIV for the insult to his ambassador, the cardinal could see many of the paintings and tapestries originally owned by the crown of England hanging on display in the *palais Mazarin* and he was specifically shown the crown jewels, including the *miroir de Portugal* and the *grand Sancy*. He was so impressed by the jewels that when he got back to Italy, he advised the Cavaliere Bernini, who was about to go to France, to make sure to ask to see them. It is almost as if the malfeasances of Cardinal Mazarin were an open secret that no one could admit to sharing—no one that is, except Nicolas Fouquet, and even he had to handle them with care. The threat to implicate the king was the one last card that he held in his hand, but only if he didn't play it.[12]

Where was Antoine-Hercule Picon all this time? Characteristically, he stayed out of the picture as much as he could, but we can still catch glimpses of him if we look hard enough. He was being sued by Hache, presumably for false imprisonment. Around this time Antoine-Hercule's father, Georges, purchased the *château* of Pouzilhac near Uzès, and began styling himself as the Sieur de Pouzilhac. Antoine-Hercule himself got married. The lady he chose was Marguerite, daughter of Michel de Villedo, Louis Le Vau's principal assistant in the construction of of Vaux-le-Vicomte. Apparently, the fall of Fouquet had not cast any shadow upon the courtship, and the contract, signed on December 20, 1662, also indicated that the families stood well with the instruments of power. The side of the bridegroom was honored by the signatures of Pierre Séguier, Charles Marquis de Saint-Simon, and Jean-Baptiste Colbert. Signing for the daughter was Guillaume de Lamoignon and two other presiding judges. Picon, moreover, was also acquiring a mixed reputation both as a drunkard and as Colbert's right-hand man. The two qualities came together in May of 1664, if we are to believe the gossipy historian Courtilz de Sandras. According to him, Picon got inebriated at the very same time that Colbert was attempting to repurchase nearly all of the municipal bonds issued by the *Hôtel de Ville* of Paris at bargain basement prices. This attempt created a furor among the investors, and Picon, according to Sandras, woke up from a hangover, screaming that they were trying to choke him. The furious Colbert—if we are to believe Sandras—dismissed Picon but after a few years reinstated him. The story may have been inflated, but it is useful for the purposes of our investigation. It shows us that by this time Picon was a notorious figure, and notorious figures have identifiable valets.[13]

By October of 1663, the trial of Fouquet had reached the point where the chamber could proceed to the verification of the reports it had compiled on each of its accusations, a process in which the chamber allowed the accused to intervene. Fouquet, for his part, began the year 1664 by attempting to recuse the chancellor, by decrying the forgeries in the documents, and by replying to Talon's most recent generalizations in another duel of printed debates. Louis and Colbert were not amused. Toward the end of June, when the court moved to Fontainebleau, they forced the chamber to transfer itself there, assigned Fouquet to another prison, and made it more difficult for him to meet with his lawyers. It was there in late July that Ormesson began reading his report on the entire trial (*rapport du procès*), which continued after August 18 when the chamber returned to Paris. But in drawing up its evidence on the infamous pension of 120,000 *livres*, the prosecution had altered the documents so ineptly that Ormesson, who, to the increasing nervousness of Louis XIV, insisted on being fair, immediately caught the forgery. In the next few days, Ormesson reported on an ordinance for six million *livres* in which Fouquet allegedly had his clerks usurp the functions of the royal treasurers and then went on to deal with other accusations and the charge of treason. Through all of these vicissitudes, Fouquet refused to break. He replied to the charge of treason that his flight of fancy was a far cry from Mazarin's vast designs on behalf of his heirs. He even introduced into evidence a copy of the testament of Cardinal Mazarin—we can only wonder which text—and on October 7 asked the chamber to subpoena an authentic copy from the notary, which Séguier summarily refused. On October 12, in defending himself against the accusation that his clerks had affixed their names in the place of royal treasurers, he retorted that Colbert, Picon, Mariage, Le Bas, Hervart, and other agents of Cardinal Mazarin had done exactly the same thing both for their own affairs and for those of Mazarin. Shortly thereafter Fouquet submitted a new defense on the pension of 120,000 *livres*, complained bitterly about having been refused a copy of the testament, and introduced into evidence Barbès's *mémoire* to the Duke de Mazarin on the malfeasances of Mazarin and Servien. But, close as Fouquet was getting, he went no further in what would have been the perilous tactic of involving the throne in the accusations against Cardinal Mazarin.[14]

In the course of Fouquet's trial, moreover, an even more noisy skeleton began to rattle. As early as May of 1662 Charles II had designated one of his most prominent subjects, Denzil Holles, to go to France as his ambassador to Louis XIV. Holles was a curious choice. Beginning as a revolutionary in the English Civil War, he ended up as an enemy of Oliver Cromwell. Holles's instructions are lost, but he seems to have been informed of the King of England's debts. Once the new ambassador arrived in France, during the summer of 1663, he must have felt the urge to make up for his revolutionary past. Early in 1664 he reported to Henry Bennet, minister of Charles II, about tapestries of the late king in the possession of the widow of the former ambassador Bordeaux and jewels currently in the possession of the Duke de Mazarin, which Holles suggested could enter into any settlement of the debts. Apparently, he did not get much of a response. However, in the summer of 1664 a bizarre collection of plaintiffs, including a woman claiming to be the widow of Boudin-Fontenay, a former equerry of Charles I, brought suit in the *Balliage du Palais* in Paris against a certain Mathurine Desfontaines, widow of the Sieur de La Pasnière, in whose house Boudin-Fontenay had died. The plaintiffs claimed that Desfontaines had murdered Fontenay and absconded with his diamonds in collusion with a jeweler named Robert Hoyau. The case was being investigated by Robert Hourlier, the *lieutenant général* of the court, who was holding her in the prison of Saint-Eloy, when she came to the attention of Charles II's sister Henrietta, Duchess d'Orléans, and of Holles himself, and by September the eager ambassador empowered his secretary Petit—a nephew, we should recall, of Cromwell's agent, Augier—to enter the case. What complicated it even further was that around this very same time a certain Duchemin, one more valet of the Count de Charost for us to keep track of, approached his master with an offer to free Fouquet from prison. Charost immediately demonstrated his loyalty by denouncing him to the king and, in the process of the investigation, someone denounced the jeweler Hoyau for having been part of the conspiracy. Confined to the Bastille, where he was questioned by the *lieutenant civil* of the *Châtelet*, Hoyau denied everything except that he had once lent some money to Duchemin but, suspiciously, in the course of Hoyau's imprisonment, we find Mathurine Desfontaines temporarily out of jail and running into Hoyau's son-in-law in, of all places, the antechambers of Michel Le Tellier, where she later claimed she had been, endeavoring to obtain the liberation of Hoyau. Were they both there, possibly, to warn Le Tellier that Denzil Holles was getting too close for comfort? If so, it would seem as if an English ambassador may have been too prestigious to put into an iron mask, but Louis, through Le Tellier, soon consigned Desfontaines to the Bastille as well, where she and Hoyau both faced the charges that they had murdered Fontenay and stolen his jewels. They denied them vociferously, even though one witness insisted that she had seen in the possession of Hoyau a crystal ship belonging to the King of England, and a sequence of witnesses came forward to support the accusations. On November 8 one witness dropped the name Thomas Gambleton, an English jeweler from whom he had bought the crystal ship, after which he had sold it to François Lescot, who, of course, was the jeweler of Cardinal Mazarin. The witness also admitted that he had in his possession a sapphire that had belonged to the late King of England. Holles felt he was hot on the trail and on November 2/12, 1664, he wrote to Bennet:

> Duke Mazarin, I thinck, if the truth were knowen, he & his uncle Cardinal have had—for some they have disposed of—as much of his Ma[ies] jewels & hangings and pictures as the money w[ch] was lent, . . . when I went to the Hotel Mazarin, furnished as it was for the Cardinal Legat, I saw three rich suites of Hangings that were our late king's and many pictures.

This same day another witness confirmed that this same Gambleton had sold numerous jewels in France belonging to the English crown. Obviously under pressure from Holles, on December 3 the *procureur du roi* of the *Baillage du Palais* asked Hourlier to seize various tapestries belonging to the crown of England, and about the same time the eccentric Duke de Mazarin had the temerity to chat amiably with Holles about the outcome of Gomont's mission of 1663 and inform him that Cardinal Mazarin, by his testament, had bequeathed the now incriminating crystal ship to the Duchess d'Aiguillon.

If this is true—and the duke is the least reliable of witnesses—these are still more provisions of Mazarin's testament that have not come down to us but, excited by his success and incited by a Protestant parvenu who called himself the Marquis de Montbrun, Holles then pressed his court for a specific order to pursue the case. So here, in the midst of the Fouquet trial, was a festering investigation in a minor tribunal, pursued by an overzealous ambassador, that might reopen the entire question of the heirlooms of the crown of England.[15]

Meanwhile, the trial of Fouquet was reaching its climax. Between November 14 and December 4, 1664, Fouquet himself testified before the chamber. It was a cold-blooded exposé of the hypocrisy of power, highlighted by his comparison of his innocent *mémoire* to himself with Séguier's participation in the government of Paris during the expiring days of the *Fronde*. Then, on December 9, Ormesson launched into a detailed analysis of the charges. Amazingly, by this time, he was sounding more and more like a defense attorney, emphasizing the questionable quality of the evidence and continually involving Mazarin in Fouquet's operations. But, combining his impartiality with his loyalty to his king, Ormesson concluded five days later, with as little inconsistency as he could muster, that Fouquet had been sufficiently irresponsible to be banished from the kingdom for life. The second reporter, Sainte-Hélène, concluded for the death penalty, as did Séguier and a number of other members of the chamber, but Ormesson had done his damage, and on December 20 the court, by a vote of 13 to 9, concurred in his recommendation. That, of course, was even worse than acquittal, for it left Fouquet free to wander from capital to capital, selling his secrets to the highest bidder. Needless to say, Louis XIV was enraged, and the courage of Ormesson condemned him to a life of exclusion from public service, but he had saved the life of Fouquet, and all that the king could do was to "amend" the sentence of banishment to one of perpetual imprisonment. On December 27 D'Artagnan picked up Fouquet at the Bastille to deliver him some 500 miles away into the citadel of Pinerolo, while the Chamber of Justice continued its work in pursuit of other malefactors. It was perhaps all for the best for the monarchy to have avoided the spectacle of high-profile executions which had marred the reign of Louis XIII, but what is noteworthy for our investigation is that the relegation of Fouquet seems also to have relieved some of the fears of the government over the secrets that he might have divulged. The trial was still proceeding when Madame Fouquet asked the king for permission to publish a complete edition of his defenses. It was ignored, but she proceeded anyway to offer them to Elzevir in the Dutch Republic, much to the disgruntlement of Colbert. The government let it pass, and their extensive publication continued to haunt it until 1668. But no sooner was Fouquet out of the way in the *donjon* of the citadel than we begin to see the pressure letting up on some of the minor offenders. In January 1665 Barbès was released from the Bastille. It would seem, however, as if the valets always paid the piper. Duchemin was sent to to galleys.[16]

Denzil Holles, on the other hand, was intent upon embarrassing both his own king and the court of France. As we have seen, Charles II had other priorities. He refused, through Bennet, Holles's request for a specific order to pursue the case. Louis XIV was in an even better position to put an end to the nonsense. On March 28, 1665, he issued, through Le Tellier, a *lettre de cachet* ordering the governor of the Bastille to release Hoyau into the hands of the bearer. We do not know who this bearer was, but on the 30th he delivered his letter and Hoyau was released. On the very next day Holles, through Petit, agreed to submit the dispute to arbitration. The case against Hoyau, by a bizarre set of coincidences, was falling apart. Three of the accusers who came to visit Holles at his embassy took the occasion, according to Holles himself, to steal two expensive handkerchiefs. On July 7 the judge dismissed the charges against Hoyau, after which two of the handkerchief suspects, one of whom found himself in the Bastille, proceeded to retract their testimony, accusing other accusers of having bribed them. The self-styled Marquis de Montbrun claimed that Hoyau had been in collusion with the arbitrators and had bribed the accusers to make their retractions but, by what was looking less and less like a coincidence, during the very same days that the accusers were retracting themselves, this same pseudo-marquis found himself in the Bastille on the grounds that he had tried to prevent his son from converting to Catholicism.[17]

This assortment of circumstances, therefore, brings three questions to mind: (1) Could it be that it had been someone close to Fouquet who had apprised Holles of the case against Desfontaines and Hoyau? (2) Could it be that someone in great authority had ordered the interruption of the investigation of Hoyau for attempting to free Fouquet the moment that it was beginning to spread into a search for the heirlooms of the English crown? (3) And could it be that this same someone had intervened to put pressure upon the perjurers to retract their testimony? I cannot answer these questions definitively, but in September of 1665 Mathurine Desfontaines was also freed from the Bastille, thus bringing an end to this highly suspicious incident.[18]

⌒

Colbert had triumphed. Le Tellier's former clerk had now eliminated his nemesis, and his own program for the regeneration of the French finances was in full swing. But as so often happens when one attains one's peak, one also begins one's decline. Louis XIV had for his own reasons supported Colbert in all of his reforms, but the king had no intention of stopping with peace and prosperity. He was interested in conquest and glory. He had not forgotten Mazarin's failed effort to acquire the Spanish Low Countries, and the cocky young king aspired to succeed where his spiritual father had failed. He could not, however, attack the Spanish without a pretext and, moreover, in September of 1664 the Duke of York attacked New Amsterdam, thus setting off a war between England and the Dutch Republic, in which a treaty between France and the Dutch committed Louis to intervene. The pretext to attack the Spanish, however, emerged on September 17, 1665, right in the middle of this war, when Louis's father-in-law, Philip IV of Spain, died, leaving his throne in the hands of a sickly three-year-old son and giving the French lawyers the opportunity to dig up an obscure "law of devolution," a local custom under which the King of France could claim a good part of the Spanish Low Countries on behalf of his wife, Maria Theresa.[19]

Claude Roux, of course, was living in a much more private world. I find him in Paris on June 28, 1663, calling himself "Sieur de foncouverte," helping the widow of a bankrupt Protestant banker named Spon recover some of her lost property. But it was not as private as all that. If Roux had indeed become a collector of wine taxes in the generality of Soissons, he would certainly have come into contact with Claude Le Clerc, a zealous agent of the Chamber of Justice in that generality, who would likely have extracted some penalties from him, and this supposition lends credence to Roux's claim that the king owed him some money for a transaction into which he had entered in that area. I also have grounds for believing that some time after the French declaration of war against England, Roux established contact with a certain John Riordan, an Irish Catholic royalist who, with the support of the Duchess d'Orléans and the ministers of Charles II, had engineered the assassination of an English regicide in Switzerland. I do know that Roux was now promising the duchess to use his Swiss connections to engineer more assassinations of English regicides, while Riordan was now promising the English ministers that he could, in the midst of the war, raise all of southern France in revolt against Louis XIV. Couldn't Roux, therefore, also have gotten to Holles with similar proposals? That, it will be remembered, is precisely what Roux told Morland and, interestingly, we find Holles in October of 1665 as optimistic as Riordan and Roux about the prospects for a revolution in France. When, in January of the following year, Louis actually declared war against England, Holles had to return there and Roux may have lost his friend, but Roux was not discouraged. In that year Louis began to hold a number of reviews of his troops in preparation for his war against Spain where, as might be expected, an accident occurred. A soldier accidentally discharged his firearm, wounding a spectator. No one thought much about the incident but, putting all of my evidence together, I would venture with ever increasing confidence to assert that this soldier was Eustache de La Salle, who had just purchased the office of *exempt* in the royal bodyguard in the company of the Count de Charost. We now have enough evidence to dismiss the possibility that the Count de Charost was behind the discharge of the firearm, but there is no question that La Salle was the man to whom Claude Roux was referring when he confided to Morland in 1668 that a royal guard had almost assassinated Louis XIV. We can thus conclude that in the 1660s, an angry and vengeful Roux was running around Paris not only in Protestant and financial but also in diplomatic and military circles, and the more we find out about him, the more his apparent exaggerations turn out to contain elements of truth.[20]

The English and Dutch were still keeping each other busy when, since the Spanish refused to take his claims seriously, Louis XIV began his War of Devolution. Without even declaring it, in May of 1667 he invaded the Spanish Low Countries at the head of an army of 85,000 men, undertaking a series of surgical sieges which, in a period of less than three months, occupied seven major cities. The governor of the Spanish Low Countries, the Marquis de Castel Rodrigo, simply did not have the resources to stop him, and it seemed as if the King of France was in a position to take over the entire Spanish Low Countries in the next campaign. His ministers, however, were not all that sanguine. Colbert did not want to imperil his domestic reforms and Lionne did not want to threaten the stability of Europe. They were also concerned for themselves because Louis's principal general Turenne and Le Tellier's son the Marquis de Louvois were taking advantage of the war in order to advance themselves in the king's estimation. At the same time the foreign powers were stirring. The Dutch were particularly alarmed at the prospect of the French becoming their next-door neighbors and rushed to make their peace with England, obliging the French to do the same. Lionne, however, pulled a secret treaty with the Holy Roman Emperor out of a hat, by which Louis could acquire the Spanish Low Countries in case the child king of Spain, who was not expected to live for long, should die without issue. Thus even though the Dutch went on to make a Triple Alliance with England and Sweden, which threatened to go to war against France if Louis continued his conquests, the secret treaty with the emperor proved to be sufficient to make Louis swallow his pride and settle for the compromise peace of Aix-la-Chapelle on May 2, 1668.[21]

Antoine-Hercule Picon may have been an alcoholic, but the position that he had acquired in the inner circle of Colbert more than made up for his intemperance. Toward the end of 1665 Paul Pellisson, after nearly four years in the Bastille, attempted to mend his fences with the persecutor of his former patron. He wrote to Colbert begging for an interview or, failing that, he offered to meet with the following: Gomont, Foucault, Berryer, and *Picon*. By this time Picon must have managed to dispose of the most incriminating of his account books for, early in 1666, Colbert turned over what can only have been a selected few of these books to the Duke de Mazarin and even obtained an *arrêt* from the council of finances, which relieved both himself and Picon from any further responsibility for Mazarin's estate. The Picons, moreover, were consolidating their social position. In the face of one of Louis XIV's periodic searches for tax dodgers who claimed to be nobles, the Picons now produced some fanciful evidence that they were descendants of a thirteenth-century patrician family from Savona in Italy, whose descendants in the following century had presumably become nobles and warriors for the King of France. This evidence meshed rather badly with the humble paralegal Picons, whom we encountered in chapter 6, none of whom appeared in the genealogy. But the renown of the Picons had reached a point where a frustrated novelist in search of her pension wrote a poem about Antoine-Hercule in which, after ironically praising his generosity, sincerity, and indefatigability, she adds that "for all these wonderful qualities, he is known to all." Is it not likely that on her numerous visits to his antechambers she and many others like her may have become acquainted with his valet, Eustache Dauger?[22]

While the Picons were thus enjoying their fame and fortune, the King of France was losing his patience. His little nephew in Spain was refusing to die, and almost immediately after the peace, Louis instigated a number of incidents along the border with the Spanish Low Countries, designed to provoke the Spanish into retaliating. His more pacific ministers, fearful that this would expand the Triple Alliance and renew the war, did their best to hold him back. While they were trying to do so, they were both aided and frustrated by Charles II of England. He had not forgotten his first priority, which was to declare his Catholicity, and he had, in the process, come to the conclusion that he could only do so—and against English public opinion— with the assistance of the King of France. Early in 1669, therefore, the King of England sent the Earl of Arundel, a Catholic peer, to France with a request for financial support. To the peace party in the council this was a wonderful opportunity to hold off Louis's bellicosity, to the war party a wonderful way to inflame it. To the King of France, who thought he was smarter than anyone else, this was the perfect way to obtain the Spanish Low Countries immediately. He considered that if he offered to help Charles with his declaration in return for a joint attack on the Dutch Republic, the Spanish would be forced to come to the aid of the Dutch and the King of England would inevitably be drawn into a war against Spain, which would permit Louis to consummate his conquest of the Spanish Low Countries. This, as I think I have shown in my book on the origins of the Dutch War, was his principal motive for going to war against the Dutch. Charles, who had no knowledge of this and who had his own grievances against the Dutch, fell in with the offer. But, for our investigation of the mystery of the iron mask, the secret negotiations for the war against the Dutch had another consequence. All of a sudden the fulfillment of the most powerful passion for the King of France became dependent on the good will of the King of England. It thus became imperative to eliminate any person, any distraction, any slight impediment that might imperil the negotiation with England.[23]

One such person, of course, was the ubiquitous Claude Roux because, while Louis XIV was doing his best to get himself into a war against Spain, Claude Roux was doing his best to stir up all Europe against Louis. We cannot exactly trace Roux's movements after the War of Devolution, but it would appear that he did have various connections, more imaginary than real, in the Spanish Low Countries, in Liège, in Cologne, in the Dutch Republic, and in Switzerland, and was assuring them all that the Kingdom of France was ripe for revolt. He had apparently just been in the Spanish Low Countries to obtain the support of Castel Rodrigo when he moved on to England, where he obtained some conferences with the Earl of Arlington. Roux had, of course, picked the worst moment in the seventeenth century to mount such a conspiracy. Thus when, in May of 1668, he had gone to visit his old acquaintance Samuel Morland, this former Cromwellian had immediately called in his fellow Protestant the French ambassador, who was even more horrified at such sacrilege. We can now imagine, even more than when I first related it, how the report of Roux's ranting struck the King of France. Regicide was bad enough. Trying to break up the planning for the Dutch War was even worse. There followed, as we have seen, a Europe-wide hunt for Roux. Colbert's brother Colbert de Croissy, now ambassador to England, looked for him vainly in that country. Mouslier, the French resident to the Swiss cantons, had an equally difficult time, but the guard who, according to Roux, fired the random shot must have been very easy to identify as Eustache de La Salle, and he was kept under very close surveillance without, however, revealing that he was under suspicion, for I find him in notarial acts of July

25 and August 21, 1668, still qualifying himself as an *exempt*. However, by December 10, in the last of his notarial records that I can find, he is no longer identified as a member of the royal bodyguard. He must have been obliged to resign between these last two dates, without being given any reason. It was only after Roux was securely in Paris and about to be executed that, on June 16, 1669, Le Tellier signed the order for La Salle to be arrested and imprisoned in the Bastille and. even then, his arrest was colored with an extremely dubious story that he had married the daughter of a prostitute, gone to the Low Countries to serve in the Spanish army, married the daughter of a banker in Liège, and then returned to Paris with his second wife to resume his relations with his first. It was also rumored that he had known about the Roux conspiracy, but had failed to denounce it. The conspiracy of Roux was thus smothered under the heading of a cheap scandal.[24]

The primacy of the war in the mind of Louis XIV also explains the otherwise incomprehensible failure to investigate the details of the Roux conspiracy. It would have taken a quick order to the Intendant of Languedoc to find every relative of Roux in Nîmes, a quick order to the Intendant of Dauphiné to identify Roux's wife and children in Montélimar, an order to the Intendant in Soissons to identify the Crommelins in Saint-Quentin, and a letter to Colbert du Terron to open the mouth of Pierre Rode in La Rochelle, but none of these actions were taken by the agents of the King of France. On the contrary, when Colbert de Croissy suggested that he might seek the permission of Charles II in order to abduct Roux's accomplices, Lionne told him not to bother. The reason for this level of neglect now becomes clear. Louis XIV did not want to know too much. If he uncovered a conspiracy in which Charles II was too heavily involved, this might take all of the pleasure out of an alliance with him against the Dutch. And if the King of France was prepared to forgo his own security in order to achieve the conquest of the Spanish Low Countries, he was certainly prepared to place an insignificant valet in perpetual confinement.[25]

Unless we have completely miscalculated, we are now also ready to set the stage for the arrest of Eustache Dauger. It is very doubtful that he had been consorting with Claude Roux. It is equally doubtful that Eustache Dauger had been conspiring with Eustache de La Salle. But what is absolutely not doubtful is that Louis XIV would react violently to the slightest interference with his grand design. All that Eustache Dauger had to do was to get drunk in a cabaret and make some allusion as to what he had seen in Picon's account books, at what he had been employed in the execution of Cardinal Mazarin's testament, or anything about his past life prior to the arrest of Fouquet, and this would have been sufficient to arouse the fury of the Sun King.

But what to do with him? He had collaborated in facilitating the succession of Cardinal Mazarin. He had not tried to plot against Louis XIV. Eustache Dauger had simply been indiscreet, a quality that had even been permissible in a person of a higher social rank. A good drubbing might have sufficed, but not as far as the King of France was concerned. Picon was too well known for his valet to be ignored. Arresting Eustache Dauger and keeping him at the Bastille would immediately have called attention to the reason. This, at least, is how Louis saw it. It had to be done out of town. But where? Well, if Eustache Dauger was accustomed to performing private services for Colbert, there was no less suspicious place than Calais, and there was no more trust-worthy person in Calais to witness the arrest than Dominique Fly and, since D'Artagnan was in Paris, no more efficient officer to carry out the arrest than Captain Vauroy of the garrison of Dunkirk. Clearly Eustache Dauger was set up. Vauroy was told exactly when and where he could perform the arrest, the letters were prepared, the deed was done.[26]

Lest one might wonder how it could be that Louis XIV would go to such extremes in order to ferret away the miserable Eustache Dauger, we have only to follow the destiny of another indiscreet individual with a bothersome con-nection to the heirlooms of the crown of England, namely, René Petit, Denzil Holles's assistant in the prosecution of Mathurine Desfontaines and Robert Hoyau. Shortly after Louis's declaration of war against England, Holles, as we have seen, left France, leaving Petit, who was a French subject, at Louis's mercy. Claiming that Petit had been critical of the French government and had been employed by the English ministers on a variety of missions, Louis, in June of 1666, banished him to Pinerolo. It is not clear whether he was relegated to the city or imprisoned in the citadel with Nicolas Fouquet. How-ever, he remained there until the end of the War of Devolution, at which time, on the recommendation of Henrietta Maria's old friend Henry Jermyn, Louis permitted him to return. This was a period of growing suspicions about the King of France's bellicose intentions and, apparently, Petit contributed to them by furnishing the gazetteers with materials against the policy of France. This was also a period when Croissy in England was advancing the negotiation over the war against the Dutch. Finally, on November 10, 1669, Lionne took the action of writing to Croissy, instructing him, on behalf of Louis, to ask Charles II to order Petit to leave Paris, even without telling him the reason. Charles, who was also interested in pursuing the negotiation with Louis, complied, relegating Petit to Rouen. Thus we can see how the entire mystery of the iron mask was part and parcel of an extended cover-up stemming from the legacy of Cardinal Mazarin and the perpetual quest for the Spanish Low Countries.[27]

CHAPTER NINE

~

Was Eustache Dauger Gay?

From the very first rumors that leaked out about him, the mystery of the iron mask has been complicated by its incredibility. It was almost impossible for anyone to conceive that such extraordinary measures could have been taken to imprison anyone other than a person of great importance or the holder of some earthshaking secret. It was equally difficult to attribute any pettiness over trifles to such national icons as Cardinal Mazarin and Louis XIV. This mind-set, I think, has prevented many historians from asking the necessary questions until the recent researches into the fortunes of the elite have opened the path to a more cynical perspective. A similar mind-set in regard to morality and sex has also prevented the asking of some obvious questions in regard to Eustache Dauger's imprisonment, namely, how a human being could survive thirty-four years of psychological and physical duress without going insane. I cannot provide as clear-cut an answer to this question as I have attempted in regard to the identity of Eustache Dauger, but I would like to consider the possibility, as speculative as it may be, that in the course of his imprisonment, Eustache Dauger, performed homosexual services for the people with whom he did come into contact.

Sexuality is one of those phenomena that is steeped in ignorance and, in the case of human sexuality, one of its unique characteristics is that, at some early point in their prehistory, humans began to associate it with morality and religion. The motive is clear enough. Sexuality is a powerful force and it was in the interest of any society to control it. This was not easy. When children exhibited libidinal signs in their play, the society was tolerant enough, until such time as it could begin to terrify their impressionable minds with ominous taboos. When adults got the urge, it was different. Crimes of difficult proof, as Beccaria noted, are difficult to enforce, and with the development of class distinctions the double standard emerged. Sexual taboos, of course, varied. The Hebrews were among the first to look upon homosexuality with horror, the Greeks among the first to see it as a form of birth control, but whatever the taboos, the double standard persisted. What the privileged could do, the underprivileged could not. It is extremely difficult to categorize or even to document—except for particular localities—the periods when prosecutions were carried out with extraordinary fervor. By the time of Mazarin in France, however, it was possible to practice sodomy with relative impunity, except that the outcasts and the weak would intermittently be executed for it.[1]

Given the double standard, it should hardly be surprising if the practice of homosexuality has been particularly common between masters and slaves, aristocrats and servants, rich and poor. Where the historical record is lacking, literary satire has confirmed the phenomenon, and it is unfortunate that no study of the history of homosexuality has documented it in detail. It is most certainly applicable to the age of absolutism. In a Europe where anarchy and revolution had gone out of fashion, whoever was in authority exercised it as absolutely as he or she could get away with, and no one was more vulnerable to exploitation than domestic servants. We are in a particularly good position to examine this phenomenon at close range in the context of a prison, and in the context of the behavior of Louis XIV toward his most famous prisoner, and of this famous prisoner in his relationship to his valets.[2]

From his position at the very top of this pyramid, the King of France could exploit his self-righteous desire to know and to control, and he did. Thus Louvois even had informers in the *donjon* of Pinerolo to make sure that Saint-Mars was following orders. Fouquet found himself deprived of all communication with the outside world, not even allowed pen and paper, and limited to one book at a time in his possession. Still, in keeping with the double standard, he was housed in an apartment with a view, right below that of Saint-Mars and his wife; provided with a valet, whose name was Champagne; and even provided with a doctor . . . whenever Saint-Mars saw fit. The only vestige of his inalienable rights remaining to Fouquet was his opportunity to go to heaven. Thus he had a confessor four times a year to confess him and a chaplain to celebrate mass. But even in a high-security prison, absolutism had its practical limitations. Fouquet responded by exploiting every vestige of independence that he still retained. He set about immediately to corrupt his confessor, his priest, and his valet, and while he seems to have failed with the first two, he had some success with the third. An amateur chemist, he found ways to produce ink, to write on anything, and to sew his scribbles into his clothing. Saint-Mars played his part just as assiduously. He was the arche-typical policeman, only as violent as he needed to be. He watched Fouquet like a hawk, did his best to corrupt his valet, and made the town of Pinerolo as unwelcome as possible for suspicious strangers.[3]

About four months after Fouquet's arrival, this dreary life was interrupted by an event that may have been enough to convince him that God was on his side. Late in June of 1665 a bolt of lightning struck the powder magazine of the citadel. A number of soldiers were killed, Fouquet's own apartment was demolished, that of Saint-Mars and his wife damaged, but Fouquet and his valet miraculously survived. Saint-Mars, who also survived along with his wife, made frantic efforts to find a secure lodging for Fouquet and his valet in the city, but this precaution was not good enough for Louis XIV, who imme-diately ordered them both to be transferred as quickly as possible to another French enclave, the nearby *château* of La Pérouse.[4]

During this interlude, Fouquet redoubled his efforts to communicate with the outside word, in close collaboration with his valet, much to the discom-fiture of both Saint-Mars and Louis XIV. Apparently, in the society of the seventeenth century, no one considered requiring Fouquet to make his own bed, so that this same comedy continued in the *château* of La Pérouse itself. When Champagne became seriously ill, Louis himself ordered that he should be released as soon as he recovered and that Saint-Mars could provide Fou-quet with another valet. Saint-Mars did not even wait before hiring what he hoped would be a more reliable replacement. His name was La Rivière, but Fouquet lost no time in winning him over as well. What is amazing about all this is that Louis, who was so intent on keeping Fouquet incommunicado, would so casually have permitted the liberation of a valet whom Fouquet had presumably corrupted. Even more amazing is that Fouquet, who was so bent on communicating with the outside world, did not jump at this chance to do it. Most amazing, however, is that Champagne did not budge. Either he was not well enough, or he did not wish to leave.[5]

It is hard to imagine that a king who was in the middle of a war against Eng-land and getting ready for another one against Spain would devote so much attention to the daily life of Nicolas Fouquet and his valets, but that is precisely what Louis XIV was doing. In July of 1666 he ordered Saint-Mars to return with his prisoner to Pinerolo, where the repairs were approaching completion. They did so in the middle of August, and soon after they returned, the new va-let La Rivière also got sick. The question of which valet to keep now assumed center stage in the correspondence between Louis, Louvois, and Saint-Mars. First, Louis ordered that if the new valet (La Rivière) wanted to leave, Saint-

Mars should keep him for three to four months so that "time would break up the measures he might have taken with Mister Fouquet." Then Louis permitted Saint-Mars either to give the first valet (Champagne) back to Fouquet or to decide which one Saint-Mars would prefer to keep. In the middle of all this Le Tellier wrote to Saint-Mars telling him to free the valet who has served Fouquet (probably referring to La Rivière), but to keep him in the citadel for a little while longer. By January 18, 1667, however, Louis seems to have changed his mind, ordering Saint-Mars to let the sick valet (probably referring to La Rivière again) back with Fouquet once he recovered. Meanwhile Saint-Mars was discovering that Fouquet, in collaboration with his valets, was trying to contact somebody on the outside, and the exasperated Saint-Mars proposed keeping the two valets locked up with Fouquet, not to be released "until death." Louis agreed. The desperate hope behind this juggling, apparently, was that one of the two valets would inform on the other.[6]

As the battle of wits went on, during the winter of 1667 Fouquet became seriously ill. The illness continued throughout the next year and Fouquet, being perfectly aware that he could have no confidence in his confessor, took advantage of the emergency to ask Saint-Mars for a new one to whom he could confess himself more regularly. For this purpose Fouquet suggested a superior of the Jesuits or a guardian of the Capucins and Recollets of Pinerolo. Saint-Mars refused and Louvois, writing from the *château* of Chambord on the Loire, congratulated him on the grounds that Fouquet "might have some other end in mind besides devotion."[7]

The citadel of Pinerolo was thus the perfect microcosm of the monarchy of Louis XIV: a terrifying monarch in terror of his most helpless subject; a standard of conformity impossible to enforce; subjects who could do nothing with their rage except to suppress it. Yet in such a prison a man could still find ways to maintain his sanity. Fouquet, as we have seen, had even managed to corrupt at least one of his valets. This leads me to put forward two reflections. One is that what Fouquet had observed as an executor of Mazarin's testament—or what Louis feared he may have observed—might have been even more damaging than we have been able to establish. Another is that if Fouquet had corrupted one of his valets, he may also have corrupted the other, and that there was more going on inside of his apartment than is dreamt of in our histories.

⁓

This was the little world that Eustache Dauger entered in 1669, and the condition prepared for him was even worse. The instructions called for complete isolation in a cell separated by enough doors so that no guard could hear him, his meals served by Saint-Mars, and, in a perpetual reminder of his original sin, threat of immediate execution if he revealed anything about his past. Saint-Mars followed his orders to the letter and placed him in the *tour d'en bas* (lower tower), although there is some debate as to which tower that was. He did not even have a view, or at the most a barred window with a view of the wall. Just like Fouquet, Eustache had no chance to exercise, but he carried the added psychological burden of being deprived of an identity. Except, of course, before God! On September 10, 1669, Louvois made sure that he would have no impediment to saving his soul by allowing him to have a prayer book, to listen in hiding to the mass that was being celebrated for Fouquet, and to confess himself three or four times a year. It is hard to imagine how such generosity could have been sufficient to permit a prisoner to maintain his sanity.[8]

Shortly after Dauger's arrival the Fouquet family made its most energetic effort to liberate him. They sent La Forêt, Fouquet's faithful valet from before his arrest, along with a gentleman named André Marmer de Valcroissant to Pinerolo. La Forêt tried to enlist in Saint-Mars's company of guards while Valcroissant posed as a valet, going by the name of Honneste. They were successful in communicating with Fouquet, but an officer of the guard ultimately stopped them. Eustache Dauger was not forgotten in this attempt. Someone tried to contact him, and we might wonder at this point why Fouquet's family should have had any interest in contacting Eustache if they did not know who he was and why he was there. In any event he passed the test. He told the interloper that he wanted to be left in peace. The two culprits fled to Turin, but they were arrested there by the authorities and returned to Pinerolo. Fouquet's valets were punished. La Forêt was tried before the highest court in the city and executed by hanging. Valcroissant, not being a valet, came out much better. He was sentenced to five years at the galleys and then got off through the intercession of influential friends. The outcome of this event crushed Fouquet. It also unsettled Louis XIV. In August of 1670 he sent Louvois down to Pinerolo for an inspection tour whose purpose no one could quite understand.[9]

Even though the fate of Fouquet demonstrated that it was not prudent to embarrass Louis XIV, it did not discourage his more intrepid subjects from following suit. Such a person was the Count de Lauzun. The king considered him a favorite and even elevated him to the post of colonel general of the cavalry. Louis XIV was not the only one who enjoyed his company; so also did Mademoiselle de Montpensier, one of the richest heiresses of France. We may remember her from the Battle of the Faubourg Saint-Antoine during the *Fronde*, where she had bailed out the Prince de Condé. Both before and after that time, she had rejected one eminent suitor after another, but she had fallen madly in love with Lauzun, who did not consider himself unfit for the honor. He had his friends approach the king to obtain his permission for marrying a princess of the blood and, incredibly, the king gave his approval. However, just as Lauzun was being congratulated by his friends, Louis had second thoughts about this unequal marriage and called it off. Lauzun did not take this rebuff lightly. At this time the king was planning for his war against the Dutch, and Lauzun knew enough about it to attempt to plot his revenge, he and a friend taking an innocent excursion to Brussels in order to warn the Dutch resident there. Louis found out and Lauzun too ended up in Pinerolo, imprisoned in a room right below that of Fouquet under very similar conditions. Let us note that he was there for exactly the same infraction as Eustache Dauger . . . getting in the way of the Dutch War![10]

Lauzun was athletic, resourceful, and truculent. He was a soldier who could handle a sword, and Saint-Mars knew immediately that he would be a problem. Not only that, but he would need a valet, and Saint-Mars, who had no idea about Eustache's previous life at the court, quickly suggested him to Louvois as a good valet for Lauzun: "I don't think he would tell Mr de Lauzun where he is from, once I tell him not to. I am sure that he will not give him any news, nor will he want to get out like all the others do." It was, as we might well imagine, a suggestion that Louvois immediately rejected. More evidence that Eustache was a model prisoner emerges in a letter of December 30, 1673, to the effect that he "lives content, as a man totally resigned to the will of God and the king."[11]

By that time Louis XIV was in the second year of his war against the Dutch, and it was not going as well as he had hoped. For one thing, early in 1674 his ally Charles II abandoned him, retreating into an ambiguous neutrality. Whether this made the King of France appreciative or furious at his cousin is difficult to determine, but it does appear as if Louis was relenting in his hostility to Fouquet. In April of that year Louvois wrote to Saint-Mars telling him that the king would allow Fouquet to exchange letters with his wife twice a year, as long as they were censored by Saint-Mars. Louis's attitude toward Eustache Dauger was also softening. Thus when, toward the end of 1674, Champagne died and Saint-Mars again suggested that the king allow him to use Eustache, the king agreed, but only to serve Fouquet and only if his other valet, La Rivière, died. But why exclude Eustache as a valet for Lauzun and yet tolerate him for Fouquet? Having come as far as we have in our investigation, we can now tell exactly why, if we recall that they had both participated in the execution of Mazarin's testament and they already shared many of its secrets.[12]

The permission to write to his wife must have been a godsend to Fouquet. We have what is probably the second of these letters, written on February 5, 1675. Although we can certainly imagine that he was limited in expressing all of his feelings, it is still very touching and also very revealing. He complains bitterly to his wife about not having a confessor whom he could trust. He feels all the more in need of such support because of his "enforced idleness, the mother of all despair, temptations, and constant agitation," to which he must add the declining state of his health. He amazingly admits to his crimes, but says he has been punished enough, and asks his wife to beg for permission to come to see him. But for our investigation, perhaps the most remarkable aspect of this heart-wrenching letter is the entire section that he devotes to his relationship with his valets. He had come to love the loyal Champagne, and we can now get a better idea of why this valet chose to remain with Fouquet even after Louis had permitted his release from Pinerolo:

> Since the feast of our lady in September, when one of my two valets named Champagne died, I have had no joy or good health. He was a diligent and affectionate boy whom I loved tenderly, whom I cared for and who cared for me.

Fouquet thought much less of La Rivière and was much less sympathetic about his constant illnesses. He was grumpy and a miserable companion. Fouquet cannot hide the rage he felt at having lost his last consolation. But perhaps the most revealing detail in this letter is that he makes no mention of Eustache, which, considering the context of the subject, Fouquet certainly should have if Eustache had been around. Thus we can deduce that Saint-Mars had followed Louvois's orders faithfully and only let Eustache out during some interval when La Rivière was completely incapacitated. When he did, of course, it must have been a new world for Eustache. After over five years of solitary confinement, he was now able to move from his cell into Fouquet's apartment, and even more he was able to converse daily with a person who knew who he was. It must have been a new world for Fouquet, who now had recovered a servant who was, from everything we have learned about him, docile. Let us note that from this time forward, Fouquet's attempts to establish outside contacts appear to cease. Can we attribute this to the contact with his wife? Or can we attribute it to his having found a new valet to comfort him? Perhaps to both.[13]

In their emerging generosity, however, Louis, Louvois, and Saint-Mars had almost forgotten about the ingenuity of Lauzun, who made them pay for it. Under the guise of an erratic behavior and an unkempt appearance, he had figured out how to transform his chimney into a passageway leading to the apartment of Fouquet directly above him, so that one fine day, or more probably night, Fouquet, Eustache, and maybe also La Rivière, must have been flabbergasted to see Lauzun emerging like Santa Claus from the fireplace. These irruptions must have become regular occurrences, because we have the description of one such reunion given many years later by Lauzun to Courtilz de Sandras, author of sporadically authoritative biographies of famous people. Fouquet, writes Sandras,

> listened with attention to everything that the other told him, but when he came to his marriage with Mlle de Montpensier, how the king, after having consented to it, had gone back on his word, how sad he had been for this princess, he [Fouquet] could not keep from turning toward *another prisoner of state who had come to join them* [italics mine], tapping his finger against his head, as one does when one means that someone is touched. Mr Lauzun acted as if he hadn't noticed and went on to the other adventures of his life, which only confirmed Mr Fouquet in his opinion.

Who could this other prisoner have been? It could not have been the grumpy La Rivière. It had to be Eustache. And Lauzun knew who he was. Without Eustache having said a word—and we know how prudently he kept his mouth shut—Lauzun had identified him as a *prisoner of state*. Moreover, he was not there as a servant. He was accepted by Fouquet as an equal participant in the reunion, perhaps even a friend, in front of whom one could ridicule a social superior.[14]

Lauzun was not finished with his subterfuges. In March of 1676 he managed to twist a bar and break a window pane in his apartment through which he lowered himself with a rope. He was apparently aided by his valet and must have done this over a number of nights, since a guard only caught Lauzun as he was attempting to break through the outer wall of the citadel. This little escapade resulted in a reprimand for Saint-Mars and some terrifying moments for Lauzun's valet, who was questioned, threatened with hanging, and replaced, but the Dutch War was going better, and Louis found himself in an even more indulgent mood. Thus when Lauzun's uncle the Duke de La Force died and left Lauzun a modest bequest, the king permitted Lauzun's elder sister and his younger brother to come to see him in Pinerolo so that he could sign some legal papers. The interview did not speak well for the air of the citadel. Lauzun came in looking like death warmed over, held up physically by Saint-Mars. He spoke very well of Saint-Mars, though, whom, he admitted, was only doing his job.[15]

It is difficult to explain Louis's softening attitude. Perhaps the evidence that Fouquet had given up his efforts to escape was having its effect. Perhaps a succession of victories in the latter years of the Dutch War was making any potential disclosures from either Fouquet, Eustache, or Lauzun seem less threatening. A little later Louis attributed his change of attitude to "compassion." In any event, in December of 1677 he decided to allow Fouquet and Lauzun to walk around the grounds of the citadel together, under the watchful eye of Saint-Mars. Apparently, the well-meaning warden then also requested that the two valets of Fouquet, namely, La Rivière and Eustache, be allowed to promenade with him, and the king did not object, as long as Lauzun was not there. Moreover, in the fading months of 1678 Louis was emerging in high spirits from the Dutch War. Thus it may be no coincidence that it was on December 23, 1678, that Louvois sent Fouquet the eye-opening letter inquiring whether Eustache had spoken in front of his fellow valet about "what he has seen," "what he was employed at doing," and "his past life." Apparently, Fouquet's reply passed muster. On January 20, 1679, he was permitted to correspond freely (through Saint-Mars) with his wife and family, to visit with Lauzun (who was accorded similar privileges), to socialize with the officers of the garrison, and to walk around the citadel (still under the supervision of Saint-Mars). It is at this time, too, that Louis attributed these liberties to compassion and he was even contemplating extending them in the near future but, we need to note, this compassion did not extend to Eustache. The moment anyone came to visit Fouquet, Louvois reminded Saint-Mars, he was to remove Eustache. This prohibition is very revealing. If Lauzun could communicate with Fouquet and not with Eustache, it suggests that Fouquet had less to reveal to Lauzun than did Eustache. In other words, Eustache, in his past life, had been in a position to learn even more dangerous secrets than Fouquet.[16]

The king was true to his intentions. In May of 1679 Louis permitted Fouquet's wife, his children, and his brother to go to Pinerolo and visit with him without any guards being present, even permitting his wife to stay in his room and sleep there as many times as she wanted. His family could also accompany him on his walks, under a little tighter surveillance. He was allowed to correspond, as long as the correspondence continued to pass through the hands of Saint-Mars. Louis was even more gracious to Lauzun. He could write to anyone he wanted without being censored. The Fouquet family and Lauzun could have their meals brought in and receive guests from the town, and if any visitors came down from Turin to dine with Saint-Mars, he could invite the entire Fouquet clan and Lauzun to join them. Suddenly, the entire citadel of Pinerolo took on the aspect of a family reunion, except, of course, for Eustache Dauger, who had to sit it out in the lower tower.[17]

The former fearful, suspicious, and vindictive Louis XIV, however, had far from disappeared. In the midst of the festivities at Pinerolo, he added another prisoner to his collection. This was Ercole Mattioli, the confidence man in the employ of the current Duke of Mantua, who had pretended to sell his stronghold of Casale to the King of France. Mattioli was, as Roux-Fazillac had discovered, kidnapped on the outskirts of Turin, spirited away to Pinerolo, and subjected to conditions of imprisonment even harsher than those of Fouquet. There were other signs that Louis was hardening. After proclaiming himself eminently satisfied with his war against the Dutch, he began to feel cheated by its results, and sought to make up for them by adopting what John B. Wolf has called "a polity of violence and terror." Disgrace of the minister who had obtained the peace for him, religious persecutions at home, unilateral annexations of territories along his frontiers, confrontations with the Holy See . . . he was becoming hated all over Europe.

We cannot tell whether this change of attitude would have destroyed Fouquet's chances of release. In the midst of these events, on March 23, 1680, he died. It was bad news for La Rivière and Eustache, who found themselves relegated to the lower tower. Moreover, in clearing up Fouquet's belongings, Saint-Mars discovered evidence of Lauzun's ingenuity. He confessed his discovery to Louvois, asking him what he should tell Lauzun if he inquired as to Eustache's whereabouts. Fouquet was followed in death, in 1683, by his arch enemy Colbert. By this time however, the threats to Mazarin's legacy were rapidly going up in smoke. The most embarrassing of Picon's account books had disappeared. The foreign threats were diminishing. Charles II of England had a succession problem. His legal successor was his Catholic brother who might well need the assistance of Louis XIV in order to secure his throne. The house of Mantua was in disarray, especially after the Mattioli fiasco. Eustache Dauger remained the only domestic threat to the legacy of Cardinal Mazarin, but the words of Marshal de Richelieu to the Abbot Soulavie should now be ringing in our ears: "The prisoner was not as important when he died as he had been at the beginning of the personal reign of Louis XIV, when he was arrested for great reasons of state." Louvois merely replied to Saint-Mars to tell Lauzun, if he inquired, that Eustache had been released.[18]

In April of 1681 Louis XIV did release Lauzun. One thing is certain—it was not out of compassion. The king had three illegitimate children, for whom he wanted to provide. The opulent Mademoiselle de Montpensier was in a position to be of assistance if it could purchase the release of Lauzun. She therefore settled the rich Principality of Dombes and County of Eu upon the king's favorite, the Duke de Maine, and Lauzun emerged, chastened and wiser, out of the citadel. La Rivière and Eustache had no such patroness. In June of the same year the governor of the frontier stronghold of Exilles, some sixty miles to the northwest of Pinerolo, died, and the king decided to replace him with the diligent Saint-Mars. It was a measure of the importance that La Rivière, by virtue of his association with Fouquet, had acquired and Eustache, independently of his association with Fouquet, had retained that of all of the prisoners in Pinerolo, it was these two whom Louis continued to entrust to the care of the new governor, while ordering him specifically to refer to them as the prisoners of the lower tower (*tour d'en bas*). Saint-Mars immediately complied in announcing his appointment to the French ambassador in Turin, the letter glossed over by Marius Topin, referring to the prisoners as "jailbirds" and "gentlemen of the lower tower." Not only that, but Saint-Mars went on to specify "Mattioli will remain with two other prisoners!" The transfer of La Rivière and Eustache was so secret that it took place without any public notice. On their arrival, they occupied a cell together, and they were held under the usual conditions of strictest isolation, but six and a half years later, La Rivière died in Exilles, so that after seven, maybe even eleven, years of relative utopia, Eustache had to resume a life of absolute solitude.[19]

In January of 1687 Saint-Mars received another promotion, this time to the island of Sainte-Marguerite, and he was to take his prisoner with him. The precautions for the transfer were as rigid as they had ever been, if not more so. There were extensive discussions over the mode of transport, how to keep the prisoner hidden without asphyxiating him, and how to prepare his quarters. It took until April 18 to be ready. The voyage was long, some 233 miles. Eustache rode in a litter, hidden by curtains like the wife of a sultan, and was carried by eight men. He complained about being stifled, and indeed it made him so sick that it took twelve days to complete the trip. So much, then, for the iron mask! Once in Sainte-Marguerite, Saint-Mars congratulated himself on the beauty and security of the accommodations for the prisoners in a letter that we owe to Loiseleur, which letter may explain the rumors about the Duke de Beaufort or the son of Oliver Cromwell. In July of 1691 Louvois died. He was succeeded by his son Barbézieux, who merely ordered Saint-Mars to continue as before. Three years later Saint-Mars and Eustache were joined by four other prisoners from Pinerolo, one of them being Mattioli, who promptly died, and another being Mattioli's valet, who continued in captivity. What is amazing is that the aging Louis XIV, who had now blundered into his biggest war yet, would not give up on the monotony of his torments. We have a report from Saint-Mars, also discovered by Loiseleur, and it is evident that the routine for the prisoners had scarcely changed since Pinerolo. Some interesting details do emerge. For one thing, Eustache was always the first prisoner served. For another, each prisoner returned his dirty dishes, which were passed on to an officer of the guard, who examined them for any writing. So much, if this is true, for throwing them out of the window! We have another report of life in Sainte-Marguerite that is even more interesting. It comes from a cousin of Saint-Mars named Blainvilliers, who had served under him at Pinerolo, and who claimed that on a visit to Sainte-Marguerite he had substituted himself for a sentinel so that he could observe the prisoner through an open window throughout the night. Blainvilliers recalled that the prisoner

> went by the name of *La Tour*. . . . He was fair complexioned, tall, and hand-some, his lower leg a little chubby and [his hair] prematurely gray . . . that he was always dressed in dark clothes, that he was given fine linen and books, that the governor and officers remained standing and with their hats off until he had them take them off and sit down, and that they often went to keep him company and eat with him.

Blainvilliers told his story on numerous occasions to the grandnephew of Saint-Mars, Guillaume-Louis de Formanoir, Sieur de Palteau, at whose *château* Saint-Mars stopped in 1698 with his prisoner on his way to the Bastille and who had apparently obtained from his own father a description of the visit itself, in which the treatment of Eustache is very consistent with the treatment described by Blainvilliers. If Blainvilliers was telling the truth—and let us note his familiarity with the code name of *La Tour*—then Saint-Mars in his official report was not. And why would Saint-Mars and his officers treat a valet with such respect if he was not an object of their fantasies?[20]

The Paris to which Eustache finally returned in 1698 had not changed very much since the time when he had left it. The landmarks were still there. Antoine-Hercule Picon was still alive, barely. He had purchased an estate some twenty-nine miles from the capital and assumed the title of Vicomte d'Andrezel. He must have known about Eustache's arrival since the news had even made it to Amsterdam. Louis XIV would not have needed to read a newspaper either, and would certainly have preferred that no one else did. He had just gotten out of his last war by the by the skin of his teeth, and many of his subjects were thoroughly sick of him. Who knows if anyone filled in Eustache on the state of public opinion? He was initially kept in a dingy apartment on the third floor of one of the towers of the Bastille. It had a view of the Faubourg Saint-Antoine, although it is not clear how long he remained in those particular quarters. He seems to have experienced more than his previous human contact, if we are to believe a number of people who claimed to have seen him. It is doubtful whether anyone bothered to tell him of Picon's death on October 6, 1699, even though it was noted in high society. He must certainly have heard of the outbreak of Louis's final war, the War of the Spanish Succession, which began in 1701. If so, he only heard about its first two years, during which nothing much happened. If only he could have imagined as he lay dying that he would go down in legend as the twin brother of the king! The ironic joke was on Louis XIV, whose entire reign was a succession of unintended consequences.[21]

In attempting to penetrate into the inner life of four high-security prisons, I have been obliged, just like the sister-in-law of Louis XIV, Voltaire, and Soulavie, to rely on a great deal of hearsay and legend. But, for the purposes of history, hearsay and legend, too, carry their modicums of truth, and we do not need to ignore these when there is some harder evidence to back them up. In all of our knowledge about Eustache Dauger there is an absolute consistency about his complacency, his docility, and his resignation. He never gave Saint-Mars the remotest trouble. Either the prisoner had super-human stoicism, or he had managed to make the conditions of his captivity somewhat bearable. This permits me to conclude my speculations with the assistance of one last bit of hearsay.

In the course of putting together his rumors, Voltaire also addressed himself to a fellow historian, Jean-Baptiste Dubos, proudly describing his own philosophy of history and flaunting the privileged information that he had already accumulated:

> I am sufficiently informed on the adventure of the man in the iron mask who died in the Bastille. I have spoken to people who served him.

Dubos, however, was a considerably more scrupulous historian than Voltaire and had been a propagandist for the Marquis de Torcy, Louis XIV's last secretary for foreign affairs. In these capacities, I must admit, he was not privy to secrets of state, and notably to such privileged ones. Yet he had been a habitué of the secretariat and must have been familiar with the prevailing scuttlebutt. Therefore, his cautious and straightforward answer to Voltaire merits our careful consideration:

> As to the masked man, I heard when he died twenty years ago that he was only a servant of Mister Fouquet. If you have some proof of this fact you will do well to present it. But if your proofs are not persuasive, my opinion is that you should not unmask this man. What I have heard about his status should not be put to paper. Mister Thieriot, to whom I have said a little more than I write to you, seems to be of my same opinion.

Dubos was fifteen years off on the date of Eustache's death, but he is the first person to assert that Eustache had been the valet of Fouquet, and in this, of course, Dubos was absolutely right. Even more important he did not discourage Voltaire from uncovering any state secrets. On the other hand, Dubos admits that he knows more about this man's *status*, as if it were something too *sordid* to put on paper. What other evidence, therefore, is Dubos guessing that Voltaire might discover if not that Eustache Dauger had served for the libidinal relief of his superiors?[22]

Voltaire ignored the valet information and stayed away from the smut, both of which would have invalidated his own hypothesis. Likewise in his *Siècle de Louis XIV*, Voltaire omitted another critical detail that Chamillart had in all probability included in his answer, which would have completely contradicted Voltaire's theory, namely, that the man in the iron mask "possessed all the secrets of Fouquet." Yet Voltaire had heard it, since he included it in his *Supplément au Siècle de Louis XIV*, where he was more interested in flaunting his knowledge than in maintaining his consistency. On the other hand, after the first publication of his *Siècle de Louis XIV*, the same admirer from Avignon who embellished the story of the pewter plate also passed on to him the testimony of a certain Madame Cassis. She told him that she had obtained permission from Saint-Mars to pay her respects to the mysterious prisoner prior to his departure for Paris. According to her, he received her very graciously, took off his glove, and touched her hand. "It was," she remembered, "the fairest and softest of skins, the hand of a woman." The gentleman also passed on other prevailing rumors to the effect that the prisoner was a princess and that he loved to do his hair. A carriage merchant who had lent Saint-Mars a stretcher joined in this chorus. Voltaire had no reason to exploit this information for any of his purposes, so it is not surprising that he kept it out of his subsequent writings. However, it is consistent with the hypothesis that I am proposing.[23]

But one might ask, why put so much stock in the reply of Dubos? Why rely on the evidence from a retired propagandist in the secretariat of foreign affairs? Had not the bulk of the correspondence regarding the man in the iron mask taken place between Saint-Mars and the secretary of war? Yes indeed, and even it had never touched on such delicate questions. But this is all the more reason to believe in Dubos if one considers the man for whom he had been working. Who was the Marquis de Torcy? He was the son of Charles Colbert, brother of Jean-Baptiste, one-time intendant of Alsace and Torcy's predecessor at the foreign affairs. Outside of Antoine-Hercule Picon and his collaborators, if there was any place in France which might have retained an intimate recollection of Eustache Dauger, it was in the secretariat of foreign affairs, where the Colberts and their retainers had been in charge since 1679. Nor was the unexpurgated statement of Chamillart without authority. He had been controller-general and secretary for war. There must have been some memory of Eustache in both departments. Voltaire, like his imitator Soulavie, had done the right thing by asking widely. Neither one of them, however, had chosen to listen.

Conclusion

It has been a long search for the man in the iron mask, and it will never be over. No human knowledge is ever complete, no human memory can re-create all human experience, and the secrets that died with Eustache Dauger on November 19, 1703, can never be uncovered. Yet I believe that I have put forward some things about the mystery of this remarkable survivalist that we can all agree upon with a fair degree of probability. One is that his name was indeed Eustache Dauger. If it was not, his jailers would never have bothered to bury him under an assumed name. Another is that he was a valet, and a very docile one. Our most reliable sources as well as our least reliable concur on that. The third is that he had participated in a conspiracy, and that his captors must have been in on it. If he had been any more guilty than his accomplices, they would not have hesitated to kill him. But what conspiracy? To hide the fact that he was the brother of Louis XIV? Ridiculous.

The more we look, however, the more we discover that Cardinal Mazarin lies at the heart of the mystery. He had led a double life—one as a statesman, the other as a loan shark—and one of his most embarrassing clients had been the widow of Charles I of England. Who was in the best position to know where every jewel, every work of art, every penny of Mazarin's fortune had been stashed but his treasurer? Who was his treasurer? Antoine-Hercule Picon, an ambitious nobody from the depths of Languedoc.

I went there and I discovered, among other things, that Picon's family had been servants of a noble lady who became the wife of a governor of the city of Senlis, close to Paris. We begin to suspect that this was the only way Picon could have managed to get himself to the court of France and become the treasurer of Cardinal Mazarin. This suspicion is confirmed by the governor's name on the marriage contract of Antoine-Hercule Picon, who had, after Mazarin's death, gone to work directly for Mazarin's alter ego, Jean-Baptiste Colbert. But where did the valet come from? During one of my visits to Languedoc, I looked everywhere for anyone with a name like Dauger in the continuum of the Picon family. No luck. But when I finally got to Senlis in the jurisdiction of the governor, I found a bunch of them. We know from Colbert that Picon had begun working for him shortly after disappearing from Languedoc. That would have been just the right time for Picon to pick up a valet. While Mazarin was in the south of France sixteen years later, such a valet reappears in the form of Picon's "man." After Mazarin dies, we examine his will and discover that it had been altered. In the postmortem additions, the name of Picon appears on numerous occasions. Trust Colbert, it reiterates, and I don't want any of my executors to see Picon's books.

When Louis XIV starts governing for himself, he flippantly orders his ambassador in England to stonewall the queen's son, who is now King Charles II, should he ask for any of his father's and mother's possessions to be returned. Clearly, Louis is in on the take, and he is not much worried about irritating his cousin. But, as time goes by, Louis wants desperately to enlist Charles II in a war against the Dutch and is terrified that anything to do with Mazarin's estate will enter into the negotiations. Need I say more? I will. Eustache Dauger was the valet of Mazarin's former treasurer Antoine-Hercule Picon. The poor Eustache had opened his mouth at the wrong time and said something about his participation in the disposition of the fortune of Cardinal Mazarin. This is why he was threatened with death if he revealed anything about his past.

I am perfectly aware that I have not been able to produce matches of Eustache Dauger's DNA from the *palais Mazarin*, the citadel of Pinerolo, the fortress of Exilles, the island of Sainte-Marguerite, or the Bastille. Some of those places are no longer even there. But I do believe that I have a proposal that covers all the evidence, and I cordially invite anyone who can find any contradiction in it to suggest a better hypothesis because, in all three instances, we would all then have contributed something, either to the advancement of historical method or to the movie industry.

Abbreviations Used in the Notes

AAE		France, Archives du Ministère des Affaires Etrangères
	CP	Correspondance Politique
	MD	Mémoires et Documents
AC		France, Archives Condé
AD		Archives Departmentales
AG		France, Archives de la Guerre
AGT		Archivio Generale dei Teatini
AM		Archives Municipales
AN		France, Archives Nationales
	MC	*Minutier Central*
Andilly		*Journal inédit d'Arnauld d'Andilly*, ed. Halphen
Anselme		Anselme, *Histoire généalogique et chronologique de la maison royale de France*
APW		*Acta Pacis Westphalicae*, ed. Konrad Repgen
AR		France, Bibliothèque Nationale, *Catalogue général des livres imprimés: Actes royaux*
ASF		Italy, Archivio di Stato di Firenze
	CM	*Codice Mediceo*
ASM		Italy, Archivio di Stato di Mantova
	AG	*Archivio Gonzaga*
ASN		Italy, Archivio di Stato di Napoli
	CF	*Carteggio Farnesiano*

AST		Italy, Archivio di Stato di Torino
	MPLM	Materie Politiche, Lettere Ministri
ASVat		Vatican, Archivio Segreto
ASVen		Italy, Archivio di Stato di Venezia
Aumale		Aumale, Duc d', *Histoire des Princes de Condé*
BArsenal		France, Bibliothèque de l'Arsenal
Besterman		
	VC	*Voltaire's Correspondence*, ed. Besterman
	CW	*Complete Works of Voltaire*, ed. Besterman et al.
BI		France, Bibliothèque de l'Institut
BL		British Library
	Add. Ms.	*Additional Manuscript*
	Egerton Ms.	*Egerton Manuscript*
	Harl. Ms.	*Harleian Manuscript*
BM		Bilbiothèque Municipale
BMaz		France, Bibliothèque Mazarine
BNF		France, Bibliothèque Nationale
	Ms. Baluze	*Manuscrit Baluze*
	Ms. Cangé	*Manuscrit Cangé*
	Ms. CCC	*Manuscrit Cinq Cents Colbert*
	Ms. Clair.	*Manuscrit Clairambault*
	Ms. Dupuy	*Manuscrit Dupuy*
	Ms. Fr.	*Manuscrit français*
	Ms. It.	*Manuscrit italien*
	Ms. MdT	*Manuscrit Morel de Thoisy*
	Ms. Mél. Col.	*Manuscrit Mélanges de Colbert*
Bod. Lib.		Oxford University, Bodleian Library
	Clar. Ms.	*Clarendon Manuscript*
Brachet		Brachet, *Le Roi chez la Reine*
Brienne HA		*Mémoires de Henri-Auguste, Comte de Brienne*
Brienne LH		*Mémoires de Louis-Henri, Comte de Brienne*, ed. Bonnefon
BSHF		*Bulletin de la Société de l'Histoire de France*
BSorbonne		France Bibliothèque de la Sorbonne
BUP		Bibliothèque de l'Université de Paris
Bussy-Rabutin		
	HAG	*Histoire amoureuse des Gaules*
	Mémoires	*Mémoires de Roger de Bussy, comte de Rabutin*, ed. Lalanne
Champollion-Figeac		*Documents historiques*, ed Champollion-Figeac

Chéruel
    Minorité   *Histoire de France pendant la minorité de Louis XIV*
    MF   *Mémoires sur Fouquet*
Choisy   *Mémoires de l'abbé de Choisy*
Conrart   *Mémoires de Valentin Conrart*
Cosnac
    RPM   *Richesses du palais Mazarin*
    SRLXIV   *Souvenirs du règne de Louis XIV*
Delort
    Détention   *Histoire de la détention des philosophes*
    MdF   *Histoire de l'homme au masque de fer*
Demotier   Demotier, *Annales de Calais*
Dubuisson-Aubenay   Dubuisson-Aubenay, *Journal des guerres civiles*
Dulong
    Comptes Bleus   Comptes Bleus du Cardinal Mazarin
    Fortune   *Fortune de Mazarin*
    Processus   Processus d'enrichissement du Cardinal Mazarin
Estrades   Estrades, *Lettres, mémoires et négociations*
Foisil   Héroard, *Journal*, ed. Foisil
Fouquet   Fouquet, *Défenses*
GAH   Gemeente Archief, The Hague
GAM   Gemeente Archief, Maastricht
    MNA   *Minuutakten Notariële Archieven* 1484
    OA   *Oud Archiev* 67, 94
Gazette   *Gazette de France*
Gourville   *Mémoires de Gourville*
Greene   *Letters of Henrietta Maria*, ed. Greene
Grouchy   Grouchy, *Un administrateur au temps de Louis XIV*
Grouvelle   *Oeuvres de Louis XIV*, ed. Grouvelle
Guizot   Guizot, *Histoire de la république d'Angleterre*
GvP   *Archives . . . de la maison d'Orange Nassau*, ed.
                          Groen van Prinsterer
Hanotaux   Hanotaux, *Histoire du Cardinal Richelieu*
Haussonville   Haussonville, *Histoire de la réunion de la Lorraine à*
                          la France
Hermant   Hermant, *Mémoires de Godefroi Hermant*
IAD   Inventory after Decease (*Inventaire après décès*)
Isambert   *Recueil général des anciennes lois françaises*, ed.
                          Isambert
Iung   Iung, *La Vérité sur le masque de fer*

Jal	Jal, *Duquesne et la marine de son temps*
Joly	*Mémoires de Guy Joly*
La Borde	La Borde, *Le Palais Mazarin*
La Châtre	*Mémoires du comte de La Châtre*
La Fare	*Mémoires et réflexions*
La Gorgue-Rosny	La Gorgue-Rosny, *Recherches généalogiques*
La Porte	*Mémoires de P. de La Porte*
La Rochefoucauld	*Mémoires de La Rochefoucauld*
Le Boindre	*Débats du Parlement de Paris*
Lefèbvre	Lefèbvre, *Histoire . . . de Calais*
LIM Colbert	Colbert, *Lettres, instructions et mémoires,* ed. Clément
LM	Mazarin, *Lettres du cardinal Mazarin pendant son ministère,* ed. Chéruel and D'Avenel
LM PdP (1690)	Mazarin, *Lettres du cardinal Mazarin où l'on voit le secret de la négotiation de la paix des Pyrenées* (1690)
LM PdP (1693)	Mazarin, *Lettres du cardinal Mazarin où l'on voit le secret de la négotiation de la paix des Pyrenées,* seconde partie (1693)
LR	Richelieu, *Lettres, instructions diplomatiques, et papiers d'état du cardinal de Richelieu,* ed. D'Avenel
Mercure	Mercure François
Michaud	Michaud, *Biographie universelle*
Mongrédien	Mongrédien, *Masque de Fer*
Montglat	*Mémoires du marquis de Montglat*
Montpensier	*Mémoires de mademoiselle de Montpensier*
Moote	
Louis XIII	*Louis XIII, the Just*
Revolt	*Revolt of the Judges*
Moreau	*Bibliographie des Mazarinades,* ed. Moreau
Choix	*Choix des Mazarinades,* ed. Moreau
Motteville	*Mémoires de madame de Motteville*
M&P	Michaud and Poujoulat
Ms.(s)	*Manuscrit(s)*
NSHA	Niedersächsisches Hauptstatsarchiv
Celle Br.	*Celle Brief*
Ormesson	Ormesson, *Journal,* ed. Chéruel

Patin
    R-P   *Lettres de Guy Patin*, ed. Réveillé-Parise
    Jestaz   *Lettres de Guy Patin à Charles Spon*, ed. Jestaz
P&M   Petitot and Monmerqué
Pinard   Pinard, *Chronologie militaire*
PRO   Great Britain Public Record Office
    CSPD   *Calendar of State Papers Domestic*
    HCA   *High Court of Admiralty*
    SPD   *State Papers Domestic*
    SPF   *State Papers Foreign*
Rabinel   Rabinel, *La Tragique aventure de Roux de Marcilly*
Ravaisson *AB*   Ravaisson, *Archives de la Bastille*
Ravenel
    LMR   *Lettres de Mazarin à la Reine*
Retz   Retz, *Oeuvres*, ed. Feillet
RI   *Recueil des instructions données aux ambassadeurs et ministres de France*
Richelieu   *Mémoires du cardinal de Richelieu*
Roux-Fazillac   Roux-Fazillac, *Recherches historiques et critiques sur l'homme au masque de fer*
Saint-Maurice   Saint-Maurice, *Lettres sur la cour de Louis XIV*, ed. Lemoîne
SHF   Société de l'Histoire de France
s.l.n.d.   sans lieu ni date (without place or date)
Sottas
    Gouvernement   "Le Gouvernement de Brouage et La Rochelle sous Mazarin"
    Maladie   "La Maladie et mort du cardinal Mazarin"
Talon   Talon, *Mémoires*
TSP   Thurloe, *Thurlow State Papers*
Turenne   *Mémoires du Maréchal de Turenne*

~

Notes

Introduction: The State of the Question

1. Saint-Mars to Louvois, August 21 and 31, 1669, letters accessible only through Pierre Roux-Fazillac, cited in note 9, below, 105–106.

2. Saint-Mars to Louvois, January 8, 1688, accessible in Champollion-Figeac, III, 645–646. The duke had died in 1669. Henry Cromwell, Oliver's fourth son, in 1674. *Les Amours d'Anne d'Autriche, épouse de Louis XIII, avec M. Le C.D.R. le véritable père de Louis XIV, ou on voit au long comment on s'y prit pour donner un héritier à la Couronne, les ressorts qu'on fit jouer pour cela et enfin tout le dénuement de cette comédie* (Amsterdam, 1692, 1693, and 1696). *Gazette d'Amsterdam*, LXXX and LXXXI, October 6 and 9, 1698, confusingly cited by Iung, 422. Elizabeth Charlotte to Sophie, October 10 and 22, 1711 [pub. in *Aus den Briefen der Herzogin Elizabeth Charlotte von Orleans an die Kurfürstin Sophie von Hannover* ed. Eduard Bodemann (Hannover, 1891) II, 288–289].

3. Voltaire to Thieriot, May 13 1732, VC II, Letter 472, pp. 315–317 or Besterman CW, LXXXVI, D488 pp. 187–188. *Sottisier:* Russia, National Library, Saint Petersburg Ms. *Voltaire* 5, fol. 1ᵛ (first mention) fol. 20ʳ (second mention) [pub. in Besterman CW LXXXI, 211 (first mention) 245 (second mention). Jean-Christian Petitfils, in his *Masque de fer* (Paris, 2003) makes the interesting suggestion that Voltaire got the elder brother story from the mistress of the Marquis de Barbézieux, secretary of war, whom I discuss in chapter 9 of this book. Voltaire, *Siècle de Louis XIV* (Berlin, 1751), ch. 24].

4. Antoine Pecquet, *Mémoires secrets pour servir à l'histoire de Perse* (Amsterdam, 1745). This interesting publication also helps us to keep up with the writing of Voltaire's *Siècle de Louis XIV* most of which he sent to Frederick of Prussia in 1739 and first published in 1751. If he had written his account of the man in the iron mask after 1745 he would in all likelihood have borrowed Pecquet's account, since Voltaire did not scruple to include the same story when the admirer in Avignon, mentioned in the next paragraph, called it to his attention.

5. Voltaire, *Siècle de Louis XIV* (Dresden, ([1752] 1753) II, ch. 24, (Leipzig [Paris] 1752) II, ch. 24. Avignon gentleman to Voltaire, October 16, 1763, L.M.C. [Chesnay] "Lettre inédite à M. de Voltaire d'un gentilhomme d'Avignon sur le Masque de fer avec la réponse," *Bulletin*

polymathique du Muséum d'instruction publique de Bordeaux (October 1815), xiii, 384–385. Also pub. in Besterman *VC* LIII, letter 10637, pp. 83–84 and Besterman *CW* CXI, Letter D11464, pp. 33–34. The Avignon gentleman is identified as a M. de Valbene in Voltaire's reply of November 11, 1763 [nineteenth-century copy in BNF Ms. *Fr.* 12944, fol. 48, which identifies the writer, pub. in Besterman *VC* LIII, letter 10667, pp. 114–115, which does not and Besterman *CW* CXI, letter D11495, p. 56, which does].

6. Henri Griffet, père, *Traité de différentes sortes de preuves qui servent à établir la vérité de l'histoire* (Liège, 1769), 300–327. Voltaire, *Questions sur l'Encyclopédiei,* "Anecdote sur l'homme au masque de fer" (London 1771–1772), I, 218–224. His editor added that Voltaire "doubtless meant to say 'elder brother' of Louis XIV," which is, of course, exactly what Voltaire had written some thirty years before in his scrapbook [also in Besterman *CW* XXXVIII, 298–303)].

7. Baron de Heiss to *Journal encyclopédique,* Phalsbourg, June 28, 1770.

8. Jean François-Mussot, alias Arnould, *L'Homme au Masque de fer ou le souterrein,* first performed on January 7, 1790, which ran for fifty-seven performances. On Soulavie, compare the *Mémoires du Maréchal Duc de Richelieu,* ed. abbé Jean Louis Giraud Soulavie (Paris, 1790), 4 vols. and especially III, 66–105, on the iron mask with the much shorter *Mémoires authentiques du maréchal de Richelieu,* ed. Arthur Boislisle Jean de Boislisle, and Léon Lecestre (Paris, 1918) SHF, which contains nothing on the iron mask. If Soulavie needs any further discrediting, we might note that Voltaire, who was on cordial terms with the Marshal de Richelieu, never makes any mention of ever having discussed the man in the iron mask with the marshal. See also Jérôme Le Grand, *Louis XIV et le masque de fer ou les princes jumeaux,* first performed on September 24, 1791, in the *Théatre de Molière* and ran for thirty-two performances. For these runs, see André Tessier, *Les spectacles à Paris pendant la révolution* (Geneva 1992–2002) I, 125 and 243.

9. Pierre Roux-Fazillac, *Recherches historiques et critiques sur l'homme au masque de fer, d'où résultent des notions certaines sur ce prisonnier, ouvrage rédigé sur des matériaux authentiques* (Paris, 1800–1801).

10. Joseph Delort, *Histoire de la détention des philosophes et des gens de lettres à la Bastille et à Vincennes* (Paris, 1829), 2 vols., and *Histoire de l'homme au masque de fer* (Paris, 1925). Even though the first book was published after the second, it seems to me that this cannot be the order in which Delort wrote them, since he inserted annotations in the 1825 book that refer to the printed 1829 one. Yet the publication dates are certainly correct.

11. "L'Homme au masque de fer," *Le Constitutionnel,* August 2, 1831, announcing the first performance. The play ran for five performances. August-Jean-François Arnould appears to have been the grandson of Jean François-Mussot, alias Arnould, the author of the earlier pantomime.

12. The letter was published in Paul Lacroix (alias Jacob), *L'Homme au masque de fer* (Paris, 1837). For Dumas's conception of history see his interesting article in *La Presse* N° 13, July 15, 1836, [accessible on BNF/Gallica]. Alexandre Dumas, et al., *Crimes célèbres* (Paris, 1839–1840) VIII, 249. Dumas and his collaborators may have had other motives as well, since Louis Philippe, the King of France at that moment, had grabbed the throne from a direct descendant of Louis XIV.

13. The *Trois Mousquetaires* was published in *Le Siècle* from March 14 to July 14, 1844, the *Vingt ans après* from January 21 to September 2, 1845. The *Vicomte de Bragelonne* from October 20, 1847, to January 10, 1850.

14. Jules Loiseleur, "Le Masque de fer devant la critique moderne," *Revue contemporaine,* ser. 2 LVIII (July 31, 1867), 193–239 and "Un dernier mot sur le masque de fer," *Revue contemporaine,* ser. 2 LXXII (December 15, 1869), 385–405. Marius Topin, *L'Homme au masque de fer* (Paris, 1869). See the letter on pp. 329–330. Théodore Iung, *La Verité sur le masque de fer (les empoisonneurs) d'après les documents inédits des Archives de la Guerre et autres depôts publics* (Paris,

1872). See esp. 187, 203. For the number of theories by 1872 see Jean-Christian Petitfis, *Le Masque de fer: Entre histoire et légende* (Paris, 2003).

15. François Ravaisson (*AB* III, 209), who made a habit of sloppy citation, cited the letter to the Archives of War without any more specific reference than its date. Jules Lair, *Nicolas Foucquet* (Paris, 1890) II, 453–452.

16. Franz Funk-Brentano, "L'Homme au masque de velours noir dit le masque de fer," *Revue historique* LVI (November–December 1894) 253–303. Andrew Lang, *The Valet's Tragedy and Other Studies* (London, 1903). Andrew Stapylton Barnes, *The Man of the Mask: A Study in the By-Ways of History* (London, 1908). See esp. 293. Maurice Duvivier, *Le Masque de fer* (Paris, 1932), blown up by Antoine Adam, "Un document inédit au dossier du masque de fer," *Revue d'histoire de la philosophie et d'histoire générale des civilisations*, nouvelle série XXIV (1938), 359–361. Georges Mongrédien, *Le Masque de fer* (Paris, 1952), 190. Jean-Christian Petitfis, *L'Homme au masque de fer* (Paris, 1970), 163–165.

1. The Sex Life of Anne of Austria

1. Claude Dulong, *Anne d'Autriche: Mère de Louis XIV* (Paris, 1980). Ruth Kleinman, *Anne of Austria: Queen of France* (Columbus, 1985). Elizabeth Wirth Marvick, *Louis XIII: The Making of a King* (New Haven and London, 1986). Lloyd Moote, *Louis XIII, the Just* (Berkeley, Los Angeles, London, 1989).

2. BNF *Ms. Fr.* 4022–4027 (Héroard's *Journal*) [pub. by Foisil]. Armand Bachet, *Le Roy chez la Reine: Histoire secrète du mariage de Louis XIII et d'Anne d'Autriche* (Paris, 1866), 2nd ed. Reported consummation: BNF *Ms. Fr.* 4025, fol. 224 [pub. in Foisil, II, 2330], *but* "Non hebbe effetto alcuno, anzi che lo lasciò con particolar disgusto," according to Bentivoglio of January 30 cited in the next note.

3. Victor Cousin, *Madame de Chevreuse et Madame de Hautefort* (Paris, 1856) and *Madame de Chevreuse* (Paris, 1862), 2nd ed., Louis Battifol, *La Duchesse de Chevreuse: Une vie d'aventures et d'intrigues sous Louis XIII* (Paris, 1913), and especially Hugh Noel Williams, *A Fair Conspirator, Marie de Rohan, Duchesse de Chevreuse* (New York and London, 1913). Ejaculations: BNF *Ms. Fr.* 4026, fol. 133, Héroard's *Journal* of January 25, 1619 [pub. in Foisil II, 2591]. Dissemination: ASVen *Francia* 51 N° 11 [sola], Angelo Contarini to Senate, January 27, (transcript in BNF *Ms. It* 1771, fols. 303–304) [pub. in Bachet, op. cit. 374–377]. Guido Bentivoglio to Cardinal Borghese, January 16 and 30, as published in *La Nunziatura di Francia del Cardinale Guido Bentivoglio*, ed. Luigi di Stefani (Florence, 1863–1870) III, 173–174, and incompletely translated in Brachet, 369–371, *Mercure françois* V (1619), 85, reported for January 24. More sex: BNF *Ms. Fr.* 4026, fol. 137, Héroard's *Journal* of February 3 (twice). fol. 145, February 25 (twice). fol. 146, February 28 (twice), fol. 148, March 5 (once), fol. 151, March 14 (once), and finally fol. 152, March 18 (once) after which Héroard writes, "Cum sua [. . .] voluptate, nihil exit utriusque" [pub. in Foisil II, 2593, 2598, 2598 again, 2599, 2601, and 2602].

4. For the nomination of Armand du Plessis, see BL *Add. Ms.* 6873, fols. 115–116, Louis XIII (own hand) to Paul V, August 29, 1620 [pub. in *LR* I, 655].

5. Miscarriage: BNF *Ms. Fr.* 4027, fol. 27, Héroard's *Journal* of March 16, 1622 [pub. in Foisil II, 2815]. Compare, for example, BNF *Ms.* CCC 98, p. 155, Louis's letter to Marie de Medici with p. 154, his letter to Anne of Austria, both of April 16, 1622 [pub. in Eugène Griselle, *Lettres de la main de Louis XIII* (Paris, 1914) I, 192–194]. Richelieu's hat: Hanotaux II, 518. Push for marriage: See the note in Richelieu's *Mémoires* (SHF III, 283).

6. For the future Cardinal de Richelieu's anti-Spanish advice, see his *Mémoires* for 1622 and 1623, P&M ser. 2 XXII, 233–236 and 253–254 or M&P ser. 2 VII, 271–272 and 277 or SHF III, 264–268 and 289–290.

7. Early admirers: Motteville P&M ser. 2 XXXVI, 339–342 or M&P ser. 2 X, 17–18. The only eyewitnesses to the scuffling in the garden were Anne and the Duke of Buckingham, so that the Duchess de Chevreuse, who was among those who came running, is our next best source. Anne's account, however, comes to us through her later confidant, Madame de Motteville, who was a child at the time and not even there, and who in a more detailed version of her *Mémoires* (fragment in BArsenal Ms. 5421 pp. 300–303) places the incident at night, and in an apparently final version (P&M ser. 2 XXXVI, 342–346 or M&P ser. 2 X, 18–20) in the daylight. In both versions, Anne and the duke are only out of sight for a few seconds, until the attendants intervened. More incriminating are the statements of Buckingham and Chevreuse, which come to us through the *Mémoires* of Cardinal de Retz. She claimed, according to Retz, that Anne and Buckingham had gone off alone "a little." It was Chevreuse who supposedly told Retz that Buckingham bragged that he had loved three queens, and browbeaten them all (Retz, III, 517–520). What makes this claim more credible is that Chevreuse also supposedly told Retz that the morning after the incident. Anne complained to her about Buckingham being a brute and asked her to find out from him if he had gotten her pregnant. One might attribute this statement to Retz's tendency to exaggerate, but in this same segment of his *Mémoires* he goes on to relate Chevreuse's considered conclusions that this was the last affair that Anne had and that her later relationship with Mazarin was most probably platonic. Another intriguing aspect of Retz's *Mémoires* is that he places his version of the incident at the Louvre in Paris, which is the last place where Anne and Buckingham could have found any privacy, but I believe there is an easy explanation for this error. Retz is writing his *Mémoires* around 1662 and does not have a clear recollection of time and place, but a clear recollection of what Chevreuse told him about the event is much more likely to have stuck with him. Another source, La Porte, Anne's faithful cloak bearer, who was in Amiens but not in the garden, describes the scene in his *Mémoires* (P&M ser. 2 LIX, 296–297 or M&P ser. 3 VIII, 7) written about the same time as Retz's similarly to Motteville and placing it in the evening. The Count de Brienne, another loyal friend of Anne, who is very reliable, comes up in his *Mémoires* (Brienne HA P&M ser. 2 XXXV, 402 or M&P ser. 3 III, 36), also written about the same time, with the interesting statement that both he and Chevreuse had advised Anne to stay with her ailing husband, whereas Madame de Vervet advised her go with the party. He was not in the garden either and does not even mention the incident there. The crux of the question is how long Anne and the duke were out of sight, and the sources are too vague to settle it. This incident, however, did inspire the one-time Jacobin Jean-Baptiste Regnault-Warin, in a novel he published in 1804, to ascribe the paternity of the man in the iron mask to the Duke of Buckingham.

8. Monsieur in council: Andilly, 16. Arrest of Ornano: Ibid., 19–20. Alliance with Condé: AAECP *France* 782, fol. 160, *Ce que Monsieur le Prince dit de M. le Cardinal à Limours en mai 1626* [pub. in Richelieu, SHF VI, 54 note 1]. Chalais interrogations: *Pièces du procès de Henri de Talleyrand, comte de Chalais* (London, 1781), 137–138, 164–169, 192–194. Monsieur's interrogation: AAEMD *France* 782, fols. 222–228, *Diverses choses que Monsieur a avouées au Roi* [pub. in Victor Cousin, *Mme de Chevreuse* (1862), 2nd ed., 364–372]. Monsieur's marriage: *Mercure françois* (1626), 379–380. Anne's interrogation: ASVen *Francia* 66 N° 87, Simon Contarini to Senate, September 11, 1626, says it took place "in vista della partenza Sua da Nantes" (transcript in BNF *Ms. It.* 1787, fols. 8–16). Her wisecrack: Motteville P&M ser. 2 XXXVI, 351–357 or M&P ser. 2 X, 21–23. La Porte P&M ser. 2 LIX, 302 or M&P ser. 3 VIII, 9 agrees that it was before leaving Nantes. Chevreuse's threat of revenge: BNF *Ms. Fr.* 6551, fol. 96 *Copie des raisons que l'on a données a M. le cardinal pour lesquelles il doit prendre garde a sa personne* [pub. in LR II, 265–268]. Return: See Richelieu, SHF VI, 191.

9. Intercepted letters: AAEMD *France* 255, fols. 205–212 and 348–351, BNF *Ms. Fr.* 3747. Louis's infatuation with Hautefort and La Fayette: Motteville P&M ser. 2 XXXVI, 378–393 or

M&P ser. 2 X, 29–34. I would suspect that it was at this time that stories began to be bandied within Anne's lonely circle, about how she had given the Duke of Buckingham a silver stud and how Richelieu had almost caught her at it. It is there, I believe, that one of the queen's young admirers, the future Duke de La Rochefoucauld, heard this tall story, which he later inserted in his *Mémoires* (P&M ser. 2. LI, 338–344, 347–349 or M&P ser. 3 V, 381–385) and that Alexandre Dumas embellished even further in *The Three Musketeers*.

10. Elpidio Benedetti, *Raccolta di diverse memorie per scrivere la vita del cardinale Giulio Mazarini romano* (Lyon, n.d.), 36–44. For Mazarin's meeting with Richelieu, see the *Mercure françois* XVI (1630), 20 and AAECP *Sardaigne* 13, fols. 352–353, *Propositions apportées par Mr Masarini Avec les reponces qui ont esté resolues et données aud~ Masarini le 2 Sep^{re} 1630*. For Anne's introduction to Mazarin see Tallemant des Réaux, *Historiettes* N° 68 "Vie du Cardinal Richelieu." The account of Mazarin's appearance before the armies kept getting better with the passage of time. Compare the first account in the *Mercure françois* XVI (1630), 724, with the more florid description in Valeriano Castiglione's *Alla Maestà Christianissima di Luigi XIII il giusto Rè di Francia per la prosperità delle sue armi*, 21–22, with the most florid relation in the anonymous life of Mazarin published by Luigi Chiala in the *Rivista contemporanea* IV (September–November 1855) and Andilly, 552–553, which has him racing across the battle line waving a crucifix and yelling, "Pace, Pace!" Victor Cousin, *La Jeunesse de Mazarin* (Paris, 1865).

11. More intercepted correspondence: BNF *Ms. Fr.* 3747, fol. 32, Anne (copy) to Mme du Fargis, March 6, 1637, fol. 38, Mme du Fargis (copy) to Anne, May 23, fols. 41–43, Anne (copies) to Mme du Fargis July 9, 23, and May 28, 1637, BNF *NAF* 4334, fols. 1–31 (includes La Porte under surveillance, interrogation of La Porte, and Anne's confession of April 17, 1637) reproduced in Richelieu, P&M ser. 2 XXX, 195–204 or M&P ser. 2 IX 221–224, La Porte P&M ser. 2 LIX, 344–380 or M&P ser. 3 VIII, 22–34, who told it to Motteville. See her *Mémoires* P&M ser. 2 XXXVI, 394–398 or M&P ser. 2 X, 34–35, as well as Montglat, P&M ser. 2 XLIX, 177–180 or M&P ser. 3 V, 60–61. Brienne HA, P&M ser. 2 XXXVI, 62–65 or M&P ser. 3 III, 68–69. La Rochefoucauld, P&M ser. 2 LI, 352–359 or M&P ser. 3 V, 386–388, See also Griffet, *Histoire du règne de Louis XIII* (Paris, 1758), III, 45–54 and Victor Cousin, *Mme de Chevreuse* (Paris, 1862), 2nd ed., 419–421. Conception of Louis: Montglat P&M ser. 2 XLIX, 180–181 or M&P ser. 3 V, 61. Sloppier account in La Porte P&M ser. 2 LIX, 380–381 or M&P ser. 3 VIII, 34 and Motteville P&M ser. 2 XXXVI, 393–394 or M&P ser. 2 X, 34.

12. Anne's changing sides: BNF *Ms.Fr.* 174 (Carnet 8) p.14, where Mazarin writes disparagingly of Monsieur's wife (sister of the Duke of Lorraine) "M^a ha piu di gioia e di dolore nelli buoni e cattivi successi della Casa d'Austria che non haveva la Regina quando non haveva figli." Disgrace of Mme de Hautefort: Montglat P&M ser. 2 XLIX, 237–243 or M&P ser. 3 V, 80–82, Brienne HA P&M ser. 2 XXXVI, 70–71 or M&P ser. 3 III, 71. Victor Cousin, *Madame de Hautefort* (Paris, 1868), 38–49. Last days of Louis XIII: Motteville P&M ser. 2 XXXVI, 422–424 or M&P ser. 2 X, 43–44.

13. For this sequence of events, see Motteville P&M ser. 2 XXXVII, 5–13 or M&P ser. 2 X, 46–49, Brienne HA P&M ser. 2 XXXVI, 84–86 or M&P ser. 3 III, 78, La Châtre P&M ser. 2 LI, 206–209 or M&P ser. 3 III, 281–283 or La Rochefoucauld P&M ser. 2 LI, 376–377 or M&P ser. 3 V, 393–394. See also BM Rouen, *Ms.* 3268 (Coll. Leber 5775), *Observations de Monsieur le Comte de Brienne Ministre et Secretaire d'Etat, Sur les memoires de Monsieur de la Chastre*, first published in *Recueil de diverses pièces curieuses pour servir à l'histoire* (1664).

14. BNF *Ms. Baluze* 174 (Carnet 2) pp. 51–52.

15. For the breakup of the cabal, see BNF *Ms. Baluze* 174 (Carnet 3) pp. 4, 8–13, 17–36, 43–63, Mottevile P&M ser. 2 XXXVII, 32–45 or M&P, ser. 2 X, 55–58 and La Châtre P&M ser. 2 LI, 237–238 or M&P ser. 3 III, 290–291. La Rochefoucauld P&M ser. 2 LI, 377–387 or M&P

ser. 3 V, 394–397. For her stay in Kempen, see Wolter Heinrich von Streyersdorff, *Beschreibung der Kölner Diöcese* (Cologne, 1670).

16. For Mazarin's conduct of the war and of the delegation in Westphalia please see my *Mazarin's Quest: The Congress of Westphalia and the Coming of the Fronde* (Cambridge, MA, 2008).

17. *Mazarin's Quest*, ch. 7, and specifically AAECP *Allemagne* 85, fols. 59–70, Mem^re (Lionne minute) *du Roy a M^rs les Plenipot^res*, August 16, 1647 (Brienne minute in Ass. Nat. Ms. 273, fols. 416–427, copies in AAECP *Allemagne* 88, fols. 603–608, and *Allemagne* 101, fols. 264–281) [pub. in APW II B 6, 285–302]. See also AAECP *Allemagne* 85, fols. 86–93, Mem^re (Lionne minute) *du Roy a M^rs les Plenipot^res*, August 23, 1647 (Brienne minute in Ass. Nat. Ms. 273, fols. 434–440, copies in AAECP *Allemagne* 89, fols. 14–25 and *Allemagne* 101, fols. 323–329) [pub. in APW II B 6, 323–329]. Mazarin first mentioned the plots in the *mémoire* of August 16 and then described them in great detail in the *mémoire* of August 23. After having done this, however, he decided to cross out the details of the Raré plot and replace them by a more sanitized relation because, ostensibly, he did not want "such diabolical things" go out in the king's name. Mazarin did permit Lionne to insert the details in his personal letter to Servien (AAECP *Allemagne* 103, fols. 332–333) [pub. in APW II B 6, 329–330] of the same date, with orders to burn it. Servien did not. We can thus read the details in both places.

18. Arrival of relatives (September 11, 1647): Motteville P&M ser. 2 XXXVII, 270–275 or M&P ser. 2 X, 129–13. The relatives were his nieces Laura Martinozzi, Laura and Olympia Mancini, and a nephew, Paul Mancini. Fault of *parlement*: BNF Ms. *Baluze* 174 (Carnet 9) fols. 39–44. Feeling sorry for himself: AAECP *Allemagne* 109, fols. 146–149, Mazarin (Lionne minute) to Servien, August 14, 1648 (copy sent in *Allemagne* 121, fols. 337–341). Outbreak of *Fronde*: Moote, *Revolt*, 151–219 and more specifically, *Arrêt de la cour de parlement, donné, toutes les chambres assemblées, le huictième jour de janvier 1649, par lequel il est ordonné que le cardinal Mazarin videra le royaume, et qu'il sera fait levée de gens de guerre pour la sûreté de la ville et pour faire amener et apporter sûrement les vivres à Paris* (Paris, 1649) [Moreau N° 217], *Arrêt de la cour de parlement, portant que tous les biens meubles ou immeubles et revenus des bénéfices du cardinal Mazarin seront saisis, et commissaires, séquestres et gardiens commis à iceux Du 13 janvier 1649* (Paris, 1649) [Moreau N° 224], *La Custode de la reyne qui dit tout* (1649) [Moreau: N° 856]. Hubert Carrier *Les Mazarinades* (Geneva, 1989–1991) II, 340. *Le silence au bout du doit* (1649) [Moreau N° 3674], *Requeste Civile contre la Conclusion de la Paix* (1649) [Moreau N° 3468], which I believe was written at the instigation of Gondi by Marigny. Chevreuse and Kerpen: See note 15, above. Laigues's mission: BNF Ms. *Fr* 3854, fol. 10, *Instruction pour Mr de Laigue: Plein pouvoir et instruction donnée par moy a Mr de Laigue . . . faict a Paris.ce 3e iour de fervier 1649* s/Armand de Bourbon and fol. 15 *Plein pouvoir a M^r le Marquis de Noirmoutier pour traitter avec Monsr l'Archiduc. . . . Du 10 feb^er 1649* also s/Armand de Bourbon. See also Retz II, 362–364. Return of Chevreuse (April 12, 1649) BNF Ms. *Fr.* 25025, fol. 21, news letter of April 16. Alliance with Mazarin: AAEMD *France* 864, fols. 390–398, Le Tellier (letter sent) to Mazarin, July 4, 1649. Alliance with Condé: Dubuisson, II, 58 for April 21, who reports that Chevreuse told the queen that on January 18, 1651, she had signed a treaty (not clear with whom) with Retz's collaboration for the marriage of her daughter to the Prince de Conti.

19. *Arrêt de la cour de parlement, pour la liberté de messieurs les princes et l'éloignement du cardinal Mazarin hors du royaume de France, Du 7 février 1651* (Paris, n.d.) [Moreau N° 289], *Arrêt de la cour de parlement, toutes les chambres asemblées, portant que le Cardinal Mazarin, ses parents et domestiques étrangers vuideront le royaume de France; autrement permis, aux communes et autres, de courir sus, avec autres ordres pour cet effet. Du jeudi 9 février, 1651.* [Moreau N° 290], *Arrêt de la cour de parlement, toutes les chanbres assemblées, contre le cardinal Mazarin. Du samedi 11 mars. 1651* (Paris n.d.) [Moreau N° 293] (copy in Motteville P&M ser. 2 XXXIX, 171–173 or M&P ser. 2 X, 384–385). Fears of abandonment: BNF Ms. *Fr.* 6886, fols. 68–69, Mazarin

(letter sent) to Le Tellier, February 18, 1651 (copy in Ms. Fr. 4209, fols. 203–205) [extract in LM IV, 31–32]. Complaints against Le Tellier: AAEMD France 267, fol. 327, Mazarin (copy) to Lionne, March 17, 1651 [extract in LM, IV, 78–82]. Divisions among Frondeurs: AAEMD France 267, fol. 331. Mazarin (copy) to Lionne March 21, 1651 [extract in LM IV, 82–85]. Treaty of Mazarin with Frondeurs (July, 1651): Motteville P&M ser. 2 XXXIX, 274–277 or M&P ser. 2 X, 416–418. Moote, Revolt, 293–298.

20. Rumors of broken engagement: Dubuisson II, 51–52 (April 5, 1651). Caused by Duchess de Longueville: AAEMD France 874, fols. 237–238, Nouvelles de Paris, April 12, 1651. Plotted by Servien and Lionne in conjunction with Condé: Motteville P&M ser. 2 XXXIX, 181–182 or M&P ser. 2 X, 388. Condé denials: Dubuisson II, 55 (April 15, 1651). Longueville and Condé denials: Retz III, 297–298. Anne's doing: BNF Ms. Fr. 25025, fols. 414–415, news letter of April 21, 1651. For the Duchess de Chevreuse's approach to Mazarin, see AAEMD France 267, fol. 376 copy of her letter to Noirmoutier, April 20, 1651 [pub. in Chéruel, Minorité IV, 327–328]. Treaty of Mazarin with Frondeurs (July 1651?): See Motteville P&M ser. 2 XXXIX, 274–277 or M&P ser. 2 X, 416–418 [also pub. in Victor Cousin, Madame de Longueville pendant la Fronde (Paris, 1859), 388–389]. See also Hugh Noel Williams, A Princess of Intrigue, Anne Geneviève de Bourbon, Duchess de Longueville (London, 1907) and Régis Chantelauze, Le Cardinal de Retz et l'affaire du chapeau (Paris, 1878), 2 vols. Treaty of Condé with Spain: BNF Ms. Fr. 6731 (Portefeuille du Prince de Condé) fols. 26–40 Copie du traicté de Monseigneur le Prince avec le Roy d'Espagne, November 6, 1651. Horror of Mazarin: AAEMD France 268, fols. 204–206, Mazarin (copy) to Brienne, September 5, 1651 [pub. in LM IV, 412–415]. Louis (own hand letter sent) to Mazarin of September 9, 1651: Benjamin Fillon, Inventaire des autographes, ser. I & II, (Paris, 1877) 36–37.

21. For the money, positions, and relatives see ch. 5. For the negotiations with Spain see Jules Valfrey, La Diplomatie française au xviie siècle: Hugues de Lionne, ses ambassades en Espagne et en Allemagne: La Paix des Pyrénées (Paris, 1881). For the negotiations with Cromwell see ch. 4.

22. Mazarin's threats: AAEMD Espagne 61, fols. 11–16 Mazarin (copy) to Louis and many other copies, July 16, 1659 [pub. in Lettres du cardinal Mazarin où l'on voit le secret de la négotiation de la paix des Pyrenées & la relation des conférences qu'il a eües pour ce sujet avec D. Louis de Haro, ministre d'Espagne . . . (Amsterdam Chez André Pierrot 1690), 14–27]. See also BNF Ms. Baluze 328, fols. 120–131. Mazarin (own hand letter sent) to Louis, August 28, 1659 [pub. in LM IX, 252–261]. Note that Brienne and Motteville believed that he would have favored the marriage of the niece.

23. Navailles incident: Motteville P&M ser. 2 XL, 168–174, 192–207, and 212–304 or M&P ser. 2 X, 534–539, Patin to Falconet, September 12, 1664, pub. in Patin R-P III, 482–483. La Fare P&M ser. 2 XLV, 156–162 or M&P ser. 3 VIII, 262–263. Illness: Patin to Falconet, May 18, June 6 and 19, 1663; February 13, April 28, June 9, and November 20, 1665; January 19 and 21, 1666, pub. in Patin R-P III, 436–442, 511–513, 524–527, 537–540 and 564–566, 578–581. See also Ruth Kleinman, "Facing Cancer in the Seventeenth Century: The Last Illness of Anne of Austria," Advances in Thanatology, IV No 1 (1977), 41–44.

2. The Candidacy of Claude Imbert

1. Archivio di Stato di Firenze CM 4660, fols. 842–845, Bonsi to Gondi. See also 4891, Avvisi of April 30 and May 7, 1658. ASF CF 186 II fascicolo 5, Bentivoglio to Lampugnano, May 10, 1658. See also Patin to Spon, July 16, 1658, pub. in Patin R-P, II, 406–409.

2. BI Ms. 1332, fols. 41–48, Retz to Charrier, November 7, 1651; fols. 183–184, Nicolas de Lingendes (the mutual friend) to Charrier, February 16, 1652, and fols. 170–171, Imbert to

Charrier, both of February 16, 1652 [pub. in Retz, VIII, 34–40, 121–122, and 124]. Ligendes's letter is unsigned, bur his identity emerges from fols. 145–146, his brother Jean de Ligendes, Bishop of Mâcon to Charrier, February 1, 1652. On Imbert's marriage, see AN MC LXXIII 412 (Saint-Vaast), October 2, 1652. A second act signed by Imbert on the same date follows. The first document is mentioned in the *Documents du Minutier central concernant l'histoire littéraire:1650–1700*, ed. Madeleine Jurgens et al. (Paris, 1960), 192. On Imbert following Retz to Nantes, see the *Lettre d'un conseiller de Nantes à son ami, sur l'évasion du cardinal de Retz* (Nantes, 1654), reprinted in Retz, .VI, 516–525. On the escape in general see BNF Ms. Fr. 10276, fols. 171–176 [pub. in Retz, VI, 507–516]. On Imbert and the escape, see BI Ms. Godefroy 288, fols. 155–156, anonymous letter of August 11, 1654. See Also AD Loire Atlantique B 6953 (investigation of Retz's escape) published for the most part in Léon Maître, *L'Evasion du cardinal de Retz hors du château de Nantes, d'après des documents inédts, information judiciaire: 1654* [Nantes, 1903], also published in the *Bulletin de la Société historique et archéologique de la Loire-Inférieure*, XLIV [1903], 30–113. On Imbert at the conclave, See AAECP *Rome* 129, fols, 279–314, anonymous "relation du conclave." The printed propaganda piece was titled, *Lettre escrite à M. le cardinal de Retz par un de ses confidants .de Paris, dont la copie a esté envoyée de Rome*, and ran for sixty-one pages. See a copy in *Rome* 126, fols. 489–520, the quote about Imbert being on p. 61 or fol. 520.

　　3. BNF *Ms. Fr.* 10325–10327 *Mémoires du cardinal de Retz*. Joly P&M ser. 2 XLVII. See esp. 307–316, 388–392, and, 403–425 or M&P ser. 3 II. See esp. 101–103, 127–128, and 131–138.

　　4. Squabbles in Munster: Claude de Mesmes, comte d'Avaux, *Lettres de messieurs d'Avaux et Servien, ambassadeurs pour le Roi de France en Allemagne concernant leurs différends et leurs responces de part et d'autre en l'année 1644* (1650). Mission to Transylvania: Jean Hudita, *Repertoire de documents concernant les négociations entre la France et la Transylvanie au XVIIᵉ Siècle* (Paris, 1926). See also Antoine Fouquet-Croissy's *Le Courrier du Temps, Apportant ce qui se passe de plus secret en la cour des princes de l'Europe* [Moreau Nᵒ 825]. His alignment with Condé: See the treaty of January 1651 from the Ms. *Caffarelli*, pub. in Retz, III, 549–556. Peace negotiations: AAEMD *France* 878 and BNF Ms., *Baluze* 175, fols. 9–12 and 46–49 (copies in Ms. *Baluze* 187, fols, 321–324, and BNF Ms. Fr. 3855, fols. 83–86 and 87–90). His first arrest: Patin to Spon, January 30, 1654 [pub. in Patin R-P, II, 106–110]. His first release: BNF Ms. Fr. 10276, p. 9. His travels: See Retz, V, 81–89, Joly P&M ser. 2 XLVII, 372–420 or M&P ser. 2 III, 122–137, and Jules Valfrey, *La Diplomatie française au XVIIᵉ siècle: Hugues de Lionne, ses ambassades en Italie: 1642–1656* (Paris, 1877), 338–341. His claims of innocence: BI Ms. Godefroy 288, fols. 217–220, *Lettre de Croisy Foucquet au duc de Brissac pour S excuser de ce qu'on lui Imputoit a Legart du Card. de Retz . . . May 1658*. His second arrest: AAEMD *France* 280, fol. 47, Mazarin (Rose minute) to Le Tellier, August 10, 1659, and *France* 281, fols. 495–498, Mazarin to Lamoignon, December 4, 1659 [pub. in LM IX, 230–231 and 430–433]. Analysis of *parlement* and *Requêtes du Palais*: BNF Ms. CCC 212, fols. 173–200 [pub. in Georg Depping, *Correspondance administrative sous Louis XIV* (Paris, 1850–1855), II, 33–70]. Collection de documents inédits sur l'histoire de France. This analysis is clearly datable for around 1660, since it speaks of Nicolas Fouquet as *procureur général*, although Depping dates it for 1663. Copies are in BNF Ms. *Baluze* 115, fols. 106–140, BArsenal Ms. 3723, fols. 141–158, and Ms. 4549, the last two of which date the analysis for 1660, and BNF Ms. Fr. 10952, fols. 1–24, incomplete, uninformed and attractive, which dates the analysis for 1662. Conditions of his release: AG Aᴶ 168, fol. 397, Le Tellier to Person, May 14, 1661, and AC, Cabinet de Livres Nᵒ 565 (*Mémoriaux du Conseil*) June 21, 1661 [pub. in Jean de Boislisle, *Mémoriaux du Conseil de 1661* (Paris, 1905–1907) II, 83 and 79]. See also Carré de Busserolle, *Dictionnaire géographique, historique et biographique d'Indre-et-Loire* (1882) and André Montoux, *Vieux logis de Touraine* (1987).

5. BNF *NAF* 1700, *Journal du Congrès de Munster, par François Ogier, Aumonier du Comte d'Avaux (1641–1647)*. It was published by Auguste Boppe (Paris, 1893). See also Ogier's *Eloge ou panégyrique de monsieur d'Avaux* (Paris, 1652), his *Actions publiques* (Paris, 1652), which includes a number of his sermons, and Patin to Belin *fils*, June 15, 1652, and October 10, 1654, to Spon, December 30, 1653, and March 26, 1655, to Falconnet, February 4, 1655, pub. in Patin R-P, I, 183–185 and 212–213; II, 94–99 and 158–163, and Jesatz, II, 541–543. There are two copies of Ogier's letter (with Retz's response) in existence. One is in BI *Ms*. 1326 (*Recueil* of Retz's letters), fols. 75–77 and the other is in *Ms*. 4454 (*Mémoires* of Claude Joly), 175–179. In the first, Ogier's letter is unsigned and Retz's is signed and dated March 25, 1662. In the second Ogier's letter is signed, "Ogier, prêtre et prédicateur de l'église de Paris" and Retz's, also signed, is dated March 27, 1662. Régis Chantelauze, apparently using *Ms*. 1326, first published these letters in his *Le Cardinal de Retz et ses missions diplomatiques à Rome* (Paris, 1879), 53–57, attributing the Ogier letter to Antoine Arnauld. Chantelauze, however, used both copies in the *Oeuvres du cardinal de Retz*, VI, 441–445, and corrected his first attribution. See also Patin to Falconet, December 28, 1665, March 14 and April 30, 1670, in the above cited R-P III, 573–575, 733–735 and 742–743. Ogier died in 1670.

6. AAECP *Angleterre* 91, fols. 265–271, Ruvigny to Louis XIV, May 25, 1668. For the hunt, see the correspondence between Lionne and Mouslier in AAECP *Suisse* 44 and AAEMD *France* 416, fols. 97–98, *Memoire du Roy pour Servir d'Instruction au Sr de la Grange Exempt des Gardes du Corps de S. M^{te} . . . 28e Jour de 7bre* 1668. Portions of this documentation have been published in Emile Laloy, *Enigmes du grand siècle: Le Masque de fer, Jacques Stuart de La Choche, l'abbé Prignani, Roux de Marsilly* (Paris, 1913) and in Aimé-Daniel Rabinel, *La Tragique aventure de Roux de Marcilly* (Paris, 1969).

7. ASVen *Francia* 144 N°s 84 and 86, Morosini to Senate, May 29 and June 5, 1669 (transcript in BNF *Ms. It* 1867, fols. 168–169 and 174–175), NSHA, Celle Br. 161 *Frankreich* N° 31, fols. 239–240 and 245–246, Pavel Rammingen to George William, June 7 and 23, 1669. BNF *Ms. Mél. Col*. 153bis, De Fita to Colbert, June 22, 1669 [pub. in Ravaisson *AB* (Paris, 1866–1686), VII, 321], 153bis, fols. 680–683, *Arrêt du Châtelet de Paris Condamnant Claude Roux, Sieur de Marcilly à estre rompu vif*, and 153bis, fols. 684–687 (Gallyots report on the execution) [pub. in Ravaisson *AB* VII, 321–323]. See also Ormesson, II, 566–567. PRO SPF 101/16, fols. 346–351 and 78/126, fol. 270, Petit news letter of June 12/22 1669 [fol. 270 pub. in Ravaisson *AB* VII, 320–321] and 101/16, fols. 360–363, Petit news letter of June 16/26, 1669 [pub. in Ravaisson *AB* VII, 326–7]. Archivio di Stato di Genova. *Archivio Segreto* 2193 (Francia 17), Della Rovere to Government, June 29, 1669.

8. BArsenal *Mss*, 11334 and 12472 (La Salle dossiers). PRO SPF 101/16, fols. 402–403, Oldenburg news letter, June 28, 1669, SPF 78/127, fol. 16, Montagu to Arlington and 101/17, fols. 36–41, Petit news letter, both of July 7/17, 1669 [extract of the last pub. in Ravaisson *AB* VII, 331], NSHA Celle Br. 161 *Frankreich* N° 31, fols. 248–250 and 257–259, Pavel-Rammingen to George William, June 28 and July 25, 1669, the first of which also describes Roux's trial and execution, AST MPLM *Francia* 84 (207, 208), Saint-Maurice to Charles Emmanuel, June 28, 1669 [pub. in Saint-Maurice I, 316–318], Ormesson II, 567. For the decision to arrest Eustache Dauger, see ch. 8.

9. For the manuscript of Guy Joly's *Mémoires*, see AAEMD *France* 84, fol. 54 [pub. in Joly P&M ser. 2, XLVII, 100 or M&P ser. 3 II, 34].

10. To add insult to injury, there are also in the same *liasse* 538, six more acts, dated January 10, June 21, June 25, and August 9, 1674; December 14, 1675; and September 17, 1676, and in *liasse* 539 one act dated January 27 1676, each signed either by Imbert, Anne Marie Marès, or both.

3. The Fouquet Connection

1. Councilor at Metz: BNF *Pièces originales* 1219 27 349, fol. 393. Master of Requests: Ibid. Position for cousin: Ibid. Marriage to Louise Fourché: AN MC LI /504 (Cousinet), January 10, 1640. Army of North intendancy: *LM*, I, 872. Bishopric of Agde: ASV Archivio Concistoriale, Processi Concistoriali 42, fol. 157, June 23, 1643.

2. Intendancy of Dauphiné: BMaz Ms. 2214, fol. 210, Mazarin (copy) to Nicolas Fouquet, July 1, 1644, Ormesson, I, 200–201, July 30, 1644, BNF Ms. *Dupuy* 631, fols. 249–259 (Fouquet's own report). Intendancy in Catalonia (1646): AG A^1 100 fols. 212, 215. Intendancy in Flanders (1647): A^1 103 fol. 311, BMaz Ms. 2216, fol. 403, Mazarin (copy) to Fouquet, September 30, 1647. Intendancy in Paris: Dubuisson-Aubenay, I, 15. For Fouquet's advice, see AAEMD *France* 848, fols. 266–267, *Touchant les harangues du parlement,* and fols. 290–291 *Touchant les assemblées du parlement,* both written around June 26, 1648.

3. Nicolas in support: Dubuisson-Aubenay, I, 175–177, February 26, 1649, and 216–217 [February 1650]. We first run into the abbé Fouquet in op. cit. February 8, 1650, 220–221, helping to chase the Duke de La Rochefoucauld out of Damvilliers, then in BNF Ms. *Fr.* 25025, fols. 270 and 276, news letters of August 12 and 19, 1650, where the abbot is ambushed with a party of his friends by one of his mother's relatives, who kill a valet and get away with it.

4. For the early life of Jean-Baptiste, see Ormesson II, 487, Courtilz de Sandras's *Vie de Colbert* (Paris, 1695), 3–4, Charles Perrault, *Memoires de Charles Perrault* (Avignon, 1759), 172, and Jean-Louis Bourgeon, *Les Colbert avant Colbert: Destin d'une famille marchande* (Paris, 1973), 224–225. See also AG A^1 58, N° 545, Sublet de Noyers (letter sent) to Colbert, May 24, 1640, and BNF Ms. *Baluze* 331, fols. 99 and 30, Colbert (own hand minutes) to Le Tellier, April 12 and June [23], 1650 [pub. in *LIM Colbert* I, 8–10 and 14–15, the last also in *BSHF* II, pt. 2, 114–115]. Colbert's advice: BNF Ms. *Fr.* 6883, fols. 310–313 Colbert (letter sent) to Le Tellier, August 9, 1650 [pub. in *LIM Colbert* I, 24–28]. See also the interesting article by Ernest Lavisse, "Colbert, Intendant de Mazarin," *Revue de Paris* (September 1, 1896).

5. Confidence in Queen: Compare BNF Ms. *Fr.* 6888, fols. 128–216, the interrogatories of the *parlementary* commission on the trail of Cardinal Mazarin, with the suspicions he expresses privately in AAEMD *France* 267, fols. 327–338, Mazarin (copies) to Lionne, March 17 and 21, 1651 [extract in *LM*, IV, 78–85]. Suspicions of Servien and Lionne: BNF Ms. *Baluze* 329, fols. 60–67, Mazarin (own hand minute) to Anne, May 12, 1651 and attached *mémoire,* which we have only as pub. in *BSHF* II, pt. 2, 1–22. Taking orders: AAEMD *France* 268, fols 112–113, Mazarin (copy) to Brienne, May 23, 1651 [extract in *LM*, IV, 200–201, dated 22nd]. Breisach: AAEMD *France* 267, fols. 434–438, Mazarin (copy) to Lionne, and BNF Ms, *Fr,* 6886, fol. 174 (letter sent) Mazarin to Le Tellier, both of June 6, 1651 (copy of the last in Ms, *Fr,* 4209, fols. 248–255) [extracts of both in *LM*, IV, 242–251]. Dismissal of Servien, Lionne, and Le Tellier: Dubuisson-Aubenay, I, July 18, 1651. Complaint about Brienne: AAECP *France* 268, fols. 228–230, Mazarin (copy) to Brienne, September 25, 1651 [extract in *LM*, IV, 438–442].

6. Marriage to Marie-Madeleine de Castille: AN MC XIX (Baudry) 443, February 4, 1651. Stalling tactics: BNF Ms. *Fr.* 6888. fol. 249, Fouquet (own hand) to Commissioners, April 29, 1651. Lifting of seizure and emergence of Basil: BNF Ms. *Fr.* 23202, fols. 3–4, Mazarin (letter sent with own hand addition) to Basil Fouquet, May 16, 1651 (copy in AAEMD *France* 268, fols.108–109) [extract in *LM*, IV, 184–186]. See also Colbert to Mazarin of October 21, 1651, cited in ch. 5 note 13, BNF Ms. *Fr.* 23202, fol. 5, Mazarin (own hand letter sent) to Basil Fouquet, May 23, 1651 [pub. in *BSHF* II, pt. 2, 45]. Bluster in *parlement*: BUP Ms. 68, (Lallemant extracts) fols. 13–14, August 1, 1651. Assurances of friendship: AAEMD *France* 878, fols. 281–283, Mazarin (copy) to Basil Fouquet, August 13, 1651 (letter sent in BNF Ms. *Fr.* 23202, fols. 13–14 [extract in *LM*, IV, 389–391]. Basil's negotiations with Gondi and Chevreuse:

Compare AAEMD *France* 877, fols. 364–367, Basil Fouquet (own hand letter sent) to Mazarin, December 7, 1651, BNF Ms. *Fr.* 23202, fols. 24–25 and 17–18, Mazarin (letters sent) to Basil Fouquet, December 15 and 22, 1651 (copies in AAEMD *France* 268, fols. 393–395 and 413–414) [excerpts in *LM*, IV, 543–545 and 562–564] with Retz, IV, 226, who makes no mention of his own dealings with Basil during this period. Valet: BNF Ms. *Fr*, 23202. fols.26–33, Mazarin (letter sent) to Basil Fouquet, December 26, 1651 (copy in AAECP *France* 268, fols. 437–439 [extract in *LM*, IV, 577–582].

7. For these concerns see ch. 5. Colbert's self-promotion: BNF Ms. *Baluze* 363, fols. 1–2 Colbert (own hand minutes) to Mazarin, February 17, 1651 [pub. in *LIM Colbert* I, 66–68], BNF Ms. *Fr.* 6886, fols. 79–80, Mazarin (letter sent) to Le Tellier, March 1, 1651 (copy in Ms. *Fr.* 4209, fols. 208–213) [pub. in *LM*, IV, 46–48], BNF Ms. *Baluze* 363, fols. 3, 6 /4, 9–11, 12–15, 16, 23–24, 21–22, 25–27, and 28–29, Colbert (own hand letters sent) to Mazarin March 3, April 14 and 21, May 4 and 19, June 2, 9/10, 16, and 20 [pub. in *LIM Colbert* I, 68–95], Ms. *Baluze* 332, fols. 108–111, Mazarin (own hand letter sent) to Colbert, May 16, 1651 [pub. in *LM*, IV, 187–188], BNF Ms. *Fr.* 6886, fols. 161–162, Mazarin (letter sent) to Le Tellier, May 23, 1651 (copy in Ms. *Fr.* 4209, fols. 240–245) [pub. in *LM*, IV, 201–204]. Self-righteousness: BN Ms. *Baluze* 332, fols. 118–120, Mazarin (letter sent) to Colbert, June 13, 1651 [extract pub. in *LM*, IV, 268–269]. For the new council as early as 1651 compare Ms. *Baluze* 363, fols. 31–34, Colbert (own hand minute) to Mazarin, July 1, 1651 [pub. in *LIM Colbert* I, 96–99] with the statement in the third text of Mazarin's will that he had called Gomont into his council "il y a dix années presque entières," Massac "il y a plusieurs années." Appropriation of confidence: BNF Ms. *Baluze* 363, fols. 58–59, Colbert (own hand minute) to Mazarin, September 16, 1651 (amended letter sent in AAEMD *France* 876, fols. 452–453) [extract of minute pub. in *LIM Colbert* I, 128–130].

8. Fouquet's *faux pas:* AAEMD *Framce* 877, fols. 235–236, Fouquet (copy) to Colbert, November 8, 1651 [pub. in *LIM Colbert* I, 165]. First critique of Fouquet: BNF Ms, *Baluze* 323, fol. 84, Colbert (own hand minute) to Mazarin, November 10, 1651 [pub. in *LIM Colbert* I, 163–169]. See also BNF Ms. *Baluze* 363, fols. 88–91, Colbert (own hand letters sent) to Mazarin, November 20 and December 1, 1651 [pub. in *LIM Colbert* I, 172–177].

9. Services of Nicolas: Dubuisson-Aubenay II, 160 (February 6, 1652). Appreciation: AAEMD *France* 887, fols. 37–38, Mazarin (Roussereau minute) to Basil Fouquet, February 13, 1651 [extract pub. in *LM*, V, 46–49]. More mentions of valet: BNF, Ms. *Fr.* 23202, fols. 31–33, Mazarin (letter sent) to Basil Fouquet, February 16, 1652 [extract pub. in *LM*, V, 58–60], AAEMD *France* 887, fols. 59–60, Mazarin (Roussereau minute) to Basil Fouquet, April 15, 1652 (copy sent in BNF Ms. *Fr.* 23202, fol. 275 and copy in AAAEMD *France,* 269, fols. 91–92 [pub. in *LM* ,V, 86–87]. Capture of Basil: Dubuisson-Aubenay II, 209–210.

10. Compare Bussy-Rabutin *HAG* (1856–1876) I, 216 or (1857) II, 390, who emphasizes the sweet talking of Basil with AAEMD *France* 887, fol. 74, Mazarin (Roussereau minute) to Basil Fouquet, April 30, 1652 (copy in AAEMD *France* 269, fols. 110–112) [extract pub. in *LM*, V, 99–101]. See also *France* 269, fols. 119–120, Mazarin (copy) letter to Basil Fouquet, May 5, 1652 [pub. in *LM*, V, 105–106].

11. La Porte P&M ser. 2 LIX, 432–433 or M&P ser. 3, VIII, 51. Compare with the *Collection complète des Oeuvres de Monsieur de Voltaire* (Geneva, 1768–1777), Collection alphabétique de la plupart des écrivains français qui ont paru dans le *Siècle de Louis XIV*, 116.

12. Fouquet's note: AAECP *France* 883 (own hand), fols. 170–174. For the battle (July 2, 1652) see Turenne I, 202–206, Montpensier P&M ser. 2 XLI, 252–274 or M&P ser. 3 IV, 117–124, Conrart P&M ser. 2 XLVIII 107–113 or M&P ser. 3 IV 565–567. Monsieur's order: BN Ms. *Baluze* 208, fol. 59 [facsimile in Henri Marcel *et al. La Bibliothèque nationale* (Paris, 1907), 104].

13. Turning point: Montpensier P&M ser. 2 XLI, 274–285 or M&P ser. 3 IV, 124–128, Conrart P&M ser. 2 XLVIII, 107–151 or M&P ser. 3 IV. 565–579. Compare with the *Gazette* N° 82 July 6, 1652, which makes no mention of the firing upon the royal troops, while concluding with the pillaging of the Hôtel de Ville. See also BUP Ms. 70 (Lallemant extracts), fols. 105–121 [pub. in Edouard Maugis, "La Journée du 4 juillet 1652 à l'Hôtel de Ville de Paris: Relation de Pierre Lallemant," *Revue historique* CXXXIII (1920), 62–72] and BL *Egerton* Ms. 1682, fols. 286–313 [pub. in Le Boindre II, 495–507]. Nicolas Fouquet's suggestion: AAEMD *France* 883 (copy) fols. 125–126, undated. Insincere negotiations: *Egerton* Ms. 1682, fols. 313–335 [pub. in Le Boindre II, 507–517], BUP Ms. 70 (Lallemant extracts), fols. 121–180, the *Second extrait des registres du parlement 25 Juin jusqu; au retour de Saint- Denis* [Moreau N° 3608], and *Le Véritable arrêt de la cour de Parlement donné, toutes les chambres assemblées, les vendredi et samedi 19 et 20 juillet 1652* (Paris, 1652) [Moreau N° 3920].

14. Colbert activities. Trading company: AAEMD *France* 885, fol 173, Colbert (cypher) to Mazarin, October 13, 1652. Entry into Paris: *France* 885. fols. 328–329, Colbert (duplicate) to Mazarin, November 1, 1652 [all pub, in *LIM Colbert* I, 195–198]. Candidacies: AAEMD *France* 892, fols. 26–27, Servien (letter sent) to Mazarin, January 1, 1653 and AAEMD *France* 892, fols. 39–40, Fouquet (letter sent) to Mazarin, January 2, 1653. On the superintendancy: AAEMD *France* 892, fols. 32–33, Colbert (letter sent) to Mazarin, January 2, and fol. 55, Colbert (own hand letter sent) to Mazarin, January 4 1653 [the second pub. in *LIM Colbert* I, 198–200].

15. *Gazette* N° 18, February 8, 1653. Commission (February 8, 1653): BNF Ms. CCC 235, fols. xxii–xxiii [pub. in Chéruel MF I, 236–237 note 2]. Devaluation: *Declaration . . . portant réglement pour l'exposition et décry des monnoyes* (Paris, 1653). Mazarin appreciation: BNF Ms. Fr. 23202, fols. 131 and 316, Mazarin (letters sent) to Basil and to Nicolas, August 8 and 16, 1654. See also Basil's letter of September 25 cited in the next note. Division of functions (December 24, 1654): BNF Ms. CCC 235, fols. xxiii–xxv. Other devaluations: *Declaration pour la fabrication des espèces nouvelles d'or et d'argent appelles lys* (March 1655).

16. Basil Fouquet plot: BNF Ms. Fr. 3857, fols. 32–35 [pub. in *BSHF* II pt. 2, 127–131]. Condé counter plot: AAEMD *France* 892, fols. 336–337 and 369–372, Basil Fouquet (own hand letters sent) to Mazarin, September 16 and 25, 1653 [excerpts in Chéruel MF I, 241–245]. Plot against Basil: AAEMD *France* 891, fols. 281–282 and 259–260, Basil Fouquet (own hand letters sent) to Mazarin, October [?] and 18, 1653. Rights of succession: BNF Ms. Fr. 10276, p. 185 (Metz was c. June 13 and Paris on August 11, 1654), BNF *Dossiers Bleus* 270, fol. 46. Hocquincourt treason: BNF Ms. Fr. 23202, fols. 306–307, Duchess de Châtillon (own hand note) to Condé, October 17, 1655 [pub. in Chéruel MF I, 546–548], AAEMD *France* 272, fols. 54, 55, and 56–57, Mazarin (copies sent) to Anne, November 5, 7, and 8, 1655 (other copies in *France* 896, fols. 319–320, 323, and 325–327 [all pub. entirely or in extract in *LM*, VII, 122–125], *France* 894, 411–414, Basil Fouquet (own hand letter sent) to Mazarin, November [10], 1655, BNF Ms. 23202, fols. 169–170, Mazarin (own hand letter sent) to Basil Fouquet, November 11, 1655 (extract in *LM*, VII, 132–133] which contains the quote, and AAEMD *France* 272, fol. 60, Mazarin (copy) to Anne, also of November 11, 1655, AAECP *Pays Bas Espagnols* 37, fol. 164, Mazarin (copy) to Turenne and AAEMD *France* 272, fol. 61, Mazarin (copy) to Anne, both of November 12, 1655 (copy of the letter to Anne in *France* 896, fol. 337 [extracts pub in *LM*, VII, 134–135], AAEMD *France* 272, fols. 62, Mazarin (copy) to Anne, November 13, 1655 [pub. in *LM*, VII, 135–136]; BNF Ms. Fr. 23202, fols. 171–172, Mazarin (own hand letter sent) to Basil Fouquet, November 14 [extract pub. in *LM*, VII, 137], AAEMD *France* 895, fols. 356–358, Mazarin (minute) to Anne and *France* 895, fol. 359 Mazarin (copy) to Nicolas Fouquet, both of November 22 (copy of letter to Anne in *France* 272, fol. 66 [extract to Anne and letter to Fouquet pub. in *LM*, VII, 139–143], *France* 894, 417–418, Basil Fouquet

(own hand letter sent, November [26], 1655, *France* 272, fol. 71, Mazarin (copy) to Anne, November 27, 1655 [extract pub. in *LM*, VII, 155–156]. See also BNF Ms. Fr. 10276, pp. 440–444, which claims the payment was 1,200,000 *livres*. Montglat P&M ser. 2 XLIX, 468–469 or M&P ser. 3, V, 309–310 has it at 600,000. See also Bussy-Rabutin *HAG* (1856–1876) I, 234–237 and 248–252 or (1657) II, 397–399 and 405–407.

17. AAEMD *France* 891, fols. 242–243, Colbert (letter sent) to Mazarin, October 14, 1653, BNF Ms. *Baluze* 216, fols. 275–279, Mazarin (Rose hand letter sent) to Colbert, October 16, 1653 [extract pub. in *LM*, VI, 61–61]. First two column letter: Ms *Baluze* 216, fols. 298–299, Colbert (letter sent) to Mazarin, October 21, 1653, with Mazarin's own hand reply, undated [extract pub. in *LIM Colbert* I, 208–209, attributed to incorrect folio].

18. Anatole France, *Le Château de Vaux-le-Vicomte, suivie d'une étude historique, par J. Cordey* (Paris, 1933).

19. Edicts of March 20, 1655: *Edict . . . portant aliénation des droits seigneuriaux, censives et justices du parisis des droits aliénes et autres droits appartenans à S.M. avec création d'intendants et commis des chartres. Vérifié en Parlement . . . le 20 mars 1655, et en la Chambre des Comptes* (Paris, 1655) F 23612 (239). *Edict . . . portant création de divers officiers de chancellerie, de judicature et des postes, avec un règlement des ports de lettres. Verifié en Parlement . . . le 20 mars 1655* (Paris, 1655) F. 23612 (236) (237), MdT 433, fol. 241. *Edict . . . portant création en tiltre d'offices, de 46 conseillers secrétaires du Roy, de 4 conseillers trésoriers payeurs et de 4 conseillers controlleurs des gages desdits secrétaires, de 2 huissiers en la Grande Chancellerie, de 5 huissiers ès Conseils de S.M, de 4 conseillers conservateurs des hypotèques . . . en chacun bailage et sénéchaussée; de 12 banquiers royaux . . . de 4 conseillers intendans . . . des postes . . . en chacune Généralité. et règlemens et taxes des ports de lettres et pacquets . . .* (Paris, n.d.), F 23612 (238). *Edict portant establissement d'une marque sur le papier et parchemin, pour la validité de tous les actes qui s'expédieront par tout le Royaume, Vérifié en Parlement . . . le 20 mars 1655, en la Chambre des Comtes et Cour des Aydes* (Paris, 1655). Louis XIV's speech (April 13, 1655): AN X^{1a} 8390 fols. 89–90 and U 2107, fols. 64–65. Mazarin pressures: BNF Ms. Fr. 23202, fol. 320, Mazarin (letters sent) to Nicolas Fouquet, May 27; fols. 154- 157, fol. 158, and fol. 159 to Basil, June 22, June 30 (copy in AAEMD *France* 896, fol. 75), and July 11, fol. 365 to Superintendants, July 14, all of 1655, fols. 324–325, to Nicolas, March 4, 1656. Valenciennes: Compare Turenne, II, 43–56 and *Gazette* N° 92, July 22, 1656, with the *Relación verdadera de la felicissima victoria, que Dios Nuestro Señor se ha servido de conceder a las católicas armas de Su Magestad, gobernadas del Serenisimo señor don Juan de Austria, contra las de el Christianisimo Rey de Francia, que se hallava sobre el sitio de la Ciudad de Valencienes, Ciudad del Pais de Henau, en los Estados de Flandes, Sucedida el Sábado 15 de julio de este año de 1656* (Seville, 1656), also in Biblioteca Nacional de España Ms. 2384, pp. 395–396 [pub. in Ruiz Rodriguez, Ignacio, *Don Juan José de Austria en la monarquia hispánica entre la politica, el poder y la intriga* (Madrid, 2007), 191–192]. Efforts of Fouquet: Mazarin to Fouquet, July 24, 1656 in *Défenses* XII, 379–389. Appreciation of Mazarin: BNF Ms. Fr. 23202, fols. 205–206, Mazarin (own hand letter sent) to Basil Fouquet, July 24, 1656 [pub. in *LM*, VII, 295–296]. Benefits to Fouquet family: BNF Ms. Fr. 10277 (December 1656) pp. 231–232. Charost-Fouquet marriage: AN MC LI/542 (Cousinet) February 11, 1657. More Mazarin pressures: BNF *Baluze* 176, fols. 279–280, Colbert (letter sent) to Mazarin, May 18, 1657, with Mazarin own hand reply of May 19, BNF Ms. *Baluze* 176, fols. 300–301, Mazarin (letter sent) to Colbert [extract in MF I, 325–326] and AAEMD *France* 274, fol. 312, Mazarin (copy) to Nicolas Fouquet, both of June 12, 1657, BNF Ms. *Baluze* 176, fols. 308–309, Colbert (letter sent) to Mazarin, June 22, 1657, with Mazarin's own hand reply of June 25, 1657 [pub. in *LM*, VII, 528–533]. Mazarin tolerance of Basil: BNF Ms. *Mél. Col.* 51a, fol. 43, Mazarin (minute) to Basil Fouquet, June 20, 1657 (copy sent in Ms. Fr. 23202, fols. 226–227) [pub. in *LM*, VII, 513–514]. For Mazarin's criticism of Nicolas see the next note.

20. AAEMD *France* 902, fols. 119–127, Nicolas Fouquet (own hand letter sent) to Mazarin, June 26, 1657 [extract pub. in *LIM Colbert* I, 501–503]. Confidential *mémoire*: BNF CCC 235, fols. 85–94 [pub. in Chéruel MF 488–501]. There is a printed *Copie figurée* in BNF Ms. CCC 235, fols. 86–93 and in BNF Lb³⁷ 344D and another copy in BNF Ms. Fr. 17048, fols. 340–352. To place this project further in context, we can note that in AAEMD *France* 904, there is an unfoliated letter of Fouquet to Mazarin of July 11, 1657, in which Fouquet makes an effort to imitate Colbert's style of sending his letters in two columns, and Mazarin replies in his own hand on the 16th. There is a facsimile of this exchange in Feullet de Conches's *Causeries d'un curieux*.

21. BNF Ms. *Baluze* 176, fols. 323–324 and 331–332, Colbert (letters sent) to Mazarin, July 8 and 21, 1657, with Mazarin's replies of July 15 and 25.

22. Basil's antics: Bussy-Rabutin, *Mémoires* I, 88 HAG (1856–1876) I, 142–276) or (1857) II, 372–419, Montpensier P&M ser. 2 XLII, 173–180 and 296–298 or M&P ser. 3 IV, 249–251 and 288–289. Mazarin's reprimand: AAEMD *France* 274, fols. 412–413, Mazarin (minute) to Basil Fouquet, July 21, 1657 [extract in *LM* VIII, 55–58].

23. Family tensions: BNF Ms. *Fr.* 23202 appears originally to have contained an anonymous letter to Basil, neither bound nor foliated, dated September 23, 1657, warning him that Mazarin was beginning suspect a rift between him and Nicolas. Lair, in his *Nicolas Foucquet* I, 424, quotes from the letter, without providing the folio number, and there is no gap in the foliation. De Lorme crisis: AAEMD *France* 275, fols. 74–78, Fouquet (copy) to Mazarin, October 5, 1657, with copy of Mazarin's reply of October 16 [extract of reply pub. in *LM*, VIII, 185–187], See also Gourville I, 145–152. Acquisition of Belle-Isle: Fouquet, *Défenses* II, *Brevet du Roy pour l'Acquisition et fortification de Belle-Isle* (August 20, 1658), 361–362. Revised *mémoire*: See the copies in BNF Ms. *Fr.* 17848 fols. 340–352 and LB³⁷ 344D. Solicitation of Colbert: The only letter of Mazarin to Colbert that I can find is in BNF Ms. *Mél. Col.* 52b, fol. 281, a secretarial minute of September 27, 1659, does not ask him for any advice on what to do about the finances. Thus I can only conclude that Mazarin must have sent him a note in his own hand, because Colbert's *mémoire* cited in the next note begins with "Votre Eminence m'ayant ordonné de luy dire ce que je pouvois scavoir concernant l'estat present des finances."

24. BNF Ms. *Mél. Col.* 32, fols. 446–460 (copy in BM Rouen Ms.1894, Collection Montbret 164) [pub. in *LIM Colbert* VII, 164–183]. It was forwarded with BNF Ms. *Fr.* 10249, fols. 1–2, Colbert (copyist hand letter sent) to Mazarin, October 1, 1659, with Mazarin reply of October 21 [pub. in Champollion-Figeac II, 498 and *LIM Colbert* I, fols. 380–383 and 514–516].

25. BNF Ms. *Fr.* 10249, fols. 8–9, Colbert own hand minute) to Mazarin, November 28, 1659 [pub. in Champollion-Figeac II, 504 and *LIM Colbert* I, 390–394].

4. Calais

1. Stanislas Brugnon, "L'Identité de l'homme au masque de fer," in *Il y a trois siècles le masque de fer: Actes du colloque international sur la célèbre énigme: 12–13 septembre 1987* (Cannes, 1989), 27–38. He quotes, without citation, from the record of payment cited in ch. 8, note 26.

2. BI *Harl. Ms.* 7379, fol. 86b. Henrietta to Charles, May 1642 [pub. in Greene, 63–65]. Heenvliet to Frederick Henry, July 24, 1642 [pub. in GvP, IV, 50–52] provides a list amounting to 1,265,300 florins, which matches very well with *The Lord George Digby's Cabinet and Dr. Goff's Negotiations; Together with His Majesties, the Queens, and the Lord Jermins, and Other Letters, Taken at the Battle at Sherborn in Yorkshire about the 15th of October Last. Also Observations upon the Said Letters* (London, 1646), 44, which set the value at 1,281,700 florins. See also Bod. Lib. *Clar. Ms.* 23, fol. 107, Goring to Henrietta Maria, January 15, 1643/4 to the effect that he

had raised some additional money on the jewels. We can date the 100,000 *livres* transfer mentioned by Cantarini in ch. 5 note 6 to this time because of his mention of the presence of Henry Jermyn, as well as to Mazarin's enigmatic letter to her in BMaz Ms. 2214, fol. 32, Mazarin (copy to Henrietta, March 19, 1643) [pub. in *LM* I, 138] in which he refers to "le petit service que j'ay tasché de rendre a V.M^té." She also borrowed 200,000 livres from the Duke d'Epernon (see her act of November 11, 1646, to Epernon cited in the following note and her acknowledgment of September 18, 1656, to Mazarin, cited in ch. 5 note 23). See also Motteville P&M ser. 2 XXXVII, 112–118 or M&P ser. 2 X, 80–82.

3. Last letter from Falmouth: BI *Harl. Ms.* 7379, fol. 96, Henrietta Maria to Charles, July 9/19, 1644 [pub. in Green, 249–250]. Sympathy: *Harl. Ms.* 7379, fol. 99, Henrietta Maria to Charles, August 3/13, 1644 [pub, in Green, 250–252]. Pension: ASVen *Francia* 101, N° 36 III, Nani to Senate, August 16, 1644 (transcript in BNF Ms. *It.* 1822, fols. 200–202). Reception in Paris: BNF *NAF* 9747, fol. 175. See also Motteville P&M ser. 2 XXXVII, 126–128 or M&P ser.2 X, 84–85. Attempts to borrow from Mazarin in 1645: BNF Ms. *Baluze* 174 (Carnet 7), fol. 30. Condition in 1646: Motteville P&M ser. 2 XXXVII, 186–190 or M&P ser. 2 X, 104 and AN MC XCVI/47 (Beauvais), November 11, 1646. This act was not originally listed in the notary's repertory 7, and there is a note at the bottom of the page of this repertory written in another hand, which says, "La reyne d angleterre a Monsieur le duc d esperon n^a que cette oblig~ a este aportee par Mr Thevenin po~ la grossoier et/garder la minutte ce cinq^e mars 1654." The transfer of the two jewels is acknowledged before the same notary on December 4, 1647, according to the marginal note on the act of March 23, 1654, cited in note 9 below, which Beauvais and Le Fouyn inserted on May 19, 1657, and through the copy of the procuration of Charles II of September 6, 1655, attached to the Le Fouyn act of May 19, 1657 indicated in ch. 5 note 24. Grant by the *parlement* (January 13, 1649): Talon P&M ser. 2 LXI, 392 or M&P ser. 2 VI, 322, Dubuisson-Aubenay I, 116, and Retz, I, 197 with different details. Escape of York: *Autobiography of Anne Lady Halkett* (1875). His arrival in Paris: Dubuisson-Aubenay I, 147.

4. BNF Ms. *Baluze* 174 (Carnet 14), p. 72, which I would date for 1650, AAECP *Angleterre* 60, fols. 390–394, *Projet* (Servien's hand) *d'instruction pour Mr Gentillot allant en Angleterre, 20 jan^er 1651* and fols. 404–409 [pub. in Guizot I, 458–461]. Instruction (sec. hand with Lionne additions) for Gentillot, *Febr 1651* [pub. in Guizot I, 462–470 and *RI Angleterre* I, 94–104]. Cromwell offer: Estrades (1719) I, 94–96 or (1743) I, 103–105, Estrades to Mazarin, February 5, 1652. Belated change of mind: AAECP *Angleterre* 61, fols. 26–30, *Projet* (Servien minute) *de response po~ Mr de Gentillot . . . 3 mars 1652* (clean copy fols. 31–36, dated *Mars 1652*, clean copy with additions in Servien's hand fols., 20–25, dated *Mars 1652*) [pub. in *RI* XXIV *Angleterre* I, 110–119]. Capitulation of Dunkirk: *Gazette* N° 114, September 27, 1652. See also the remarkable recollection of this incident in Louis XIV's own *Mémoires* for 1662. Capitulations of Barcelona and Casale (October 10 and 21, 1652) *Gazette* N° 130 and 134, November 2 and 9, 1652 giving earlier dates.

5. Offer to Cromwell of alliance: AAECP *Angleterre* 61, fols. 276–277, *Mémoire* in Servien's hand, dated 1653, and fols. 257–260 *Mémoire donné à Monsieur de Brienne pour envoyer à Monsieur de Bordeaux à Londres, Le X Juillet 1653* [pub. in *RI* XXIV, *Angleterre* I, 164–150]. Petit's correspondence in this period, including many of his news letters, is in *TSP* II, III, and IV. For the negotiation, Guizot's *Histoire de la république d'Angleterre et de Cromwell* and Gardiner's *History of the Commonwealth and Protectorate* are still good reads. For Morland's mission, see ch. 6 note 15. There are numerous copies of the Franco-English treaty in AAECP *Angleterre* 66, fols. 122–138 (in Latin), fols. 139–160 (in French), fols. 161–188 (in Latin and French—printed—without secret article), fols. 194–200 (in French), plus another copy in *Angleterre* 67, fols. 65– 73 (in French). Interestingly enough, however, the French government continued to provide a pension for the English princes.

6. Order of sale by *parlement* (March 23, 1648): BI *Harl. Ms.* 4894, Inventory of the pictures, medals, agates, etc., sold by order of council from 1649 to 1662, AAECP *Angleterre* 59, fols. 377–380, Croullé (letter sent) to Mazarin, May 23, 1650, enclosing *Angleterre* 60, fols. 277–281, *Estat de quelques tableaux exposés en vente a la maison de Sommerset* [May 1650] and *Estat des tapisseries du deffucnt Roy et de la Reyne d'angleterre a present exposées en vente a la maison de Sommerset* [pub. in Guizot I, 410–411 and *RPM*, 413–420]. For evidence that Mazarin quickly acquired six pieces of the Acts of the Apostles, see AAEMD *France*, 884, fols. 254–255, a copy, unsigned, of Colbert to Mazarin, September 8, 1652. On Jaback, compare Carlo Gambarini, *A Description of the Earl of Pembroke's Pictures* (Westminster, 1731), 83–84 with Fouquet, *Défenses* cited in ch. 8 note 10. For the *History of David* see Bordeaux's letter of March 10 cited below in this note. Bordeaux and exchange rates: See Mazarin's letter of November 17, 1653 and Bordeaux's letter of March 22, 1654 cited below in this note. **Dürer:** AAECP *Angleterre* 61, fols. 175–177, 184–185, 200–201, 208–209. Bordeaux (own hand letters sent) to Mazarin, March 10, April 3 and 18, and May 5, 1653 [excerpts in *SRLXIV* VI, 248–252 and *RPM*, 169–171]. See also *Angleterre* 63, fols. 127–129, 148–149, 312–315, and *Angleterre* 64, fols. 188–190 and 287–290, Bordeaux (own hand letters sent except for first and third,) February 23, March 16, April 16, September 3, and December 24, 1654 [extracts in *RPM*, 212–213, 215–216, 222, 227, 232–233]. **Rubens:** Letters of April 3 and 18 just cited, and *Angleterre* 61, fols. 208–209. See also Bordeaux (own hand letter sent) to Mazarin, May 5, 1653 [excerpts both in *SRLXIV* VI, 252–253 and *RPM*, 172–173]. **Holbein:** AAECP *Angleterre* 63, fols. 168–170, 306–307, and 326–327 March 19, April 14 and 20, 1654 [excerpts in *RPM*, 216 and 222–223. **Raphael:** Letter of May 5 just cited, See also *Angleterre* 61, fols. 338–340, 386–389, and 404–405, Bordeaux (own hand letters sent) to Mazarin, November 17 and December 11 and 15, 1653 [extracts in *SRLIX* VI, 273–277 and *RMP*, 195–200]. **Correggio:** Letter of May 5 just cited. See also *Angleterre* 61, fols. 314–316, 317–318, and 325–326, Bordeaux (own hand letters sent) to Mazarin, October 23 and 27, and November 3, 1653 [excerpts in *SRLXIV* VI, 265–272 and *RPM*, 186–193], Letter of November 17 just cited, *Angleterre* 61, fols. 348–349, Mazarin (secretary's minute) to Bordeaux, November 17, 1653 [excerpt in *RPM*, 194–195]. Letters of *December* 11 and 15 just cited. **Busts:** *Angleterre* 61, fol. 220, Bordeaux (own hand) *Memoire des Bustes que J'ay trouvé* [pub. in *SRLXIV* VI, 255 and *RPM*, 177]. **Titian:** Letter of December 15 just cited, *Angleterre* 61, fols. 406–408 and 410–411, Bordeaux (own hand letters sent) to Mazarin, December 18 and 22, 1653 [excerpts. in *SRLIXV* VI, 277–280 and *RPM*, 200–204]. **Romano:** Letter of October 23 just cited, *Angleterre* 63, fols. 148–149, and 152–153, Bordeaux (own hand letters sent) to Mazarin, March 12 and 16, 1654 [extracts in *RPM*, 213–216], fol. 160, Mazarin (minute) to Bordeaux, March 22, 1654 [pub. in. *RPM*, 217–218], *Angleterre* 63, fols. 360–363 and *Angleterre* 64, fols. 251–254, Bordeaux (own hand and sec. hand letters sent) to Mazarin, April 27 and November 16, 1654 [extracts in *RPM*, 224 and 231]. **Van Dyck:** AAECP *Angleterre* 63, fols. 127–129, 144–146, 148–150, 168–170 (also cited above), 183–184, and 279–287, Bordeaux (first in secretary's hand all other in Bordeaux's own hand letters sent) to Mazarin, February 23, March 12, 16, 19, 22, and April 13 [extracts in *RPL* 212–217 and 221], *Angleterre* 64, fols. 57–59, 235–237, 242–243, 249–250, 251–254 also cited above, 255–258, 264–266, 275–277, and 296–298, Bordeaux (own hand letters sent except for fols. 57–59, 242–243, and 251–254 which are (secretary's hand letters sent) to Mazarin, May 25, October 29, November 9, 11, 16, 19, 23, December 14 and 31, 1654 [extracts in *RPM*, 225 and 228–233]. See also *Angleterre* 64, fols. 437–440, Bordeaux (own hand letter sent) to Mazarin, April 25, 1655 [extract in *RPM*, 236]. Death of Pietro Mazzarino: November 14, 1654. Collaboration of Charost, Letters of April 18, 1653 and December 31, 1654 just cited.

7. See AN MC LXVI/74 (Paisant), March 18, 1636; LXVI/75 (Paisant), August 6, 1636; and LXVI 81 (Paisant), May 11, 1638. Lescot family acts are mainly in Etudes LXVI and XLVI.

BNF Ms. *Baluze* 174 (Carnet 7) 1645, "Lescot de la Reyne farlo chiamare." During the *Fronde*: BNF Ms. *Baluze* 363, fols.84–85 and 90–91, Colbert (own hand minutes) to Mazarin, November 10 and December 1, 1651 [pub. in *LIM Colbert* I, 163–169 and 173–178].

8. First arrival: AAECP *Angleterre* 64, fols. 449–451, Bordeaux (own hand letter sent) to Mazarin, May 13, 1655, and AAEMD *France* 894, fol. 108, Colbert (own hand letter sent) to Mazarin, May 19, 1655. First acquisitions: AAECP *Angleterre* 64, fols. 463–466, Bordeaux (own hand letter sent) to Mazarin, May 20, 1655. Lescot in England: AAEMD *France* 894, fol.112, Colbert (own hand letter sent) to Mazarin, May 21, 1655, AAECP *Angleterre* 66, fol. 85, Mazarin (Rose minute) to Bordeaux, July 9, 1655. AAEMD *France* 894, fol. 220, Colbert (own hand letter sent) to Mazarin, July 12, 1655 [pub. in *LIM Colbert* I, 235–236], BNF Ms. *Mél. Col.* 51, fol. 480, Mazarin (minute) to Colbert July 14, 1655, AAECP *France* 894, fol. 221, Colbert (letter sent) to Mazarin, July 14, 1655, AAECP *Angleterre* 67, fols. 10–12, Bordeaux (own hand letter sent) to Mazarin, September 2, 1655. For the citation, combine AAECP *Angleterre* 66, fol. 106, Mazarin (Rose hand) to Bordeaux, September 8, 1655, *Angleterre* 69. fol. 106, *Addition de la main de Son E. a la lettre de M. le President de Bordeaux du . . . "non seulement c'est un des plus grands serviteurs que le Roy ayt, mais un de mes meilleurs amys"* and *Angleterre* 67, fols. 18–19, Bordeaux (own hand letter sent) to Mazarin September 10, 1655. AAECP *Angleterre* 67, fols. 29–31, Bordeaux (own hand letter sent) to Mazarin, September 30, 1655, to get the entire picture. First evidence of return: BNF Ms. *Baluze* 176, fols. 208–209, Colbert (letter sent) to Mazarin, May 30, 1656, with Mazarin reply, undated.

9. Arrival of Henry (May 21): BNF Ms. *Fr.* 25026, fol. 224, news letter of May 23, 1653. New loan: AN MC XCVI/61 (Beauvais), March 23, 1654. Treaty of Paris: March 2, 1657.

10. Michaud XL, 430–435 "Sully" and IV, 407 "Béthune, Philippe de," Pinard I, 81 83.

11. Incident: Dubuisson-Aubenay I, 47–50, 100. Pinard I, 83.

12. AN MC XCV/4 (Le Fouyn), July 4, 1651.

13. Charost duties: AAEMD *France* 1683, fol. 109 Mazarin (Silhon minute) to Charost, January 22, 1654. AG A^I 157, N^{os}, 15, 21 Charost (sec. hand letters sent) to Le Tellier, July 1, and 3 1654, AG A^I 157, N°s. 83 and 127 Charost (sec. hand letters sent) to Le Tellier, July 18 and 22, 1654. Congratulations from Mazarin: BNF Ms. *Mél. Col.* 51, fol. 49, Mazarin (minute) to Charost, July 26, 1654 (copy in AAECP *Pays Bas Espagnols* 34, fol. 95), *Gazette* N° 91, July 29, 1654 *La Prise du Fort Philippes pres de Gravelines, par le Comte de Charost, Gouverneur de Calais.* AG A^I 157, N°s. 127 and 173, Charost (sec. hand letter sent) to Le Tellier, July 24 and 29, 1654. See also *TSP* II, 181 Bordeaux (intercepted translation) to Charost, August 6, 1654, AG A^I 157, N° 201, Charost (sec. hand letter sent) to Le Tellier August 12, 1654, *TSP* II, 527, 554, 656, 664, and 665, Charost (intercepted translation) to Bordeaux, August 17, 30, October 17, 22, and 23, 1654. Lefèbvre, 581–582, mentions neither Cancer nor Fly.

14. **Courtebonne**: AM Calais BB 32 (1663–1664) fol. 28. **Launoy**: AD Pas-de-Calais 4 E 55 (Pierre Danjan) begins appearing (1658), AD Pas-de-Calais 4 E 52/252 (Anquier), "Lieutenant du roi dans la citadelle" (1662), AD Pas-de-Calais 4E 55 (Charles Danjan) (1662), AD Pas-de-Calais 4 E 52/259 (Anquier), cf Lefèbvre, 713–714. **Pignan**: AD Pas-de-Calais 4 E 55 (Charles Danjan) has "Dominique de Cancer, Seigneur de Pignam Lieutenant d'une compagnie de chevaux legers estant en cette ville," November 22, 1656, with Isabelle Fly signing in his absence, but this same notary has him as captain of the regiment of Espagny with a number of Flys in February of 1668, cf. La Gorgue-Rosny, I, 321. **Raoult family**: Demotier, p. 400, Lagorgue-Rosny III, 1220–1221. **Hache family**: AD Pas-de-Calais 4 E 55 (Pierre Danjan) "Jacques Hache, con^{er} du Roy tresorier receveur de son domaine" (1665), AD Pas-de-Calais 4 E 55 (Pierre Danjan) Jacques Hache (1658), AM Calais BB 29 (1658–1660) Jacques Hache mayor in 1636 and 1660, AD Pas-de-Calais 4 E 52/351 (Théru) Hache mayor in 1658, cf. Lefèbvre, 613, AM Calais BB 32 Thomas Hache, mayor in 1666–1668 (cf. Demotier 400). AD Pas-de-Calais 4 E 52/355 (Théru)

"Dominique Hache Conseiller du Roi et Receveur de son domaine" (1668). **Costé**: AM Calais BB 26 (1650–1653) fol. 33, Pierre Costé, "Seign de La Motte Warin, named *"procureur de la justice*," AD Pas-de-Calais 4 E 52/351 (Théru) Costé (1658), cf Lefèbvre, 613. **Thosse family**: AD Pas-de-Calais 4 E 52/249 (Anguier) Pierre de Thosse (1659), AD Pas-de-Calais 4 E 52/352 (Théru) Pierre de Thosse (1660) AD Pas-de-Calais 4 E·52/254 (Anquier), Pierre de Thosse (1664), AD Pas-de-Calais 4 E/55 (Pierre Danjan) "François de Thosse Con^er du Roy en ses Conseils d'estat, President et Juge general de la Jusice et administration de Calais" (1663–1664), AD Pas-de -Calais 4 E 52/355 (Théru) Pierre Thosse (1667–1668), cf. La Gorgue-Rosny III, 1419–1420. **Fly**: See note 22 below. **Caussien**: AM Calais CC 20, fol. 36 (1650) "Louis Caussien, greffier de la ville," CC 25 (1665–1667) "Louis Caussien, greffier."

15. For the marriage contract, see ch. 3 note 19.

16. AN MC LXXXVII/196 (Nonnet), Procuration for Antoine Houdan, October 11, 1665 (copy in AD Pas-de-Calais 4 E 55 (Caussien), AD Pas-de-Calais 4 E 55 (Caussien), November 7, 1665, settlement. AN MC LXXVII/2 (Thomas), Antoine Houdan and Jeanne Dumont *don mutuel*, December 11, 1675, MC LXXVII /10, *Hôtel de Ville à Antoine Houdan*, July 5, 1679, MC LXXVII/17, *Hôtel de Ville à Antoine Houdan*, October 6, 1681. These last two are *constitutions de rentes*. AN MC XX//331 (Sainfray), Descharge for François Augier, February 3, 1668.

17. Turenne II, 70–103, writes as if Mazarin was in good faith. Attack by Spanish on Calais: *Gazette* N° 82, July 7, 1657. Mention of Fly: Demotier, 189–191.

18. Arrival in Calais: *Gazette* N° 63, June 1, 1658. Battle of Dunes (June 14, 1658): Turenne II, 120–129 and *Gazette* N° 75, June 31, 1658. Capitulation of Dunkirk (June 24): *Gazette* N° 76, July 3, 1658. Siege of Bergues: Turenne II, 130–133 and *TSP* VII, 143–144, Lockart to Thurloe, June 2, 1658.

19. Antoine Vallot, *Journal de la Santé du roi Louis XIV*, ed. le Roy (Paris, 1862). More doctors: BNF Ms. Mél. Col. 52, fol. 474, Mazarin (minute) to Colbert, July 4, 1658. For Louis's dying words and the arrival of the doctors see ASN CF 186 II (fascicolo 5), Bentivoglio to Lampugnano, July 9, and 16, 1658. By the canons of modern medicine Louis had simply become dehydrated, requiring nothing more than liquids and a little rest for a full recovery. By these same canons, had Louis not been blessed with an extremely robust constitution, he would most certainly have died from the repeated bleedings. Madame de Motteville seems to have had a better grasp of the problem than any of the doctors. See Motteville P&M ser. 2 XXXIX, 430–431 or M&P ser. 2 X, 465–466.

20. Capitulation of Gravelines: *Gazette* N° 106, September 4, 1658. Capitulation of Oudenarde: *Gazette* N° 116, September 25, 1658. Capitulation of Ypres (September 26, 1658): *Gazette* N° 123, October 10, 1658. Approval of Turenne: BN Ms. Mél. Col. 52a, fol. 284, Mazarin (minute) to Turenne, September 24, 1658 [pub. in *LM* IX, 64–66].

21. Mellowing: See his letters to Fly, Robertot, and Lange in notes 23 and 24. AAECP *Lorraine* 37, Mazarin (minute) to Miromenil, January 15, 1655 [excerpt in Grouchy (1883) 77 and (1886) 27]. Robertot, Fly and the Frigate: AAECP *Pays Bas Espagnols* 47, fols. 296–301, Robertot (own hand letter sent) to Mazarin, January 28, 1659 [excerpt in Grouchy (1885) 47 and (1886) 288]. For Robertot and Talon's involvement in Mazarin's private purchases see Colbert's letter to Mazarin of February 25 and Mazarin's response of March 6 cited in note 25 below.

22. BN Ms. Fr. 6408, pp. 1–121, *Inspection maritime de M. d'Infreville sur les côtes françaises de l'océan* (1629). Lease for Admiralty rights: AN MC LXXVI/307, N° 37 (Parque II), April 14, 1632 *Etats au vrai de la recette et dépense faite par Mr François Leconte, Conseiller du Roy, Trésorier Général de la marine de ponant, pour l'exercice et Fonction de sa charge de l'année mil six cent trente cinq* [both pub. in *Correspondence de Henri d'Escoubleau de Sourdis*, ed. Eugène Sue, III, 171–221 and 359–527 from a lost ms. in the Dupuy collection]. Two-year lease: MC XXVI/68 (Monenhault). Money from Calais: See above note 6, the letter of December 18. Defense

of Calais: Lefèbvre II, 591. Contacts in England: *TSP* III, 629–630, Bordeaux to Fly, July 19, 1655, *TSP* VI, 584–585, Ormesson to Bordeaux, November 10, 1657 and *TSP* VI, 633 and 638, Fly to Bordeaux, December 5 and 8, 1657.

23. Place to stay: BNF Ms, *Mél. Col.* 52a, fol. 53, Mazarin (minute) to Charost, August 1, 1658 (copy in AAEMD *France* 1683, fol. 401). New mailing address: AAEMD *France* 905, fols. 365–366, Colbert (letter sent) to Mazarin, August 11, 1658, with Mazarin's own hand reply of August 14. Continued relationship: BNF Ms. *Mél Col.* 52a, fol. 268, Mazarin (minute) to Fly, September 14, 1658. Package for Lockhart and letter to Robertot: BNF Ms. *Mél. Col.* 52a, fol. 273, Mazarin (minute) to Fly, September 18, 1658 (copy in AAECP *Pays Bas Espagols* 45, fol. 333). Growing collaboration: BNF Ms. *Mél. Col.* 52a, fols. 282–283, Mazarin (minute) to Fly, September 24, 1658. Expression of confidence: BNF Ms. *Mél. Col.* 52a, fols. 308–309, Mazarin (minute) to Fly, October 5. 1658. Additional responsibilities: AAECP *Pays Bas Espagnols* 45, fols. 430–432, Mazarin (copy) to Fly, October 9, 1658. Functions of commissioner of war for Gravelines and Ypres: BNF Ms. *Mél. Col.* 52a, fols. 366–368, Mazarin (minute) to Fly, October 28, 1658. Dissemination of propaganda: Compare BNF Ms. *Mél. Col.* 52a, fols. 335–336, Mazarin (minute) to Robertot, October 29, 1658 (copy in AAECP *Pays Bas Espagnols* 45, fols. 471–474) with AAECP *Pays Bas Espagnols* 47, fols. 132–135, Robertot (own hand letter sent) to Mazarin, November 22, 1658 [excerpt in Grouchy (1886) 254–259 with omission on Lange]. On the personal funds see AAECP *Pays Bas Espagnols* 49, fols. 497–498, Fly (own hand letter sent) to Mazarin, December 24, 1660: "Monsieur de Villacer (f) me donne advis par Sa lettre du 5ᵉ de ce mois que j'ay receu Le xxiᵉ Que Votre Eminence m'ordonne par ung billet de paier a M. Charron Les xᵍʳ en argent blanc que vre Eminence m a confié c est ce que Je feray en mesme temps que le billet me Sera presenté." For the money still there in 1661 see Mazarin's *IAD* and Le Bas's *Compte*.

24. First mention of Lange: BNF Ms. *Mél. Col.* 43, fol. 188, Mazarin (minute) to Seyron, October 19, 1656. Marriage: AN MC LXXI/64/ (Roussel) no longer contains the minute, although it is recorded in his Repertory 2 under the date of December 23, 1657. *Mazarin italien*: Ms. *Mél. Col.* 51a, fol. 495, Mazarin (minute) to La Contour, January 5, 1658. Payment of Troops: Ms. *Mél. Col.* 52, fol. 43, Mazarin (minute) to Lange, January 28, 1658. Frigate at Dunkirk and hospital: Ms. *Mél. Col.* 52a, fol. 291, Mazarin (minute) to Lange, September 22, 1658 [extract in Grouchy (1886) 285]. The frigate later became known as the *Eminente* (see Jal I, 224, 244). More duties: Ms. *Mél. Col.* 52a, fols. 297–298, Mazarin (minute) to Lange, September 24, 1658, fols. 314–316, Mazarin (Rose minute) to Lange, October 9, 1658 (copy in AAECP *Pays Bas Espagnols* 45, fols. 413–415) [excerpt in Grouchy (1886) 223]. Hospital and confidence in Robertot and Talon: Ms. *Mél. Col.* 52a, fol. 320, Mazarin (minute) to Lange, October 12, 1658. Lange in Ypres: Ms. *Mél. Col.* 52a, fols. 325–326, Mazarin (minute) to Lange, October 17, 1658. Lange illness: Mazarin to Robertot of October 29 cited in previous note. Recovery: Ms. *Mél. Col.* 52a, fols. 371–372, Mazarin (minute) to Robertot, October 31, 1658 [excerpt in Grouchy (1886) 234]. Acquisition of Frigate: Robertot to Mazarin of November 22 cited in previous note. Lange in Ypres: AAEMD *France* 279, fol. 240, Mazarin (own hand letter sent) to Colbert, December 18, 1658. Warm relations: AAECP *Pays Bas Espagnols* 47, fols. 185–189, Lange (own hand letter sent) to Mazarin, December 21, 1658, *Pays Bas Espagnols* 48, fols. 47–54, Mazarin (copy) to Lange February 4, 1659, and *Pays Bas Espagnols* 47, fols. 364–368, Lange (own hand letter sent) to Mazarin, February 22, 1659 [extract in Grouchy (1885) 48 and (1886) 258], *Pays Bas Espagnols* 48, fols. 74–75, Mazarin (copy) Robertot, March 7, 1659, Mazarin to Lange, March 7, 1659 and fols. 77–83, Mazarin (copy) to Lange, March 7 1659. Paintings and Tapestries: *Pays Bas Espagnols* 47, fols. 288 and 462–465, Lange (own hand letters sent) to Mazarin, both undated, but answered in his letter of April 18, cited in the next note) [extract of the second in Grouchy (1885) 67 and (1886) 309].

25. Requests for books: AAECP *Pays Bas Espagnols* 48, fols. 130 and 162–163, Mazarin (own hand letter sent and copy) to Lange, April 18 and June 6, 1659. Complaints about accounts: *Pays Bas Espagnols* 38, fols. 438 and 441, Mazarin (copies) to Lange, February 4 and 13, 1660. Robertot and Talon vs. Lange: *Pays Bas Espagnols* 49, fols. 338–339, Robertot (own hand letter sent) to Mazarin, February 17, 1660 and fols. 351–354, Talon (letter sent) to Mazarin, February 22, 1660, BNF Ms. *Baluze* 332, fols. 222–223, Colbert (letter sent) to Mazarin, Paris, February 22, 1660, with Mazarin's own hand response from Marseilles, March 6, 1660. See also *Pays Bas Espagnols* 49, fols. 445 and 460–467, Talon (letter sent) to Mazarin, May 1 and 23, 1660.

26. ASTorino MPLM *Francia* 87, N° 103/5 Charles Emmanuel II (minute) to Saint-Maurice August 15, 1670 [pub. in Gaudenzio Claretta, *Storia del regno e del tempo di Carlo Emanuele II, duca di Savoia* (Genoa, 1877–1878) II, 630–631 n. 1].

27. Sherlock Holmes would also keep in mind that between July 1661 and June 22, 1669, we find thirty letters in the *Mélanges Colbert* of Dominique Fly to Jean-Baptiste Colbert and that in 1664, he also served as mayor of Calais (see AM Calais BB 34, fol. 91).

5. Follow the Money

1. Léon de La Borde, *Le Palais Mazarin et les habitations de ville et de campagne au dix-septième siècle* (Paris, 1846). Madeleine Laurain-Portemer, "Mazarin, militant de l'art baroque au temps de Richelieu," *Bulletin de l'Histoire de l'Art Français* (1975), 65–100. Daniel Dessert, "Pouvoir et finance au XVIIᵉ siècle: La Fortune du cardinal Mazarin," *Revue d'histoire moderne et contemporaine* XXIII N°. 2 (April–June, 1976), 161–181. The citations are from Dessert's *Louis XIV prend le pouvoir* (Paris, 1989), 33 and Dulong's *Fortune de Mazarin* (Paris, 1990), 49.

2. Fortune on arrival: Mazarin to Lionne cited in note 13, below. On Mondin see Dulong, *Processus*, 355. On Euzenat see Mazarin to Colbert of May 16, 1651, cited in ch. 3 note 7 and June 19/20, 1651, cited in note 13 below.

3. Official salaries: See the *Estats des biens* cited in note 25 below. Dulong quite sensibly attributes this core income to him in the 1640s and raises his entire income to 893,735 *livres* by 1648. See her "Fortune d'un ministre" in the *Annuaire-Bulletin de la Société de l'histoire de France* (1995), 19–36, and her "Comptes bleus du cardinal Mazarin," *Revue d'histoire moderne et contemporaine* XXXVI (October–December, 1989), 537–558. Superintendent of the *Compagnie du Nord*: AAEMD *France* 852, fol. 151, *Brevet portant permission a M. le Card^al Mazarini de prendre un present de la Somme de 180000^# de la Comp^ie establie pour la pesche et fonte des Baleines et Chiens des mers . . .* October 5, 1645. Benefices: Joseph Bergin, "Cardinal Mazarin and His Benefices," *French History* I (1987), 3–26. For Anne's bounty, see BNF Ms. Baluze 328, fols. 22–31, *Memoire sur les deniers dotaux et douaire de la Reyne mère*, AAECP *France* 852, fols. 76–77, Infreville (letter sent) to Mazarin, August 14, 1645, fols. 135–136, *Estat des Vaissaux qui ont esté equipez armes Et Radoubez de charpente et Calsatz a toullon en l année 1645* and especially fols. 287–289, *Estat de la Recepte faicte par Pierre Maillesez recepveur des droits d admirauté en provence des deniers appartenans au Roy a cause des prises faictes par les Vaissaux de Sa M^té nommez en [?] par aucuns des Messieurs Les capp^nes de La marine ez années 1643 1644 et La pñte 1645.* See also Dulong, *Fortune,* 25.

4. For his army, see Louis Susane, *Histoire de l'ancienne infanterie française* (Paris, 1853), VIII, 165, 377; *Histoire de la cavalerie française* (Paris, 1874), II, 146, and Pinard, VI, 94. His navy: AAECP *Suède* 12, fols. 203–204, Chanut (copy) to Cerisantes, October 12, 1647 [extract pub. in Jal. I, 161] and Mazarin to Colbert, of June 19/20, 1651, cited in note 13 below. Speculation in military supplies: BMaz Ms. 2214, fols. 53–54, Mazarin (copy) to Migènes, June 15, 1643. Copper: Colbert's letter of November 10, 1651 cited in ch. 3 note 8. Boutiques: Testimony of

Carteron, cited in note 13 below. Luxury goods: AAEMD *France* 846, fols. 101 and 102, *Memoire de M^r L'Abbé Mondin touchant des reliques de St Charles que la Reine mere avoit laissées a M^r L'Ev. de Gand . . . Mars 1643* and fol. 102, *Memoire sur le Voyage de L'Abbé Mondin en flandre.* In market for diamonds: AAECP *Hollande* 32, fols. 53–55, Brasset (letter sent) to Mazarin, September 12, 1644. Personal collection: AC *Ms*.1293 *Inventario delli argenti dorati e bianchi, giove, christali e altro dell Em^{te-} e Rev^{mo} cardinale Giulio Mazarini* (1645). Lescot expedition: AAEMD *France* 261 fol. 252, Mazarin (copy) to Lanier, January 29, 1647. Lescot remained until the summer of 1648. Escape from tolls: *France* 261, fols. 326–327, Mazarin (copy) to Mondin, May 17, 1647. Council: Dulong, "Mazarin et l'argent: Banquiers et prête-noms," *Mémoires et Documents de l'Ecole des Chartes* LXVI (2002), 105–106. First mention of Jobart: AAEMD *France* 267, fols. 145–149, Mazarin (copy) to Jobart, April 2, 1650. First mention of Girardins: BNF *Ms. Mél. Col.* 74 (Le Bas *Compte*) cited in ch. 7 note 22, referring to a transaction of September, 1650. For Le Bas, see Contarini's *Esclarsissement* cited in note 10 below, fol. 32, where he disburses 25,000 *pistoles* to Le Bas and a colleague on behalf of Mazarin around March of 1648, and Fouquet, in his *Défenses*, IX idenfifies Le Bas as a *commis* of Jean-Baptiste Colbert's distant cousin, Eduard Colbert de Villacerf and specifically accuses Le Bas of participating in Mazarin's appropriations.

5. Claims of advance: BMaz *Ms.* 2214, fol. 38, Mazarin (copy) to Mauroy, April 27, 1643. Payment to Schomberg: See *Estat de diverses parties* cited in note 10 below and recalled in Mazarin to Lionne cited in note 13 below. Gifts to Venetians: 102, N° 192 I, Nani to Senate, July 27, 1645 (transcript in BNF *Ms. It.* 1825, pp. 621–638), also recalled in Mazarin to Lionne cited in note 13 below.

6. See her acknowledgment in note 23 below. To substantiate this, we have two sets of accounts given by Cantarini to commissioners of the *parlement* of Paris in 1649 and 1651. The first set, cited in note 10 below, shows him and his partner furnishing on behalf of Mazarin "pour une lettre de quatre vingts mil florins pour la Reyne d'angleterre payab. a amsterdam L. 100,000" then going on to clarify "et Mr Cardinal m'en a donné l'ordre verballe et promis de me f~ payer ou la payer luy mesme en la pñce du Sr Milord Germain & Mr de Lionne Mr Ondedei et autres." The second set (cited in note 13 below) shows entirely different payments to "Mr de Montagu pour la Reine d'Angleterre 50,000 *livres*" and to "La Reine d'Angleterre en Hollande 7,200 *livres*." All this, of course, is far less than Henrietta and her son admitted to having received, which suggests either that Cantarini was lying or that the other funds he gave her in Mazarin's name were not from Mazarin. For Mazarin's own estimate, see Mazarin letter to Lionne cited in note 13 below. List of jewels: AAECP *Angleterre* 61, fols. 96–98, *Liste des Joyaux de Sa Ma^{ite} de la Reyne d'Angleterre engages en hollande.* Epernon: Acts of November 11, 1646 and December 4, 1647, cited in ch. 4 note 3.

7. AN K 1311, N° 122, September 26, 1645, manuscript contract drawn up by Guénegaud and Brienne, published as *Contract de mariage du roy de Pologne avec la princesse Marie* (Paris, 1645). Involving Carlo II: AN E 1689 N° 77, *Arrêt* of November 7, 1645, AN MC/LXXIII/381 (Saint-Vaast), Quittance of Anne de Gonzague for 900,000 *livres* to Cantarini and Serrantoni, and to Louis XIV for 300,000 *livres*, both of November 21, 1645. Claude Dulong has brilliantly exposed these transactions and penetrated into Mazarin's intentions in her "Processus d'enrichissement," 410–141, and her *Fortune de Mazarin*, 103–116.

8. Recollections of services: Compare AAECP *Suède* 7, fols. 427–428, Mazarin (copy) to Chanut, March 6, 1648 [extract in *LM* III, 81–83] with the recollections in Mazarin to Brienne, and Mazarin to Lionne cited in note 13 below. Money for Naples: Bibliothèque Municipale de Chartres *Ms.* 534, Mazarin (letter sent) to Fontenay, February 7, 1648 [extract in *LM* III, 27–33] or AAEMD *France* 118, N° 200, Mazarin (minute) to Infreville, November 27, 1648. Tapestries from Flanders: AN MC XCVI/51 (Beauvais), August 8, 1648. More money for

Germany: Compare BMaz Ms. 2215, fols. 271–275, Mazarin (copy) to Turenne, August [blank] 1648 [pub. in LM III, 190–197] with the sale to Cantarini, described in AAEMD France 878, fols. 251–253, Mazarin (minute) to Colbert, July 21, 1651 (copy sent in BNF Ms. Baluze 332, fol. 186. See also note 10 below. Amber and musk: AAEMD France 264, fols. 211–212, Mazarin (copy) to Lanier, November 22, 1648. For Colbert's recollection of advances see his letter to Mazarin of December 1, 1651, cited in ch. 3 note 8. Laura Mancini for Turenne: BMaz Ms. 2215, fols. 291–295, Mazarin (copy) to Turenne, January 12, 1649 [pub. in LM III, 260–266].

9. Isabelle Aristide, La Fortune de Sully (Paris, 1990), 93–95, which estimates his fortune at 3.8 million livres. Joseph Bergin, Cardinal Richelieu: Power and the Pursuit of Wealth (New Haven, 1985), 248–249, which estimates his fortune at 20 to 22.4 million livres. For Mazarin's fortune of some thirty-five to thirty-eight million, see the works of Dessert (179) and Dulong (133) cited above in note 1.

10. For the commission see BNF Ms. Fr. 6881, fols. 26–35, 24–25 and 44–45, which includes an Estat de diverses parties qui Sont deubes a moy Cenamy par Monsr le Cardinal Mazarin tant pour argent fourny pour son compte par^er que pour le Service du Roy Sur Ses ordres et Sur Ses promesses Verballes et par escript and an Esclaircissement sur l'estat de diverses parties qui sont deues a moy Cantariny par Monsr le Cardinal Mazarini tant pour argent fourny pour son compte par^er que pour le Service du Roy Sur Ses ordres et Sur ses promesses verballes et par escript. Cantarini's explanation of his purchase from Mondini is on fol. 45.

11. Inventaire des merveilles du monde rencontrées dans le palais du cardinal Mazarin (Paris, 1649) [Moreau N° 1729 also pub. in La Borde, 166–168]. Lettre d'un religieux envoyée a monseigneur le prince de Condé à Saint Germain en Laye contenant la vérité de la vie et les moeurs du cardinal Mazarin, avec exhortation audit seigneur prince d'abandonner son parti, 18 janvier 1649 (Paris, 1649) [Moreau N° 1895, pub. in his Choix I, 102–109]. Lettre d'un secretaire de S. Innocent a Iules Mazarin (Paris, 1649) [Moreau: N° 1896]. Le Courrier du temps, apportant ce qui se passe de plus secret en la cour des princes de l'Europe (Amsterdam, 1649) fictitious imprint. [Moreau N° 825, extract in his Choix I, 507–514].

12. Offer to Mercoeur: BNF Ms. Fr. 25025, fol. 25, news letter of April 30, 1649. Estates of Burgundy: recalled in Mazarin to Colbert of June 28, 1651, cited in the following note. Death of Mondini (March 20, 1650): Ms. Fr. 25025, fol. 188, March 25, 1650. Offer to Epernon: Mazarin (copy) to Duke d'Epernon, June 6, 1649 [extract in LM III, 346–347]. Governorship of La Fère: Ms. Fr. 25025, fol. 226, news letter of June 3, 1650 [pub. with the recollection in Mazarin's mémoire of May 12, 1651, cited in ch. 3 note 5]. Loss of Jules: See the Instruction for Gentillot cited in ch. 4 note 4 and in Mazarin to Colbert of June 28, 1651, cited in the following note. Anna: Compare AAECP Suède 9, fols. 442–446 and 496–499, Chanut (letters sent) to Mazarin, February 1 and April 4, 1648, with Mazarin's letter of June 19/20, 1651, cited in the next note and BNF Ms. Baluze 363, fol. 30, Colbert (own hand minute) to Mazarin, June 27, 1651 (copy sent AAEMD France 875, fol. 305) [pub. in LIM Colbert I, 95–96]. Continuation of advances: Compare BNF Ms. Fr. 25025, fols. 336–341, news letter of December 23, 1650, with Mazarin to Gargan of April 23, 1651, cited in the following note and Mazarin to Colbert of June 8, 1651, also cited in the following note. Distribution of assets: BNF Ms. Baluze 363, fols. 41–42 and fol. 88, Colbert (own hand minutes) to Mazarin, July 28, and November 20, 1651 [pub. in LIM Colbert I, 109–112 and 172–173], AAEMD France 874, fols. 46–48, Jobart (letter sent) to Mazarin, February 9, 1651, and France 875, fols. 9–13, Jobart (letter sent) to Mazarin, May 6, 1651. In hands of Chevreuse: BNF Ms. Baluse 363, fol. 83, Colbert (own hand minute sent) to Mazarin, November 8, 1651 [pub. in LIM Colbert I, 159–161]. We have no record of the queen giving him the governorship of Haute and Basse Auvergne. We do know, however, that it was vacant in February of 1651, at which time Mazarin sent the brevet to the Duke de Candale. See AN O^1 8, fols. 1–3, February 1, 1651, and BNF Ms. Fr.25025, fol. 361,

news letter of February 3, 1651. See also Mazarin's pretensions in AAEMD *France* 267, fols. 380–391, copy of his letter Lionne of May 9, 1651 [pub. in *LM* IV, 165–171], in the *mémoire* of May 12, cited in Ch. 3 note 5, and in Colbert to Mazarin of November 20 cited in this note. Moreover, the provisions of 1658 cited in note 25 below indicate that Mazarin had preceded Candale as governor. Manicamp in La Fère: compare BNF *Ms. Fr.25025*, fols. 374–376, news letter of February 17, 1651, with BNF *Ms. Fr.* 6891 fol. 17, Mazarin (own hand minute) to Le Tellier September 2, 1652 [pub.in *LM* V, 198–200]. Recollection of attempts to get guarantees: BNF *Ms. Baluze* 332, fols. 108–111, Mazarin (own hand letter sent) to Colbert, May 16, 1651 [extract in *LM* IV, 187–188, omitting the relevant point].

13. See the *arrêts* of March 2 and 11, 1651 cited in ch. 1 note 18. Interrogatories: BNF *Ms. Fr.* 6888, fols. 90–94 (Jehan Carteron), fols. 97–106 (Jean Baptiste Ludovicy), fols. 116–125 (François Juliennes), fols. 251–260 (Jacques Charton), fols. 261–265 (courier), fols. 51–55 (books), fols. 285–295 (treasurer of the navy). For Mazarin's side, see BNF *Ms. Baluze* 332, fol. 94, Mazarin (letter sent) to Colbert, March 23, 1651, AAEMD *France* 268, fols. 69–76, Mazarin (copy) to Brienne, March 24, 1651, BNF *Ms. Baluze* 332, fols. 97–98, Mazarin (copy to Colbert) to Gargan, April 23, 1651, BNF *Ms. Fr* 6886, fols. 115–121, Mazarin (letter sent) to Le Tellier May 1, 1651 (copies in *Ms. Fr.* 4209, fols, 220–240), *Ms. Baluze* 332, fols. 101–103 [extract in *LM* IV, 152–162, dated May 2], AAEMD *France* 268, fols. 69–75, Mazarin (copy) to Brienne, March 24, 1651 and *France* 267, fols. 420–423, Mazarin (copy) to Lionne, May 26, 1651 [pub. in *LM* IV, 90–107 and 220–224], BMaz *Ms.* 2218, fols. 174–176, Mazarin (copy) to Cantarini, May 29, 1651, AAEMD *France* 878, fols. 192–194, Mazarin (minute) to Colbert, June 8, 1651, *France* 878, fols. 204–206, Mazarin (minute) to Jobard, June 13, 1651, *France* 878, fols. 214–215, Mazarin (minute) to Colbert, June 19, 1651 (letter sent in BNF *Ms. Baluze* 332, fol. 121–129, dated the 20th), AAEMD *France* 878, fols. 224–228, Mazarin (minute) to Colbert, June 28, 1651 (copy sent in BNF *Baluze* 332, fols. 126–129). Mercoeur-Mancini marriage: AAEMD *France* 267, fols. 397–399 [extract in *LM* IV, 181–184]. Mazarin's *Mémoire touchant le mariage de M. le duc de Mercoeur*, May 12, 1651, and BMaz *Ms.* 2218, fols. 217–219, Mazarin (copy) to his father, July 9, 1651 [extract in *LM* IV, 315–316]. Wavering of *parlement*: AAEMD *France* 874, fols. 290–291, *Arrêt du Parlement a l effect De la Creation d'un Syndiq . . . pour les creanciers Du Cardinal Mazarin, 21 avril 1651*, establishing syndicate for Mazarin's creditors. BNF *Ms. Fr.* 6888, fols. 319–330, *Arrest de la cour de parlement donné en faveur des creanciers du Cardinal Mazarin . . . 7 sept. 1651*. Contarini's counter attack: BNF *Ms. Dupuy* 775, fols. 89–92, *Abregé du compte de la recepte faitte sous le nom de Monsieur Le Cardinal Mazarin depuis 1641 jusques en l'année 1648* and *Abregé du compte de la depense faitte soubs le nom de M. le Card^l Mazarin depuis l'an 1641 jusques a l'an 1648* [pub. in Dulong, *Comptes bleus*, 552–557]. Colbert's appeal: *Arrêt* of October 11, 1651, described in BNF *Ms. Baluze* 363, fol. 70, Colbert (own hand minute) to Mazarin, October 21, 1651 [pub. in *LIM* Colbert I, 146–148].

14. *La Mazarinade:* March 11, 1651 [Moreau N°, 2436]. For the attribution to Paul Scarron, his knowledge of the jewels only confirms the conclusions of Paul Morillot, *Scarron, étude biographique et littéraire* (Paris 1888) and Henri Chardon, *Scarron inconnu* (Paris, 1903–1904). For Gondi's claim see Retz II, 197–199.

15. Governorship of Breisach: AAEMD *France* 269, fols. 101), Mazarin (copy) to Harcourt, April 16, 1652 [pub. in *LM* V, 87–88]. Governorship of Vincennes: AAEMD *France* 885, fols. 121–122, Colbert (letter sent) to Mazarin, October 10–11, 1652, only the second half of which is pub. in *LIM Colbert* I, 194]. Marriage alliances: Compare BNF *Ms. Fr.* 25026, fols. 196, 198, 210, and 224, news letters of February 28, March 18, May 2, and May 23, 1653, with AAEMD *France* 891, fols. 305–306, Mazarin (minute) to Servien, November 9, 1653 [extract in *LM* VI, 77–79 but miscited]. The relatives were Mazarin's sisters Geronima Mancini and Laura Margherita Martinozzi, and their five children, Hortense Mancini, Maria Mancini, Filippo

Mancini, Alfonso Mancini, and Anna Maria Martinozzi. See Maria Mancini's *Apologie, ou les véritables Mémoires de Madame Marie Mancini, Connestable de Colonna Ecrits par Ellle même* (Leyden, 1678), 4–19. On the commerce raiding, see Colbert's correspondence with Mazarin of July 5 and October 21, 1656, cited in notes 21 and 22 below. Cantarini's declaration, dated May 23, 1653, is mentioned in the act of April 22, 1654 cited in note 19. BNF Ms. *Fr.*15526, fol. 63 indicates that the letters by which the queen made him lieutenant-general were registered in *parlement* on July 26, 1653, whereas the letters that made him governor were issued in the name of the king on May 27, 1654. Establishment of Terron: BNF Ms. *Baluze* 216, fols. 255–256, Mazarin (Rose hand) to Colbert du Terron, September 10, 1653. See also Sottas, Gouvernement XXXIX, 48–56, 141–154, and 207–219.

16. BNF Ms. *Baluze* 216, fol. 215 *Memoire Sur le change d'hollande*, fol. 217 also titled *Memoire sur le change de hollande*, both in Colbert's hand. Fol. 217ᵛ has the designation: *Memoire envoyé a S.E. le 8 may 1653* in a secretary's hand. *Baluze* 216, fols. 212–214, Colbert (minute preceded by letter sent) to Mazarin, May 8, 1653. See also *Baluze* 216, fols. 220–222, Colbert (in same order) to Mazarin, May 10, 1653.

17. Recovery of La Fère: BNF Ms. *Baluze* 216, fol. 231, Colbert (minute) to Mazarin, July 19, 1653 [pub. in *LIM Colbert* I, 206–207]. AAEMD *France* 891, fols. 157–158, Mazarin (Roussereau minute) to Colbert (letter sent in BNF Ms. *Baluze* 216, fols. 232–235) [pub. in *LM* V, 642–645], AAEMD *France* 891, fol. 158, Mazarin (Roussereau minute) to Anne [pub. in *LM* V, 641–642], and BNF Ms. *Baluze* 216, fols. 236–237, Mazarin (Rose and Mazarin hand) to Colbert, all of July 19, 1653, plus AAEMD *France* 891, fol. 159, Mazarin (Roussereau minute also transcribing a Louis XIV PS) to Anne, July 21, 1653 [pub. in *LM* V, 646–647]. For the confusion between personal profit and public expense see Colbert's letter of October 25 cited in the following note. AC Ms. 1294 *Inventaire de tous les meubles du cardinal Mazarin: Dressé en 1653* [pub. by d'Aumale with same title in London, 1861].

18. AAEMD *France* 891, fols. 242–243, Colbert (letter sent) to Mazarin, October 14, 1653, BNF Ms. *Baluze* 216, fols. 275–279, Mazarin (own hand letter sent) to Colbert, October 15, 1653, *Baluze* 216, fols. 298–299, Colbert (letter sent) to Mazarin, October 21, 1653, with Mazarin's own hand response, undated [extract pub. in *LIM Colbert* I, 208–209, incorrectly cited]. *Baluze* 216, fols. 302–304, Colbert (letter sent) to Mazarin, October 25, 1653, with Mazarin's own hand response, undated. *Baluze* 176, fols. 11–14, Colbert (letter sent) to Mazarin, June 7, 1654, with Mazarin own hand response, undated. For the anxiety see *Baluze* 176, fols. 88–89, Colbert (letter sent) to Mazarin, July 14, 1654, with Mazarin's response, undated, *Baluze* 176, fols. 118–119, Colbert (letter sent) to Mazarin, August 2, 1654, and fols. 123–124, Mazarin (Rose and own hand letter sent) to Colbert, August 6, 1654.

19. Conti-Martinozzi marriage: (February 22, 1654): *Gazette* N° 26, February 28, 1654. Demand for first option: ASM AG 685, fols. 232–233 and 235, Bellinzani to Dalla Valle and to Charles II, April 17, 1654. Copy of declaration of Contarini: AN MC XCV/23 (Le Fouyn) April 22, 1654, brought to Le Fouyn on January 11, 1659. Contract on Mayenne: BNF Ms. *Fr.* 3949, fols. 179–185, gives the sum of "sept cens cinquate mil livres tournois francs deniers." Hervart transfer: MC XCV/23 (Le Fouyn) July 26, 1654, BNF Ms. *Baluze* 176, fols. 112–113, Colbert (letter sent) to Mazarin, July 28, 1654, with Mazarin's reply of August 25 [pub. in *LIM Colbert* I, 225–226]. Breisach: Treaty of Basel (May 21, 1654), *Relatione del Baron di Lisola di quanto ha operato nella negotiatione di Brisach, dall anno 1651 sin al fine dall anno 1654*, pub. in Alfred Francis Pribram, *Paul Freiherr von Lisola (1613–1674) und die Politik seiner Zeit* (Leipzig, 1894), 68–70. La Fère: AN E 1703, fols. 166–170, dated September 16, 1654 (copy in AD Aisne B 745, including other documents and governorship, dated December 14, 1654). Este-Martinozzi marriage (May 30, 1655): *Gazette* N° 72, June 5, 1655. Appointment of Charles Colbert: AAEMD *France* 895, fol. 304, Mazarin (copy of a *billet*) to Charles Colbert, September 23, 1655.

20. AAEMD *France* 891, fol. 198, Mazarin (minute) to Basil Fouquet, September 29, 1653 (letter sent in BNF Ms. *Fr.* 23202, fols. 95 and 96) [extract in *LM* VI, 47–49]. AAEMD *France* 891, fol. 254 and *France* 291, fol. 277, Mazarin (copies) to Chevreuse, October 16 and 29, 1653, BNF Ms. *Baluze* 176, fols. 146–147, Mazarin (own hand letter sent) to Colbert, August 22, 1654, fols. 158–159, Mazarin (first part in Rose hand second in Mazarin's own) to Colbert, October 9, 1654, fols. 161–162, Colbert (own hand letter sent) to Mazarin, October 13, 1654, with Mazarin's own hand reply, undated, AAEMD *France* 894, fol. 220, Colbert to Mazarin of July 12, 1655, cited in ch. 4 note 8, *France* 896, fols. 193–194, Mazarin (copy) to Chevreuse, August 14, 1655, *France* 896, fol. 245, Mazarin (copy) to Chevreuse, September 7, 1655, *France* 894, fol. 337, Colbert (own hand letter sent) to Mazarin, September 30, 1655, *France* 896, fol. 335, Mazarin (copy) to Superintendants of Finances, November 9, 1655, *France* 896, fol. 336, Mazarin (copy) to Chevreuse, November 9, 1655, BNF Ms. *Baluze* 176, fol. 165, Colbert (own hand letter sent) to Mazarin, November 24, 1655, with Mazarin's own hand reply, undated.

21. House of La Porte-Meilleraye: See Anselme IV, 619–626. Investment in Madagascar: Compare BNF Ms. *Baluze* 176, fols. 228–229, Colbert (letter sent) to Mazarin, July 5, 1656, with Mazarin reply, undated, and Colbert to Mazarin of October 21 cited in the following note with Francheville, *Histoire générale et particulière des finances* (Paris 1738–1746) III, 610. For Mazarin's shifting positions, carefully examine Colbert's letter of July 5 just cited, with AAEMD *France* 894 fols. 415–416, Basil Fouquet (own hand letter sent) to Mazarin, undated in 1655 and BNF Ms. *Baluxe* 176, fols. 232–233, Colbert (letter sent) to Mazarin, July 13, 1656, with Mazarin's reply of July 16.

22. Compare BNF Ms. *Baluze* 176, fols. 208–209, Colbert (letter sent) to Mazarin, May 30, 1656, with Mazarin reply, undated and fols. 224–225, Colbert (letter sent) to Mazarin June 10, 1656, with the appointment as governor cited in note 25 below. Valenciennes: See ch. 3 note 19. Collection of advances: AAEMD *France* 900, fols. 261–262, Colbert (own hand letter sent) to Mazarin, August 7, 1656. Lescot to the Spanish Low Countries: *France* 900, fol. 379, Colbert (own hand letter sent) to Mazarin, September 30, 1656 and *France* 274, fol. 195, Mazarin (Roussereau hand letter sent) to Colbert, October 5, 1656. More tapestries: *France* 900, fol. 394, Colbert (own hand letter sent) to Mazarin, October 21, 1656. Marriage: *Gazette* N° 24, February 24, 1657. Finally see BNF Ms. *Baluze* 329, fols. 230–235, *Estat des biens et revenus et effects appartenans a Monseigneur en la presente année 1656*.

23. Jermyn affair: BNF Ms. *Baluze* 176, fol. 149, Colbert (letter sent) to Mazarin, August 5, 1656, with Mazarin reply July (*sic*) 6, fols. 265–266, Colbert (letter sent) to Mazarin, September 10, 1656, with Mazarin reply, September 11, *Baluze* 176, fols. 274–275, Colbert (letter sent) to Mazarin, September 17, 1656, with Mazarin reply, September 18. For Henrietta's confirmation see Monaco S 17, the acknowledgment of September 18, 1656, further confirmed by Charles II in Bruges on December 1, 1656.

24. First Lescot voyage: AAECP *Hollande* 57, fols. 10–13 and 14–15, De Thou (own hand letters sent) to Mazarin, April 1 and 5, 1657, AAEMD *France* 902, fols. 73 and 74, *Extrait de la lettre de lescot escritte D'amstedam le 8ᵉ may 1657* and Colbert (own hand letter sent) to Mazarin, May 11, 1657, *France* 274, fol. 230, Mazarin (copy) to Colbert, May 14, 1657, BNF Ms. *Baluze* 176, fols. 279–280, Colbert (letter sent) to Mazarin, May 18, 1657, with Mazarin's own hand reply, May 19. Second Lescot voyage: BNF Ms. *Baluze* 176, fols. 291–292, Colbert (letter sent) to Mazarin, May 29, 1657 with Mazarin's own hand reply, May 31 [extract pub. in *LIM* Colbert I, 272–273, without the relevant passage]. Henrietta offer to Epernon: AN MC XCV/25 (Le Fouyn), undated. Sale to Hervart: XCV/25 (Le Fouyn), *obligaòn*, May 19, 1657, with procuration of Charles II attached, *Promesse de fe~ la vente*, May 19, 1657, *Vente de deux diamants*, May 30, 1657. Hervart's disclaimer: XCV /25 (Le Fouyn), *Declaraòn* May 19 and 30, 1657. Delivery to Mazarin: BNF Ms. *Baluze* 176, fols. 285–286, Colbert (letter sent) to Mazarin, May 23, 1657,

with Mazarin's own hand reply, undated. Mystery resolved: BNF Ms. *Baluze* 176, fols. 289–290, 294–305, and 308–309, Colbert (letters sent) to Mazarin, May 27, June 14, and 22, 1657, with Mazarin's own hand replies of May 30, June 22, and June 25. End of tether: BNF Ms. *Baluze* 176, fols. 315–318, Colbert (letter sent) to Mazarin, July 1, 1657, with Mazarin's own hand reply, undated [pub. in LIM *Colbert* I, 274–276].

25. The *arrêt* of September 7, 1657, is mentioned in the *arrêt* of March 29, 1659 cited below. If there is any doubt about the way in which Mazarin was manipulating the motions of Cantarini, see ASM AG 685, fols. 1188–1189, Bellinzani (copy) to Tarachia, June 21, 1658. BL *Egerton Ms.* 1903, fols. 87–89, *Sur la cause a plaider contre M. de Mantoue*, January 9, 1659, ASM AG 686, fols. 47–50, Sannazaro (own hand letter sent) to Charles II, June 7, 1659, and AN X^{1b} 5917 (Plaidoiries), *Arrêt* of March 29, 1659. I have also found two printed copies of this *arrêt* in ASM. AG 707 and AG 710. Contract for Sale of Duchy of Nevers: Archvives Communales de Nevers [pub. in Henri Crouzet, "Droits et privilèges de la Commune de Nevers," *Publication de la Société Nivernoise* ser. 1 (Nevers, 1858), 198–247]. Colbert's worries: BNF Ms. *Baluze* 331, fols. 145–148, Colbert (letter sent) to Mazarin, July 13, 1659. Donations: AD *Haut-Rhin* 2929. Governorship of Auvergne: BI Ms. *Godefroy* 310, fols. 17–18, February 26, 1658 [pub. in Dulong *Fortune*, 167–169]. For the classic résumé of Mazarin's wealth in 1658 see BNF Ms. *Baluze* 329, fols. 210–218, *Estat des biens, Revenus et Effects appartenans a Monseigneur en la presente anée 1658* Collationné ce 22 Juin 16$\underline{58}$ [pub. in LIM *Colbert* I, 520–530]. Purchase from Servien: BNF Ms. *Baluze* 331, fols. 18–19, Colbert (minute) to Mazarin and fols. 173–176, Colbert (letter sent to Mazarin) August 3 1659, with Mazarin's own hand reply of August 11, 1659 [excerpt pub. in Clement LIM *Colbert* I, 334]. Fictitious purchase from Le Normant: AN MC XCV/25 (Le Fouyn) September 4, 1659. For the exact descriptions of these items see ch. 7 note 21.

26. Preliminary treaty: AAECP *Espagne* 38, fols. 34–81, Tratado de paz entre los Señores Reyes Catholico et Cristianissimo convenido y accordado entre el Señor Cardinal Jullio Mazarinj, y don Antonio Pimentel de Prado, June 4, 1659 [copy pub. in Abreu y Bertodano VI, 407–454]. Preparations: BNF Ms. *Baluze* 351, fols. 118–122, Mazarin (own hand letter sent) to Colbert, June 28, 1659. Chevreuse: AAEMD *France* 280, fol. 204, Mazarin (copy) to Duchess de Chevreuse, no date. Negotiations: Compare AAEMD *Espagne* 61, fols. 150–153, Mazarin (copy) plus many other copies to Le Tellier, September 4, 1659, with BNF Ms. *Mél. Col.* 52b, fols. 169–170, Mazarin (Roussereau minute) to Anne of Austria, September 8, 1659 (copy in BMaz 2216, fols. 294–296) [pub. in LM IX, 284–285]. Bullying: AAEMD *Espagne* 61, fols. 216–219, Mazarin (copy) plus many other copies to Lionne, September 27, 1659 [pub. in *Lettres du cardinal Mazarin où l'on voit le secret de la négociation de la Paix des Pyrénées* (Amsterdam, 1693), pt. 2, 148–154, incorrectly dated]. More Chevreuse: See the letter of the 27th just cited and BNF Ms *Mél. Col.* 52b, fol. 217, Mazarin (Russereau minute) to Mme de Chevreuse, September 28, 1659, AAEMD *France* 281, fol. 193, Mazarin (copy) to Claude Avry, October 17, 1659 [pub. in LM IX, 375–376]. Treaty of Pyrenees: Henry Vast, *Les Grands traités du règne de Louis XIV* (Paris, 1893–99), I, 93–167. Alsace and Haguenau: AD *Haut-Rhin* 2929.

27. Bodleian Library, *Calendar of Clarendon State Papers* (Oxford, 1869–1970), III, 417, 421, and 516. Charles to Monck, July 11 (21), 1659, in Richard Baker, *A Chronicle of the Kings of England* (London, 1684), 651. John Evelyn, *Memoirs illustrative the life and writings of John Evelyn . . . comprising his diary from the year 1641 to 1705–6, and a selection of his familiar letters* (London, 1827), II, 148–149.

6. A Tale of Two Families

1. Georges Rivals, "Les Conditions économiques et sociales de la Réforme dans le Bas-Languedoc," *Cahiers d'histoire et archéologie*, XIII (1938), 41–66. Albert Puech, *La Renaissance*

et la Réforme à Nîmes (Nîmes, 1883). BNF Ms. Fr. 4102, fols. 121–122. The *Estat des deniers que le Roy veut et entend estre payez pour la solde des gens de guerre, estats et entretenement de gouverneurs estans en garnison es viles et places baillées en garde à ceux de la Religion pretendue refformée* . . . *Rennes, 14 may 1598* gives exactly forty-eight. Jouanna Arlette, *La France du XVIe siècle* (Paris, 1996).

2. Mathellin Roux, spelled variously "Matelin," "Maturin," and "Mathurin" and signing himself as "MR": For a clear identification of MR compare AD Gard 2 E 1/289 (Jean Ursi le jeune), August 31, 1596, AD Gard 2 E 1 /291 (Jean Ursi le jeune), May 10 and 31 and September 13, 1597, AD Gard 2 E 1/292 (Jean Ursi le jeune), January 31 and March 25, 1598, with ibid., March 30, 1598, and with Jeanne Rousse to her father in AD Gard 2 E 39/124 (Isaac Barre), April 19, 1608. Claude Roux–Anne Pepine marriage: The original act was in AD Gard 2 E 57/55 (Solignac, notary of St Hyppolite), July 16, 1611, but it is now accessible only through the notation in AD Gard 1 E 424 (old E 1274). Etienne Pepin: AD Gard 2 E 216/2, born November 28, 1574. Anne Pepine: AD Gard 2 E 216/ 2, born December 24, 1591. Claude Roux as merchant: AD Gard 2 E 39/324 (Isaac Barre), April 19, 1608. His children—Claude (*female*) Roux: AD Gard UU 94, fol. 240, born May 2, 1612. Jean Roux: AD Gard UU 94, fol. 384, born January 21, 1614. Etienne Roux: AD Gard UU 95, fol. 4, born April 18, 1616. Jeanne Rousse: AD Gard UU 95, fol. 101, born December 24, 1618. Deceased: AD Gard UU 118, fol. 218, June 5, 1620. Claude Roux: AD Gard UU 95, fol. 210, born June 1, 1622. Antoine Roux: AD Gard UU 95, fol. 300, born October 30, 1625. Catherine Roux: AD Gard UU 95, fol. 349, born February 18, 1628. Claude Roux as Consul (1631): See Léon Ménard, *Histoire civile, ecclésiastique et littéraire de la ville de Nismes* (Paris, 1758), VI, 37. This was the very year that the king restructured the consulate in Nîmes (beginning in 1632) to make it more favorable to the Catholics. Jean Roux–Isabeau de Philip contract: AD Gard 2 E 10/857 (Durand, notary of Sommières), June 10, 1638, and marriage: AD Gard UU 97, fol. 9, July 18, 1638. Emancipation: AD Gard 2E 39/335 (Paul Barre), October 23, 1638. Jean and Etienne as merchants: Ibid., January 20, 1639. Death of Isabeau: AD Gard 2E 37/117 (Ducros), fols. 218–220, May 17 1639. If one consults Aimé-Daniel Rabinel's *La Tragique aventure de Roux de Marcilly* (Toulouse, 1969) one will observe that he ignores many of the sources that I bring forward in this book.

3. Picons in La Figère: AD Ardeche 2 E 21869 (Desaufres), *Commᵒⁿ passée entre Mʳ estienne Picon p~ticien d une part et anthoine La balme tuteur de feu anthoine Picon d aûe*, January 4, 1588. The claim of marriage between Pierre Picon "escuyer" and Jeanne Dalmeras in 1593 in the proofs of nobility cited in cited in ch. 8 note 22 is dubious and I have been able to identify neither the locality nor the notary. Pierre Picon and Jeanne Almerasse appear to have had two sons, Antoine and Georges (see the dubious proofs of nobility), prior to having a third, Henry, in 1612, which is documented in AD Ardeche, Baptêmes, Mariages, Sépultures (1612–1695), and a daughter, Jeanne. In the baptismal record, Pierre is not styled with any title. Marriage of Jacques Coste and Hélipse Plantier: AD Gard 2 E 4/51 (Froment), at Portes March 16, 1608. AD Gard 2 E 16/283 (Vincent), testament of the elder Jacques Coste of September 26, 1617. I can only find the marriage of Georges Picon to Alix de Coste without indication of place or notary in the dubious proofs of nobility. However in AD Gard 2 E 16/285 (Vincent), June 24, 1623, Georges Picon purchases a two-story home in Rivières, presumably for himself and his new wife. AD Gard 2 E 16 /285 (Vincent), Procuration, identifying Georges Picon as brother of Pierre, still in La Figère and uncle of Georges Picon, who is given the power of attorney, December 6, 1623. My only source for the date and place of birth of Antoine-Hercule Picon is Clément *LIM Colbert* IV, 334. However, for the ages of the rest of his children I have AD Gard *Rivières* 201, which contains parish registers as well as two indispensable lists of parishioners the second of which is titled *Roosle de tous les paroissiens de rivieres* and which I date for 1654. AN K 572, Nᵒˢ 35–36, Budos-Crussol Marriage contract (October 28, 1626), Nᵒ 37: Celebration of

Marriage (March 24, 1627). See also Jean-Bernard Elzière's excellent *Histoire des Budos Seigneurs de Budos en Guyenne et de Portes-Bertrand en Languedoc* (Jean-Bernard Elzière, 1978).

4. Jean Roux in Paris: See AD *Hérault* 2 E 55/127 (Laune), December 19, 1651, which seems to place Jean Roux in Paris earlier than March 4, 1642. See also AN MC XXIV/421 (Chapelain), July 8, 1642, MC XXIV/423 (Chapelain), October 22, 1643, along with two other acts signed by Jean Roux. Claude Roux in army: AD Gard C 647, pp. 1023–1040. Revue, dated August 5, 1642, has a Claude Roux as coming from Beaucaire, pp. 1059–1086, other copy also dated August 5, 1642, titled *Departement des dix Compagnies du Regiment de Nismes* has the name Claude Roux crossed out. Charles Chappuzeau, *De la justice et de la paix, de l'injustice de la guerre; de l'injustice et fin luctueuse des guerres Civiles & Etrangeres; Et qu'il n'y a rien au monde plus desirable que la Paix* (Paris, 1627). Marriage of Jean Roux and Marie Chappuzeau; AN Y 183, October 21, 1643; December 18, 1643; and February 3, 1644. Charles Chappuzeau as Condé's lawyer: Samuel Chappuzeau, *Entretiens familiers pour l'instruction de la noblesse étrangère* (Paris and Geneva, 1665, 1671), 328. Enghien in Catalonia: AC M XXVII, fols. 182–183, Duke d'Enghien (own hand letter sent) to Prince de Condé, Narbonne, April 14, 1642.

5. Charles de Saint-Simon-Louise de Crussol marriage: AN MC XVI /342 (Le Cat), which may contain minute of the contract, signed on September 11, 1634, is not communicable. The marriage took place on September 14 according to the *Gazette* N° 99, September 23, and was registered at the *Châtelet* on September 27, according to AN K 572 N° 33 and Y 175, fols. 152–153. See also Jal, 1137. The act designates Emanuel de Crussol as *chevalier d'honneur* and Louise as *dame d'honneur* of Anne of Austria. Georges Picon in Portes: Mairie de Portes 1 CC 1–3, *Compoix de Portes, 1640*, where he is identified as "Regent." Both Georges and Gabriel Picon in Rivières: AD Gard *Rivières* 201, Registre des Baptesmes en L Egl[ise] Paroiss[ale] de St Privas de Rivieres: "*Ce xxiiii mai 1643 . . . Son parrin Mre George Picon Regent dans le marquisat de portes . . . L an mil six cens quarante quatre et le Septiesme jour du mois de fevrier . . . son parrain a esté Gabriel Picon.*" AD Gard 2 E 16/300 (Pouzols), Georges Picon, regent of Theyrargues, concerning sale of a dovecote, February, 27, 1644. This same volume has over thirty-eight acts signed by Saint-Simon and George Picon, mainly *arrentements*, May 16, 1644, to May 31 1644. As a further indication of how Antoine-Hercule got to Paris, see his marriage contract signed by Saint-Simon cited in ch. 8 note 13. For the time at which Antoine-Hercule began working for Colbert, see the exact recollection in Colbert to Mazarin of October 28, 1659, cited in note 25 below.

6. Claude Roux in Chilleurs: AD Loiret 3 E 10008 (François Bonhomme), February 3 and 23, 1644, two acts, the first of which mentions the servant. Claude Roux violence: Loiret 3 E 10038 (Hüet), September 10, 1644. Charles d'Aumale-Haucourt Seigneur de Chilleurs: GAH 28 (Pieck), fol. 306, November 6, 1644. See also AD Loiret 3 E 10039 (Hüet), July 16 and especially July 22, 1648, which employs Charles's procuration of April 7, 1648 to his brother Nicolas. Charles died in 1652 as is apparent from GAH 170 (Rietraet), fol. 128, May 27, 1652.

7. For Charles de Saint-Simon's relations with Mazarin, begin with AAEMD *France* 848, fols. 242–243, Charles de Saint-Simon (own hand letter sent) to Mazarin, January 6, 1645. For the Augers in Senlis see AD Oise 1 Mi/ECA 612 R 11 (Paroisse Saint-Martin), Michel d'Auger as a godfather at a baptism, April 20, 1615, *EDT* 1/GG 72 (Paroisse Saint-Aignan), fol. 21, the burial of Jehan Augier "manouvrier," July 12, 1649, 2 E 287/5 (Desaintlieu); N° 2/210, where Marie Flamen, widow of Jean Auger apprentices her son Jean Auger to a hatmaker, July 18, 1649. In *EDT* 1/GG 73 (Paroisse Saint-Aignan), the father is posthumously referred to on April 22, 1652, as "compagnon masson" for the engagement of his son, Jehan (*sic*) Auger, who is now a hatmaker, with his name spelled Jehan Auge (or Augé) and getting married on May 2. In the same register, on November 18, 1652, the father is referred to as "feu Jehan Hauger" and as "masson" in the marriage of his daughter Catherine. And in the same register, on October

3, 1654, the son "Jehan Augé" remarries. According to 1 Mi/B356 (Paroisse Saint-Agnan) Catherine dies in 1656. In AD Oise 1 Mi/B 359 (Paroisse Notre Dame), a Laurent Auger is baptizing Françoise Angelique Boudrau on April 24, 1659, while on June 29 and July 6 and 13 he is publishing his marriage vows, with his name spelled "Augé." Also in AD Oise 1 Mi/ ECA 612 R11 (Paroisse Saint-Martin) we have the baptism of "Philippes Ogier" son of "Martin Ogier" on January 17, 1645. EDT 1/GG73 (Eglise Saint-Aignan) we have Jehan (sic) Auger, now a hatmaker, getting engaged on April 22, 1652 and, with his name spelled Jehan Auge (or Augé), getting married on May 2. In the same register, on October 11, 1654, with his name spelled "Jean Auger," he is remarrying.

8. Bankruptcy of Jean Roux: AN V⁶ 192, November 29, 1644. Sale of wood: AD Loiret 3 E 10008 (François Bonhomme), March 18, 1645. Death of Claude Roux senior: AD Gard UU 119, fol. 79, January 19, 1647. We have an interesting act, originally drawn up by the notary Fieffé, which shows Marie Chappuzeau as separated in property from her husband Jean, still, however working with him on June 27, 1647, the minute of which is currently in AN MC CVII/97 (Moufle), September 5, 1661. Crommelin-Rode marriage: AD Gard 2 E 39/336, (Barre), December 23, 1647. Jean Roux in Chilleurs: AD Loiret 3 E 10009 (François Bonhomme), April 9, 1648. Claude Roux–Marie Chalamel wedding: AD Gard UU 97, fol. 119, February 24, 1649 and AD Drôme 2 E 15686 (Bon), March 6, 1649. Roux's limited wealth in Montélimar emerges in his marriage contract and in AD Drôme 2E 15672 (Brey-nat). Investiture with Claude Roux as witness, April 14, 1649, 2E 15686 (Bon), April 17, 1649, acknowledgment of 221 livre debt to Claude Roux, with payment recorded August 21, 2E 15686 (Bon), April 26, 1649, acceptance of 500 livres in cash and goods belonging to his wife's dowry. Setting up of Society (May 20, 1651): recalled in AD Gard 2 E 37/163 (Privat), Cession et Remission au Sʳ Claude Roux, September 14, 1651, accepted by Claude Roux on the 16th. His legal troubles begin almost immediately and may be followed in AD Vaucluse B 43 (Parrlement d' Orange), 147 and 43. Espinasse–Laubre wedding: AD Drôme 2 E 15689 (Bon), fols. 45–47, January 5, 1653.

9. AAEMD France 848, fols. 242–243, Claude de Saint-Simon (own hand letter sent) to Mazarin, January 6, 1646, France 267, fols.123–124, Mazarin (copy) to Claude de Saint-Simon, February 28, 1650, BNF Ms. Fr 25025, fols. 177, 215, 218 and 222, news letters of March 4 and May 13, 20, and 27, 1650, BMaz 2216, fols. 444–445, AN KK 1221, fol. 296, and BMaz 2216, fols. 444, 445, Mazarin (copy) to Claude de Saint Simon, May 26, 1650 [pub. in LM III, 541–544], BNF Ms. Fr. 4208, fols. 41–42, Mazarin (copy) to Le Tellier, June 18, 1650 [extract in LM III, 563–564 misfoliated], BNF Ms. Fr. 25025, fols. 252–254, July 15, 1650, BNF Ms. Fr. 6883, fols. 205–206 Mazarin (letter sent) to Le Tellier, July 26, 1650 (copy in BNF Ms. Fr. 4208, fols. 126–129 [pub. in LM III, 625–629], BNF Ms. Fr. 25025, fols. 264, 281–284, and 293, news letters of August 5 and 26 and September 9, 1650. AAEMD France 888, fols. 388–390, Claude de Saint-Simon (own hand letter sent) to Servien, December 23, 1652, and AAEMD France 891, fols. 136–137, Claude de Saint-Simon (own hand letter sent) to Servien, May 23, 1653. For Picon's continuing connection with the Saint-Simons, see his marriage contract in ch. 8 note 13.

10. AD Gard LL 23 (Registres des délibérations du conseil de Nîmes), fols. 75–77. Actions by Council of State: AN E 1700, fols. 457–460, August 31, 1653. Ruvigny compromise: AN E 1700, fols. 534–535, Arrest pour Vals envoye par M. de Ruvigny, October 2, 1653. See also Elie Benoist, Histoire de l'Edit de Nantes (Delf, 1693–1695) III, 162–163. For the revolt in Nîmes, beware of Aimé-Daniel Rabinel, "Le Mouvement protestant contre l'impôt à Nîmes en 1653: Jean Roux frère ainé de Roux de Marcilly," Bulletin de la Société de l'Histoire du Protestantisme Français (1968), 33–65. Ravenel, who has now gotten to more documents in the AD Gard, has not used them to identify two Jean Roux in Nîmes, nor is he aware of the evidence from the

AN, AD Loiret, Drôme, and Vaucluse which invalidates his claim. The Thurloe State Papers, cited in the bibliography, contain numerous reports on the troubles in the Vivarais and Nîmes in volumes 1 and 2, which cover this period.

11. Legal troubles in Orange: AD Vaucluse B 43 (*Parlement d'Orange*), fols. 738–741. Fictitious cession: Acknowledged in AD Gard 2E 1/440 (Pepin), fols. 359–360, June 2, 1653. See also AD Vaucluse B 147 (*Parlement d' Orange*), fols. 864–870, October 2, 1653, where Claude Roux failed to appear in his case against de Laurens and Roux's lawyer stated he was no longer representing him.

12. Georges Picon in Rivières: AD Gard *Rivieres*, cited in note 5, passim. Antoine-Hercule and Gabriel at court: BNF Ms. *Baluze* 216, fols. 257–258, Rose (own hand letter sent) to Colbert du Terron, September 10, 1653. Amazing document: See the Le Bas *Compte* cited in ch. 7 note 22. See also AN XCV (Le Fouyn), Repertory 1 under November 19 and December 28, 1653, two *procurations* in which Picon acts for Cardinal Mazarin, for which we no longer have the minutes. Moreover, Terron's letter to Jean-Baptiste Colbert of March 1, 1656, cited in note 17 below, gives some excellent examples of Picon's acting as a treasurer between May 24 1654 and September 10, 1653. Picon acts: AN MC XCV /23 (Le Fouyn), March 27 and April 18, 1654.

13. First appearance of Berryer: See AN MC XCV (Le Fouyn), Repertory 1 under December 29, 1653, a *procuration* in which Berryer acts for Jean-Baptiste Colbert for which we no longer have the minute. Girardins: Colbert to Mazarin of January 2, 1653 cited in ch. 3 note 14, AAEMD *France* 891, fol. 156, copy of a portion of a letter from Servien to Mazarin, July 19, 1653, fols. 157–158, Mazarin (minute) to Colbert, July 19, 1653 (letter sent in sec. and Mazarin's own hand, PS in BNF Ms. *Baluze* 216, fols. 232–235) [pub. in *LM* V, 642–645]. Unsuccessful contracts: AN MC XCV/25 (Le Fouyn), Contracts on Grand Selve and Moissac before Toulouse notary Jonquet on June 6, 1654. Offer to Girardin: AAEMD *France* 893bis, fols. 77–79, Servien (letter sent) to Mazarin, June 19, 1654. Le Bas: AAEMD *France* 891, fols. 261–262 and 270–271, Claude Auvry (own hand letter sent) to Mazarin, October 21 and 26, 1653. Mariage: AN MC XCV/23, June 27, 1654. In Mazarin's council: BL: *Egerton Ms*. 1902–1903.

14. *Declarations* [June 12 and September 27, 1649, April 30 and July 1 1654] *du Roy pour la fabrication en ce Royaume des Liards de cuivre, valans trois deniers et Décry des Doubles & Deniers qui ont eu cours iusques à present, à l'exception des Deniers qui ont esté faits par ordre de sa Majesté, Certifiées en la Cour de Monnoyes le 7 Aoust & premier Octobre 1649, 3 Juin & 11 Juillet 1654* (Paris, 1654) (Lyon, 1654). Jean Roux in court: AD Vaucluse B 148 (*Parlement d' Orange*), fols. 248–250, October 31, 1654.

15. For Morland's mission, see, *TSP* III, IV, and V. For the citation, see Pell to Thurloe, June 9/19, 1655, pub. in Robert Vaughan, *The Protectorate of Oliver Cromwell and the State of Europe during the Early Part of the Reign of Louis XIV* (London, 1839) I, 192–196. At no point in their correspondence do either Pell or Morland make the slightest mention of Claude Roux.

16. Jean Roux in Orange AD *Vaucluse* 3 E 51/210 (Turc), July 5, 1655, *Procuraòn pour Guillaume donnadieu au Sr Jean Roux*. Currency manipulation: *Edict pour la fabrication de nouvelles especes d'or et d'argent appellées lys, et pour le décry des espèces d'or et d'argent tant de France qu'estrangeres* . . . December 1655 and AN E 1704, fols. 9–10, *Arrêt* of February 1, 1656. Jean Roux in Corbeil: AN Z^{1b} 342, fols. 3–5 *Estat faict a Jean Roux procureur d Isaac Blandin . . . depuis le iiiie Janvier 1656 jusques au xxviie juillet aud~ an* and . . . *depuis le dernier Juillet 1656 Jusques au trentie~ decembre aud~ an* and *depuis Neuf Janvier 1657 Jusques a la fin de lad~ année*. Claude out of Orange: AD Drôme B 708, *Inventaire general des papiers du greffe royal de la presente ville de Mon^ar Sentences de l'année 1656* "Noble Phelipes Guilhaume de Laurent Contre Claude Roux." Dissentions in Nîmes: AN E 1706 N° 11, fols. 23–24, February 11, 1656 and N° 27, fols. 59–61. On the *liards* in Nîmes see especially AN E 1706 N° 60, fols. 172–173, *arrêt* of August 19, 1656.

Condé and *liards*: AC P XVI, fols. 49–50, 174–177, 201–202, 257–258, 283–284, 334–335. Pierre Caillet to Jacques Caillet February 2, May 12 and 29, July 21 and 30, August 11 and 30, and September 19, 1656.

17. Quittance for Le Normant: AN MC XCV/23 (Le Fouyn), October 31, 1654. Saint-Denis: XCV /24 (Le Fouyn), May 25, 1655. Saint-Medard: XCV /24 (Le Fouyn), September 28, 1655. Quittances signed by Picon: XCV/24 (Le Fouyn), November 8, and 24, 1655. Election of Sables: See BNF Ms. *Mél. Col.* 101, fols. 13–14, Colbert du Terron (letter sent) to Jean-Baptiste Colbert, February 1, 1656. Posters for salt: BNF Ms. *Mél. Col.* 101, fols. 15–16, Terron (letter sent) to J-B Colbert, February 9, 1656. Quittance by Picon: AN MC XCV/24, February 22, 1656. His rising status: BNF Ms. *Mél. Col.* 101, fols. 22–24, Terron (letter sent) to J-B Colbert, March 1, 1656. Picon and Rode: Ms. *Mél. Col.* 101, fols. 33–34, Terron (letter sent) to J-B Colbert, March 8, 1656. Picons, Rode, and taxes: Ms. *Mél. Col.* 101, fols. 47–50, Terron to J-B Colbert, May 18, 1656 with J-B's response of May 23. Waiting for Gabriel: BNF Ms. *Mél. Col.* 101, fols. 51–53, Terron to J-B Colbert, May 21, 1656 with J-B's reassurance on May 27. See also fols 64–65, Terron to J-B Colbert, July 26, 1656, with J-B's reply of August 4.

18. First letter to Picon: BNF Ms. *Mél Col.* 51, fol. 218, Mazarin (Roussereau minute) to Picon, September 1, 1656. Transport signed by Picon: AN MC XCV/24, September 21, 1656. See also BNF Ms. *Mél. Col.* 101, fols. 77–80, Colbert duTerron (letter sent) to Jean-Baptiste Colbert, December 2, 1656, with J-B's answer, undated. Convention signed by Picon: ANMC XCV/24, December 3, 1656. Gabriel Picon in Sables d'Olonne: BNF Ms.*Mél. Col.* 101, fols. 81–82, Terron to J-B Colbert, December 18, 1656 with J-B's marginal reply of December 24. Loan to Duke of Mantova: AN MC XCV/24 (Le Fouyn), December 29, 1656.

19. Rode's contract in La Rochelle is mentioned in his contract with Picon, which is in AN MC XCV/25 (Le Fouyn), Declaraòn, May 12, 1657. Association over the *taille*: See the interrogatory cited in note 23 below.

20. Berryer nomination: AN MC XCV/24 (Le Fouyn), November 4, 1653. For him and Béchamel, see François Dornic, *Une ascension sociale au xviie siècle: Louis Berryer, agent de Mazarin et de Colbert* (Caen, 1968), 53. Death of Jobart: AAEMD *France* 901, fol. 96, Mazarin (letter sent with Mazarin's own hand last paragraph) to Colbert, July 2, 1656 [extract pub. in Cosnac, *Mazarin et Colbert*, II, 86, dated 3rd]. Girardins in La Rochelle: J-B's reply to Terron of May 18, 1656, cited in note 17 above. Girardins in Normandy: See the *Estat des biens for 1656*, cited in ch. 5 note 22. One year contract: AN MC XCV/25 (Le Fouyn), June 1, 1656. A copy of the contract from 1657 to 1659 is attached to the contract of December 23, cited below. Kidnapping of Girardin: BNF Ms. *Baluze* 176, fols. 289–290, Colbert (letter sent) to Mazarin, May 27, 1657, with Mazarin own hand response of May 30. Condé on Girardin: AC P XVII, fols. 301–302, Condé (letter sent) to Auteuil, August 8, 1657. Search for new administrator: AN MC/XCV/25 (Le Fouyn), November 2, 1657, Bail for Pierre Gervaison, backed by Odoart de Gomont, for Grand Selve and Moissac "avant midi," replaced by a procuration for Gomont to administer the temporal revenue of the same benefices and choose any subodinates, dated "apres midi" same day. MC/XCV/25 (Le Fouyn), November 6, 1657, Procurations for Odoart de Gomont one for Grand Selve and one for Moissac. MC/XCV/25 (Le Fouyn), December 23, 1657, *Traité Mr Girardin*. Orders to visit Fouquet: AAEMD *France* 275, fols. 67–68, Mazarin (Rose hand) to Picon, October 1, 1657 with copy of reply, undated. Paying off debtors of Duke of Mantua by Picon: MC CX/134 (Le Moyne), October 18, 1657, AAEMD *France*, fols. 74–77, Fouquet (letter sent) to Mazarin, October 5, 1657, with Mazarin's (own hand reply) of October 26. Disboursement for Soissons: BNF NAF 22874, fols. 5–6, November 27, 1657.

21. Closing of mints: The Blandin *registres* cited in note 16 above go only to the end of 1657. Devaluations: AN E 313b, fols. 497–498 (May 25, 1658), printed as *Arrest du Conseil d'Etat portant reglement sur le fait des liards* (Paris, 1658), AN E 314a (June 1, 1658), printed

as *Arrêt du Conseil d'Etat du Roy portant interpretaions de celuy du 25 may dernier pour le regle-ment sur le fait des liards* (Paris, 1658). AAEMD *France* 275, fols. 251–252, Fouquet (copy) to Mazarin, June 9, 1658, with copy of Mazarin's reply of June 15 on left hand margin [extract in LM VIII, 426–428]. AN AD⁺ 340, printed *Arrest du Conseil d'Etat du Roy par lequel Sa Majesté veut que les liards n'aient cours que pour deux deniers seulement du 20 juin 1658*, printed *Arrêt du conseil d'Etat du Roy par lequel sa Majesté ordonne que les liards n'auront cours que pour un denier seulement . . . Du 20 Juillet 1658* (Paris, 1658) followed by *Tres haute remonstrance au roy par les six corps des marchands de la ville de Paris sur le fait des liards* (s.l.n.d.), which seems to result in AN E 1708, fol. 239 (August 3, 1658), published as *Arrêt du Conseil d'Etat du Roy par lequel Sa Majesté ordonne que les liards auront cours par tout le royaume pour deux deniers* (Paris, 1658). Rode in La Rochelle: AD *Charente-Maritime*, 3E 315, fol. 58 (Demontreau), May 7, 1658. Dis-appearance of Roux: AD *Loiret* 3E 10013 (Pierre Bonhomme), October 12, 1659, in which Jean de Brachou Seigneur de Marcilly rents the *mestairie* of Marcilly in the parish of Chilleurs to a Pierre Tellars *laboureur*. For Roux's connection with the wine merchants of Brugge, compare the case involving the ship *Sᵗᵉ Godeliefve* in PRO HCA 30/179 and 873 with Roux's appeals to Bennet on behalf of its owners in *SPD* (Charles II) 29/187, N° 103, undated [calendared in CSPD (Charles II) VI, 423, tentatively but incorrectly dated for 1666] and *SPF* 78/125, fol. 159, Roux (own hand note) to Bennet (Earl of Arlington), January 7/17, 1669 [pub. in Ravais-son *AB* VII, 307 and Rabinel, 168–169].

22. Receipt: AN MC XCV/25 (Le Fouyn), *Quittance generale*, May 1, 1658. The sale of the office is not in the minutes, but the act, which again identifies Picon as the Sieur de La Farelle, is listed in BNF Ms. *Mél. Col.* 75 (Mazarin's *IAD*), fols. 663–664. We also get the description of the sale of the office from AN M C XCV/10 (Le Fouyn), the *Declaration* of July 31, 1658. See also the *Estat des biens* of 1658, cited in ch. 5 note 25. Gabriel Picon in Sables: BNF Ms. *Mél. Col* 101, fols. 136–137 and 140–143, Colbert du Terron (letters sent) to Jean-Baptiste Colbert, with replies of March 17 and 31. Bankruptcy of Hache: Ms. *Mél. Col.* 101, fols. 268–271, Ter-ron (letter sent) to J-B, September 9, 1658, with reply of September 21.

23. Mission to Libourne: BNF Ms. *Baluze* 331, fols. 137–138 and 145–148, Colbert (letters sent) to Mazarin, July 9 and 13, 1659, BNF Ms. *Fr.* 7627, fols. 72–86 *Roole de plusʳˢ parties et Sommes de Deniers Que le Roy a commandé . . . payer, Voyages*, fol. 76, July 14, 1659. Arrest of Hache: BArsenal Ms.10330, fols. 113–114, Louis (*lettre de cachet* countersigned by Le Tellier) to Besmaux, July 28, 1659. The interrogatory of this case originally in AN Xᶦᵇ 9440 is no longer there, so I can only cite it from Ravaisson *AB* I, 180–199.

24. Picon's man: BNF Ms. *Baluze* 331, fols. 214–217, Colbert (letter sent) to Mazarin, Sep-tember 3, 1659, with Mazarin's own hand response of September 12 [extract pub. in Clément *LIM Colbert* I, 367–368 without the relevant passage]. More on Picon: AN MC XCV/25 (Le Fouyn), September 4, 1659, purchase of the Acts of the Apostles from Jacques Le Normant by Gilles Petit, who declares he has done it for Mazarin by order of Colbert and has been paid by Picon. See also, *Baluze* 331, fols. 218–231, Colbert (letter sent) to Mazarin, September 7, 1659, with Mazarin's own hand response of September 18, telling Colbert that if he goes to Nevers, he can leave Picon in Paris to forward anything that Lescot will give him for Mazarin.

25. See Colbert's letter of October 1, 1659, with Mazarin's reply cited in ch. 3 note 24. For Colbert's revealing reply see BNF Ms. *Fr.* 10249, fols. 8–9, Colbert's (own hand minute) to Mazarin, October 28, 1659 [pub. in Champollion-Figeac II, 604 and Clément *LIM Colbert* I, 390–394]. For the positive identification, see Colbert to Mazarin, January 4, 1660, pub. in Clé-ment, *LIM Colbert* VII, 183–188.

26. Demand for new ratification: ASM AG 686, fols. 358–359, Sannazaro (letter sent) to Ottavio Gonzaga, December 17, 1660. Summons to "St. Lazzare": BN *NAF* 22874, fols. 16–17

(clerk's hand with Le Fouyn in bold), January 12, 1661. Softening of Picon: ASM AG 686 fols. 419–420, Sannazaro (letter sent) to Ottavio Gonzaga, February 25, 1661.

27. Georges: AD E 409a cited in ch. 8 note 22, *"conseiller et maître d'hôtel ordinaire du roi, commissaire général des armées, et maître de requêtes de la reine."* For the last see BNF Ms. Fr. 7834, fols. 300–301 (pp. 2558–2617), Ms. Fr. 7856 (pp 1591–1642), BNF Ms. Clair. 837 (pp. 3613–3718) [pub. in Griselle, 116, which I cite in my bibliography]. Antoine-Hercule: The *Estat nouveau de la France dans sa perfection* (Loyson 1661) lists under "ESTAT DE LA MAISON de la Reine de France" p. 34. *"Deux Secretaires du Conseil:* M. Picon and M. Macé and Un Soliciteur d'affaires M. Mariage." The same is under "L'Estat de la France nouvellement corrigé & mis en meilleur ordre" (Loyson, 1663), p. 299, which also lists on p. 345, Picon (obviously A-H) as one of "Deux secrétaires du conseil" at 400 *livres*, and adds Georges Picon as a *maître des requêtes* of the queen.

7. The Testament of Cardinal Mazarin

1. Illness of 1635: Aubery I, 68, of 1644: ASVen *Francia* 101 N° 55 I, Nani to Doge, October 4, 1644 (transcript in BNF Ms. It. 1823, fols. 14–16), Motteville P&M ser. 2 XXXVII, 120 or M&P ser. 2 X, 82–83, Aubery I, 241. Crises of 1650 and 1651: AAEMD *France* 874, fols. 136–137, Vautier (own hand letter sent) to Mazarin, March 2, 1651, AAEMD *France* 878, fols. 184–185, Mazarin (copy) to Roger du Plessis-Liancourt, June 2, 1651, and Mazarin to Anne, July 20, 1651, pub. in Ravenel *LMR*, 199–203. Difficult recovery: Mazarin to Anne, January 17, 1652, pub. in Ravenel *LMR*, 483–484 and AAEMD *France* 884, fols. 133–134, Vallot (own hand letter sent) to Mazarin, August 27, 1652. Recurrences: BNF Ms. *Baluze* 216, fols. 281–282, Mazarin (own hand letter sent) to Colbert, October 5, 1653 and fols. 283–284, Rose (own hand letter sent) to Colbert, October 9, 1653, BNF Ms. Fr. 9357, fols. 146–147 and 154, Patin (own hand letters sent) to Spon, March 6 and June 2, 1654, pub. in Patin R-P, II, 118–122, misdated, and 138–141, misplaced, and Patin Jestaz, 1193–1198 and 1225–1227, AAEMD *France* 893bis, fol. 34, anonymous letter to Mazarin, May 6, 1654, *TSP* II, 246, *A Letter of Intelligence from Mr. Augier's Secretary*, April 29/May 8, 1654, AAEMD *France* 292, fol. 23, Mazarin to Anne, August 7, 1655. Reported in *Gazette* N° 146 of October 30, 1655, Patin to Spon, November 2, 1655, pub. in Patin R-P II, 217–219, AAEMD *France* 896, fols. 247–248, Mazarin (copy) to Anne, November 16, 1655 (other copy in *France* 272, fol. 64). Deteriorating health: Patin to Falconet, March 26, 1657, pub. in Patin R-P III,71–73. Motteville P&M ser. 2 XXXVI, 418 or M&P ser. 2 X, 461, AAEMD *France* 274, fol. 73, Mazarin (minute) to Nicolas Fouquet, October 16, 1657 [extract pub. in *LM*, VIII, 365–367 w/o reference to pains], BNF Ms. Fr. 9357, fols. 273–277, Patin (own hand letters sent) to Spon, October 22 and November 6, 1657 [November 6, pub. in Patin R-P II, 350–354]. Calais and Gravelines: BNF Ms. *Baluze* 331, fols. 145–148, Colbert (letter sent) to Mazarin, July 13, 1659 with Mazarin's own hand reply from Bidache, July 23, AAEMD *France* 905, fols. 286 and 305, Colbert (letters sent) to Mazarin, July 26 and August 3, 1658, with Mazarin replies of August 3 and 6. On the way to Saint-Jean-de-Luz: Compare BNF Ms. *Baluze* 331, fols. 166–167, Mazarin (sec. hand letter sent) to Colbert, July 26, 1659, with AAEMD *Espagne* 61, fols. 30–31 (and in numerous other copies of this set), Mazarin (copy) to Anne of Austria, Saint-Jean-de-Luz, August 2, 1659 [pub. in *LM PdeP* (1693), 17–19]. Return of illness: AG A¹ 162, fol. 365, Le Tellier to Grammont, August 20, 1660. Displacements: AAECP *Allemagne* 149, Mazarin (Lionne minute) to Gravel, September 3, 1660 (copy sent in *Allemagne* 148 [extract in *LM* IX, 642–644]. Gout in six places: Patin to Falconet, October 1, 5, and 8, 1660, pub. in Patin R-P III, 265–271. Lust

for life: AAEMD *France* 284, fol. 435, Mazarin (copy) to Grammont, August 25, 1660 [pub. in *LM* IX, 640]. Condition c. January 1661: Brienne LH, II, 32–33 and III, 85–86. Fire at Louvre: ASVen *Francia* 126 N° 104 I, Alvise Grimani to Senate, February 8, 1661 (transcript in BNF *Ms. It.*1849, fols. 261–263). Motteville P&M ser. 2 XL, 85 or M&P ser. 2 X, 501. Consultation: Patin to Falconnet, January 25, 1661, pub. in Patin R-P III, 312–315. See also the sections of the young Brienne's *Mémoires* cited in note 3 below. A modern physician: Sottas in his "Maladie et mort du Cardinal Mazarin," *Chronique médicale* (1925), 195–202, 227–230, 259–266, 291–300, 323–327, 355–362 and (1926), 1–9, agreed with contemporary doctors that Mazarin was suffering from the gout, but neither he nor they are taking into account the jaundice and the itching that Mazarin revealed in his letter of June 2, 1651, to Du Plessis-Liancourt, which suggest a disease of the liver.

2. Brienne's *Survivance*: AAEMD *France* 878, fols. 224–225, August 24, 1651, Louis-Henri only began putting together his *Mémoires* between 1676 and 1684 during his confinement in the monastic house of Saint Lazare, which took place between 1674 and 1692. We have them in two versions divided into three manuscripts. The first manuscript, which he began writing about 1678 and is in his own hand, is in the BNF *NAF* 6450. The second manuscript, a continuation of this version, is in a copy at the Bibliothèque Municipale d'Auxerre Ms. 102, and the second version is in the BNF *NAF* 4698. They are all and distinctly edited by Paul Bonnefon for the Société de l'Histoire de France (Paris, 1916, vols. I and II, 1–90), II, 91–354 and III, 1–270.

3. Brienne describes this memorable incident in both versions of his *Mémoires*, vol. I, 306–307 and vol. III, 88–90. In the second version he drops mention of his cousin, claims the letter was from Bordeaux, and quotes Mazarin verbatim. In vol. II, 29–30, Brienne helps us date the consultation. To the last years of Brienne's life I would also attribute a commentary on Mazarin's testament which I have found in BNF *Ms. Fr.* 11453. Brienne's clarity of mind is confirmed by the Abbot de Choisy, who visited him after his confinement and whose description in his *Mémoires* (P&M ser. 2 LXIII, 198–205 or M&P ser. 3 VI, 569–572) of Mazarin's testament and death is largely derived from what Brienne told him. Likewise, Antoine Aubery, the author of the most "official" *Histoire du cardinal Mazarin*, shows excellent knowledge of Mazarin's last days and of Text C of his will, though his interpretation of both is totally different to Brienne's. See Aubery, 597–623.

4. Amédée Renée, *Les Nièces de Mazarin* (Paris, 1856). The party had taken place in 1659 during Holy Week at Roissy. See Roger de Bussy Rabutin, *Mémoires de messire Roger de Rabutin, comte de Bussy* (Paris, 1696), II, 179–184 or in his *Mémoires* ed. Lalanne II, 89–94, Motteville P&M ser. 2 XL, 6–7 or M&P ser. 2 X, 476, and Georges Mongrédien, "La Grande débauche de Roissy," *Mercure de France* N° 1046 (October 1, 1950), 277–285. See also the exchanges between Charles and J-B Colbert over Philippe during his exile in Alsace in BNF *Ms. Mél. Col* 101, fols. 476–479 and BNF *Ms. Baluze* 178, fol. 10, June 8 and July 28, 1659, with J-B's own hand replies of June 20 and August 8 [only J-B's answers are published in LIM *Colbert* I, 346–347 and 354–355].

5. AGT (Bissaro's *Relazione distinta*) fol. 2 says 8th, BNF *Ms. Fr.*3949, fol. 233 says 7th, Joly's *Relation succinte* says 7th. See Darricau and Laurain-Portemer, "La Mort du cardinal Mazarin" in the *Annuaire-Bulletin de la Société de l'Histoire de France* (1958–59), 77 and 116. Motteville P&M ser. 2 XL, 88–89 or M&P ser. 2 X, 501–502. Futile purgations: Patin to Falconnet, February 13, 1661 [pub. in Patin R-P III, 332–333]. Projected will: ASVen *Francia* 127 N°ˢ 116 and 117, Alvise Grimani to Senate both of March 1, 1661 (transcript in BNF *Ms. It.* 1850, fols. 4–9). Fouquet visit: Fouquet, *Défenses (Suite de la continuation de la production de Mr Fouquet pour servir de réponse à celle de Mr Talon, sur le prétendu crime d'état à la fin de laquelle on a ajouté le troisième tome)*, IX, 12–13. Marriage contract: AN Y 199, fols. 266–268. Marriage: ASVat *Francia* 119, fols. 83–84 and 88–89, *Avvisi* of March 4, 1661. Ondedei officiating: Hermant IV, 608.

6. Temporary relief: Motteville P&M ser. 2 XL, 90 or M&P ser. 2 X, 502. The Brienne document is the commentary he attached to the copy of Text B of Mazarin's testament cited in note 17 below.

7. Early administration of extreme unction: ASVat *Francia* 119, fol. 90, Piccolomini (letter sent) to Cardinal Chigi, March 4, 1661, Motteville P&M ser. 2 XL 90 or M&P ser. 2 X, 502, Hermant IV, 611–613. For the copies of all the texts see note 17 below.

8. Card playing and jewel fondling: Hermant, IV, 612. Burying the Synagogue: Brienne LH II, 31 and III, 92. AGT (Bissaro's *Relazione distinta*) fol. 8 [pub. in Darricau and Laurain-Portemer, op. cit 101].

9. See below note 17.

10. The *Coustumes de la prevosté et vicomté de Paris* (Paris, 1660), Article CCXCVII, reads as follows: "Les executeurs testamentaires sont saisis durant l'an & jour du trespas du deffunct, des biens meubles demeurez de son decez pour l'accomplissement de son testament: si le relateur n'avoit ordonné, que ses executeurs fussent saisis de sommes certaines seulement. *Et est tenu ledit executeur de faire inventaire en diligence, si tost que le testament est venu à sa connoissance: l'heritier presomptif present ou deuëment apellé*" (italics mine).

11. Call for Joly: Hermant IV, 614–618. Tour of the gardens: Brienne LH, II, 31, which dates it precisely and III, 91–95, which is more sloppy. King's approval: Brienne LH, II, 36–37. Last days: BNF Ms. *Mél. Col.* 75 (Mazarin's *IAD*), fols. 39–40, Motteville P&M ser. 2 XL, 96–99 or M&P ser. 2 X, 504–505, Brienne LH, II, 34–36 and III, 94–95.

12. Brienne LH, II, 48–50.

13. Hour of death: Motteville, P&M ser. 2 XL, 99 or M&P scr. 2 X, 505. Joy of relatives: *Mémoires de Madame La Duchesse de Mazarin* (Cologne 1675), 20–21. Amusement of Brienne: Brienne LH, II, 51–52.

14. Brienne LH, II, 52–58. The council meeting was on the morning of the 9th. See Jean de Boislisle, *Mémoriaux du Conseil de 1661* (Paris, 1905–1907), I, 2.

15. See note 17 below and for a more technical demonstration, please see my "Three Testaments of Cardinal Mazarin," *French Historical Studies*, XXXVII 3 (Summer 2014), 421–436.

16. See the next note.

17. I have located seven copies of this "*Sommaire du Testament de M. le cardinal*": BNF Ms. Fr. 20162, fols. 329–333, Bibliothèque de l'Arsenal Ms. 3740, fols. 123–126, Bibliothèque de L'Université de Paris Ms.1201, fols. 11–13, and Bibliothèque Municipale d 'Aix Ms. 415, N° 2 plus AAEMD *France* 911, fols. 48–50, BNF Ms. *Mél. Col.* 103, fols. 548–551 and 542–544. These last three, which are in manuscripts assembled by Colbert, look like they derive from a copy that someone brought to him. I have also located the following copies of the testament: **TEXT A:** AAEMD *France* 911, fols. 53–59 (obtained by Colbert). Monaco S 7. BNF Ms. Fr. 20331, fols. 190–198 (coming from the congregation of Saint-Victor). BNF Ms. Fr. 4332, fols. 232–241 (coming from Philibert de La Mare). **TEXT B:** BNF *NAF* 22874 (two copies), fols. 41–56 and 33–40, the second without the brevet of March 6 (donated by Count Léon de La Borde in 1919). BNF Ms. Fr. 11453 (coming from the congregation of the Benedictins of Saint-Maur). BNF Ms. Fr.12801, fols. 37–45 (origin uncertain). Printed editions and translations of 1663, including the one in BNF Ms. Fr. 15604, fols. 168–193 (coming from Achille II de Harlay). BNF Ms. Fr. 9717, fols. 73–83 (origin uncertain). BNF Ms. *Clair.* 1144, fols. 171–182 (origin uncertain). BNF Ms. Fr. 10210. pp. 75–90 (origin uncertain). BArsenal Ms. 675, fols. 265–282 (Camus collection). BNF Ms. Fr. 10206, fols. 42–51 (origin uncertain). AN MC XCV /16 (origin uncertain). BNF Ms. Fr. 23347, fols. 374–389 (coming from President Jean Bouhier). BNF Ms. Fr. 6557, irregular foliation 171–180 (origin uncertain). **TEXT C:** BNF Ms. *Mél. Col.* 74, fols. 1–40 (Colbert's copy). *Oeuvres de Louis* XIV, ed. Grouvelle (Paris, 1806), VI, 292–345 (derived from the preceding). Copy published by the Count de Cosnac in

Mazarin et Colbert (Paris, 1892), II, 441–477, also derived from the first. AS Roma, Ufficio 18 (Francesco Pacichelli) vol. 388, fols. 354–368 (extracts concerning the succession of Philippe Mancini in Rome). BNF *Pièces originales* 1906 (two extracts concerning Philippe Mancini, at the request of the Duke de Mazarin furnished by Le Vasseur et Le Fouyn to Jacques Le Normant, notary, December 11 and 12, 1666, and printed by him). Monaco S 7 (two copies, one collated with no date, the other being a copy of a copy collated by Plastrier and de Beauvais, successor of Le Fouyn, January 17 1671, plus a third partial copy). Finally, in BNF *Ms. Dupuy* 858 there is one more copy collated by de Beauvais on March 9, 1673. I translate from Text A in AAEMD *France* 911, fols. 53–59, Text B in BNF *NAF* 22874, fols. 50–51 and Text C in BNF *Ms. Mél. Col.* 74, although the other copies of the same texts may vary slightly. For example, the Grouvelle edition mangles the name of Picon. We must also note that in Le Fouyn's repertory (AN MC XCV/95) Rep. 2, under the dates March 3, 6, and 7, 1661 we read:

> Act to which is attached the testament of His late Eminence, following which is the 1ˢᵗ codicil, both approved by His mᵗʸ by act which follows the said codicil with a Codicil also approved by His mᵗʸ by another act which follows that one, all bound together.

This suggests that this is a reference to Text A, or at the most Text B, because there is no mention of the brevet of March 18 on the occasion of the final reading of the testament before the king and the privileged parties. We should also note that on March 12 Le Vasseur and Le Fouyn made a true copy (*copie collationnée*) of the long testament and the first codicil, and on March 31 they made another true copy that incorporated all the portions, as indicated in *Mélanges Colbert* 74 and the Grouvelle edition. Thus since Text A contained the brevet of the 7th we can date the additions in the long testament and first codicil after the 7th and prior to the 12th and the shorter additions to the second codicil between the 12th and 18th. See also ASVen *Francia* 127 N° 139, Grimiani to Senate, March 29, 1661 (transcript in BNF *Ms. It.* 1850) where the Venetian ambassador writes, "Two versions are talked of, without actually knowing which is the true one." Choisy in his *Mémoires* (P&M ser. 2 LXIII, 199 or M&P ser. 3 VI, 570) reports, "On the 7th and 8th he made some change," but even if he did, he did it after the reading of Text A on the 7th.

18. Copy of king's order of March 29: BNF *Ms. Mél. Col.* 75 (Mazarin's *IAD*), fols. 3–4. First session of Inventory: Ibid. fols. 1–2.

19. The *Compte*, or report, of François Le Bas is in BNF *Ms. Mél. Col.* 74, fols. 46–383 and for the close collaboration between Le Fouyn, Le Bas, Berryer, and Picon see BNF *Ms. Mél. Col.*103, fols. 423–424, Le Fouyn (own hand letter sent) to Colbert, August 16, 1661, but there were many more things going on in the execution of the testament than meet the eye. For example, Fouquet later complained (see ch. 8 note 10) that his own credit had been used by Mazarin to purchase 300,000 *livres* worth of paintings from Jabec, which Mazarin in his testament then bequeathed to the king, expecting the testamentary executors to settle with the creditors, although there is no mention of this in either Texts A, B, or C and the activity of Jabec is independently confirmed by Brienne in his *Mémoires* I, 296. Also, the Duke de Mazarin later (see ch. 8 note 15) informed Denzil Holles that Mazarin had bequeathed a crystal ship to the Duchess d'Aiguillon and there is no mention of such a bequest in any of our copies.

20. BNF *Ms. Mél. Col.* 75 (Mazarin's *IAD*), fols. 39–41 and *Ms. Mél. Col.* 74 (Le Bas's *Compte*), fol. 66. Brienne in his *Mémoires* II, 48–49, reports that he later learned that there had been found nine million *livres* at Vincennes, five million at the Louvre, seven at the Bastille, eight at La Fère, and fifteen to twenty at Sedan and Breisach, which he believed had gone into the king's coffers. Choisy in his *Mémoires* (P&M ser. 2 LXIII, 200–201 or M&P ser. 3 VI, 570) gives five million for Sedan, two at Breisach, six at La Fère, and five or six at Vincennes.

21. **CHARLES I'S POSSESSIONS IN 1661 IAD:** Romano's *Saint Jerome*, purchased by Bordeaux for 1,500 *livres* in his letter of October 23, 1653, in 1661 *IAD* N°941 valued at 4,000 *livres*. Correggio's *Venus Satyr and Cupid* alias *The Beautiful Antiope* alias *Jupiter and Antiope*, possibly in the Somerset catalog (pub. in Cosnac *RPM*). N° 15 appraised at £80, purchased by Bordeaux for 4,000 to 6,000 *livres* in his letters of May 5, October 27, and December 11, 1653, cited in ch. 4 note 6, in the 1661 *IAD* N° 978 appraised at 5,000 *livres* and in the Louvre P 42. Correggio's *Torment of Marsyas*, acquired by Charles I from Duke of Mantua, purchased by Bordeaux in his letter of November 3, 1653, in the 1653 Inventory p. 344 appraised at 4,000 *livres*, in the 1661 *IAD* N° 994 also appraised at 4,000 *livres*, and in the Louvre Graphic Arts 5927. Sixteen pieces of the *History of David*; in the Somerset catalog there are twenty pieces valued at £6,500, Bordeaux deals for five pieces in his letters of March 10 and April 3 and 18, 1653, cited in ch. 4 note 6, sixteen pieces in the 1653 Inventory pp. 117–118, sixteen pieces in the 1661 *IAD* N° 1690 valued at 12,000 *livres*. Five pieces of the *Life and Passion of Jesus Christ*: There are thirty pieces in the Somerset catalog valued at £2,164—it is mentioned by Bordeaux in his letters of April 18, 1653, and February 23, March 16, April 16, September 4, and December 24, 1654, cited in ch. 4 note 6—five pieces are in the 1653 Inventory pp. 129–130 valued at 4,000 *livres*, five pieces in the 1661 *IAD* N° 1691 valued at 4,000 *livres* after Dürer. *Twelve Months of the Year*: there are six pieces in the Somerset catalog, six pieces in the 1653 Inventory p. 142, with "*chiffres*" of the King of England valued at 5,000 *livres*; the same six pieces are in the 1661 *IAD* N° 1700, with "*chiffres*" of the King of England valued at 5,000 *livres*. There are nine pieces from the *Acts of the Apostles* after Raphael in the Somerset catalog valued at £4,745, six pieces seized by *parlement* in 1652 valued at 13,100 *livres* in Colbert's letter of September 8, 1652, cited in ch. 4 note 6. Colbert in that letter suggests that some important person repurchase them for Mazarin, so these may be six of the seven pieces later in the hands of Servien. Bordeaux and Mazarin are searching for more pieces in letters of October 23 and November 17, 1653, also cited in ch. 4 note 6, yet there are only three pieces in the 1653 Inventory p. 129 bearing the arms of England valued at 5,500 *livres* and they cannot be Servien's, since in 1659 Mazarin purchased seven pieces bearing the arms of England from Servien's estate (see ch. 5 note 25). There are four pieces in the 1661 *IAD* N° 1704 adorned with the arms of Charles I valued at 16,000 *livres*. I would suspect, however, that the six of the seven pieces remaining in the *Mobilier national* (GMTT 16/1 and 16/3 to 16/7) are from the Servien purchase. On the other hand, the seven pieces in the 1661 *IAD* N° 1705 and currently in the *Mobilier* GMTT 19/1 to 10/7 are not from the collection of Charles I but from that of Henry Rich, Earl of Holland, who also lost his head in the English Civil War. *Horsemanship* after Rubens: Bordeaux is attempting to purchase it for about 10,000 *livres* in letters of April 3, 18, and May 5, 1653, cited in ch. 4 note 6; there are ten pieces in the 1653 Inventory p. 125–126 valued at 8,000 *livres*, and ten pieces in the 1661 *IAD* N° 1720 valued at 8,000 *livres*. Five pieces of the *Five Senses* in the Somerset catalog and five pieces in the 1653 Inventory p. 126, not appraised, which the 1661 *IAD*, fol. 443ᵛ indicates were at Vincennes, all tapestries, made it without a hint of scruple into the inventory, along with Van Dyck's *Three Children of Charles I*, in the Somerset catalog N°338 appraised at £120, in Bordeaux's letter of October 29, 1654, cited in ch. 4 note 6 as being too expensive, in the 1653 Inventory N° 169 p. 313 appraised at 1,500 *livres,* and in the1661 *IAD* N° 1003 appraised at 1,500 *livres*, but there is absolutely no evidence that this is the Louvre P 1237, which was seized in 1795 by the Directory from the house of Orange. Van Dyck's *Cardinal Infante* is in the Somerset catalog N° 204, in the 1661 *IAD* N° 1180. It is not in Louvre, but it could be in the Musée de Versailles et Trianon MV 3413 INV 1189 LP 434 attributed to Gaspard de Craye. Raphael's *Saint Michael Slaying the Demon* and *Saint George Slaying the Dragon* are in Somerset catalog N° 33 appraised at £150, in the 1653 Inventory p.

346, appraised at 2,000 *livres*, in the 1661 *IAD* N° 1177, appraised at 2,000 *livres* and in the Louvre P 608–609, all paintings. **CHARLES I'S POSSESSIONS NOT IN 1661 IAD NOR OTHERWISE ACCOUNTED FOR:** Since Mazarin, owned at least the three pieces from his 1653 Inventory and seven from the estate of Servien, all bearing the arms of England, and there are only four listed in his 1661 *IAD*, it follows that six are not in the 1661 *IAD*. Also missing are Raphael's *Young Man*, in the Somerset catalog N° 209, bought by Bordeaux in letters of November 17 and December 11 and 15, 1653, cited in ch. 4 note 6. Correggio's *Triumph of Virtue* and *Triumph of Vice* may have been bought in Bordeaux's letter of November 17, cited in ch. 4 note 6, and are in Louvre P 5926 and 5927. Titian's *Venus del Pardo* (alias *Jupiter and Antiope* alias *Venus, Satyr, and Cupid*), is a gift of Philip IV to Charles I, purchased by Bordeaux from an army officer for 7,000 *livres* in letters of December 18 and 22, 1653, cited in ch. 4 note 6, in the 1653 Inventory pp. 343–344. *Madonna of the Rabbit*, which Bordeaux is attempting to purchase for less than 4,000 *livres* in letters of December 15 and 18 cited in ch. 4 note 6, is in the Louvre P 743. Van Dyck's *Saint-Sebastian*: in Bordeaux's letter of May 25, possibly also of October 29 and November 9, 1654, cited in ch. 4 note 6 along with other Van Dycks, in the Louvre P 1233 and Giulio Romano's *Triumph of Titus and Vespasian* as from Charles I's collection purchased by Bordeaux for 800 *livres* in letters of March 12 and 23 and April 27, in the Louvre P 423, all paintings. **WORKS OF UNCERTAIN PROVENANCE ACQUIRED BY BORDEAUX:** Holbein's *Paysage*, the purchase of eight pieces of tapestry is in correspondence between Bordeaux and Mazarin of March 19, April 13, and April 20, 1654, cited in ch. 4 note 6, not in the 1661 *IAD!* *Hero and Leander* after Holbein, set of tapestry first produced in 1625 by Francis Cleyn at Mortlake for James I, is in Somerset catalog, which states that it was similar to a set owned by Charles I. There is no evidence of its purchase by Bordeaux, but it was bequeathed by Mazarin to Louis XIV's brother, Duke of Anjou/Orléans. In 2004 one piece from this tapestry seems to have been acquired by the Muzée Labenche in Brive-La-Gaillarde. It is also impossible to tell whether twenty Van Dycks that appear in the 1661 *IAD* are from the collection of Charles I. Cosnac's argument: *RPM* p. 242. My response: BNF Ms *Mél Col.* 75 (Mazarin's *IAD*), fols. 141, 152, 177, 333, 341, 367, 376, 405, 411, 436–437, 441, 443, 456, 464, 476–478, 485–486, 492–493, 499, 512, 515, 522, 539–540, 543, 594, 605–607, and 609.

22. Monaco S 10, BNF Ms. *Mél Col.* 75 (Mazarin's *IAD*). Interestingly, however, Le Bas in his *Compte*, fols. 218–227, admits that in the *IAD* the *grand Sancy* and the *miroir du Portugal*, were "not included" and indicates that they were mentioned in a "separate *état*," all of which makes the effort to obscure their transfer to the king more obvious. Le Bas may be referring to Monaco S 8, "*Lettres du Roy portant reception de 18 Diamans et de deux tantures de Tapiserie Leguées a la Couronne par M*^r *le Cardinal de Mazarin . . . 24 avril 1661*," which does identify the jewels.

23. BNF Ms. *Mél. Col.* (Le Bas' *Comte*), 74, fol. 68.

8. The Cover-Up

1. See Louis XIV, *Mémoires pour l'instruction du Dauphin* for 1661, any edition.

2. See the *Etat de la France* for 1661, the Loyson edition, where Picon begins to appear as a secretary of the council of the queen. See also the marriage contract cited in note 13 below, where Picon is designated as "*con*^er *du Roy en ses conseilz*," and "*Secretaire du Co*^d *de la Reyne*," and living in the home that Colbert had inherited on the Rue Neuve des Petits Champs. Colbert de Croissy in Alsace: BNF Ms. *Mél. Col.* 103 and AAEMD *Alsace* 18 and 19. Gabriel Picon: BNF Ms. *Fr.* 6784–6787, *Comptes de la recepte et despense qui a esté daicte par le . . . tresorier de Monseigneur le duc de Mazarin (1661–1665)*. Le Bas: BNF NAF 22874, fols. 155–166, *Inventaire des Pieces, Tiltres et contracts qui ont este dellivrez A M*^re *francois Lebas Con*^er *du Roy en*

Ses Conseils Tuteur onoraire de Tres hault & puissant Seigneur Mre Philippe Mazarini Mancini duc de Nivernois & donziois Pair de France, July 23, 1661. Gomont's brother: BNF Ms. *Mél. Col.* 103, fol. 343, Odoart Gomont (letter sent) to Colbert, August 6, 1661, accepting the position.

3. AAECP *Angleterre* 75, fols. 107–109, Estrades (letter sent) to Louis XIV, August 11, 1661 [copy sent pub. in Estrades I (1719) 159–161 or (1743), 176–178]. AAECP *Angleterre* 76, fols. 87–90 Louis (Lionne minute) to Estrades, August 26, 1661 (copy on fols. 215–220) [copy sent, pub. in Estrades I, 192–198 and Grouvelle V, 44–50, dated August 25].

4. Early plans to arrest: See Louis to Anne of Austria in note 6 below. In counting up the reasons for the arrest of Fouquet, I am consciously ignoring the rumors that he had tried to step in between the king and Mlle de La Vallière.

5. For Fouquet's state of mind, compare Gourville SHF, 179–186 with young Brienne's *Mémoires*, which are contradictory. Gourville makes it clear that Fouquet was oblivious to warnings and was intent on selling the office of *procureur général*, whereas young Brienne (SHF III, 53–56) claims that Fouquet was anticipating his arrest and regretted the sale. Voyage to Brittany: Patin to Falconet, June 24, 1661, pub. in Patin R-P III, 377–378. Sale of the office: Patin to Falconet, July 12, 1661, pub. in Patin, R-P III, 379–382, who reports on Fouquet's initial attempts. Final establishment of Harlay as *procureur général* (August 20, 1661): AN X^1a 8392, fols. 418–419. Festival at Vaux (August 17, 1661): Brief mention in *Gazette* N°99, August 20, 1661.

6. Arrest: Louis to Anne of Austria, c. September 5, 1661, pub. in Grouvelle V, 50–54 and Louis *Mémoires* Text D for 1661 (see the Grouvelle or my own edition), BNF Ms. CCC 235, fols. III–VIII *Recit de ce qui S'est passé a L'Emprisonnement de Mre Nicolas Fouquet ci devant Surjntendant des Finances* [pub. in Clément, *Histoire de l'administration monarchique en France* II, 444–454 and *Mémoires complets et authentiques de Saint-Simon* VIII, 447–453]. Seizures: Compare BNF Ms. *Fr.* 17398, fols. 122 and 132, La Fosse to Séguier, September 23 and 29, 1661, with Fouquet, *Défenses* I (*Recueil des défenses*), 1–45. Fouquet letter to Le Tellier: Félix Feuillet de Conches, *Causeries d'un curieux* (Paris, 1862–1868), II, 532.

7. *Edict du roy portant creation et establissement d'une Chambre de Justice, pour la recherche des abus & malversations commises dans les Finances de sa Majesté, depuis l'année 1635* (Paris, 1661). *Commission du Roy Contenant les noms des Juges et Officiers qui composent la Chambre de Justice . . . 15 Novembre 1661, Commission pour Messieurs du Grand Conseil . . . 15 Novembre 1661.* These published documents are also in BNF Ms. *Clairambault* 766 and are copied by hand into BNF Ms. CCC 228, fols. 14–23, 8–13, and 13–14 (Foucault's *Journal*, December 3, 1661). The *Commission du Roi* is also published in Ormesson II, LXXVI–LXXX. See the first two interrogatories in BNF Ms. *Fr.* 7621, fols. 2–250 and the first three in AN 144 AP 60 (156Mi 6 and 7), Dossiers 1–3. The first interrogatory is also in Fouquet, *Défenses* (*Conclusion des défenses*), 1–258.

8. Reformation of finances: BNF Ms. *Fr.* 7755, Colbert's *Mémoire sur les affaires de finance de france pour servir à l'histoire* [pub. in LIM Colbert II, 17–68]. Alexandre de Saint-Léger, "L'Acquisition de Dunkerque et de Mardyck par Louis XIV," *Revue d'histoire moderne et contemporaine* (1900), I, 233–245. For the incident in Rome, please see my *Louis XIV's View of the Papacy: 1661–1667* (Berkeley and Los Angeles, 1964), 30–31. For the sun king title, see Louis XIV, *Mémoires* for 1662, any edition.

9. Pellisson's writings: *Discours au Roy par un de ses fidèles sujets sur le procès de M. Foucquet* (s.l., n.d.) plus another similar writing, untitled. They were again published in *Oeuvres diverses de Monsieur Pellisson* (Paris, 1735), II, 13–199 and III, 1–68. See also BArsenal Ms. 5421, pp.1029–1030, *Jugement sur les deux défenses imprimées en faveur de M. Fouquet.* Family pressures: pub. in *Formulaire des inscriptions et souscriptions des lettres dont le roy de France est traité par les potentats & dont il les traite réciproquement, on a adjouté à la fin une harangue de Mad. Fouquet au Roi* [Utrecht, 1680]. This is in all probability the document referred to in BArsenal Ms. 10304, *Titres des ouvrages et libelles imprimés sans permission qui ont été saisis en vertu des ordres du roi depuis*

l'année 1660 jusqu'en 1718, which dates it for July 30, 1662. Chamber relents: BNF Ms. CCC 229, fols. 21–23 and 26 September 25 and 26, and October 4, 1662. Ormesson and Sainte-Hélène as reporters: Ormesson II, 22, October 12, 1662. Removal of Lamoignon: Ormesson II, 27, December 7, 1662. Fouquet writings: *Mémoires et Remarques Sur une partie du procedé qui a esté tenu à mon égard depuis le cinquième Septembre 1661 jusqu'au 9 Decembre 1662*, published in Fouquet, *Défenses (Conclusion des Defenses)*, 261–335. Attack on Colbert: *Défenses sur tous les poincts de mon Procés, que j'aurois à proposer, si j'estois devant mes juges naturels*, 14, first published in January of 1663, according to La Fontaine to Fouquet, January 30, 1663, in La Fontaine *Oeuvres diverses* (Paris, 1729) II, 24–25 [also in BNF Ms. MdT, 399, fols. 257–324, later published in Fouquet's *Défenses (Défenses de M. Fouquet sur tous les points de son procez)* II, 25–26]. Interestingly enough, the young Brienne, in the second portion of his *Mémoires* (SHF II, 37), refers to Mazarin's testament in exactly the same terms as Fouquet. More Fouquet writings: *Requête de Fouquet (25 May 1663) à l'effet d'obtenir communication de la production du procureur général et des papiers saisis par ordre de la chambre de justice commencant par ces mots: A noseigneurs de la Chambre de Justice, supplie très humblement Nicolas fouquet . . . disant que par le procès verbal de MM. les Commissaires de la chambre du 20 Septembre dernier* (s.l.n.d.) [also in BNF Ms. MdT 402, fols. 523–540]. BNF Ms. CCC 236, fols. 84–85 (January 20, 1663) indicates that this request was announced to the chamber on that date and not on May 25. It is printed in Fouquet, *Défenses* I, 1–60. Ms. CCC 236, fols. 85–90 (January 30, 1663), *Requeste de recusation proposée par Mr foucquet contre Mr Talon, procureur general de la chambre*, Ms. CCC 236, fols. 92–95, 97–101, and 102–106 (January 31, 1663), *Requeste de recusation proposée par Mr foucquet contre moy, Requetste de recusation proposée par M. foucquet contre Mr Pussort, Requeste de recusation proposée par M. foucquet contre Mr Voisin*. Right to copies: Ms. CCC 236, fols. 111–113, *Arrêt* of February 3 1663. Charges: BNF Ms. Fr. 7626, fols. 1–123 and fols. 162–395, *Inventaire de la production que baille par devant Vous Messieurs de la chambre de Justice le Procureur general du Roy en ladicte chambre demandeur et accusateur*. See also BNF Ms. CCC 229, fols. 127–129, April 10, 1663 and Ormesson II, 42. Fouquet prints this "production" in his *Défenses (De la Production de M. Fouquet contre celle de Mr Talon)* III and V along with his lengthy responses. *Lettres Patentes* moving Chamber to Arsenal: BNF Ms. CCC 229, fols. 216-217, dated May 28, 1663.

10. Lionne's (own hand minute) to Estrades, March 15, 1663, ordering him to complain about efforts to print a *libelle* titled *Le Testament du Cardinal Mazarin* in the Dutch Republic is neither in AAECP *Hollande* 68 nor in Estrades's papers in BNF Ms. *Clair.* 580. However, in *Hollande* 68, fols. 271–276, Estrades (letter sent) to Louis XIV, March 22, 1663, Estrades informs Louis that the "Estats ont fait des deffences tres expresses a tous les imprimeurs d'imprimer aucuns lettres ny exemplaires deffendus en france" and on fol. 265 there is a copy of the *mémoire* that he presented to the States-General on March 19. Both Lionne's letter and Estrades's *mémoire* appear in published form in Estrades II, (1719), 120–123 or (1743), 147–150. This *libelle* was in all probability the origin of *Le Testament du defunt cardinal de Mazarin, duc de Nivernois, etc. (7 mars) Juxte la copie* (Cologne, 1663) (Paris, 1663). Its appearance in Paris and impact is described in PRO *SPF* 101/13, fols. 153–155, Chavaran (own hand newsletter) Paris, June [blank] 1663. Bussy-Rabutin in his *Mémoires* claims that he was accused of distributing it and deprived of his pension. For the foreign translations see *Het testament van miin heer de cardinael Jul. Mazarin, duc de Nivernois . . . etc traduict du français suivant la copie*, and *The Last Will and Testament of the Renowned Cardinal Mazarini, Deceased February 27, 1660, Together with some Historical Remerques of His Life* (London, 1663). Talon's bid: *Requête du procureur général Talon, du 25 juin 1663, contenant un résumé des charges du procés, et demandant qu'il soit passé outre au jugement en se bornant aux neuf procès verbaux mentionnés dans la requête, commençant par ces mots: A MM. de la chambre de justice, Supplie le procureur général du roi, disant que dans les abus et malversations* (s.l.n.d.). There is a printed

copy of this in BNF Ms. *Fr.* 7626, fols. 138–161. Report on Fouquet's first rebuttal: Ormesson II, 42, July 9, 1663, published as *Première partie de la production de M. Foucquet contre celle de M. Talon* (s.l.n.d.). It was also published in Fouquet's *Défenses* (*De la Production de M. Fouquet contre celle de Mr Talon première partie*), III and followed by a second part in BNF Ms. *Fr.* 7622 and 7623, two copies of *Inventaire des pieces que baille Pardevant vous Nosseigneurs de la Chambre de Justice Mre Nicolas Fouquet. . . . Contre M^r le procureur gñal en la Chambre.* The cited passage is in Ms. *Fr.* 7622, fols. 14–15 and 7623, fol. 14 and also in AN 144 AP 69 [partially published as *Seconde partie de la production de M. Foucquet contre celle de M. Talon* (s.l.n.d.)], also in BNF Ms. *MdT* 401 fols. 288–357 and published in Fouquet, *Défenses* (*De la Production de Mr Fouquet contre celle de Mr Talon, seconde et troisième partie*), V, with the cited passage on p. 25 along with a third part. Talon's counter reply is inserted and rebutted by Fouquet in his *Reponse de Mr Fouquet à la replique de Mr Talon* cited in note 14 below. New prosecutors: BNF Ms. CCC 230, fols. 175 or 236, fol. 5 and Ormesson II, 60–61, November 27, 1663, *Commission pour MM. Hotman et Chamillard pour la fonction d'avocat et procureurs généraux en la chambre de justice*, December 1, 1663 (s.l.n.d.). For Chamillart's son's full statement as reported to Voltaire see ch. 9 note 23.

11. Barbès in court: BNF *Carrés d'Hozier 57.* For the content of his *mémoire* to the Duke de Mazarin see Fouquet's *Production nouvelle* cited in note 14 below. *Lettre de cachet:* BL Add. Ms. 15890, fol. 118. Mme Barbès: BNF Ms. *Mél. Col.* 116bis, fols. 794–795, E. M. Barbès (letter sent) to Colbert, August 19, 1663.

12. ASR Ufficio 18/388 (Pacichelli) exhibited on June 10, 1662. AN MC XLVI/90 (Charles), *IAD* of François Lescot. The inventory states that the seals were placed on March 7, 1664 and admits that Lescot "Seroit deceddé des Le mois de Mars de L année dernier mil Six cens Soix^{te} trois." For Gomont's mission see AAECP *Angleterre* 81, fol. 265, Lionne (own hand letter sent) to Comminges, June 16, 1663, which beautifully encapsulates Louis's ambiguity: "encore que le Roy n'ayt pas pour quelques raisons considerations Jugé a propos de parler de M. Gomont dans la lettre que Sa M^{te} escrit au Roy de la Grande Bretagne neantmoins Sa M^{té} a approuvé qu'il fasse ce voyage." We only know of the outcome of Gomont's mission through the Duke de Mazarin who revealed it in 1664 to Denzel Holles. See his letter to Bennet of November 30/December 10, 1664, cited in note 15 below. Chigi in his correspondence with the court of Rome makes no mention of seeing the crown jewels. However, he was sufficiently impressed by them that in 1665, when the Cavaliere Bernini was about to go to France, Chigi recommended that he ask to see them. Bernini got an eyeful. On June 4 at Saint-Germain-en-Laye, day of the feast of Corpus Christi, he happened to see the tapestries of the Acts of the Apostles on display and on October 19 Colbert proudly showed him the crown jewels, including the *miroir de Portugal* and the *grand Sancy*. See BI Ms. 1043 *Journal du voyage du Cavalier Bernin en France* [pub. in Paul Fréant de Chantelou, *Journal du Voyage du Cavalier Bernin en France*, ed. Ludovic Lalanne (Paris, 1885), 16 and 251–252].

13. Legal troubles: Ravaisson *AB* I, 185-199 (July 16-September 19, 1661). Purchase of Pouzilhac (December 18, 1661): Aubais, *Pièces fugitives pour servir à l histoire de France* (1759), I part 2, 308. Picon's marriage: AN MC XVI/477 (Séjournant), December 30, 1662. Mixed reputation: Gatien Courtilz de Sandras, *Vie de Colbert* (Paris, 695), 33. The act that precipitated the discontent was the *Arrêt du conseil royal des finances du 24 mai 1664 par lequel Sa Majesté ordonne que les proprietaires & posesseurs des rentes assignées sur les deniers des fermes représenteront les titres justificatifs de leur propriété, pour être par messieurs les commissaires dressé procès-verbal de la représentation à iceux, & par leur rapport incéssamment procéder à la liquidation & remboursement desdites rentes.* A subsequent imaginative historian embellished the story by claiming that Colbert purposely got Picon drunk in order to discredit him before Louis XIV. See BNF *NAF* 13799 (Mémoires de Robert Challe), fols. 55–56 [pub as Robert Challe, *Mémoires, Correspondance*

complète, Rapports sur l'Acadie et autres pièces, ed. Frédéric Deloffre (Geneva, 1996), 178–179].
Challe attributes to Picon Sandras's *Testament Politique de Jean Baptiste Colbert*.

14. *Vérification des procès verbaux*: BNF Ms. CCC 236, fols. 163–170, October 22, 1663.
Recusation of Chancellor: Ormesson II, 72, January 7, 1664. *Inscription en faux*: BNF Ms. CCC
236, fols. 211–212 and Ormesson II, 75–76, both of January 18–19, 1664. Reply to Talon:
Published as *Reponse à la replique de M. Talon* in BNF Ms. MdT 402, fols. 573–689 and also as
Reponse de Mr Fouquet à la replique de Mr Talon in Fouquet, *Défenses* IV. See also Ormesson II,
77 (January 26, 1664). Ready with *rapport du procès* and *procès-verbaux*: Ormesson II, 185–188,
July 28, 1664. Reading of reports: BNF Ms. CCC 236, fols. 325–327 and Ormesson II, 213–215,
both of September 5–10, 1664. Fouquet's reply on the charge of treason and submission of
Mazarin's testament: Fouquet, *Défenses* (*Suite de la continuation de la production de Mr Fouquet
pour servir de réponse à celle de Mr Talon, sur le prétendu crime d'état à la fin de laquelle on a ajouté
le troisième tome*), IX. See esp. 10–26 and Ormesson II, 223–225 (September 30–October 4).
Request for testament: BNF Ms. CCC, fol. 342 and Ormesson II, 227, both of October 7, 1664.
New productions of Fouquet: BNF Ms Fr. 7624, fols. 1–9 and 1–412, Fouquet's *Continuation
de la Production Sur les Procès-Verbaux* and *Procès verbal de l'ordonnance de six millions*, also in
BNF Ms. MdT 401, fols. 358–566 and AN 144 AP 69 [156 MI 21], which seems to have been
read between October 13 and 20, 1664. See BNF Ms. CCC 236, fols. 344–350 and Ormesson
II, 230–232 and the published version in Fouquet's *Défenses* (*Continuation de la Production Sur
les Procès Verbaux, Tome Quatrième de la Suite*, p.162), X. BNF Ms. Fr. 7625, fols. 187–210,
Production Nouvelle Sur le premier chef d'Accusation Concernant La pension des gabelles, also in
AN 144 AP 69 [156 Mi 22] Dossier 5, announced on October 23 and read on October 24 and
25, according to BNF Ms CCC 236, fols. 355–358 and Ormesson II, 235. Fouquet repeats the
Barbès accusation in BNF Ms. Fr.7625, fols. 213–377, *Response A la Requeste de Contredits de
M. Talon Sur le Faict de la Pension des Gabelles*, also in AN 144 AP 69 [156 Mi 23] Dossier 7,
fols. 1–167, also read on the 25th according to Ormesson II, 235.

15. Holles's appointment: PRO SPD (Charles II) 29/81 N° 134[1], May, 1662, *CSPD* (Charles
II) III, 306. His eagerness: PRO SPF 78/118, fol. 57, Holles (own hand letter sent) to Bennet,
February 17/27, 1664. See AN Z² 2926 for the complete case. The initial imprisonment in
Saint-Eloy is referred to in Desfontaines's testimony of December 3, 1664. Initial witnesses:
AN Z² 2926, Anne Thomasson, Jeanne Giroux, Jacques Collin; July 3, Eduard Bonnet, Jeanne
Bertrand; July 7, Adam Perrot; September 1, 1664. Desfontaines to *Consièrgerie*: AN Z² 2926
September 1, 1664. Hoyau to Bastille: BArsenal Ms. 10333 (September 2, 1664, countersigned
by Le Tellier. Interrogation regarding Duchemin: BN Ms. Fr. 7067, September 2, 1664 [pub.
in Ravaisson AB II, 214–217. Le Tellier inquiry about Hoyau: BL Add. Ms. 15890 fol. 162, Le
Tellier (letter sent) to Besmaux, October 20, 1664, September 3, 1664 [pub. in Ravaisson AB
III, 470]. Holles's procuration for Petit: AN Z² 2926, September 3, 1664. Desfontaines must
have been temporarily released from the Conciergerie, since she cannot be making up her
encounter with Hoyau's son-in-law in Le Tellier's antechamber, which I can only date between
September 2 and October 27, which she recalls in AN Z² 2926, her testimony of November
24, and December 3, 1664. Thus, I cannot accept the record in BArsenal Ms.12725, fol. 25,
claiming that she was sent to the Bastille on September 2, 1664, accepted by Ravaisson in AB
I, 346, because Louis orders her transfer from the Conciergerie to the Bastille to be confronted
with Hoyau in BL Add Ms. 15890, fol. 179. Louis (*lettre de cachet* countersigned by Le Tellier)
to Besmaux, October 27, 1664 [pub. in Ravaisson AB III, 473]. Interestingly, her name is left
blank in the letter (just as it originally was for Eustache Dauger) and she is merely identified as
"*une feme*" in a note on the back of the letter. More accusations: AN Z² 2926, (Jeanne Giroux,
Phelippere Baulme) both of October 16, 1664. Desfontaines and Hoyau denials: AN Z² 2926,
October 30, 1664 (Desfontaines) and October 31, 1664 (Hoyau). Testimony of Sylvestre Bosc:

AN Z^2 2926, November 8, 1664. Evaluation of the Duke de Mazarin's holdings: PRO SPF 78/119, fols. 126–127, Holles (own hand letter sent) to Bennet, November 2/12, 1664 [trans. in Ravaisson AB III, 473–475]. Testimony of Jean Catillon: AN Z^2 2926, November 12, 1664. Plea by the *procureur du roi*: AN Z^2 2926, December 3, 1664. Duke de Mazarin's chat with Holles: PRO SPF 78/119, fols. 160–161, Holles (own hand letter sent) to Bennet, November 30/ December 10, 1664 [extract in Ravaisson AB III, 477–478]. On Montbrun, see Courtilz de Sandras, *Mémoires de Monsieur le Marquis de Montbrun* (Amsterdam, 1701) and the *mémoire* cited in note 17. Holles alludes to his request for special orders in his letter of February 11/21, 1665 cited in the same note below.

16. Fouquet on the witness seat: BNF CCC 237, first folio not foliated plus fols. 1–146, Ms. Fr. 7628, Ormesson II, 245 [partially pub. in Ravaisson AB II, 225–302], *Relation de ce qui s'est passe dans la Chambre de Justice au jugement de M. Fouquet* in *Défenses* (*Conclusion des Défenses*). Ormesson's presentation: Ormesson, II, 266 and BNF CCC 237, fols. 151–171 [pub. in Ormesson II, 776–799]. Mme Fouquet: BArsenal Ms. 5421 pp. 1021–1028, *Placet présenté au Roy par madame Fouquet pour obtenir permission de faire imprimer les défenses de son Mari 1664*. Discomfiture of Colbert: Van Beuningen to de Witt, February 27 and March 13, 1665, published in Johan de Witt, *Brieven geschrieven ende gewisselt tusschen den Heer Johan de Witt, raedt pensionaris en groot-segelbewaerder van Hollandt, en West Vriesland, ende de gevol-maghtigden van den staedt der Vereennighde Nederlanden: so in Vranckryck, Engelandt, Sweden, Danemarcken, Poolen, enz, beginnende met den jaere 1652, tot het jaer 1669 incluys* (The Hague, 1723–1726), II, 49 and 66–69. Publication: Fouquet, *Défenses* (Amsterdam 1665–1667/8) 13 vols. and conclusion, republished (Paris, 1696), which must tell us something about the later reign. Barbès: AN MC XLIV/19 (Loyer), May 8, 1668, which refers to eighteen months in the Bastille. Duchemin: BL Add. Ms. 15890, fol. 186, *lettre de cachet*, January 27, 1665 [pub. in Ravaisson, AB III, 368].

17. PRO SPF 78/120, fol 35, Holles (own hand letter sent) to Bennet, February 4/14, 1665 [pub. in Ravaisson AB III, 483], PRO SPF 78/120, fols. 42–43, Holles (own hand letter sent) to Bennet, February 11/21, 1665 [extract in Ravaisson AB II, 482], PRO SPF 78/120, fols. 49–50, Holles (own hand letter sent) to Bennet, February 22/March 4, 1665. Release of Hoyau: see BL Add. Ms.15890, fol. 200, Louis (*lettre de cachet* countersigned by Le Tellier) to Besmaux, March 28, 1665, and BArsenal Ms.10333 for the release date. Submission to arbitration: AN Z^2 2926, March 31, 1665. Hoyau accusations against accusers: AN Z^2 2926, April 30; May 1, 7, 13, and 23; and June 2, 1665. Guichard in Bastille: BArsenal Ms. 12725, fol. 23 (June 1– December 27, 1665). PRO SPF 78/120, fols. 183–184, Petit (own hand letter sent) to Bennet, June 3/13, 1665, defending the arbitration and PRO SPD (Charles II) 29/125, fols. 127–130, *Extraict des depositions des tesmoings ouis en l'Information faicte pendant Le Juge Bailly du Pallais Contre Mathurine desfontaine & Robert Hoyau orfevre Accusés* with a *mémoire*, apparently by Montbrun, criticizing the artibration, attached [calendared in CSPD (Charles II) IV, 455]. Theft of handkerchiefs: AN Z^2 2926 (Holles's complaint). Dismissal of charges: AN Z^2 2926, July 7, 1665 (*Défaut à Hoyau*). Retractions: AN Z^2 2926, August 13 and 25, 1665 (*Retractations de Joachin Hue, dict Beauregard*), August 21, 1665, and retraction of Nicolas Guichard, August 21, 1665. Montbrun in and out of Bastille: BL Add. Ms. 15890, fols. 234 and 238, Louis to Besmaux, August 22 and 28, 1665, the last exiling him to Bayeux with fol. 237, Montbrun's signed promise of August 28 to comply. Release of Desfontaines: BL Add. Ms. 15890, fol. 240, Louis (*lettre de cachet* countersigned by Le Tellier) to Besmaux, September 4, 1665.

18. Release of Desfontaines: BL Add. Ms. 15890, fol. 240, Louis (*lettre de cachet* counter-signed by Le Tellier) to Besmaux, September 4, 1665.

19. Please see my *Louis XIV and the Origins of the Dutch War* (Cambridge and New York, 1988).

20. In Paris: AN MC L/85 (Chaussière), procuraòn Anne Baillergeau vᵉ Spon, à Le Roux foncouverte, June 28, 1663. Investigation: I wish I could cite the original AD *Aisne* Baillage de Vermandois 176, the *Information faite à Guise par Claude Leclerc, Commissaire député par la chambre de Justice, pour rechercher les abus et malversations commises dans les finances en l'étendue du Baillage de Laon, Coucy, et Laon, de 1661 à 1664*, in Amédée Combier, *Etude sur le Baillage de Vermandois, et Siège Présidial de Laon*, who also describes other documents on the Le Clercs, all destroyed during the First World War, but I can point out that Laon was in the generality of Soissons. Assassination of Lisle (August 11, 1664): PRO *SFP* 78/119, fols. 51–52, Riordan (own hand letter sent) to Bennet, August 26, 1664. Revolt in France: PRO *SPF* 78/117, Riordan (own hand letter sent) to Robert Lye, May [blank] 1665. Holles on Revolution in France: PRO *SPF* 78/121, fols. 122–123, Holles (own hand letter sent) to Bennet, October 18/28, 1665 [extract in Lister's *Life and Administration of Edward, First Earl of Clarendon: With Original Correspondence, and Authentic Papers Never before Published* (London, 1837–1838), III, 413–414]. The proof of Roux's connection with La Salle emerges in the notarial acts cited in note 24 below, especially the act of August 21, which gives us the year of La Salle's entrance into the guards. French declaration of war (January 26, 1666): *Gazette* Nº 15, January 30, 1666.

21. Please see my *Louis XIV and the Origins of the Dutch War*, op. cit.

22. Pellisson's appeal: Pellisson to Colbert, November 29, 1665 [pub. in Delort, *Détention*, I, 113–114]. Amazing document: AN E 1731, Nº 21, *Arrêt* of February 4, 1666, reproduced in BNF *Ms. Mél. Col.* 74 (Le Bas *Compte*) fols. 343–374, *Proces Verbaux de Mʳˢ d'aligre et de Seve contenant la descharge des comptes des maison et affʳᵉˢ de feu S. E. et pieces Justificatives d'iceux . . . ce 18 febʳ 1666*. This title is in the hand of Le Fouyn. Proofs of nobility: AN E 409a, fols. 207–210, June 4, 1668 (copy in BNF *Nouveau Hozier* 265, Dossier 6063). Marie-Catherine Desjardins (Madame de Villedieu), *Nouveau recueil de quelques pièces galantes* (Paris, 1669), dedicating to Picon her sardonic "Relation d'une Revue des Troupes de l'Amour."

23. Please see my *Louis XIV and the Origins of the Dutch War*, op. cit.

24. For these movements, we have the letter of Ruvigny cited in ch. 2 note 6 and the connection of Roux with the merchants of Brugge cited in ch. 6 note 21. For the business in Liège, Cologne, and the Dutch Republic, see GAM *MNA* 1484 (Corstius) notarial acts of September 19, September 22, and December 31, 1667, signed by Roux, *OA* 94 (Requestboeken), September 20, and *OA* 67 (Raadsverdragen) September 26, 1667, mentioning Roux [the act of September 22 is pub. in Rabinel, *La Tragique aventure de Roux de Marcilly* (Toulouse, 1969), 92]. Search for Roux in England: Compare PRO *SPF Entry Book* 104/30, fol. 37, June 22/July 2, 1668, and AAECP *Angleterre* 91, fol. 312, Ruvigny (own hand note sent) of July 3, 1668. Search in Switzerland: AAECP *Suisse* 44, Nº 102, 109 and *Suisse* 45, Nº 57, Mouslier (letters sent) to Lionne, August 10, 1668; September 7, 1668; and May 17, 1669. La Salle still *exempt:* MC LXVIII/202 (Laurent), July 25 and August 21, 1668. No longer *exempt:* MC LXVIII/203 (Laurent), December 10, 1668, *Compte*. Neither the *Etat de la France* for 1665 nor the one for 1669, published by Loyson in each of those years, includes Eustache de La Salle among the *exempts* in the *Gardes du Corps*. However, AN Z¹ᵃ 499, which contains later copies of the rosters of various companies of the *Gardes du Corps du Roy* taken from the records of the *Maison du Roi* (the current Series O) and includes the entire roster of Charost's company for the years 1658, 1668, and 1671 includes under the year 1668 the entry: *Exempts* "Eustache de la Salle Ecuyer." Arrest of La Salle: BArsenal Ms. 12472, June 16, 1669, PRO *SPF* 101/16, fols. 402–403, Oldenburg (secretary's hand) news letter, AST MPLM *Francia* 84, fols. 207–209, Saint-Maurice (letter sent) to Charles Emmanuel, both of June 28, 1669 [pub. in Saint-Maurice I, 312–318]. I cannot speak to La Salle's intimacies, but he was clearly in France at least until December 10, 1668. Thus he would have had to move to the Spanish Low Countries between that date and June of 1669, which would not have given him much time both to enlist in the Spanish army

and to find a wife in Liège before returning to France. We do not have detailed records of the composition of the Spanish army in the Low Countries for this period. However, we do have some evidence that in 1669 the Marquis de Castel Rodrigo was dismissing troops. Moreover, my investigation in the Archives de l'Etat in Liège shows no sign either of Roux's presence there or of Eustache de La Salle's marriage, although some of the parish records are missing.

25. See, for example, AD Gard 2 E 39/ 81 (Daubanel), September 11, 1668, which identifies "Sieur pierre Rodes con^ee du Roy Receveur des tailles hañt en la Ville de la rochelle" and is signed by "E. Roux de Pérél." AAECP *Angleterre* 95, fols. 6–9, Croissy (letter sent) to Lionne, July 1, 1669 and fol. 24, Lionne (own hand minute) to Croissy, July 13, 1669.

26. BNF M*s. Clair.* 581, pp. 107–110, Louvois (Calpatry hand letter sent) to Estrades, July 19, 1669, asking him to grant Vauroy leave "ayant des affaires." AN K 120a, N° 67, Louvois (letter sent) to Saint-Mars, July 19, 1669 [pub. in Delort, *Détention* I, 155–156]. AG A*¹* 234, fol. 271, Louis (minute) to Vauroy and fol. 272 (minute) to Saint-Mars, both of July 28, 1669, both with name left blank (letter sent to Saint- Mars in AN K 120a, N° 338 with name filled in by Calpatry and countersigned by Le Tellier]. AG A*¹* 234, fol. 274, Louis (minute) to Piennes (Governor of Pinerolo) announcing the arrival, with name left blank, but presumably it was also filled in and the letter countersigned by Le Tellier. The voyage is also recorded in BNF M*s. Mél. Col.* 281, fol. 276, record of payment for 3,000 *livres* to go from Dunkirk to Calais with three other men (*lui quatriesme*) and from Calais to Pinerolo with four men (*lui cinquiesme*) and for another 3,000 *livres* for having returned from Pinerolo to Dunkirk (*lui quatriesme*).

27. For the life of Petit after Holles's departure, compare AAECP *Angleterre* 96, fol. 105, Lionne (own hand letter sent) to Croissy, November 10, 1669, with PRO *SPF* 101/17 fol. 53, Perwitch to Williamson, November 30, 1669 [pub. in *The Despatches of William Perwich, English Agent in Paris: 1669–1677*, ed. M. Berryl Corran (London, 1903), 47]. One can follow Petit's subsequent services to the English crown in PRO *SPD* (Charles II) 29/287, 289–293, 295, 336, 337 and SPF *Entry Book* 104/ 35A, calendared in *CSPD* (Charles II) XIV and XVI and especially the details in PRO *Warrants not relating to money* IV, 31–33 [pub. in *Calendar of Treasury Books* (London 1904–1957), IV, 789] which are extremely consistent with the details given by Lionne.

9. Was Eustache Dauger Gay?

1. David Hume, *An Enquiry Concerning the Principles of Morals* (London, 1751). Daniel Holbrook, "Fidelity to the Marriage Bed: An Inquiry into the Foundation of Sexual Ethics," *Electronic Journal of Human Sexuality* X, 2007. E. William Monter, "La Sodomie à l époque moderne en Suisse romande," *Annales* N° 4 (July–August 1974), 1023–1033, translated in Tom Betteridge, *Sodomy in Early Modern Europe* (Manchester, 2002), 94–111. Luiz Mott, "Justitia et Misericordia," in Harold Johnson and Francis Dutra, *Pelo Vaso Traseiro: Sodomy and Sodomites in Luso-Brazilian History* (Tucson, 2007), 63–104.

2. Colin Spencer, *Homosexuality in History* (London, 1995). Marc Daniel, *Hommes du grand siècle: Etudes sur l'homosexualité sous les règnes de Louis XIII et Louis XIV* (Paris, 1957) [English translation "A Study of Homosexuality in France during the Reigns of Louis XIII and Louis XIV" in *Homophile Studies* 4, 125–136]. Robert Oresko "Homosexuality and the Court Elites of Early Modern France: Some Problems, Some Suggestions and an Example," *Journal of Homosexuality* XVI 1–2 (1988), 105–128, republished in "The Pursuit of Sodomy: Male Homosexuality in Renaissance and Enlightenment Europe," ed. Kent Gerard and Gert Hekma (New York and London, 1989) with same pagination. *Pelo Vaso Traseiro:* cited in the previous note. See also the more clinical observations in Magnus Hirschfeld, *Die Homosexualität des Mannes und*

des Weibes (Berlin, 1914), 499–500 [English translation, *The Homosexuality of Men and Women* (Amherst, NY, 2000), 568].

3. Initial arrangements: AN K 120a Nº 1, Louis (letter sent) to Saint-Mars, December 24, 1664 [pub. in Delort, *Detention* I, 24–27], K 120a Nᵒˢ 2–11, Louvois (letters sent) to Saint-Mars, January 29, February 10, 20, 24, March 3, 15, April 17, 24, June 8, and 18, 1665 [pub. in Delort, *Detention* I, 85–93]. For the informers on Saint-Mars, see the letter of Louvois to Saint-Mars of September 10, 1669, and March 16, 1670, cited in notes 8 and 9 below. For the location of Fouquet's apartment, see the letter of Louvois to Fouquet of March 9, 1676, cited in note 15 below. For his devices, see the letter of Louvois to Saint-Mars of July 16, cited in the following note, as well as his letter to Barbézieux of January 6, 1696, cited in note 20 below.

4. AN K 120a, Nᵒˢ 12, 13 and 334, Louvois (one letter sent) and Louis (two letters sent) to Saint-Mars, all of June 29, 1665 [pub. in Delort, *Detention* I, 93–100]. See also Nᵒˢ 14–16, Louvois (letters sent) to Saint-Mars, July 10, 14, and 26, (*sic*) 1665 [pub. in Delort, *Detention* I, 101–104.].

5. Valets and La Pérouse: AN K 120a, Nᵒˢ 18–19, Louvois (letters sent) to Saint-Mars, August 21 and 29, Nº 336, Louis (letter sent) to Saint-Mars, October 11, and Nᵒˢ 22–23, Louvois (letters sent) to Saint-Mars, October 15 and 26, 1665 [pub. in Delort, *Detention* I, 105–107, and 110–112]. Louis's intentions: K 120a Nᵒˢ 25–27, 36–37, and 40, Louvois (letters sent) to Saint-Mars, December 12, 18, and 25, 1665; May 21, June 4, and June 30, 1666 [pub. in Delort, *Detention* I, 115–117, 122–127, and 129–130].

6. Return to Pinerolo: AN K 120a, Nº 337, Louis to Saint-Mars, July 15, 1666, Nº 41, Louvois to Saint-Mars, July 17, 1666, and Nº 43, Louvois to Saint-Mars, September 3, 1666 (all letters sent) [pub. in Delort, *Detention* I, 131–135]. Debate over valets: K 120a, Nᵒˢ 44 and 45, Louvois (all letters sent) to Saint-Mars, September 23 and October 8 and Nº 46, Le Tellier to Saint-Mars, October 23, 1666, Nº 47, Louvois to Saint-Mars, January 18 and February 14, 1667 [pub. in Delort, *Detention* I, 136–139].

7. AN K 120a, Nᵒˢ 52 and 55, Louvois (letters sent) to Saint-Mars, December 22, 1667, and October 1, 1668 [pub. in Delort, *Detention* I, 147 and 148].

8. For the instructions, see Louvois to Saint-Mars of July 19, 1669, cited in ch. 8 note 26 and Saint-Mars to Louvois, August 21, 1669, found only in Roux-Fazillac, 105. Lair (II, 453) claims the tower was the one above the governor's cellar. Other scholars (Petitfils) identified it as the middle tower of the *donjon* facing south, but more recent excavations have suggested a rounded foundry lying between the same face of the *donjon* and the outer wall of the citadel. References to the lower tower keep recurring in Louvois's letter to Saint-Mars, May 12, 1681, and Saint-Mars to Abbot Estrades, June 25, 1681, both cited in note 19 below. See also AG A¹ 235, whose fol. 76 originally contained Louvois (minute) to Saint-Mars September 10, 1669) whose theft was noted by an archivist on February 5, 1968. The letter sent, however, is in AN K 120a, Nº 68 [pub. in Delort, *Detention* I, 157].

9. AN K 120a, Nᵒˢ 72 and 73, Louvois (letters sent) to Saint-Mars, December 17, 1669, and January 1, 1670 [pub. in Delort, *Detention* I, 159–161]. Sevigné to Grigman, June 25, 1670, Sevigné *Lettres de Madame de Sevigné*, ed. Monmerqué (Paris, 1862–1868) II, 1–3. AN K 120a, Nº 78, Louvois (letter sent) to Saint-Mars, March 16, 1670 [pub. in Delort, *Detention* I, 167–168]. Inspection tour: ASTorino, MPLM *Francia* 86, Nº 146, Saint-Maurice (own hand letter sent) to Charles Emmanuel, August 29, 1670 [pub. in Saint-Maurice I, 481–484].

10. For the treason of Lauzun, please see my *Louis XIV and the Origins of the Dutch War* (Cambridge, 1988), 129–130, 152, and 173, AN K 120a, Nᵒˢ 92, *lettre de chachet*, November 25, 1671, signed Louis/Le Tellier and Nº 93, *Instruction pour ce que je dois observer pour la garde de monsieur de Lauzun le 26ᵉ novembre 1671* [pub. in Delort, *Detention* I, 176–178].

11. Problems with Lauzun: AG A¹ 264, Nᵒˢ 218 and 227, Saint-Mars (own hand letters sent) to Louvois, September (actually December) 22 and December 30, 1671. First suggestion

of Dauger: AG A¹ 299 N° 67, Saint Mars (letter sent) to Louvois, February 20, 1672 [pub. in Ravaisson AB III, 117–119]. Resignation of Dauger: AG A¹ 355, N° 237, Saint-Mars (letter sent) to Louvois, December 30, 1673.

12. For Louis's changing moods during and after the Dutch War please see my "Louis XIV's *Mémoires pour l'histoire de la guerre de Hollande*," *French Historical Studies* VIII, 1 (Spring 1973), 68–78, and "Louis XIV and the Dutch War," in *Louis XIV and Europe*, ed. Ragnhild Hatton (London, 1976), 153–178. Softening on Fouquet: AN K 120a, N° 154, Louvois (letter sent) to Saint-Mars, April 10, 1674 [pub. in Delort, *Detention* I, 229]. Approval of Dauger: AG A¹ 421, N°. 540 and A¹ 423, fol. 158, Louvois (minutes) to Saint-Mars, January 30 and March 11, 1675 (letters sent) in AN K 120a, N°ˢ 167 and 168 [pub. in Delort, *Detention* I, 233–234].

13. BNF Ms. Fr. 10958 (copy of D'Ormesson's *Journal*), fols. 234–238, Fouquet (copy) to Mme Fouquet, February 5, 1675, where he talks about the death of Champagne and adds, "The other valet is dying here with his medicines and has as many and needs them more than I." This is obviously a reference to La Rivière, and if Eustache had also been serving Fouquet at this time, he would certainly have mentioned it.

14. *Mémoires de M. L.C.D.R. concernant ce qui s'est passé de plus particulier sous le ministère du cardinal de Richelieu et du cardinal Mazarin, avec plusieurs particularités remarquables du règne de Louis le Grand* (Cologne, 1687), 225.

15. AG A¹ 472, fols. 28–29, Louvois (minutes) to Saint-Mars, March 2, 1676 [pub. along with a letter of March 9, but not presently in the same volume, both in Ravaisson AB III, 184–188]. There is also a suspicious redating and refoliating between March 9 and 10, which suggests that someone has tampered with the file. AS Torino *Archivio Notariale di Pinerolo*, vol. 768 (Lantieri), Procuration de Monsieur Anthoine de Lausun àla Comtesse Dame Charlotte de Caumont, November 1, 1677. BNF Ms. Clair. 634–635, fols. 133–139, *Recit de l'entrevue de la Comtese de Nogent avec le Comte de Lauzun Son frère prisonnier à Pignerol en 1677.*

16. AN K 120a, N° 228, Louvois (letter sent) to Saint-Mars, December 26, 1677 [pub. in Delort, *Detention* I, 271–272]. AG A¹ 581, fol. 418, Louvois (minute) to Fouquet, December 23, 1678 [pub. in Ravaisson AB III, 208]. AG A¹ 617, fols. 513–514, Louvois (minute) to Fouquet, January 20, 1679, AG A¹ 617, fols. 515–518, *Mémoire de la manière dont le Roy desire que Mᵣ de Saint Mars garde a l'advenir les prisonniers qui sont a sa charge* [pub. in Delort, *Detention* I, 280–285].

17. AN K 120a, N°ˢ 272–274, Louvois (letters sent) to Saint-Mars, May 10, 18, and 29, 1679 [pub. in Delort, *Detention* I, 295–298].

18. Discovery: AN K 120a, N° 302, Louvois (letter sent) to Saint-Mars, April 8, 1680 [pub. in Delort, *Detention* I, 317–320]. Picon, however, had not disappeared from sight. In December of 1685, the *Mercure galant* reports his having received a pension of 2,000 *écus* (6,000 *livres*) for his services under Colbert and under Colbert's successor Claude Le Peletier. It would seem this was a kind of severance payment.

19. Appointment to Exilles: AG A¹ 684, fol. 232, Louvois (minute) to Saint-Mars, May 12, 1681 [pub. in Delort *MdF*, 268–269, Iung, 396–397, and Mongrédien, *MF*, 90–91]. Saint-Mars's compliance: BNF Ms. Clair. 589, pp. 361–365, Saint-Mars (own hand letter sent) to Abbot Estrades, June 25, 1681 [pub. in Ravaisson AB III, 214–215]. Conditions of imprisonment: Saint-Mars to Louvois, July 12 and March 11, 1682 [pub.in Delort *MdF*, 273–274 and 279–281, and Mongrédien, 95–97 and 105–106]. Death of La Rivière: AG A¹ 779, fol. 281, Louvois (letter sent) to Saint-Mars, January 13, 1687 [pub. in Iung, 404].

20. Appointment to Sainte-Marguerite: AG A¹ 779, fol. 114, Louvois (minute) to Saint Mars, January 8, 1687 [pub. in Iung, 404–405 and Mongrédien, 114]. See also Saint-Mars to Louvois, January 20, 1687, pub. in Roux-Fazillac, 114–115 and Delort *MdF*, 282, AG A¹ 779, fol. 506, Louvois (minute) to Saint- Mars, February 1, 1687 and AG A¹ 781, fol. 235, Louvois

(minute) to Saint-Mars, March 16, 1687. Difficulty of trip: Compare Saint-Mars to Louvois, March 23, 1687, pub. in Roux-Fazillac, 115 and Delort *MdF*, 283–284, and Saint Mars to Louvois, May 3, 1687, pub. in Roux-Fazillac, 116 and Delort *MdF*, 284–285 with BNF *Ms. Fr.* 23498 (*Nouvelles ecclésiastiques*), September 4, 1687 (copy in Bibliothèque Sainte-Geneviève *Ms* 1477, fol. 396 [pub. in Xavier Azéma, *Un prélat janséniste: Louis Fouquet, évêque et comte d'Agde: 1656–1702* (Paris, 1963), 150]. Saint-Mars to Louvois, January 8, 1688, pub. in Jules Loiseleur, "Un dernier mot sur le masque de fer," *Revue contemporaine*, Dix-huitième année, 2ᵉ série LXXII (1869), 391. Administration of Barbézieux: AG *A¹* 1034, fol 246 and *A¹* 1242, fol. 96, Barbézieux (minute) to Saint-Mars, August 18 and February 4, 1694. New Arrivals: AG *A¹* 1272, fol. 125, De Maisonel to Barbézieux, April 24, 1694. Death of Mattioli: AG *A¹ 1245*, fol. 139, Barbéxieux (minute) to Saint-Mars, May 10, 1694 [pub. in Iung, 91 and Mongrétien, 183–184]. Louis's pettiness: AG *A¹* 1303, fol. 108, Barbézieux (minute) to Saint-Mars, December 20, 1695, and Saint-Mars to Barbezieux, January 6, 1696, pub. in Jules Loiseleur, "Un dernier mot sur le masque de fer," cited above in this note, 399–400. We find Blainvilliers in Louvois's letter of December 17, 1669, cited in note 9 above, where Blainvilliers is relaying orders from Louis XIV on how to deal with La Forêt and Valcroissant, in AN *K* 120a Nº 238, Louvois to Saint-Mars, July 29, 1678, where Louis permits Blainvilliers to come to Paris to take care of Saint-Mars's personal affairs, Nº 264, Louvois to Saint-Mars, March 28, 1679 [pub. in Delort, *Detention* I, 275 and 293], where Blainvilliers is relaying orders from the king on how to lodge Lauzun, in Saint-Mars to Louvois, October 9 and 16, 1680, pub. in Delort *MdF*, 264–265, where Blainvilliers reports Mattioli for trying to bribe him with some diamonds. Return trip: Palteau to Fréron, *Année littéraire* (1768), IV, 351–354.

21. For Picon's death see AD Seine-et-Marne, GG 3 (1 Mi320 R1), fol. 200, as well as the *Journal du Marquis de Dangeau avec les additions du duc de Saint-Simon*, ed. Eudoxe Soulié et al. (Paris, 1854–1860), VII, 165–166, and Souches *Mémoires*, ed. Cosnac V, 192. On the ironies of Louis XIV's reign, please see my "Some Mischievous Questions about the Treaty of Ryswick," *Journal of Early Modern European History* IV, Nᵒˢ 3–4 (2001), 452–455.

22. Voltaire to Jean-Baptiste Dubos, October 30 [1738] Besterman *VC* VII, Letter 1569, pp. 424–427 or Besterman *CW* LXXXIX, Letter D1642, pp. 344–346 and Jean-Baptiste Dubos to Voltaire, December 3, 1738, Besterman *VC* VIII, Letter 1597, pp. 5–7 or Besterman *CW* LXXXIX, Letter D1672, 388–390.

23. Voltaire, *Supplément au Siècle de Louis XIV* (Dresden, 1753) or Besterman *CW*, XXXIIc, 291–382. For the Avignon gentleman see the introduction note 5.

Bibliography

Manuscript Sources

England
Bodleian Library, Oxford University
  Clarendon Manuscript 23
British Library
  Additional Manuscript 15890, Original Lettres de Cachet Egerton Manuscripts.
    1681–1682, *Débats du Parlement de Paris*: 1641–1652
    1902–1903, Register for the Council for the Estates
  Harleian Manuscript 7379, Letters to King Charles I from his Queen: 1643–1645
Public Record Office (National Archives)
  High Court of Admiralty 13/176, 30/179, 30/873
  State Papers Domestic (Charles II) 29/81, 125, 287, 289–293, 295, 306, 336–337
  State Papers Foreign
    Entry Book 104/30, 35A
    France 78/121 and 125-127
    Newsletters 101/13 and 16–17
  Treasury: Warrants not regarding Money 4

France
Archives Condé
  Cabinet de Livres N° 565 (*Mémoriaux du Conseil*)
  M XXVII
  Ms.1088–1090 (Peace of Pyrenees)
  Ms.1293 *Inventario delli argenti dorati e bianchi, giove, christali e altro del l Em^te- e Rev^mo cardinale Giulio Mazarini* (1645)
  Ms.1294 *Inventaire de tous les meubles du cardinal Mazarin: Dressé en 1653*
  P XVI–XVII

211

Archives de la Guerre (Service Historique de l'Armée de Terre)
  A[1] 100, 101, 103, 157, 159, 160, 162, 168, 234, 235, 355, 421, 472, 581, 617, 684, 779, 781, 1034, 1242, 1245, 1272, 1303
Archives Departmentales
  Aisne
    B 745
  Ardèche
    2E 21869, 21870 (Desaufres)
    Baptêmes, Mariages, Sépultures (La Figère): 1612–1695
  Charente-Maritime
    3E 315 (Alexandre Demontreau)
  Drôme
    2 E 15672 (Pierre Breynat)
    2 E 15686, 15689 (Hector Bon)
    B 708, *Inventaire général des papiers du greffe royal de la presente ville de Mon^ar Sentences de l'année 1656*
  Gard
    1 E/424 (old E 1274)
    2 E 1'289, 291–292 (Jean Ursi le jeune)
    2 E 1/440 (Daniel Pepin)
    2 E 4'51 (Jean Froment)
    2 E 10/857 (Jean Durand)
    2 E 16/283, 285, 288–290 (André Vincent)
    2 E 16/296, 300 (Guillaume de Pouzols)
    2 E 37 117 (Jacques Ducros)
    2 E 37/163 (Claude Privat)
    2 E 39/81 (Jean Daubanel)
    2 E 39/124, 324 (Isaac Barre)
    2 E 39/335–336 (Paul Barre)
    2 E 216/2 (Baptêmes, Mariages, Sépultures) Monoblet
    C (Admiistration Provinciale) 647
    E Depôt
      126/1 Déliberaòns des habitans de Rivières: 1655
      126/4 Inventaire de St Privat de Rivières: 1696
      126/7 Compoix de Rivières de Theyrargues: 1655
    GG 19 (Baptêmes, Mariages, Sépultures)
    LL 19–24 (Archives Municipales de Nîmes, Déliberations des Consuls 1621–1667)
    Rivières 201
    UU 94, 95, 97, 118, 119 (Baptêmes, Mariages, Sépultures)
  Haut-Rhin
    Ms. 2929
  Hérault
    2 E 55/127 (Jean Laune)
  Loire-Atlantique
    B 6953
  Loiret
    3 E 10008, 10009 (François Bonhomme)
    3 E 10013 (Pierre Bonhomme)
    3 E 10038, 10039 (Nöel Hüet)

Oise
  1 Mi B 356–357, 359 (Tables)
  EDT 1/GG 69–79
  1 Mi *ECA* 612 *R* 11
  2 *E* 28/75 (Martin Desaintlieu)
Pas-de-Calais
  4 *E* 52/249–250, 252, 259 (Pierre Anquier)
  4 *E* 52/351–356 (Charles Théru)
  4 *E* 55 (Pierre Danjan)
  4 *E* 55 (Charles Danjan)
  4 *E* 55 (Louis Caussien)
Rhône
  B 73, 107 111
Seine-et-Marne
  GG (Régistres Paroissaux) 3 (1Mi320 R1)
Vaucluse
  B (Parlement d'Orange) 43, 147, 148
  3 *E* 51/210 (Jean Turc)
Archives du Ministère des Affaires Etrangères
  Correspondance Politique
    Allemagne 85, 88, 89, 101, 103, 109, 121, 148, 149
    Angleterre 60, 61, 64, 66, 67, 69, 75, 81, 91
    Espagne 35, 38
    Hollande 32, 57, 68
    Lorraine 37
    Pays Bas Espagnols, 29, 34, 45, 47, 48, 49
      Rome 64, 126, 129
      Sardaigne 13
      Suède 12
      Suisse 44
  Mémoires et Documents
    Alsace 18, 19
    Espagne 60–63
    France 118, 259–285, 416, 846–911, 1593, 1683
Archives Municipales
  Calais
    BB (for 1636) 29 (1658–1660), 30 (1661–1662), 32 (1664–1670)
    CC 20, 25
  Portes
    1 CC 1–3 *Compoix de 1640*
Archives Nationales
  Archives Privées
    144 *AP* 57 (156Mi3) Item 2 *"Journal de M. d'Ormesson pendant la chambre de justice
      establie en décembre 1661 dans la chambre des révisions de la chambre des comptes"*
    144 *AP* 60–74 (156Mi 6–30) Documents concernant le procès Fouquet
  AD+ (Textes Administratifs)
    340
  E (Conseil du Roi)
    313b, 314a, 409a, 1689, 1700, 1703, 1704, 1705, 1706, 1731

H^{2*} (Déliberations du Bureau de la ville de Paris)
    1799 (1616–1620), 1800 and 1801 (1620–1624), 1801 (1624–1628), 1803 (1628–
      1632)
H^2 (Déliberations du Bureau de la ville de Paris)
    1797–1806 (1615–1643), 1810 (1648–1652)
K (Monuments Historiques)
    120a (Ordres au gouverneur de Pignerol 1661–1682)
    572 (Titres de la maison de Budos)
    1309–1317 (Pologne)
KK (Monuments Historiques)
    1217–1221 (Correspondence de Mazarin: 1649–1653)
Minutier Central
    XVI/372 (Philippe Le Cat)/477 (Louis de Séjournant)
    XX/331 (Charles Sainfray)
    XIX/443 (Nicolas Baudry)
    XXIV/421, 423 (Jean Chapelain)
    XXVI/68 (Jean de Monenhault)
    XLIV/19 (Christophe Loyer)
    XLVI/90 (Nicolas Charles)
    L/85 (Jean Chaussière)
    LI/504, 539, 542 (Jérôme Cousinet)
    LXVI/74, 75, 81 (Etienne Paisant)
    LVII/70–104 Repertoire 2 (Etienne Thomas)
    LXVIII/202, 203 (André Laurent)
    LXXXI/64, Repertoire 2 (Gilles Roussel)
    LXXIII/412 (Charles-François de Saint-Vaast)
    LXXIII 538–539 (Noël Le Maistre)
LXXVII/2, 10, 17, Repertoire 1a (Etienne Thomas)
LXXXVI/307 (Pierre Parque II)
LXXXVII/196 (Jean Nonnet)
XCV/4, 10, 16, 23–25, Repertoires 1, 2 (François Le Fouyn)
XCVI/47, 51, 61 (Michel de Beauvais)
CVII/97 (Benjamin Moufle)
CX/134 (Olivier Le Moyne)
O^1 (Maison du Roy)
    8
U (Extraits et Procédures Judiciaires)
    2107 (Registres du Conseil du Parlement)
V^6 (Conseil Privé)
    192
X (Parlement de Paris)
    X^{1a} (Conseil Secret) 8390, 8392
    X^{1a} (Plaidoiries) 5877, 5917
Y (Châtelet de Paris)
    175, 183, 199 (Insinuations)
Z (Juridictions Spéciales et Ordinaires)
    Z^{1a} 499 (Gardes du Corps)
    Z^{1b} (Cour des Monnaies de Paris) 342
    Z^2 (Baillage du Palais) 2926

Bibliothèque de l'Arsenal
  Ms. 675 (Testament de Mazarin)
  Ms. 3740 (Sommaire du testament de Mazarin)
  Mss. 3723, 4549 (Analyses du Parlement de Paris)
  Mss. 5414, 5421, 5426 (Collection Conrart)
  Mss. 5178–5185 (Journal autographe d'Arnauld d'Andilly)
  Ms.10304 "*Titres des ouvrages et libelles imprimés sans permission qui ont été saisis en vertu des ordres du roi depuis l'année 1660 jusqu'en 1718*"
  Mss. 10330 10333, 10334, 12472, 12721
Bibliothèque de l'Assemblée Nationale
  Ms. 273
Bibliothèque de l'Institut de France
  Ms. 55–58 (Peace of Pyrenees)
  Ms 2015 "*Voyage de Monsieur le cavalier Bernin en France*"
  Ms. 1332 (Papiers de Régis de Chantelauze relatifs à son Histoire du cardinal de Retz)
  Ms. 4454 "*Mémoires touchant les démêlés du cardinal de Retz avec la cour de France*," par Claude Joly
  Ms. *Godefroy*, 288, 310 (Pièces diverses et mélanges)
Bibliothèque de Sainte-Geneviève
  Ms. 802 (Peace of Pyrenees)
  Ms. 1477 *Nouvelles ecclésiastiques*
  Ms. 2014 "*Relation succinte de ce qu s'est passé à la mort de M. le Cardinal Mazarini premier ministre d'Estat*"
Bibliothèque de l'Université de Paris
  Ms. 64–70 Extraits des registres du Parlement, faits par Pierre Lallemant, maître des requêtes
  Ms. 1201 "*Sommaire du Testament de feu le cardinal Mazarin*"
Bibliothèque Mazarine
  Mss. 2214–2218, 2249–2253
Bibliothèques Municipales
  Aix
    Ms. 415 (Sommaire du testament de Mazarin)
  Auxerre
    Ms. *102* Mémoires of Brienne (continuation of *NAF 6450*)
  Chartres
    Ms. 534 (saved from bombing of May 26, 1944)
  Rouen
    Ms.1894 (Collection Montbret 164), "*Mémoires de M. Colbert au cardinal Mazarin sur les finances de France suivis du plan de la Chambre de justice et des affaires qui s'y traitent*"
    Ms. 3268 (Collection Leber 5775), "*Observations de Monsieur le Comte de Brienne Ministre et Secretaire d'Etat, Sur les memoires de Monsieur de la Chastre*"
Biliothèque Nationale
  Cabinet des Titres
    Carrés d'Hozier 57
    Dossiers Bleus 270
    Nouveu Hozier 265
    Pièces originales 1906

Manuscrits Baluze
115 (Cardinal de Retz, Parlement de Paris)
148 (Lettres autographes de Guy Patin)
174–175 (Carnets de Mazarin)
175–176 (Papiers de Mazarin)
178 (Papiers de Charles Colbert)
187 (Négociations diverses, Italie, Angleterre, Espagne)
208 (Mélanges)
216 (Papiers de Mazarin et Colbert: 1642–1660)
328–329, 331–332 (Correspondence de Mazarin)
351 (Papiers de Baluze)
363 (Minutes de lettres de Colbert à Mazarin: 1651)
Manuscrits Cinq Cents Colbert
98 Registre de lettres de Louis XIII et de Marie de Medicis (1619–1623)
212, Lettres patents, arrêts et autres actes concernant le Parlement 1389–1656
228–237 "*Extraicts sommaires tiréz des registres de la Chambre de Justice (1661–1665) rédigéz par Mre Joseph Foucault, greffier de la Chambre*"
Manuscrits Clairambault
579–581 (Comte d'Estrades)
634–635 (Mélanges)
837 (Maison de Louis XIII)
1144 (Testament de Mazarin)
Manuscrits Dupuy
631 Recueil de lettres et documents concernant les règnes de Henri II, Charles IX, Henri II, Henri IV, Louis XIII et Louis XIV
775 Divers mémoires d'histoire et meslanges soubz les roys Louis XI, Henry II, Charles IX, Henry III, Louis XIII, jusques en l'an 1654
858 Testament du Cardinal Mazarin
Manuscrits Français
3722 "*Registre de Monsieur Tronson, secretaire du Cabinet de plusieurs Lettres Escrittes de la main du Roy Louis treisiesme a divers Princes, Seigneurs et autres es années 1619, 1620, 1621, 1622, 1624, 1625 et 1626*"
3747 Recueil de copies de pièces
3854–3855 Recueils de lettres et pièces originales, et de copies de pièces
3949 Recueil de copies de pièces
4022–4027 "*Journal de la vie active du Roy Louis [XIII], exactement descrit depuis le premier janvier 1605 jusqu'au xxx . . . janvier . . . 1628 . . . par messire Jehan Herouand, S^gr de Vaucrigneuse, son premier medecin*"
4102 Recueil des pièces relatives aux guerres de religion sous Louis XIII
4138 "*Livre des negotiations de Mr de Sabran, envoyé resident en Angleterre pour le service du roy tres chrestien le 17e jour du mois de may 1644*"
4168–4195 Recueil de copies de pièces, formé principalement des dépêches écrites ou signées par Michel Le Tellier, sécrétaire d'État durant les dix-huit premières années du règne de Louis XIV
4208–4209 "*Depesches de S.E. [le Cardinal Mazarin] à Mgr Le Tellier depuis le 4 juin 1650 jusques au retour du voyage de Bourdeaux, a la fin du mois de decembre de la mesme années*" (copies), and "*Memoires et lettres de S.E. [le cardinal Mazarin] et de Mr Colbert, adressants à Mgr Le Tellier durant le voyage de Bourdeaux, en l'année 1650*" (copies)
4332 Testaments de roys, princes et grands seigneurs, et hommes doctes, testaments fictifs (1306 à 1669) copies

6408 Etats de dépenses et autres pour la Marine

6557 Recueil de pièces historiques du XVIIᵉ siècle Portefeuille du Prince de Condé contenant sa correspondance et les traités conclus pendant les années 1649 à 1659

6784–6787 *"Comptes de la recepte et despense qui a esté daicté par le . . . tresorier de Monseigneur le duc de Mazarin"* (1661–1665)

6880–6900 Papiers d'état de Michel Le Tellier (1640–1678)

7156 *"Lettres et mémoires du cardinal Mazarin à Messieurs Le Tellier et de Lionne, contenant le secret de la négociation de la paix des Pyrenees dans les conférences tenues à Saint-Jean de Luz en 1659"*

7607 *"Recueil des pièces qui ont été communiquées au Sʳ Foucquet pour servir a se deffendre dans les accusations faites contre luy par les accusations faites contre luy par differents faux tesmoins gagnes par ses ennemis"*

7620–7627 Pièces originales du procès de Nicolas Foucquet (1661–1668)

7628 *"Interrogatoire de Mʳ Nicolas Foucquet, ministre d'État et surintendant des finances, sur la sellette, à lArsenal"* (1664)

7755 *"Mémoires sur les affaires de Finances de France,"* par Colbert (1661)

7852–7856 *"Officiers des maisons des roys, reynes, enfans de France, et de quelques princes du sang, depuis le reigne du roy Sᵗ Louis jusqu'à Louis XIV"* and *"Table des ordonnances et estats des masons des roys, reynes, dauphins enfans et autres princes de France depuis Sᵗ Louis jusqu'à Louis XIV"* (1221–1665)

9357–9358 *"Recueil de lettres originales de Guy Patin, docteur régent dn la Faculté de médecine à Paris adressées à Charles et Jacob Spon de Lyon"* (1642–1672) and *"Recueil de lettres originales de Guy Patin, adressées au médecin Belin de Troyes, et à Charles et Jacob Spon de Lyon"* (1630–1664)

9438 *"Inventaire, prisée, et estimations des livres trouvés à St-Mandé appartenant cidevant à Mʳ . . . 1663"*

9717 Recueil de pièces historiques

10206 Recueil de pièces originales et copies concernant l'histoire de France (XVIᵉ–XVIIIᵉ siècle)

10210 Recueil de copies de pièces relatives à l'histoire de France pendant le XVIIᵉ siècle

10228–10229 *"Recueil de plusieurs pieces curieuses touchant les affaires du temps concer-nant Mʳ Fouquet et autres escrites ès années 1660,1661, 1662 et 1663 avec les suites transcrit le 9ᵉ juillet 1663 et les 8 septembre 1664"*

10249 Lettres autographes du cardinal Mazarin, de Colbert, d'Anne d'Autriche, de Philippe duc d'Orléans et de Louis XIV (1659–1674)

10273–10277 *"Remarques journallieres et veritables de ce qui c'est passé Paris et en quelques aultres endroictz du royaume et ailleurs durant l'année 1648 jusaqu'en 1657"*

10325–10328 Mémoires du cardinal de Retz

10456–10457 Mémoires du duc de La Rochefoucauld (1643–1652)

11952 Portraits des membres du Parlement de Paris en 1662

10977 Mémoire "sur le crime de leze-majesté" attributed to Chamillart

11453 *"Testament de Monseigneur le Cardinal Mazarin"*

12801 Recueil de pièces diverses sur le règne de Louis XIV en prose et en vers, chansons, épigrammes, épitaphes, sonnets, etc.

15499–15583 Recueil de pièces, manuscrits et imprimées, formé par le président Achille III de Harlay, relatives principalement à l'histoire religieuse, politique, administrative, diplomatique et littéraire des XVIᵉ et XVIIᵉ siècles

15604 Testaments, oraisons funèbres, épitaphes de rois, reines, princes et person-nages célèbres; manuscrits et imprimés (1308–1672)

17048 Portefeuille du docteur Vallant—Mélanges d'histoire . . . Pièces diverses

17367–17412 Correspondance de Pierre Séguier, chancelier de France (1663–1669)

19757 *"Lettres et memoires de M.le cardinal de Mazarin a M^{rs} Le Tellier et de Lionne, contenans le secret de la negociation de la paix des Pyrenées, dans les conferences tenues a St Jean de Luz entre ledit seigneur cardinal et Dom Louis s'Haro en 1659"*

20156–21063 Recueil de pièces sur l'histoire de France provenant des frères de Sainte-Marthe

23202 Recueil de lettres adressées par le cardinal Mazarin à l'abbé Fouquet (1651–1660)

23347 *"La négociation d'Osnabruck par M. le comte d'Avaux, Claude de Mesme (1647), plus les motifs de la France pour la guerre d'Allemagne et encore les testamens d'A.-J. Du Plessis, cardinal duc de Richelieu"* (1642) *"et de J. Mazarini"* (1661)

23496 *Nouvelles ecclésiastiques*

25025–25026 Nouvelles de Paris, de Bordeaux, etc. (25 décembre 1648–26 août 1653) [transcribed in http://www.ranumspanat.com]

Manuscrits Italiens 1771, 1823, 1825, 1849, 1850, 1867 (transcripts of ASVen *Francia*)

Manuscrits Joly de Fleury

2445–2446 Pièces historiques (1550–1665)

2502–2503 Procès de Fouquet

2520 Services de M. d'Hervart

Manuscrits Morel de Thoisy

157–158, 399–403 Procès de Fouquet

433 Postes et Messageries

Mélanges de Colbert

41–45, 51–52c Minutes de la correspondance du cardinal de Mazarin durant son ministère (1646–1650), (1654–1656)

74 Testament et comptes des exécuteurs testamentaires du cardinal Jules Mazarin (1661–1666)

75 Inventaire des meubles, cabinets, joyaux, médailles, vaisselle, tableaux, statues, tapisseries et argent du cardinal Jules Mazarin (1661)

101–176 Correspondance de Colbert (1649, 1656–1674)

281 Etats de la Recette et Dépense du Trésor Royal (1669)

Nouvelles Acquistions Francaises

1700, Journal du Congrès de Munster, par François Ogier, Aumonier du comte d'Avaux (1641–1647)

4698 Memoires de Henri-Louis de Loménie, comte de Brienne, sur le règne de Louis XIV

6450 *"Mémoires de messire Louis-Henri de Loménie, Comte de Brienne, cy-devant secrétaire d'Estat et maintenant prisonnier à Saint-Lazare" (1643–1682)*

9747 Réception d'Henriette de France, Reine d'Angleterre

13799 Mémoires de Robert Challe

22874–22875 Papiers divers, contrats, quittances, testaments (1657–1743), avec une lettre originale du cardinal Mazarin (13 juin 1659)

22877 *"Compte de la recepte et despence qui a esté faicte par le sieur de la Boudre, trésorier de Monseigneur le duc Mazarin, depuis le premier avril dernier jusau'au dernier décembre 1662"* (cf BNF Ms. Fr. 6784–6787)

Germany

Niedersächsisches Hauptstatsarchiv

Celle Br.161 *Frankreich 31*

Italy

Archivio di Stato di Firenze
  Codice Mediceo 4660, 4891
Archivio di Stato di Genova
  Archivio Segreto 2193 (Francia 17)
Archivio di Stato di Mantova
  Archivio Gonzaga 685, 686, 707, 710
Archivio di Stato di Napoli
  Carteggio Farnesiano 186 II fascicolo 5
Archivio di Stato di Roma
  Notai Capitolini, Ufficio 18/388 Francesco Pacichelli (Franciscus Pacichellus) Testament of Mazarin
Archivio di Stato di Torino
  Materie Politiche Lettere Ministri *Francia* 84, 86, 87
Archivio di Stato di Venezia
  Francia 51, 101, 102, 126, 127, 144

Monaco

Prince of Monaco
  S 5–12, 15–20

Netherlands

Gemeente Archieven
  Den Haag
    Notarieel Archief
      28 (Cornelis Pieck)
      170 (Walterus Rietraet)
  Maastricht
    Notarieel Archief 1484 (Joos Corstius)
    Oud Archief 67 (Raadsvertragen)
      949 (Requestboeken)

Russia

National Library, Saint Petersburg Ms.Voltaire 5

Spain

Archivo General de Simancas
  K 1623
Biblioteca Nacional de España
  Ms. 2384 (Sucesos de los años: 1653–1656)

Vatican

Archivio Segreto del Vaticano
  Nunziatura di Francia 119
Archivio Concistoriale
  Processi Concistoriali 42

Printed Sources

Abraham van der Doort's Catalogue of the Collections of Charles I, ed. Oliver Millar (Glasgow, 1960), Walpole Society, XXXVII.

Abreu y Bertodano, Joseph Antonio de, *Coleccion de Los Tratados de paz, alianza, neutralidad, garantia, proteccion, tregua, mediacion, accession, reglamento de limites, comercio, navegaction, &c., hechos por los pueblos, reyes, y principes de España con los pueblos, reyes, principes, republicas, y demàs potencias de Europa, y otras partes del mundo . . . Desde antes del establecimiento de la monarchia gothica, hasta el feliz reynado del rey N.S.D.* (Madrid, 1740–52), 12 vols.

Acta Pacis Westphalicae, ed. Konrad Repgen (Münster, 1962–).

Les Amours d'Anne d'Autriche, épouse de Louis XIII, avec M. Le C.D.R. le véritable père de Louis XIV, ou on voit au long comment on s'y prit pour donner un héritier à la Couronne, les ressorts qu'on fit jouer pour cela et enfin tout le dénuement de cette comédie (Amsterdam, 1692, 1693, and 1696).

Arnauld d'Andilly, Robert, *Journal inédit d'Arnauld d'Andilly* (1626), ed. Eugène and Jules Halphen I (Paris, 1905).

Arrêt de la cour de parlement, donné, toutes les chambres assemblées, le huictième jour de janvier 1649, par lequel il est ordonné que le cardinal Mazarin videra le royaume, et qu'il sera fait levée de gens de guerre pour la sûreté de la ville et pour faire amener et apporter sûrement les vivres à Paris (Paris, 1649) [Moreau N° 217].

Arrêt de la cour de parlement, portant que tous les biens meubles ou immeubles et revenus des bénéfices du cardinal Mazarin seront saisis, et commissaires, séquestres et gardiens commis à iceux Du 13 janvier 1649 (Paris, 1649) [Moreau N°· 224].

Arrêt de la cour de parlement, pour la liberté de messieurs les princes et l'éloignement du cardinal Mazarin hors du royaume de France, Du 7 février 1651 (Paris, n.d.) [Moreau N° 289].

Arrêt de la cour de parlement, toutes les chambres assemblées, contre le cardinal Mazarin. Du samedi 11 mars. 1651 (Paris, n.d.) [Moreau N° 293].

Arrêt de la cour de parlement, toutes les chambres assemblées, portant que le cardinal Mazarin, ses parents et domestiques étrangers vuideront le royaume de France; autrement permis, aux communes et autres, de courir sus, avec autres ordres pour cet effet. Du jeudi 9 février 1651 [Moreau N° 290].

Arrêt du Conseil d'Etat du Roy par lequel Sa Majesté ordonne que les liards n'auront cours que pour un denier seulement. Du 20 Juillet 1658 (Paris, 1658).

Arrest du Conseil d'Etat du Roy par lequel Sa Majesté veut que les liards n'aient cours que pour deux deniers seulement du 20 juin 1658.

Arrêt du Conseil d'Etat du Roy portant interprétations de celuy du 25 may dernier pour le règlement sur le fait des liards (Paris, 1658).

Arrêt du conseil royal des finances du 24 mai 1664 par lequel Sa Majesté ordonne que les proprietaires & possesseurs des rentes assignées sur les deniers des fermes, représenteront les titres justificatifs de leur propriété, pour être par messieurs les commissaires dressé procès-verbal de la représentation à iceux, & par leur rapport incéssamment procédé à la liquidation & remboursement desdites rentes.

Aubais, Charles de Baschi, Marquis d, *Pièces fugitives pour servir a l histoire de France* (1759), 2 vols.

Aumale, Henri, duc d', *Inventaire de tous les meubles du cardinal Mazarin: Dressé en 1653* (London, 1861).

Avaux, Claude de Mesmes, comte d', *Lettres de messieurs d'Avaux et Servien, ambassadeurs pour le Roi de France en Allemagne concernant leurs différends et leurs responces de part et d'autre en l'année 1644* (1650).

Balthazar, Jean de, *Histoire de la guerre de Guyenne*, in *Mémoires de Jacques de Saulx. Comte de Tavannes, suivis de l'histoire de la guerre de Guyenne par Balthazar*, ed. Célestin Moreau (Paris, 1858).

Bassompierre, François de, *Journal de ma vie; mémoires du maréchal de Bassompierre*, ed. M. J. A. de la Cropte Chantérac (Paris 1870–1877), 4 vols. SHF.

Benedetti, Elpidio, *Raccolta di diverse memorie per scrivere la vita del cardinale Giulio Mazarini romano* (Lyon, n.d.), 36–44.

Bentivoglio, Guido, *La Nunziatura di Francia del Cardinale Guido Bentivoglio*, ed. Luigi di Stefani (Florence, 1863–1870), 4 vols.

Bibliographie des Mazarinades, ed. Célestin Moreau (Paris, 1850–1851), 3 vols.

Bodleian Library, *Calendar of the Clarendon State Papers Preserved in the Bodleian Library*, ed. William Dunn Macray and F. J. Routledge (Oxford, 1869–1970), 5 vols.

Boislisle, Jean de, *Mémoriaux du Conseil de 1661* (Paris, 1905–1907), 3 vols.

Brienne, Henri-Auguste de Loménie, Count de, *Mémoires du comte de Brienne*. Collection des mémoires relatifs à l'histoire de France, ed. Petitot and Monmerqué (Paris, 1819–1829), ser. 2 XXXV–XXXVI, or in Nouvelle collection des mémoires pour servir à l'histoire de France, ed. Michaud and Poujoulat (Paris, 1836–1839), ser. 3 III.

Brienne, Louis Henri de Loménie, Count de, *Mémoires de Louis-Henri de Loménie, Comte de Brienne, dit le jeune Brienne*, ed. Paul Bonnefon (Paris, 1916), SHF.

Bulletin de la Société de l'Histoire de France II (Paris, 1836).

Bussy, Roger de Rabutin, Comte de, *Histoire amoureuse des Gaules*, ed. Paul Boiteau and Charles Louis Livet (Paris, 1856–1876), 4 vols.

———, *Mémoires de messire Roger de Rabutin, Comte de Bussy* (Paris, 1696), 2 vols.

———, *Mémoires de Roger de Rabutin, Comte de Bussy, édition suivie de l'histoire amoureuse des Gaules*, ed. Ludovic Lalanne (Paris, 1857), 2 vols.

Il Cardinale Mazzarino in Francia: Colloquio Italo-Francese (Rome, 1977).

Carsalade du Pont, J., *Documents inédits sur la Fronde en Gascogne* (Paris and Auch, 1883). Archives Historiques de la Gascogne, I.

Castiglione, Valeriano, *Alla Maestà Christianissima di Luigi XIII il giusto Rè di Francia per la prosperità delle sue Armi* (s.l.n.d.).

Challe, Robert, *Mémoires, Correspondance complète, Rapports sur l'Acadie et autres pièces*, ed. Frédéric Deloffre (Geneva, 1996).

Champollion-Figeac, Jacques Joseph, ed., *Documents historiques tirés des collections manuscrites de la Bibliothèque royale et des archives ou des bibliothèques de départements* (Paris, 1841–1848), 4 vols. Collection de documents inédits sur l'histoire de France.

Chantelou, Paul Fréant de, *Journal du voyage du Cavalier Bernin en France*, ed. Ludovic Lalanne (Paris, 1885).

Chappuzeau, Charles, *De la justice et de la paix, de l'injustice et de la guerre; les misères et fin luctueuse des guerres Civiles & Etrangères; Et qu'il n'y a rien au monde plus désirable que la Paix* (Paris, 1627).

Chappuzeau, Samuel, *Entretiens familiers pour l'instruction de la noblesse étrangère* (Paris and Geneva, 1665).

L.M.C. [Chesnay], "Lettre inédite à M. de Voltaire d'un gentilhomme d'Avignon sur le Masque de fer avec la réponse," *Buletin polymathique du Muséum d'instruction politique de Bordeaux* (October 1815) XIII, 384–385.

Chiala, Luigi, "Il Cardinale di Mazarino," *Rivista contemporanea*, IV (September–November, 1855), 539–584.

Choisy, abbé de, *Mémoires de l'abbé de Choisy*. Collection des mémoires relatifs à l'histoire de France, ed. Petitot and Monmerqué (Paris, 1819–1829), ser. 2 LXIII or in Nouvelle collection des mémoires pour servir à l'histoire de France, ed. Michaud and Poujoulat (Paris, 1836–1839), ser. 3 VI.

Choix des Mazarinades, ed. Célestin Moreau (Paris, 1853), 2 vols.

Colbert, Jean-Baptiste, *Lettres instructions et mémoires de Colbert*, ed. Pierre Clément (Paris, 1861–1862), 8 vols.

Commission du Roy Contenant les noms des Juges et Officiers qui composent la Chambre de Justice . . . 15 Novembre 1661 (1661).

Commission pour Messieurs du Grand Conseil . . . 15 Novembre 1661 (1661).

Commission pour MM Hotman et Chamillard pour la fonction d'avocat et procureurs généraux en la chambre de justice, December 1, 1663 (s.l.n.d.).

Conrart, Valentin, *Mémoires de Valentin Conrart*, Collection des mémoires relatifs à l'histoire de France, ed. Petitot and Monmerqué (Paris, 1819–1829), ser. 2 XLVIII or in Nouvelle collection des mémoires pour servir à l'histoire de France, ed. Michaud and Poujoulat (Paris, 1836–1839), ser. 3 IV.

Le Constitutionnel

Continuation de factum sur une production faite par M. Fouquet le 24 octobre 1664, touchant la pension de six vingt mille livres sur la ferme des gabelles; sur la requête de M. le procureur général, servant de contredite, du 4 novembre, et réponses de M. Fouquet, du 6 novembre (s.l.n d.).

Contract de mariage du roy de Pologne avec la princesse Marie (Paris, 1645).

Cosnac, Gabriel Jules de, *Mazarin et Colbert* (Paris, 1892), 2 vols.

———, *Les richesses du palais Mazarin . . . Correspondence idédite de M, de Bordeaux, ambassadeur en Angleterre. Etat inédit des tableaux et des tapisseries de Charles premier mis en vente au palais de Somerset en 1650. Inventaire inédit dressé après la most du cardinal Mazarin 1661* (Paris, 1884).

Courcillon, Philippe de, marquis de Dangeau, *Journal du marquis de Dangeau avec les additions du duc de Saint-Simon* ed. Eudoxe Soulié et al. (Paris, 1854–1860), 19 vols.

Courtilz de Sandras, Gatien, *Mémoires de M. L.C.D.R. concernant ce qui s'est passé de plus particulier sous le ministère du cardinal de Richelieu et du cardinal Mazarin, avec plusieurs particularités remaquables du règne de Louis le Grand* (Cologne, 1687).

———, *Vie de Colbert* (Paris, 1695).

Coustumes de la prevosté et vicomté de Paris, avec les notes de M. C. du Molin restituées en leur entier, ensemble les observations de Mes I. Tournet, Iacq Ioly, & Ch. L abbé, anciens Advocats de la Cour & Arrests d'icelle, par eux recueillis sur chacun article: dernière édition (Paris, 1660).

Crouzet, Henri, "Droits et privilèges de la Commune de Nevers," *Publication de la Société Nivernoise*, 1re série (Nevers, 1858), 198–247.

La Custode de la Reyne qui dit tout (1649) [Moreau: N° 856].

Dangeau, Philippe de Coucillon, Marquis de, *Journal du marquis de Dangeau avec les additions du duc de Saint-Simon*, ed. Eudoxe Soulié et al. (Paris, 1854–1860), 19 vols.

Daniel, Gabriel, *Histoire de la Milice française* (Paris, 1721), 2 vols.

Darricau, Raymond et Laurain-Portemer, Madeleine, "La Mort du cardinal Mazarin," *Annuaire-Bulletin de la Société de l'Histoire de France* (1958–1959), 58–120.

Declaration modifiant la frappe des liards de cuivre ordonnés par la declaration du 12 juin 1649, April 30, 1654.

Déclaration . . . portant règlement pour l'exposition et décri des monoyes . . . 29 avril 1653 (Paris, 1653).

Déclaration pour la fabrication des espèces nouvelles d'or et d'argent appelles lys (Paris, 1655).

Declarations (des 10 juin et 27 septembre 1649, 30 avril et 1er juillet 1654) *du Roy pour la fabrication en ce Royaume des Liards de cuivre, valans trois deniers et Décry des Doubles & Deniers qui ont eu cours iusques à preent, à l'exception des Deniers qui ont esté faits par ordre de sa Majeste, Certifiées en la Cour de Monnoyes le 7 Aoust & premier Octobre 1649, 3 Juin & 11 Juillet 1654* (Paris, 1654) (Lyon, 1654).

Delort, Joseph, *Histoire de la détention des philosophes et des gens de lettres à la Bastille et à Vincennes* (Paris, 1829), 3 vols.

——, *Histoire de l'homme au masque de fer* (Paris, 1825).

Depping, Georg, *Correspondance administrative sous le règne de Louis XIV* (Paris, 1850–1855), 4 vols. Collection de documents inédits sur l'histoire de France, ser. 3 vol. XXXII.

Desjardins, Marie-Catherine (Madame de Villedieu), *Nouveau recueil de quelques pièces galantes* (Paris, 1669).

DeWitt, Johan, *Brieven geschrhieven ende gewisselt tusschen den Heer Johan de Witt, raedt pensionaris en groot-segelbewaerder van Hollandt en West Vrieslandt, ende de gevolmaghtigden van den staedt der Vereennighde Nederlanden: so in Vranckryck, Engelandt, Sweden, Danemarcken, Poolen, enz. beginnende met den jaere 1652, tot het jaer 1669 incluys* (The Hague, 1723–1726), 3 vols.

Documents du Minutier central concernant l'histoire littéraire: 1650–1700, ed. Madeleine Jurgens et al. (Paris, 1960).

Dohna, Friedrich von, *Les Mémoires du burgrave et comte Frédéric de Dohna:1621–1688*, ed. H. Borkowski (Königsberg, 1898).

Dubuisson-Aubenay, François-Nicolas Baudot, sieur d', *Journal des guerres civiles: 1648–1652*, ed. Gustave Saige (Paris, 1883), 2 vols.

Dumont, Claude, *Factum pour Claude Dumont ci devant receveur des tailles en l'élection de Crespy-en-Valois, contre Frederick Antoine Charmolue, tresorier de France au bureau de finances de la généralité de Soissons et autres parties secrètes* (s.l., 1663).

Edict du Roy portant création et establissement d'une Chambre de Justice, pour la recherche des abus & malversations commises dans les Finances de Sa Majesté depuis l'année 1635 (Paris, 1661).

Edict . . . portant aliénation des droits seigneuriaux, censives et justices du parisis des droits aliénés et autres droits appartenans à S.M. avec création d'intendants et commis des chartres. Vérifié en Parlement . . . le 20 mars 1655, et en la Chambre des Comptes (Paris, 1655).

Edict . . . portant création de divers officiers de chancelerie, de judicature et des postes, avec un règlement des ports de lettres. Verifié en Parlement . . . le 20 mars 1655 (Paris, 1655).

Edict . . . portant création en tiltre d'offices, de 46 conseillers secrétaires du Roy, de 4 conseillers trésoriers payeurs et de 4 conseillers controlleurs des gages desdits secrétaires, de 2 huissiers en la Grande Chancellerie, de 5 huissiers ès Conseils de S.M, de 4 conseillers conservateurs des hypotèques . . . en chacun baillage et sénéchaussée; de 12 banquiers royaux . . . de 4 conseillers intendans . . . des postes . . . en chacune Généralité.. et règlemens et taxes des ports de loettres et pacquets . . . (Paris, n.d.).

Edict portant establissement d'une marque sur le papier et parchemin, pour la validité de tous les actes qui s'expeédieront partout le Royaume, Verifié en Parlement . . . le 20 mars 1655, en la Chambre des Comptes et Cour des Aydes (Paris, 1655).

Edict pour la fabrication de nouvelles especes d'or et d'argent appellées lys, et pour le décry des espèces d'or et d'argent tant de France qu'estrangeres . . . Verifié en la Cour des Monnoyes . . . le 23 decembre 1655.

Estrades, Godefroi, Comte d', *Lettres, mémoires et négociations de etc.* (The Hague, 1719).

——, *Lettres, mémoires et négociations de etc.* (London, 1743), 9 vols.

Etats de la France (in chronological order)

Estat de la France Comme elle estoit gouuenée en l'An MDCXLVIII Ou sont Contenües diverses Remarques et particularitez de l'Histoire de nostre temps, MDCXLIX.

Estat et Gouvernement de France Comme il est depuis la Majorité du Roy Louis XIV à present regnant Ou sont contenues diverses remarques et particularitez de l'Histoire de nostre temps, avec les Noms, Dignitez &t Familles principalles du Royaume, & leurs Alliances Sixieme Edition Reveuë, corrigée et augmentée. A La Haye. Au dépens d'Adrian Vlacq, 1652.

Le Vray estat de la France comme elle est Gouvernée à present Où il est traitté des principaux points du Gouvernement de ce Royaume. Avec plusieurs recherches curieuses & tres untiles pour l'intelligence de l'histoire. Nouvelle Edition, Reveue, corrigée et augmenté et mis dans sa perfection, Par le Sieur du Verdier Historiographe de France. A Paris, Chez J. Baptiste Loyson, M. DC. LIV.

Le Parfait estat de la France Comme elle est Gouvernée à Present Où il est traitté des principaux points du Gouvenmement de ce Royaume à present Derniere Edition Augmentée des Blasons, Armes & fonctions des principaux Officiers de la Couronne. Ensemble les Estats Nouveaux des Maisons du Roy, de la Royne, et de Monseigneur le Duc d'Anjou. A Paris, Chez Cardin Besogne . . . 1656.

Le Vray et nouveau estat de la France comme elle est Gouvernée en cette presente Année 1657. Où il est traitté des principaux points du Gouvernement de ce Royaume. Avec plusieurs recherches curieuses & tres utiles pour l'intelligence de l'histoire Nouvelle Edition, Reveuë, corrigée et augmenté et mis dans sa perfection Ensemble l'estat de la maison de Monseigneur le Duc d'Anjou, Par Le Sieur Du Verdier, Historiographe de France. A Lyon, Chez Jean Aimé Candy.

L'Etat de la France dans sa perfection et comme elle est a present gouvernée. Ou a esté ajousté plusieurs recherches curieuses & nécessaires pour l'intelligence de l'histoire, jusques à présent. Avec des Blasons, Armes & fonctions des principaux Officiers de la Couronne, & de plusieurs grandes & ilustres maisons de ce Royaume, Ensemble des Maisons du Roy, de la Reyne, de M. le Duc d'Anjou & de M. le Duc d'Orleans et augmenté d'un traité des conseils du roi et des personnes qui les composent. Paris, Chez Jean Baptiste Loyson, rüe S. Jacques proche la Poste, à la Croix Royale, M.DC. LVIII.

L'Estat de la France nouvellement corrigé & mis en meilleur Ordre ou l'on voit de suite les Officiers de la Couronne avec leurs Armoires, Ensemble les Noms des officiers de la Maison du Roy & le quartier de leurs services, avec leurs gages & privilege, & l'explication des Fonctions de leurs Charges, Comme aussi des Officiers des Maisons Royales, de la Reine & de Monsieur &tc. Avec pluseiurs traités pariculiers, Le tout enrichi d'un grand nombre de figures, et dedié au roi, par N. Besongne, Clerc de Chapelle & d'Oratoire du Roy, & A.D.S.M. Paris, Chez la vefve Pierre David, proche la grande porte des Augustins, au Roy David, M.DC.LXI.

L'Estat nouveau de la France dans sa perfection. Contenant toutes les paricularitez de l' Histoire, & le rang que tiennent les Princes, Ducs, & Pairs, & Officiers de la Couronne. Ensemble l'estat des Maisons Royales, Gages, Privileges, & Exemptions des Officiers Commençaux de leurs Majestez, Le tout reveu, corrigé, augmenté et mis dans un meilleur ordre que les autres Editions qui ont esté imprimées jusques à present. Enrichi de nouvelles Figures, & de tous les Blazons des Officiers de la Couronne. A Paris, Chez Jean Baptiste Loyson, rüe Saïnt Jacques, à la Croix Royale, proche la Poste, M.DC. LXI.

L'Estat de la France nouvellement corrigé & mis en meilleur ordre, ou l'on voit tous les Princes Ducs et Pairs, Maréchaux de France, et autres Officiers de la Couronne: les Chevaliers de l'Ordre, les Gouverneurs des Provnces, les Cours Souveraines, etc. Ensemble les Noms des Officiers de la Maison du Roy, & le quartier de leur service: avec leurs gages et Privileges, & l'explication des Fonctions de leurs Charges. Comme aussi des Officiers des Maisons Royales de la Reine-Mére, de la Reine, de Monsieur le Dauphin, et Mnsieur & de Madame &c. Avec plusieurs Traitex particuliers, des Archeveschez, Evéschez et Abbayes de France, du Conseil Royal des Finances etc. Dedié au Roy . . . par N. Besongne C. & A. du Roy, B, en TH. & Clerc de Chapelle & d'Oratoire de sa Majesté. A Paris, Chez Estienne Loyson, M.DC.LXIII.

L'Etat de la France ou l'on voit toutes les Princes, Ducs et Pairs, Marêchaux de France, & autres Officiers de la Courone: [sic] *les Evêques, les Gouverneurs des Provinces, les Chevaliers des Ordres, les Cours Souveraines &c. Ensemble les Noms des Officiers de la Maison du Roy, & le quartier de leur service: avecque leurs gages et Priviléges, & l'explication des Fonctions de leurs Charges. Comme* [sic] *aussi des Officiers des Maisons Roïales de la Reine, de Monsieur le Dauphin, & des Enfans de France, de Monsieur le Duc d'Orleans & de Madame. Suivant les Etats portés à la Cour des Aides. Le tout enrichy d'un grand nombre de Figures.* A Paris, Chez Estienne Guignard fils, dans la grande Salle du Palais, a l'Image Saint Jean, 1665.

L'Etat de la France ou l'on voit tous les Princes, Ducs et Pairs, Marêchaux de France, & autres Officiers de la Courone: [sic] *les Evêques, les Gouverneurs des Provinces, les Chevaliers des Ordres, les Cours Souveraines &c. Ensemble les Noms des Officiers de la Maison du Roy, & le quartier de leur service: avecque leurs gages et Priviléges, & l'explication des Fonctions de leurs Charges. Come* [sic] *aussi des Officiers des Maisons Roïales de la Reine, de Monsieur le Dauphin, & des Enfans de France, de Monsieur le Duc d'Orleans & de Madame. Suivant les Etats portés à la Cour des Aides. Le tout enrichy d'un grand nombre de Figures.* A Paris, Chez Jean Baptiste Loyson, MD. C. LXIX, 2 vols.

L'Etat de la France ou l'on voit tous les Princes, Ducs & Pairs, Marêchaux de France, & autres Officiers de la Couronne: les Evêques, les Cours qui jugent en dernier ressort, les Gouverneurs des Provinces, les chevaliers des ordres, &tc. Ensemble les noms des Officiers de la Maison du Roy, & le quartier de leur service: . . . Suivant les états portés à la Cour des Aides, Le tout enrichy d'un grand nombre de Figures. A Paris, Chés Jean Batiste Loyson, dans la Salle Dauphine, à la Croix d'or, Et Henry Loyson dans la Salle des Merciers, du costé de la Sainte Chapelle, à la Croix d'or, M.DC.LXXII, 2 vols.

L'Etat de la France ou l'on voit tous les Princes, Ducs & Pairs, Marêchaux de France, & autres Officiers de la Courone [sic]: *les Evêques, les Cours qui jugent en dernier ressort, les Gouverneurs des Provinces, les Chevaliers des Ordres, &tc. Ensemble les noms des Officiers de la Maison du Roi, & le quartier de leur service: avec leurs gages et Privileges, & l'explication des Fonctions de leur charges. Come aussi des Officiers des Masions Roïales de la Reine, de Monsieugeur le Dauphin, de Monsieur, Duc d'Orleans & de Madame. Suivant les Etats portés à la Cour de Aides Le tout enrichy d'un grand nombre de figures.* A Paris, chés Jaques le Gras, au Palais, M. DC. LXXIV.

L'Estat de la France ou l'on voit tous les Princes, Ducs et Pairs, Marêchaux de France, & autres Officiers de la Courone: [sic] *les Evêques, les Gouverneurs des Provinces, les Chevaliers des Ordres, les Cours Souveraines &c. Ensemble les Noms des Officiers de la Maison du Roy, & le quartier de leur service: avecque leurs gages et Priviléges, & l'explication des Fonctions de leurs Charges. Come* [sic] *aussi des Officiers des Maisons Roïales de la Reine, de Monsieur le Dauphin, & des Enfans de France, de Monsieur le Duc d'Orleans & de Madame. Suivant les Etats portés à la Cour des Aides. Le tout enrichy d'un grand nombre de Figures.* A Paris, Chez P. Traboüillet, M. DC. LXXVII, 2 vols.

L'Etat de la France ou l'on voit tous les Princes, Ducs et Pairs, Marêchaux de France, & autres Officiers de la Courone: [sic] *les Evêques, les Gouverneurs des Provinces, les Chevaliers des Ordres, les Cours Souveraines &c. Le tout enrichy d'un grand nombre de Figures.* A Paris, Chez Jaques Le Gras, au Palais à l'entrée de la Grand'salle, M. DC. LXXVIII, 2 vols.

L'Etat de la France ou l'on voit tous les Princes, Ducs et Pairs, Marêchaux de France, & autres Officiers de la Courone: [sic] *les Evêques, les Gouverneurs des Provinces, les Chevaliers des Ordres, les Cours Souveraines &c. Ensemble les Noms des Officiers de la Maison du Roy, & le quartier de leur service: avecque leurs gages et Priviléges, & l'explication des Fonctions de leurs Charges. Come* [sic] *aussi des Officiers des Maisons Roïales de la Reine, de Monsieur le Dauphin, & des Enfans de France, de Monsieur le Duc d'Orleans & de Madame. Suivant les Etats portés à la Cour des Aides. Le tout enrichy d'un grand nombre de Figures.* A Paris, Dedié au Roy, Chez Jacques Le Gras à l'entrée de la Grand-Salle du Palais, M.DC LXXXIII.

Evelyn, John, *Memoirs illustrative of the life and writings of John Evelyn. . . comprising his diary from the year 1641 to 1705–6 and a selection of his familiar letters* (London, 1827), 5 vols.

Fillon, Benjamin, *Inventaire des autographes et des documents historiques composant la collection de M. Benjamin Fillon* ed. Etienne Charavy (Paris, 1877–1883).

Formanoir, Guillaume-Louis de, sieur de Palteau, "Lettre à l'auteur de ces Feuilles sur l'Homme au Masque de fer," *Année littéraire* (1768), IV, 351–354.

Formulaire des inscriptions et souscriptions des lettres dont le roy de France est traité par les potentats & dont il les traite réciproquement, on a adjouté a la fin une harangue de Mad. Fouquet au Roi [Utrecht, 1680].

Fouquet, Nicolas, *Copie figurée de l'escrit trouvvé dans le cabinet appellé Secret de la Maison de Monsieur Foucquet, a Saint Mandé* (cf. BNF Ms. Fr. 17048).

———, *Défenses* (Amsterdam, 1665–1667), Elzevir, 13 vols.

I. *Recueil des défenses de Mr Fouquet* (1665–1666).

II. *Défenses de Mr Fouquet sur tous les points de son procez* (cf. BNF Ms. Fr. 10228–10229).

III. *De la Production de Mr Fouquet contre celle de Mr Talon première partie.*

IV. *Réponse de Mr Fouquet à la réplique de Mr Talon* (1665–1666).

V. *De la Production de M^r. Fouquet contre celle de Mr Talon seconde et troisième partie.*

VI. *Traité du péculat* (1666).

VII. *Production de Mr Fouquet contre celle de Mr Talon sur le fait de Belle-Isle. Tome premier de la suite* (1667).

VIII. *Continuation de la production de Mr Fouquet pour servir de réponse à celle de Mr Talon sur le prétendu crime d'état. Tome deuxième de la suite.*

IX. *Suite de la continuation de la production de Mr Fouquet pour servir de réponse à celle de Mr Talon, sur le prétendu crime d'état à la fin de laquelle on a ajouté le troisième tome* (1666).

X. *Continuation de la production sur les procez-verbaux. Tome quatrième de la suite.*

XI. *Suite de la continuation de la production sur les procez-verbaux. Tome cinquième de la suite.*

XII. *Inventaire des pièces baillées à la çhambre de justice par Mre Nicolas Fouquet contre M. le Procureur général, pour répondre à quelques procez verbaux par luy produits. Tome sixième de la suite.*

XIII *Inventaire des piéces . . . concernant les défauts des intentaires. Tome septième de la suite.*

———, *Conclusion des défenses* (1668).

———, *Défenses sur tous les poincts de mon procés, que j'aurois à proposer, si sj'i'estois devant mes juges naturels.*

———, *Première partie de la production de Mr Foucquet contre celle de M. Talon* (no place or date) [June 1663] in *Recueil de pièces imprimées concernant le procès de Foucquet* in 4$^{o.}$

———, *Reponse à la replique de Mr Talon* (s.l. n.d.) [1664].

———, *Requête de Fouquet à l'effet d'obtenir communication de la production du procureur général et des papiers saisis par ordre de la chambre de justice commencant par ces mots* « A noseigneurs de la Chambre de Justice, supplie très humblement Nicolas fouquet . . . disant que par le procès verbal de MM. les Commissaires de la chambre du 20 Septembre dernier (s.l.n.d.) [May 25, 1663].

———, *Seconde partie de la production de Mr Foucquet contre celle de M. Talon, sur le fait de la pension* (s.l.n.d.) [July 1663].

[Fouquet-Croissy, Antoine], *Le Courrier du Temps, Apportant ce qui se passe de plus secret en la cour des princes de l'Europe* [Moreau N° 825].

Gamaches, Cyprien de, *Mémoires de la mission des Capucins de la province de Paris près la reine d'Angleterre depuis l'année 1630 jusqu'à 1669*, ed. Apollinaire de Valence (Paris, 1881).

Gazette d'Amsterdam

Gazette de France

Gourville, Jean Hérauld de, *Mémoires de Gourville*, ed. Léon Lecestre (Paris, 1894–1895), 2 vols. Société de l'Histoire de France, vols. CCLXVII and CCLXXII.

Great Britain, Historical Manuscripts Commission, *Calendar of Treasury Books*, ed. William A. Shaw (London, 1904–1957), 29 vols.

———, *Fifteenth Report, Appendix, Part II: The Manuscripts of J. Elliot Hodgkin, Esq., F.S.A. of Richmond Surrey* (London, 1897).

————, Public Record Office, *Calendar of State Papers, Domestic,* Charles II (London, 1860–1947), 28 vols.

————, *Report on the Manuscripts of E. W. Leyborne-Popham, Esq. of Littlecote, Co. Wiltshire* (Norwich, 1899).

Groen van Prinsterer, Guillaume et al., *Archives ou correspondance inédite de la maison d'Orange-Nassau* (Leiden and Utrecht, 1835–1915), 25 vols.

Halkett, Anne, *Autobiography of Anne Lady Halkett* (1875), Camden Society.

Henrietta Maria, *Letters of Queen Henrietta Maria, including her private correspondence with Charles I,* ed. Mary Anne Everett Greene (London, 1857 [1858]).

Hermant, Godefroi, *Mémoires de Godefroi Hermant sur l'histoire ecclésiastique du XVIIᵉ siècle: 1630–1663* (Paris, 1905–1910), 6 vols.

Héroard, Jean, *Journal de Jean Héroard: Médecin de Louis XIII,* ed. Madeleine Foisil (Paris 1989), 2 vols.

Hudita, Jean, *Repertoire de documents concernant les négociations entre la France et la Transylvanie au XVIIᵉ siècle* (Paris, 1926).

Inventaire des merveilles du monde rencontrées dans le palais du cardinal Mazarin (Paris, 1649) [Moreau N° 1729].

The Inventories and Valuations of the King's Goods: 1648–51, ed. Oliver Miller. Walpole Society, vol. XLIII, 1972.

Joly, Claude, *Mémoires de Claude Joly,* Collection des mémoires relatifs à l'histoire de France, ed. Petitot and Monmerqué (Paris, 1819–1829), ser. 2 XLVII or in Nouvelle collection des mémoires pour servir à l'histoire de France, ed. Michaud and Poujoulat (Paris, 1836–1839), ser. 3 II.

Joly, Guy, *Mémoires de Guy Joly,* Collection des mémoires relatifs à l'histoire de France, ed. Petitot and Monmerqué (Paris, 1819–1829), ser. 2, XLVII or in Nouvelle collection des mémoires pour servir à l'histoire de France, ed. Michaud and Poujoulat (Paris, 1836–1839), ser. 3 II.

Journal encyclopédique

La Châtre, Edme, Count de Nançay, *Mémoires du comte de La Châtre.* Collection des mémoires relatifs à l'histoire de France, ed. Petitot and Monmerqué (Paris, 1819–1829), ser. 2 LI, or in Nouvelle collection des mémoires pour servir à l'histoire de France, ed. Michaud and Poujoulat (Paris, 1836–1839), ser. 3 III.

La Fare, Charles Auguste, Marquis de, *Mémoires et réflexions sur les événements du règne de Louis XIV et sur le caractère des hommes quiy ont eu la principale part.* Collection des mémoires relatifs à l'histoire de France, ed. Petitot and Monmerqué (Paris, 1819–1829), ser. 2 XLV or in Nouvelle collection des mémoires pour servir à l'histoire de France, ed. Michaud and Poujoulat (Paris, 1836–1839), ser. 3 VIII.

La Fontaine, Jean de, *Oeuvres diverses de M. de La Fontaine* (Paris, 1729), 3 vols.

La Grange-Chancel, Joseph de, "Lettre de M. de la Grange-Chancel à M. Fréron," *Année littéraire* (1759), III, 188–195.

La Porte, Pierre de, *Mémoires de P. de La Porte.* Collection des mémoires relatifs à l'histoire de France, ed. Petitot and Monmerqué (Paris, 1819–1829), ser. 2 LIX, or in Nouvelle collection des mémoires pour servir à l'histoire de France, ed. Michaud and Poujoulat (Paris, 1836–1839), ser. 3 VIII.

La Rochefoucauld, François, duc de, *Mémoires de La Rochefoucauld.* Collection des mémoires relatifs à l'histoire de France, ed. Petitot and Monmerqué (Paris, 1819–1829), ser. 2 LI–LII or in Nouvelle collection des mémoires pour servir à l'histoire de France, ed. Michaud and Poujoulat (Paris, 1836–1839), ser. 3 V.

Le Boindre, Jean, *Débats du parlement de Paris pendant la minorité de Louis XIV*, ed. Robert Descimon, Orest Ranum, and Patricia M. Ranum (Paris, 1997), 2 vols.

Le Roux de Lincy, Antoine-Jean-Victor, and Douet d'Arcq, Louis-Claude, *Registres de l'hôtel de ville de Paris pendant la Fronde, suivis de ce qui s'est passé dans la ville et l'abbaye de Saint-Denis pendant la Fronde: 1648–1652* (Paris, 1846–1848), 3 vols. SHF.

Lettre d'un Conseiller de Nantes à son Ami sur l'Evasion du Cardinal de Retz (Nantes, 1654).

Lettre d'un religieux envoyée a monseigneur le prince de Condé à Saint Germain en Laye contenant la vérité de la vie et les moeurs du cardinal Mazarin, avec exhortation audit seigneur prince d'abandonnerson parti, 18 janvier 1649 (Paris, 1649) [Moreau N° 1895].

Lettre d'un secretaire de S. Innocent à Iules Mazarin (Paris, 1649) [Moreau: N° 1896].

Lettre escrite à M. le cardinal de Retz par un de ses confidants de Paris, dont la copie a esté envoyée de Rome.

Tke Lord George Digby's Cabinet and Dr. Goff's Negotiations; Together with His majesties, the Queens, and the lord Jermins and other Letters, Taken at the Battel at Sherborn in Yorkshire about the 15th of October Last. Also Observations Upon the Said Letters (London, 1646).

Louis XIII, *Lettres de la main de Louis XIII*, ed. Eugène Griselle (Paris, 1914), 2 vols.

——, *Lettres inédites de Louis XIII à Richelieu*, ed G. La Caille (Paris, 1901).

——, *Louis XIII et Richelieu: Lettres et pièces diplomatiques*, ed. Eugène Griselle (Paris, 1911).

Louis XIV, *Mémoires de Louis XIV*, ed. Jean Longnon (Paris, 1927).

——, *Mémoires for the Instruction of the Dauphin*, ed. Paul Sonnino (London and New York, 1970).

——, *Oeuvres de Louis XIV*, ed. Grouvelle (Paris, 1806), 6 vols.

Ludlow, Edmund, *The Memoirs of Edmund Ludlow, Lieutenant-General of the Horse in the Army of the Commonwealth of England: 1625–1672*, ed. Charles Harding Firth (Oxford, 1894), 2 vols.

Maître, Léon, *L'Evasion du Cardinal de Retz hors du château de Nantes, d'après des documents inédts, information judiciaire, 1654* (Nantes, 1903), also published in the *Bulletin de la Société historique et archéologique de la Loire-Inférieure*, XLIV (1903), 30–113.

Mancini, Maria, Princess Colonna, *Apologie, ou les véritables mémoires de Madame Marie Mancini, Connestable de Colonna écrits par ellle même* (Leyden, 1678).

Mancini, Ortensia, Duchess de Mazarin, *Mémoires de Madame la Duchesse de Mazarin* (Cologne, 1675).

Mazarin, Jules, *Lettres du cardinal Mazarin*, ed. Alphonse Chéruel (Paris, 1872–1894), 9 vols. Collection de documents inédits sur l'histoire de France.

——, *Lettres du cardinal Mazarin à la reine, à la princesse palatine, etc. écrites pendant sa retraite hors de France en 1651 et 1652*, ed. J. Ravenel (Paris, 1835–1836). BSHF I–II.

——, *Lettres du cardinal Mazarin où l'on voit le secret de la négotiation de la paix des Pyrénées & la relation des conférences qu'il a eües pour ce sujet avec D. Louis de Haro, ministre d'Espagne . . .* (Amsterdam, Chez André Pierrot, 1690).

——, *Lettres du cardinal Mazarin où l'on voit le secret de la négotiation de la paix des Pyrénées & la relation des conférences qu'il a eües pour ce sujet avec D. Löuis de Haro, ministre d'Espagne, Seconde Partie* (Amsterdam, Henri Wetstein, 1693).

——, *Le Testament du défunt cardinal de Mazarin, duc de Nivernois, etc. (7 mars) Juxte la copie* (Cologne, 1663) (Paris, 1663). *Het testament van miin heer de cardinael Jul. Mazarin, Hertog van Nivernois en Ysieux etc., Na de Copye, uyt het Fransch vertaelt* (Cologne, 1663). *The Last Will and Testament of the Renowned Cardinal Mazarini, Deceased February 27, 1660, Together with some Historical Remerques of His Life* (London, 1663).

Mercure françois

Mercure galant

Montglat, François de Paule de Clermont, Marquis de, *Mémoires du Marquis de Montglat*. Collection des mémoires relatifs à l'histoire de France, ed. Petitot and Monmerqué (Paris, 1819–1829), ser. 2 XLIX–LI or in Nouvelle collection des mémoires pour servir à l'histoire de France, ed. Michaud and Poujoulat (Paris, 1836–1839), ser 3 V.

Montpensier, Anne Marie Louise d'Orléans, Duchesse de, *Memoires de Mademoiselle de Montpensier*. Collection des mémoires relatifs à l'histoire de France, ed. Petitot and Monmerqué (Paris, 1819–1829), ser. 2 XL–XLIII or in Nouvelle collection des mémoires pour servir à l'histoire de France, ed. Michaud and Poujoulat (Paris, 1836–1839), ser. 3 IV.

Motteville, Françoise de, *Mémoires de Madame de Motteville*. Collection des mémoires relatifs à l'histoire de France, ed. Petitot and Monmerqué (Paris, 1819–1829), ser. 2 XXXVI-XL or in Nouvelle collection des mémoires pour servir à l'histoire de France, ed. Michaud and Poujoulat (Paris, 1836–1839), ser. 2 X.

Nicholas, Sir Edward, *Correspondence of Sir Edward Nicholas, Secretary of State*, ed. George F. Warner (London, 1886–1920), 4 vols. Royal Historical Society Publications, Camden new ser., vols. XL, L, LVII, third ser. vol. XXXI.

Ogier, François, *Actions Publiques* (Paris, 1652).

——, *Eloge ou Panégyrique de Monsieur d'Avaux* (Paris, 1652).

——, *Journal du congrès de Munster, par François Ogier, aumonier du comte d'Avaux:1641–1647*, ed. Auguste Boppe (Paris, 1893).

Orléans, Charlotte-Elizabeth, duchesse d', *Aus den Briefen der Herzogin Elizabeth Charlotte von Orleans an die Kurfürstin Sophie von Hannover*, ed. Eduard Bodemann (Hannover, 1891), 2 vols.

Ormesson, Olivier Levèvre, *Journal d'Olivier Lefèvre d'Ormesson*, ed. Pierre Adolphe Chéruel (Paris, 1860–1861), 2 vols. Collection de documents inédits sur l'histoire de France, ser. 1, vol. X.

Patin, Gui (or Guy), *Correspondence de Gui Patin*, ed. Armand Brette (Paris, 1901).

——, *Lettres de Gui Patin*, ed. J. H. Réveillé-Parise (Paris, 1846), 3 vols.

——, *Lettres de Gui Patin*, ed. Paul Triaire (Paris, 1907), 3 vols.

——, *Les Lettres de Guy Patin à Charles Spon: Janvier 1649-février 1655*, ed. Laure Jestaz (Paris, 2006), 2 vols.

Pellisson-Fontanier, Paul, *Discours au Roy par un de ses fidèles sujets sur le procès de M. Foucquet* (s.l.n.d.).

——, *Oeuvres diverses de monsieur Pellisson* (Paris, 1735), 3 vols.

Perrault, Charles, *Mémoires de Charles Perrault* (Avignon, 1759).

Perwich, William, *The Despatches of William Perwich, English Agent in Paris: 1669–1677*, ed. M. Beryl Curran (London, 1903).

Pièces du procès de Henri de Talleyrand, Comte de Chalais (London, 1781).

La Presse

Ravaisson-Mollien, François, *Archives de La Bastille, d'après des documents inédits* (1866–1904), 19 vols.

Recueil de diverses pièces curieuses pour servir à l'histoire (1664).

Recueil des Instructions données aux ambassadeurs et ministres de France depuis les Traités de Westphalie jusqu'à la Révolution Française (Paris, 1884–), XXIV–V, *Angleterre*, I–II, ed. J. J. Jusserand (Paris, 1929).

Recueil de tous les arrêts de la cour de Parlement, lettres, déclarations et autres actes données tant pour la liberté et innocence de messeigneurs les princes de Condé, de Conty et duc de Longueville, que pour l'éloignement et sortie hors du royaume du cardinal Mazarin, avec commission aux sieurs de Broussel, Le Meusnier, Bidault et Pithou, conseillers du roi en ladite cour, pour informer des contraventions auxdits arrêts, ensemble les deliberations concernant l'exclusion des étrangers, même des cardinaux françois d'entrer les conseils de Sa Majesté, des 7m 9, 10, 20 et

25 février, 2, 11, et 16 mars 1651, quelques-uns desdits arrêts non encore publiés (Paris,1651) [Moreau N° 3045].

Relación verdadera de la felicissima victoria, que Dios Nuestro Señor se ha servido de conceder a las católicas armas de Su Magestad, gobernadas del Serenisimo señor don Juan de Austria, contra las de el Christianisimo Rey de Francia, que se hallava sobre el sitio de la Ciudad de Valencienes, Ciudad del Pais de Henau, en los Estados de Flandes, Sucedida el Sábado 15 de julio de este año de 1656 (Seville, 1656).

Requeste civile contre la Conclusion de la Paix (1649) [Moreau N° 3468].

Retz, Jean François Paul de Gondi de, *Oeuvres du Cardinal de Retz I*, ed. Alphonse Feillet (Paris, 1870–1896), 10 vols. Les Grands Ecrivains de France.

Richelieu, Armand Jean du Plessis de, *Lettres, instructions diplomatiques, et papiers d'état du Cardinal de Richelieu*, ed. Georges d'Avenel (Paris, 1853–1877), 8 vols. Collection de documents inédits sur l'histoire de France, ser. 1.

———, *Mémoires du Cardinal de Richelieu*. Collection des mémoires relatifs à l'histoire de France, ed. Petitot and Monmerqué (Paris, 1819–1829), ser. 2 XXIbis–XXX or in Nouvelle collection des mémoires pour servir à l'histoire de France, ed. Michaud and Poujoulat (Paris, 1836–1839), ser. 2 VII–IX or the partial edition by Société de l'Histoire de France (1907–), 9 vols.

Richelieu, Louis François Armand du Plessis, duc de, *Mémoires authentiques du maréchal de Richelieu*, ed. Arthur Boislisle, Jean de Boislisle, and Léon Lecestre (Paris, 1918). SHF.

———, *Mémoires du Maréchal Duc de Richelieu*, ed. Jean-Louis-Giraud Soulavie (Paris, 1790), 4 vols.

Saint-Maurice, Thomas-François Chabod de, *Lettres sur la cour de Louis XIV: 1667–1673*, ed. Jean Lemoîne (Paris, 1910), 2 vols.

Saint-Simon, Louis de, *Mémoires complets et authentiques du duc de Saint-Simon sur le siècle de Louis XIV et la régence*, ed. Adolphe Chéruel (Paris, 1856–1858), 20 vols.

Scarron, Paul, *Les Dernières oeuvres de M. Scarron divisées en deux parties, contenantes plusieurs lettres amoureuses et galantes nouvelles, histoires, plusieurs pièces tant en vers qu'en prose, comédies et autres* (Paris, 1663).

———, *La Mazarinade* [Moreau N° 2436].

———, *Roman Comique* (Paris, 1651 and 1657).

———, *Typhon, ou la gigantomanie: poème burlesque* (Paris, 1644).

Second extrait des registres du parlement 25 Juin jusqu'au retour de Saint-Denis [Moreau N° 3608].

Sevigné, Marie de Rabutin-Chantal, marquise de, *Lettres de madame de Sevigné, de sa famille et de ses amis, recueillies et annotées par M. Monmerqué* (Paris, 1862–1868), 14 vols.

Le Silence au bout du doit (1649) [Moreau N° 3674].

Souches, Louis François de Bouchet, marquis de, *Mémoires du Marquis de Souches sur le règne de Louis XIV*, ed. Gabriel Jules deCosnac (Paris, 1882–1893), 13 vols.

Sourdis, Henri d'Escoubleau de, *Correspondence d'Henri d'Escoubleau de Sourdis*, ed. Eugène Sue (Paris, 1839), 3 vols.

Streyersdorff, Wolter Heinrich von, *Beschreibung der Kölner Diöcese* (Cologne, 1670).

Tallemant, Gédéon, Sieur des Réaux, *Historiettes*, any edition.

Talon, Denis, *Requête de M. le procureur général de la chambre de justice, servant de continuation contre la partie de la production de M. Fouquet concernant les prêts par lui faits à l'épargne . . . 20 août 1663* (Paris, 1663).

———, *Requête de M. le procureur général de la chambre de justice, servant de contredits contre la première partie de la production de M. Foucquet . . . 8 août 1663* (Paris, 1663).

———, *Requête de M. le procureur général de la chambre de justice, servant de contredits contre les chefs de la production de M. Foucquet concernant les alinations des rentes, augmentations des gages, et autres biens du roi, et achats et négotiations de vieux billets d'Espargne* (Paris, 1663).

——, *Requête du procureur général Talon, du 25 juin 1663, contenant un résumé des charges du procès, et demandant qu'il soit passé outre au jugement en se bornant aux neuf procès verbaux mentionnés dans la requête, commençant par ces mots: A MM. de la chambre de justice, Supplie le procureur général du roi, disant que dans les abus et malversations . . .* (s.l.n.d.).

Thurloe, John, *A collection of the state papers of John Thurlow, Esq. secretary, first, to the Council of State, and afterwards to the two Protectors, Oliver and Richard Cromwell* (London, 1742), 7 vols.

Très haute remonstrance au roy par les six corps des marchands de la ville de Paris sur le fait des liards (s.l.n.d.).

Turenne, Henri de La Tour d'Auvergne, Vicomte de, *Mémoires du Maréchal de Turenne* (Paris, 1914), 2 vols. SHF.

Turner, James, Sir, *Memoirs of His Own Life and Times: 1632–1670* (Edininburgh, 1829). Bannatyne Club Publications, N° 28.

Vast, Henry, *Les Grands traités du règne de Louis XIV* (Paris, 1893–99), 3 vols.

Le Véritable arrêt de la cour de parlement donné, toutes les chambres assemblées, les vendredi et samedi 19 et 20 juillet 1652 (Paris, 1652) [Moreau N° 3920].

Vertue, George, *A Catalogue and Description of King Charles the First's Capital Collection of Pictures, Limnings, Statues, Bronzes, Medals, and Other Curiosities* (London, 1757).

Voltaire, *The Complete Works of Voltaire*, ed. Theodore Besterman et al. (Geneva, Oxford, 1968–), 143 vols.

——, *Collection complète des oeuvres de monsieur de Voltaire* (Geneva, 1768–1777), 30 vols.

——, *Voltaire's Correspondence*, ed. Theodore Besterman (Geneva, 1953–1965), 107 vols.

Yoshida-Takeda, Tomiko, and Lebrun-Jouve, Claudine, *Inventaire dressé après le décès en 1661 du cardinal Mazarin* (Paris, 2004). Mémoires de l'Académie des Inscriptions et Belles-Lettres.

Secondary Sources

Adam, Antoine, "Un document inédit au dossier du masque de fer," *Revue d'histoire de la philosophie et d'histoire générale des civilisations*, nouvelle série XXIV (1938), 359–361.

Anselme de Sainte-Marie, Augustin, *Histoire généalogique et chronologique de la maison royale de France* (Paris 1726–1733), 9 vols.

Aristide, Isabelle, *La Fortune de Sully* (Paris, 1990).

Arlette, Jouanna, *La France du XVIᵉ siècle* (Paris, 1996).

Armengol, Sophie, "La Commensalité à Montpellier au XVIIᵉ siècle: L'Exemple de l'apothecairerie-parfumerie royale," *Bulletin Historique de la Ville de Montpellier* N° 17 (1ᵉʳ trimestre 1993), 32–41.

Arnauld, Antoine, and Fournier, Narcisse, *L'Homme au masque de fer* (Paris, 1851).

Arnaud, Eugène, *Histoire des protestants du Vivarais et du Velay, pays de Languedoc, de la réforme à la revolution* (Paris, 1888), 2 vols.

Arvengas, Jean, *Histoire d'un village de Sologne: Marcilly-en-Villette dès origines à nos jours* (Beaugensy, l952).

Aubery, Antoine, *Histoire du cardinal Mazarin* (Paris, 1688), 2 vols. or (Amsterdam 1695), 2 vols.

Aumale, Henri d'Orléans, duc de, *Histoire des princes de Condé pendant les XVIᵉ et XVIIᵉ siècles* (Paris, 1863–1896), 7 vols.

Azéma, Xavier, *Un prélat janséniste: Louis Fouquet, évêque et comte d'Agde:1656–1702* (Paris, 1963).

Bachet, Armand, *Le Roy chez la Reine: Histoire secrète du mariage de Louis XIII et d'Anne d'Autriche*, 2nd ed. (Paris, 1866).

Badalo-Dulong, Claude, *Anne d'Autriche: mère de Louis XIV* (Paris, 1980). See also under Dulong.

Baker, Richard, *A Chronicle of the Kings of England* (London, 1684).

Bapst, Germain, *Histoire des joyaux de la couronne de France d'après des documents inédits* (Paris, 1889).

Barnes, Arthur Stapylton, *The Man of the Mask: A Study in the By-Ways of History* (London, 1908, rev. 1912).

Barthélemy, Edouard de, *Une nièce de Mazarin: La princesse de Conti* (Paris, 1875).

Baschi Aubais, Charles de, *Pièces typiques pour servir à l'histoire de France* (1759).

Battifol, Louis, *La Duchesse de Chevreuse: Une vie d'aventures et d'intrigues sous Louis XIII* (Paris, 1913).

——, *Le Roi Louis XIII à vingt ans* (Paris, 1910).

Bazzoni, Augusto, "Un nunzio straordinario alla corte di Francia nel secolo xvii," *Rivista europea: Rivista internazionale*, XIX (June, 1880), 401–418.

Béguin, Katia, *Les Princes de Condé, rebelles courtisans et mécènes dans la France du grand siècle* (Paris, 1999).

Benedict, Philip, *The Huguenot Population of France: 1600–1685, the Demographic Fate and Customs of a Religious Minority*, American Philosophical Society LXXXI (1991).

Benoist, Elie, *Histoire de l'Edit de Nantes* (Delf, 1693–1695), 3 vols.

Bergin, Joseph, "Cardinal Mazarin and his Benefices," *French History* I (1987), 3–26.

——, *Cardinal Richelieu: Power and the Pursuit of Wealth* (New Haven, 1985).

——, *The Making of the French Episcopate: 1589–1661* (New Haven, 1996).

Betteridge, Tom, *Sodomy in Early Modern Europe* (Manchester, 2002).

Boislisle, Jean de, *Mémoriaux du Conseil de 1661* (Paris, 1905–1907), 3 vols. SHF.

Bonnaffé, Edmond, *Les Amateurs de l'ancienne France: Le surintendant Foucquet* (Paris and London, 1882).

Bordeaux Paul, "Imitations des monnoyes françaises," *Revue numismatique* (1901), fourth series V, 75–103.

Bourelly, Jules, *Cromwell et Mazarin: deux campagnes de Turenne en Flandre; la bataille des Dunes* (Paris, 1886).

Bourgeon, Jean-Luis, *Les Colbert avant Colbert: Destin d'une famille marchande* (Paris, 1973).

Brugnon, Stanislas, "L'Identité de l'homme au masque de fer," in *Il y a trois siècles le masque de fer: Actes du colloque international sur la célèbre énigme: 12–13 séptembre 1987* (Cannes, 1989), 27–38.

——, *Reconstitution du registre d'écrou des prisonniers de l'île Sainte-Marguerite à compter du 30 avril 1687 et jusqu'au 19 mars de l'année 1704* (Paris, 1992).

Carré de Busserolle, Jacques Xavier, *Dictionnaire géographique, historique et biographique d'Indre-et-Loire et de l'ancienne province de Touraine* (Tours, 1882). *Mémoires de la Société Archéologique de Touraine*, XXX.

Carrier, Hubert, *La Presse de la Fronde (1648–1653): Les Mazarinades* (Geneva, 1989–1991), 2 vols.

Carruti, Domenico, *Storia di Pinerolo* (Pinerolo, 1897).

Caullery, Jules, "Notes sur Samuel Chappuzeau," *Bulletin de la Société de l'Histoire du Protestantisme Français*, LVIII (1909), 141–157.

Chantelauze, Régis, *Le Cardinal de Retz et l'affaire du chapeau* (Paris, 1878), 2 vols.

——, "Les Derniers jours de Mazarin, d'après des documents inédits," *Le Correspondant* nouvelle série, CXXIV, 10 juillet et 10 août 1881, 65–88 et 417–458, republished in his *Portraits historiques: Philippe de Commynes, Le Grand Condé, Mazarin, Frederic II, Louis XV et Mare Thérèse* (Paris, 1886), 231–352.

Chardon, Henri, *Scarron inconnu* (Paris, 1903–1904), 2 vols.

Chatelain, Urbain Victor, *Le Surintendant Nicolas Foucquet, protecteur des lettres, des arts et des sciences* (Paris, 1905).

Chéron, André, and Sarret de Coussergues, Germaine, *Une seigneurie en Bas-Languedoc: Coussergues et les Sarret* (Brussels, 1963).

Chéruel, Pierre Adolphe, *Histoire de France pendant la minorité de Louis XIV* (Paris, 1879–1880), 4 vols.

———, *Mémoires sur Nicolas Foucquet, surintendant des finances et sur son frère l'abbé Fouquet* (Paris, 1862), 2 vols.

Chesnel de la Charbouclais, Louis Pierre François Adolphe de, *Dictionnaire des armées de terre et de mer* (Paris, 1862–1864), 2 vols.

Claretta, Gaudenzio, *Storia del regno e del tempo di Carlo Emanuele II, duca di Savoia* (Genoa, 1877–1878), 3 vols.

Clark, Ruth, *Anthony Hamilton (Author of the Memoirs of Count Grammont): His Life and Works and Family* (London and New York, 1921).

Clément, Pierre, *Histoire de l'administration monarchique en France depuis l'avènement de Phlippe-Auguste jusqu'à la mort de Louis XIV* (Paris, 1855), 2 vols.

Cochin, Augustin, "Les Conquêtes du consitoire de Nîmes pendant la Fronde: 1649–1653," *Revue des questions historiques* LXIX (1903), 498–514.

———, "Les Eglises calvinistes du Midi: Le Cardinal Mazarin et Cromwell," *Revue des questions historiques* LXXVI (1904), 109–159.

Combier, Amédée, *Etude sur le Baillage de Vermandois, et Siège Présidial de Laon* (Paris, 1874).

———, *Nomenclature sommaire des archives du greffe de Laon* (Paris, 1866).

Cosnac, Gabriel Jules, *Mazarin et Colbert* (Paris, 1892), 2 vols.

———, *Les Richesses du palais Mazarin . . . Correspondence idédite de M, de Bordeaux, ambassadeur en Angleterre* (Paris, 1884).

———, *Souvenirs du règne de Louis XIV* (Paris, 1866–1882), 8 vols.

Coste, Gabriel, *Les Anciennes troupes de la marine: 1622–1792* (Paris, 1893).

Courtilz de Sandras, Gatien, *Mémoires de M. L.C.D.R. concernant ce qui s'est passé de plus particulier sous le ministère du cardinal de Richelieu et du cardinal Mazarin, avec plusieurs particularités remarquables du règne de Louis le Grand* (Cologne, 1687).

———, *Vie de Colbert* (Paris, 1695).

Cousin, Victor, *La Jeunesse de Mazarin* (Paris, 1865).

———, *Madame de Chevreuse: Nouvelles études sur les femmes illustres et la société du dixseptième siècle*, 2nd ed. (Paris, 1862).

———, *Madame de Chevreuse et Madame de Hautefort* (Paris, 1856).

———, *Madame de Hautefort: Nouvelles études sur les femmes illustres et la société du dixseptième siècle* (Paris, 1868).

———, *Madame de Sablé: Nouvelles études sur la société et les femmes illustres du XVIIe siècle* (Paris, 1859).

Crèvecoeur, Robert Saint John de, "Un personnage de Tallemant des Réaux: Montbrun-Souscarrière; 1594–1670, d'après des documents inédits," *Mémoires de la Société de l'Histoire de Paris et de l'Ile de France*, XVI (1889) (Paris, 1890), 57–103.

Daniel, Marc, *Hommes du grand siècle: Etudes sur l'homosexualité sous les règnes de Louis XIII et de Louis XIV* (Paris, 1957). [English translation, "A Study of Homosexuality in France during the reigns of Louis XIII and Louis XIV" in *Homophile Studies* 4, 125–136.].

Danjou, Félix, *Archives curieuses de l'histoire de France depuis Louis XI jusqu'à Louis XVIII* (Paris and Beauvais, 1837–1840).

Darcel, Alfred, and Guichard, Edouard, *Les Tapisseries décoratives de garde-meuble; choix des plus beaux motifs* (Paris, 1878–1881), 2 vols.

Demotier, Charles, *Annales de Calais depuis les temps les plus reculés jusqu'à nos jours* (Calais, 1856).

Depping, Georg, *Un banquier protestant en France au XVIIe siècle, Bathélémy Herwarth, contrôleur général des finances: 1607–1686*, extrait de la *Revue Historique* (1879) X, 285–338, XI, 63–800.

Dessert, Daniel, *Argent, pouvoir et société au grand siècle* (Paris, 1984).

———, *Colbert, ou le serpent venimeux* (Paris, 2000).

———, *Fouquet* (Paris, 1987).

———, *Louis XIV prend le pouvoir* (Paris, 1989).

———, "Pouvoir et finance au XVIIe siècle, La Fortune du Cardinal Mazarin," *Revue d'histoire moderne et contemporaine* XXIII N°. 2 (April–June 1976), 161–181.

Dornic, François, *Une ascension sociale au xviie siècle: Louis Berryer, agent de Mazarin et de Colbert* (Caen, 1968).

Droz, Alfred, *Le Procès de Fouquet* (Paris, 1899).

Dulong, Claude, *Banquier du roi, Barthélemy Hervart: 1606–1676* (Paris, 1951). See also Badalo-Dulong.

———, "Les Comptes bleus du cardinal Mazarin," *Revue d'histoire moderne et contemporaine* XXXVI (October–December 1989), 537–558.

———, *La Fortune de Mazarin* (Paris, 1990).

———, "La Fortune d'un ministre: Le cardinal Mazarin," *Annuaire-Bulletin de la Société de l'Histoire de France* (1995), 19–36.

———, "Mazarin et l'argent: Banquiers et prête-noms," *Mémoires et documents de l'Ecole de Chartes* LXVI (2002).

———, "Mazarin et les frères Cenami," *Bibliothèque de l'Ecole des Chartes* N° 144 (1986), 299–354.

———, "Mazarin et ses banquiers," *Atti dei Convegni Lincei*, N° 35 (1977), 17–40.

———, "Mazarin, ses banquiers et prête-noms," *La Fronde en question: Actes du 18e colloque du Centre Méridional de Rencontres sur le XVIIe siècle* (Marseilles-Cassis, 28–31 janvier 1988).

———, "Processus d'enrichissement du cardinal Mazarin d'après l'inventaire de l'abbé Mondin," *Bibliothèque de l'Ecole des Chartes* N^o148 (1990), 355–425.

Dumas, Alexandre, *Les Trois Mousquetaires* (Paris, 1844), 8 vols.

———, *Le Vicomte de Bragelonne, ou Dix ans plus tard: complément des Trois Mousquetaires et de Vingt ans après* (Paris, 1848–1850), 26 vols.

———, *Vingt ans après: suite des Trois Mousquetaires* (Paris, 1845), 7 vols.

Dumas, Alexandre, et al. *Crimes célèbres* (Paris, 1839–1840), 8 vols.

Duvivier, Maurice, *Le Masque de fer* (Paris, 1932).

Ekberg, Carl J., "Abel Servien, Cardinal Mazarin, and the Formulation of French Foreign Policy, 1653–1659," *International History Review* III N° 3 (July, 1981), 317–329.

Elzière, Jean-Bernard, *Histoire des Budos, Seigneurs de Budos en Guyenne et de Portes-Bertrand en Languedoc* (1978). Bibliotheque Privee, 2002.

Feuillet de Conches, Félix-Sébastien, *Causeries d'un curieux*, (Paris, 1862–1868), 4 vols.

Fillon, Benjamin, *Inventaire des autographes et des documents historiques composant la collection de M. Benjamin Fillon*, Series I and II (Paris, 1877).

Firth, Charles Harding, "Royalist and Cromwellian Armies in Flanders, 1657–1662," *Transactions of the Royal Historical Society*, ser. 2 XVII (London, 1903), 67–119.

———, *Notes on the Diplomatic Relatons of England and France: 1603–1688* (Oxford, 1906).

France, Anatole, *Le Château de Vaux-le-Vicomte, suivie d'une étude historique, par J. Cordey* (Paris, 1933).

Francheville, Joseph Du Fresne de, *Histoire générale et particulière des finances . . . ou l'on voit l'origine, l'établissement, la perception & la régie de touses les impositions: dressée sur les pièces authentiques* (Paris, 1738–1746), 3 vols.

Funk-Brentano, Franz, "L'Homme au masque de velours noir dit le masque de fer," *Revue historique* LVI (November–December 1894), 253–303.

Gallia Christiana

Galtier de Laroque, A. de, *Le Marquis de Ruvigny, députe général des églises et les protestants à la cour de Louis XIV: 1643–1665* (Paris, 1892).

Gambarini, Carlo, *A Description of the Earl of Pembroke's Pictures* (Westminster, 1731).

Gardiner, Samuel Rawson, *History of the Commonwealth and Protectorate: 1649–1660* (London, 1897–1901), 3 vols.

Gautier, Jean-Antoine, *Histoire de Genève dès origines à l'année 1691* (1730), 2 vols.

Gerard, Kent, and Hekmam, Gert, "The Pursuit of Sodomy: Male Homosexuality in Renaissance and Enlightenment Europe," *Journal of Homosexuality* XVI, N°s 1/2 1988. Also (New York and London, 1989).

Griffet, Henri, père, *Histoire du règne de Louis XIII, Roi de France et de Navarre* (Paris, 1758), 3 vols.

———, *Traité de différentes sortes de preuves qui servent à établir la vérité de l'histoire* (Liège, 1769).

Griselle, Eugène, *Etat de la maison du roi Louis XIII de celles de sa mère, Marie de Médicis, de ses soeurs Chrestienne, Elisabeth et Henriette de France, de son frère Gaston d'Orleans, de sa femme Anne d'Autriche, de ses fils, le dauphin (Louis XIV) et Philippe d'Orléans* (Paris, 1912).

Grouchy, Emmanuel Henri, Vicomte de, "Acquisition du duché de Mayenne par le Cardinal Mazarin," *Revue d'histoire diplomatique* II (1888), 289–292.

———, *Un administrateur au temps de Louis XIV, Thomas de Grouchy, Sieur de Robertot, conseiller au parlement de Metz: 1610–1675* (Ghent, 1886).

Grouchy, Emmanuel Henri, Vicomte de, and Marcy, Arthur, Comte de, "Un administrateur au temps de Louis XIV," *Messager des sciences historiques, ou Archives des arts et de la bibliographie de Belgique* (1883), 54–113, 152–198, 248–279, 389–416; (1885) 45–101, 165–203, 241–301, 402–414.

Guiffrey, Jules, *Inventaire général des richesses d'art de France: Monuments Civils IV, Tapisseries du Garde Meuble* (Paris, 1913).

———, *Inventaire général du mobilier de la couronne sous Louis XIV: 1663–1715* (Paris, 1886).

Guiorgazdé, Claire, "Reconstruction d'un plan parcellaire du village disparu de Portes (Gard) à partir du'un compoix de 1640," *Le Compoix et ses usages: Actes du colloque de Nîmes, les 26 et 27 nov. 1999.*

Guizot, François, *Histoire de la république d'Angleterre et de Cromwell: 1649–1658* (Paris, 1854), 2 vols.

Hanotaux, Gabriel, and La Force, Augustin, Duke de, *Histoire du Cardinal Richelieu* (Paris, 1896–1947), 6 vols.

Hirschfeld, Magnus, *Die Homosexualität des Mannes und des Weibes* (Berlin, 1914) [English translation: *The Homosexuality of Men and Women* (Amherst, NY, 2000)].

Holbrook, Daniel, "Fidelity to the Marriage Bed: An Inquiry into the Foundation of Sexual Ethics," *Electronic Journal of Human Sexuality* X, 2007.

Hume, David, *An Enquiry Concerning the Principles of Morals* (London, 1751).

Il y a trois siècles le masque de fer, Actes du colloque international sur la célèbre énigme (Cannes, 1989).

Iung, Théodore, *La Vérité sur le masque de fer (les empoisonneurs), d'après des documents inédits des Archives de la Guerre et autres dépôts publics: 1664–1703* (Paris, 1872).

Jal, Auguste, *Abraham Duquesne et la marine de son temps* (Paris, 1873), 2 vols.

——, *Dictionnaire critique de biographie et d'histoire* (Paris, 1867).

Jennings, Neil, and Jones, Margaret, *A Biography of Samuel Chappuzeau, a seventeenth century French Huguenot Playwright, Scholar, Traveller and Preacher: An Encyclopedic Life* (Lewiston, 2012).

Jouanna, Arlette, *La France du XVIe siècle: 1483–1598* (Paris, 1996).

Kleinman, Ruth, *Anne of Austria: Queen of France* (Columbus, 1985).

——, "Facing Cancer in the Seventeenth Century: The Last Illness of Anne of Austria," *Advances in Thanatology* IV N° 1 (1977), 41–44.

La Borde, Léon Emmanuel Simon Joseph, *Le Palais Mazarin et les habitations de ville et de campagne au dix-septième siècle* (Paris, 1846).

Lacroix (alias Jacob), Paul L., *L'Homme au masque de fer* (Paris, 1837).

——, *Pignerol, histoire du temps de Louis XIV* (Paris, 1836), 2 vols. [repr. 1850, 1861, 1862, 1863, 1865, 1868].

La Gorgue-Rosny, Louis Eugène de, *Recherches généalogiques sur les comtés de Ponthieu, de Boulogne, de Guines et pays circonvoisins* (Boulogne-Sur-Mer, 1874–1877), 4 vols.

Lair, Jules, *Nicolas Fouquet, procureur général, surintendant des finances, ministre d'état de Louis XIV* (Paris, 1890), 2 vols.

Laloy, Emile, *Enigmes du grand siècle: Le Masque de fer, Jacques Stuart de La Cloche, l'abbé Prignani, Roux de Marsilly* (Paris, 1913).

Lang, Andrew, *The Valet's Tragedy and Other Studies* (London, 1903).

Laurain-Portemer, Madeleine, "Mazarin, militant de l'art baroque au temps de Richelieu," *Bulletin de l'Histoire de l'Art Français* (1975), 65–100.

Laverny, Sophie de, *Les Domestiques commensaux du roi de France au XVIIe Siècle* (Paris, 2002).

Lavisse, Ernest, "Colbert, Intendant de Mazarin," *Revue de Paris* (September 1, 1896).

Lefèbvre, M., *Histoire générale et particulière de la ville de Calais et du Calaisis ou pays reconquis, précédée de l'histoire des Morins, ses plus anciens habitans* (Paris, 1766), 2 vols.

Le Grand, Jérôme, *Louis XIV et le masque de fer ou les princes jumeaux* (Paris, 1792).

Lister, Thomas H., *Life and Administration of Edward, First Earl of Clarendon: With Original Correspondence, and Authentic Papers Never before Published* (London, 1837–1838), 3 vols.

Loiseleur, Jules, "Le Masque de fer devant la critique moderne," *Revue contemporaine*, ser. 2 LVIII (July 31, 1867), 193–239.

——, "Un dernier mot sur le masque de fer," *Revue contemporaine*, ser. 2 LXXII (December 15, 1869), 385–405.

Magne, Emile, *Tallemant des Réaux* (Paris, 1921–1922), 2 vols.

Marcel, Henri, et al. *La Bibliothèque nationale* (Paris, 1907).

Martin, Ron, "On the Trail of the Iron Mask: The State of the Question," *Proceedings of the Western Society for French History* XIX (1992), 89–98.

Marvick, Elizabeth Wirth, *Louis XIII: The Making of a King* (New Haven and London, 1986).

Matte, Louis, *Crimes et procès politiques sous Louis XIV: Le Procès de Fouquet, La Conspiration du chevalier de Rohan, Le Masque de fer* (Paris, 1910).

Maugis, Edouard, "La Journée du 4 juillet 1652 à l'Hôtel de Ville de Paris: Relation de Pierre Lallemant," *Revue historique* CXXXIII (1920), 55–72.

Meinel, Friedrich, *Samuel Chappuzeau: 1625–1701* (Borna-Leipzig, 1908).

Ménard, Léon, *Histoire civile, ecclésiastique et littéraire de la ville de Nismes* (Paris, 1758), 7 vols.

Mentzer, Raymond A., "Organizational Endeavour and Charitable Impulse in Sixteenth-Century France: The Case of Protestant Nîmes," *French History* V (1991), 1–29.

Michaud, Jean-Francois and Louis-Michel, *Biographie universelle* (Paris, 1811–1882), 85 vols.

Michel, Patrick, "Mazarin et l'Espagne: Quelques rencontres," in *Arte y diplomacia de la monarquia hispanica en el siglo XVII*, ed. José Luis Colomer (Madrid, 2003), 293–312.

———, Mazarin, Prince des collectionneurs: es collections et ameublement du cardinal Mazarin: 1602–1661, Histoire et analyse (Paris, 1999).

Mongrédien, Georges, "La Grande débauche de Roissy," Mercure de France N° 1046 (October 1, 1950), 277–285.

———, Le Masque de fer (Paris, 1952).

———, "Le Problème du masque de fer, deux documents inédits," Dix-septième siècle XVII–XVIII (1953), 55–58.

Monter, E. William, "La Sodomie à l époque moderne en Suisse romande," Annales N° 4 (July–August 1974), 1023–1033.

Montoux, André, Vieux logis de Touraine (Chambray-les-Tours, 1987).

Moote, Lloyd, Louis XIII, the Just (Berkeley, Los Angeles, London, 1989).

Morillot, Paul, Scarron, étude biographique et littéraire (Paris 1888).

Mott, Luiz, "Justitia et Misericordia," in Harold Johnson and Francis Dutra, Pelo Vaso Traseiro: Sodomy and Sodomites in Luso-Brazilian History (Tucson, 2007), 63–104.

Mussot Jean-François alias Arnould, L'Homme au masque de fer ou le souterrein (Paris, 1790).

Noone, John, The Man behind the Iron Mask (New York, 1988).

Nuttail, W. L. F., "King Charles I's pictures and the Commonwealth Sale," Apollo (October, 1965).

Oresko, Robert, "Homosexuality and the Court Elites of Early Modern France: Some Problems, Some Suggestions and an Example," Journal of Homosexuality XVI 1–2 (1988), 105–128. Republished in "The Pursuit of Sodomy: Male Homosexuality in Renaissance and Enlightenment Europe," ed. Kent Gerard and Gert Hekma (New York and London, 1989), with same pagination.

Paroletti, Modeste, Sur la mort du surintendant Foucquet: Notices recueillies à Pignerol (Turin, 1812).

Pecquet, Antoine, Mémoires secrets pour servir à l'histoire de Perse (Amsterdam, 1745).

Petitfils, Jean-Christian, L'Homme au masque de fer (Paris, 1970).

———, Le Masque de fer: Entre histoire et légende (Paris, 2003).

———, "Le Masque de fer enfin démasqué," Historia N° 552 (December, 1992), 69–76.

Philips, Claude, The Picture Gallery of Charles I (London, 1895).

Pinard, François-Joseph-Guillaume, Chronologie historique-militaire, contenant l'histoire de la création de toutes les charges, dignités et grades militaires supérieurs, de toutes les personne qui les ont possédés . . . des troupes de la maison du Roi, Suite des maréchaux de France, les grands maîtres de l'artillerie, les colonels généraux (Paris, 1760–1778), 8 vols.

Poldo d'Albenas, Jean, Discours historial de l'antique & illustre cité de Nismes en la Gaule Narbonnoise, avec les portraitz des plus antiques & insignes bastimens dudit lieu, reduits à leur vraye mesure & proportion, ensemble de l'antique & moderne ville (Lyon, 1550).

Poli, Oscar de, Un regiment d'autrefois: Royal Vaisseaux (1638–1672).

Pribram, Alfred Francis, Paul Freiherr von Lisola (1613–1674) und die Politik seiner Zeit (Leipzig, 1894).

Pro Loco di Pinerolo, Pinerolo, la maschera di ferro e il suo tempo, Atti del Convegno Internationale di Studio, 28–29 settembre 1974 (Pinerolo, 1976).

———, Pinerolo, la Maschera di ferro e il suo tempo, Atti del Secondo Convegno Internazionale di Studio, Pinerolo: 13–14–15 settembre 1991 (Pinerolo, 1992).

Puech, Albert, La Renaissance et la Réforme à Nîmes, d'après des documents inédits (Nîmes, 1893).

Rabinel, Aimé-Daniel, "Le Mouvement protestant contre l'impôt à Nîmes en 1653: Jean Roux, frère aîné de Roux de Marcilly," Bulletin de la Société de l'Histoire du Protestantisme Français (1968), 33–55.

———, La Tragique aventure de Roux de Marcilly (Toulouse, 1969).

Regnault-Warin, Jean-Baptiste, *L'Homme au masque de fer* (Paris, 1804), 4 vols.

Renée, Amédée, *Les Nièces de Mazarin* (Paris, 1856).

Reuss, Rudolph, *Histoire d'Alsace* (Paris, 1916).

Rivals, Georges, "Les Conditions économiques et sociales de la Réforme dans le Bas-Languedoc," *Cahiers d'histoire et archéologie* XIII (1938), 41–66.

Rohrschneider, Michael, "Die spanisch-französichen Verhandlungen im Jahre 1649," in *Der Pyrenäienfriede: Vorgeschichte, Widerhall, Rezeptionsgeschichte*, ed. Heinz Duchhardt (Göttingen, 2010), 23–40.

Rondot, Notalis, "La Monnaye de Vimy ou de Neuville dans le Lyonnais," *Revue numismatique*, ser 3 VIII (1890), 435-445, republished (Paris, 1890).

Roux-Fazillac, Pierre, *Recherches historiques et critiques sur l'homme au masque de fer d'où résultent des notions certaines sur ce prisonnier, ouvrage rédigé sur des matériaux authentiques* (Paris, 1800–1801).

Ruiz Rodriguez, Ignacio, *Don Juan José de Austria en la monarquia hispánica entre la politica, el poder y la intriga* (Madrid, 2007).

Saint-Foix, Germain-François Poullain de, *Essais historiques sur Paris* (London, 1754–1757), 5 vols.

——, *Lettre au sujet de l'homme au masque de fer* (Amsterdam, 1768).

——, *Oeuvres complètes de Saint-Foix* (Paris, 1777), 6 vols.

——, *Réponse au R.P. Griffet, et recueil de tout ce qu a été écrit sur le prisonnier masqué* (London, 1770).

Saint-Jean de Crèvecoeur, Robert, "Un personnage de Tallemant des Réaux: Montbrun-Souscarrière: 1594–1670, d'àprès des documents inédits," *Bullettin de la Société de l'Histoire de Paris et de l'Ile de France* XVI, 57–103.

Saint-Léger, Alexandre de, "L'Acquisition de Dunkerque et de Mardyck par Louis XIV," *Revue d'histoire moderne et contemporaine* (1900), I, 233–245.

Sauzet, Robert, *Contre réforme et réforme catholique en Bas-Languedoc, Le diocèse de Nîmes au XVIIe sièle* (Louvain and Paris, 1979), 2 vols.

Schnapper, Antoine, *Curieux du grand siècle* (Paris, 1994).

——, "Encore Jabach, Mazarin, Louis XIV mais non Fouquet," *Bulletin de la Société d'Histoire de l'Art Française* (1989) (1990), 75–76.

——, "Jabach, Mazarin, Fouquet, Louis XIV," *Bulletin de la Société d'Histoire de l'Art Française* (1982) (1984), 85–86.

Sonnino, Paul, "Louis XIV and the Dutch War," in *Louis XIV and Europe*, ed. Ragnhild Hatton (London, 1976), 153–178.

——, *Louis XIV and the Origins of the Dutch War* (Cambridge and New York, 1988).

——, "Louis XIV's *Mémoires pour l'histoire de la guerre de Hollande*," *French Historical Studies* VIII, 1 (Spring, 1973), 68–78.

——, *Louis XIV's View of the Papacy: 1661–1667* (Berkeley and Los Angeles, 1964).

——, *Mazarin's Quest: The Congress of Westphalia and the Coming of the Fronde* (Cambridge, MA, 2008).

——, "On the Trail of the Iron Mask: The Candidacy of Claude Imbert," *Proceedings of the Western Society for French History* XIX (1992), 99–108.

——, "Some Mischievous Questions about the Treaty of Ryswick," *Journal of Early Modern European History* IV, 3–4 (2001), 452–455.

——, "The Three Testaments of Cardinal Mazarin," *French Historical Studies* XXXVII, 3 (Summer 2014), 421–436.

Sottas, Jules, "Le Gouvernement de Brouage et La Rochelle sous Mazarin," *Revue de Saintonge & d'Aunis*, XXXIX (1921) 48–56, 141–154, 207–219 ; XL (1923) 17–27, 60–71, 318–332); XLI (1924) 31–59, 130–143, 185–198, 273–288; XLII (1926) 5–21, 81–97, 197–214.

——, "La Maladie et mort du Cardinal Mazarin," *La Chronique médicale* VII (1925) 195–202, VIII 227–230, IX 259–266, X 291–300, XI 323–327, XII 355–362; I (1926) 1–9.

Spon, Jacob, *Histoire de la ville et de l'estat de Genève* (Lyon 1680).

Susane, Louis, *Histoire de la cavalerie française* (Paris, 1874), 3 vols.

——, *Histoire de l'ancienne infanterie française* (Paris, 1849–1853), 8 vols.

Tessier, André, *Les Spectacles à Paris pendant la révolution* (Geneva 1992–2002).

Topin, Marius, *L'Homme au masque de fer* (Paris, 1869).

Valfrey, Jules, *La Diplomatie française au XVIIᵉ siècle: Hugues de Lionne, ses ambassades en Espagne et en Allemagne: La Paix des Pyrénées* (Paris, 1881).

——, *La Diplomatie française au XVIIᵉ siècle: Hugues de Lionne, ses ambassades en Italie: 1642–1656* (Paris, 1877).

Vaughan, Robert, *The Protectorate of Oliver Cromwell and the State of Europe during the Early Part of the Reign of Louis XIV* (London, 1839), 2 vols.

Vittel, Jean, "Les Tapisseries de la couronne à l'époque de Louis XIV," *Versailles* N° 10, 2007.

Voltaire, *Questions sur l'Encyclopédie* (London, 1771–1772), 9 vols.

——, *Siècle de Louis XIV* (Berlin, 1751).

——, *Siècle de Louis VIV* (Dresden, [1752] 1753), 2 vols.

——, *Siècle de Louis VIV* (Leipzig [Paris]), 1752), 2 vols.

——, *Supplément au siècle de Louis XIV* (Dresden, 1753). Also in Besterman et al., XXXIIc 291–382.

Walpole Horace, *Anecdotes of Painting in England; with some account of the principal artists; and incidental notes on other arts; collected by the late Mr. George Vertue; and now digested and published from his original Mss.* (Strawberry Hill, 1762–1771), 4 vols.

White, Michelle A., *Henrietta Maria and the English Civil Wars* (Aldershot, UK, and Burlington, VT, 2006).

Williams, Hugh Noel, *A Fair Conspirator, Marie de Rohan, Duchesse de Chevreuse* (London and New York, 1913).

——, *Five Fair Sisters* (New York, 1906).

——, *A Princess of Intrigue, Anne Geneviève de Bourbon, Duchess de Longueville* (London, 1907).

Zeller, Berthold, *Etudes critiques sur le règne de Louis XIII: Le Connétable de Luynes, Montauban et la Valtelline, d'après les archives d'Italie* (Paris, 1879).

——, *Louis XIII, Marie de Médicis, Richelieu ministre: étude nouvelle d'après les documents florentins et vénitiens* (Paris, 1899).

——, *La Minorité de Louis XIII: étude nouvelle d'après les documents florentine et vénitiens* (Paris, 1892–1897).

——, *Richelieu et les ministres de Louis XIII de 1621 à 1624: La cour, le gouvernement, la diplomatie d'après les archives d'Italie* (Paris, 1880).

Index